Live & Work in

China & Hong Kong

Second edition 2008

Jocelyn Kan and Hakwan Lau
Revised by Diana Martin, with
contributions from Olivia Robinson

crimson

Published by Crimson Publishing, a division of Crimson Business Ltd, 2008
www.crimsonpublishing.com

4501 Forbes Blvd, Suite 200, Lanham MD 20706

Westminster House, Kew Road, Richmond, Surrey TW9 2ND

Distributed in North America by National Book Network
www.nbnbooks.com

Distributed in the UK by Portfolio Books
www.portfoliobooks.com

A catalogue record for this book is available from the British Library.

ISBN: 978 1 85458 384 0
Printed and bound in China by Everbest Printing Co. Ltd

Foreword

China exerts a fascination on people all over the world. Whether it is the exciting business opportunities, the rich culture, or the millennias of history that draw people, China never fails to deliver.

China is not merely an exotic location; it is well known that in recent years, the Chinese economy has become one of the most dynamic in the world. With a view to developing the huge potential wealth of a country populated by more than a staggering 1.3 billion people, the Chinese government has opened its doors to foreign investors, welcomed their skills and expertise and encouraged fruitful partnerships with local businesses and institutions. Vodafone has linked up with China Mobile, Shell is working with the leading Chinese oil company CNOOC, and 65% of Chinese automobile production results from international joint ventures. These developments not only serve the huge local market, but also generate exports on a massive scale. The increase in local wealth is typified by the fact that car ownership is currently doubling every four years.

Experts anticipate that by 2030 the Chinese economy will overtake that of the USA. With this in mind, the Chinese government is easing the immigration process for high-skilled personnel and has been making long-term or permanent residence a genuine aspiration for outsiders. In short, the opportunities for living and working in China are getting better all the time. Hence the need for a book like *Live & Work in China* to show where the greatest opportunities lie and to explain how best to pursue them.

China is more than just a country: it is Asia in microcosm, composed of landscapes that range from snowy mountains to subtropical jungle, via sandy desert and sweeping grasslands, and populated by a variety of ethnic groups. In area it is the third largest country in the world after Russia and Canada. Spending time in China is the only way to know what makes the country and its people tick. Better still, try and learn the language so you can communicate with people around you on their terms. You will soon understand that some of the myths about China that you brought with you are simply myths. In *Live & Work in China*, we explore some of these popular ideas about China and give readers an idea of what to expect when they look for accommodation and for work, how to negotiate business etiquette, the health system and the education system.

The book also covers the vibrant region of Hong Kong. Because of Hong Kong's colonial past and its somewhat British infrastructure, it will probably come across to most westerners as less daunting than the rest of China. But Hong Kong is by no means a watered-down version of mainland China, nor is its culture much westernised when you scratch below the surface. It is a city with its own distinct character, brimming with people, tower blocks and opportunities. It has a population of around six million, and is a multilayered city, still remaining extremely safe. In most respects it compares favourably with New York, Paris or London.

Diana Martin, Oxford
December 2007

CHINA Contents

Working in China 123

Time Off 197

About China 207

HONG KONG Contents

Why Live & Work in Hong Kong? 239

Before You Go 251

Setting Up Home 269

Daily Life 293

Working in Hong Kong 321

Time Off 357

About Hong Kong 365

Appendices 379

How to Use This Book

This book is divided into two sections: mainland China and Hong Kong. Information on Macau is given throughout the section on mainland China, and is given specific headings under each topic.

Telephone numbers:

All numbers are given from inside the country – unless the number is likely to be called from abroad.

International dialing code for China: + 86
Hong Kong: + 852

Exchange rates:

Throughout the book, currency conversions are given at the beginning of each topic. Please refer to the table below in other instances.

Chinese yuan ¥	US dollar $	British pound £	Euro €	Australian dollar A$	New Zealand dollar NZ$
1	0.14	0.07	0.09	0.16	0.18
10	1.40	0.72	0.90	1.56	1.80
100	14	7.20	9	15.6	18
1,000	143	72	90	156	180
10,000	1,480	718	904	1,560	1,807
100,000	14,280	7,180	9,040	15,600	18,073

Hong Kong dollar HK$	US dollar $	British pound £	Euro €	Australian dollar A$	New Zealand dollar NZ$
1	0.13	0.06	0.08	0.14	0.16
10	1.30	0.65	0.80	1.40	1.63
100	13	6.50	8.10	14	16
1,000	128.50	65	81.30	140.50	63
10,000	1,285	646	813	1,405	1,626
100,000	12,850	6,458	8,130	14,050	16,260

Macau dollar MOP$	US dollar $	British pound £	Euro €	Australian dollar A$	New Zealand dollar NZ$
1	0.13	0.06	0.08	0.14	0.16
10	1.27	0.64	0.80	1.38	1.60
100	12.70	6.37	8	13.86	16
1,000	126.80	63.70	80	138.65	160.50
10,000	1,268	637.30	803	1,386.50	1,605
100,000	12,680	6,373	8,026	13,865	16,050

Acknowledgements

Thanks to Beth Law, Sally Rawlings, Sarah Riddle, Andrea Boudville, Robert Law and Pierston Hawkins for use of their photos.

EXPO
2010
SHANGHAI CHINA
城市,让生活更美好
Better City,Better Life
光明
光明优+纯
订奶热

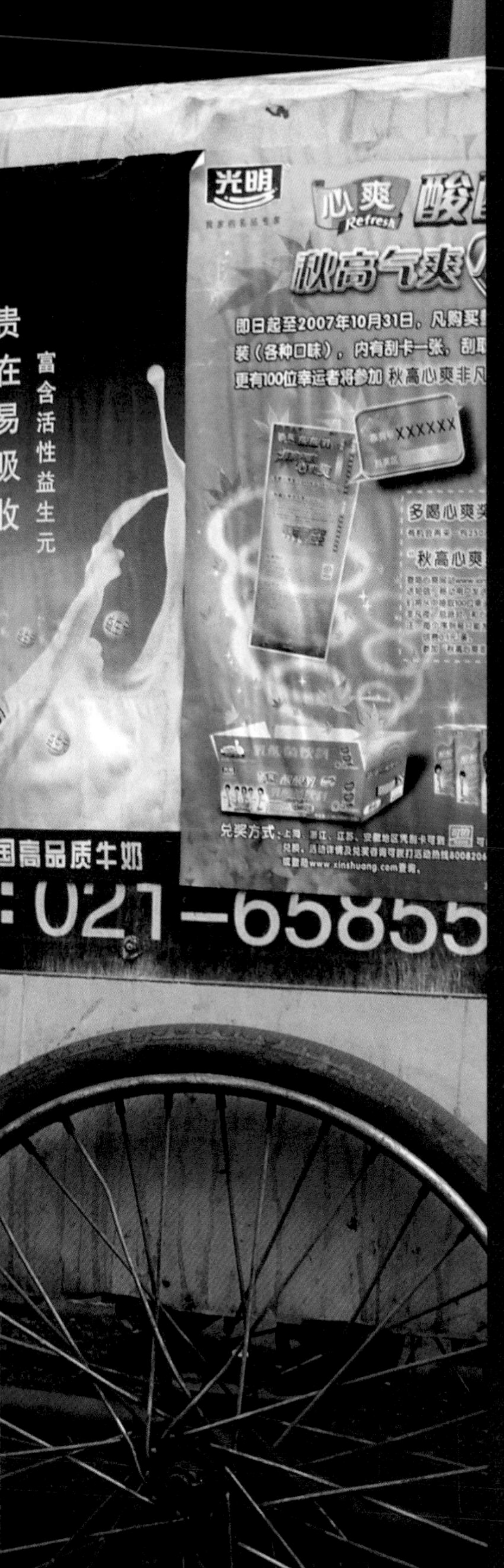

Why Live & Work in China?

ABOUT CHINA

Ever since Marco Polo's traveling account gave readers a glimpse of the distant land of China, westerners have been intrigued by this mysterious country. Part of this fascination resulted from China's reluctance to open its doors to western travellers or traders. Thus it remained a secret country. After centuries of regarding itself as the Middle Kingdom – the most ancient and most civilised culture, surrounded by lesser countries who acknowledged its superiority by paying it tribute – China was unfamiliar with, and even shocked by the idea of relations with other nations on an equal footing. China considered that it had everything it needed and desired nothing from the outside world. It was a privilege to allow foreigners to tread on Chinese soil. Much misunderstanding ensued and, as is so often the way in history, might triumphed and the technologically and militarily superior west forced China to westernise their trade. If we then jump ahead a hundred years from the 19th century to the communist regime, China once more slammed its doors on the west and on its ideas and goods for roughly 40 years. During this period, however, those westerners who were able to spend time in China as missionaries (in pre-communist times), diplomats, traders or guests wrote gripping accounts of the people and places they got to know, trying to 'explain' Chinese ways to an uncomprehending but curious west.

“China's economic transformation is one of the most dramatic economic developments of recent decades.
The Organisation for Economic Cooperation and Development”

Now, more than almost ever before, it is possible to make the journey and see for oneself: to travel around in varying degrees of comfort and safety, talk to local

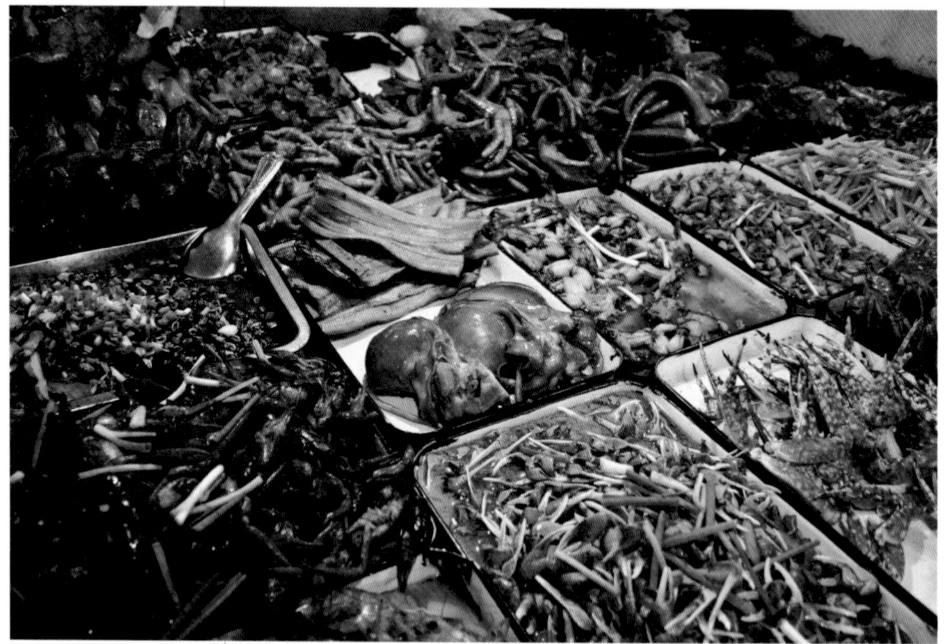

people, buy a range of goods in local shops, take a course of study, work there, even start up a business. In Beijing, if you want to, you can even do your shopping in the American Wal-Mart, French Carrefour or most recently, British Tesco.

There is no doubt that the Chinese are getter richer, even though there is still a big gap between city dwellers and people in the countryside. In the four-year period from 2001 to 2005 the average per capita disposable income of an urban resident rose from nearly ¥7,000 (£502/$999) to nearly ¥10,500. In the countryside the average per capita net income rose from just under ¥2,400 to ¥3,255. The latter represents an average annual growth of 5.3% compared with 9.6% in the towns and cities.

This change can be seen on the streets of most cities. The Chinese have long since cast off the dark blue and grey 'Mao suits' and the shapeless trousers and tunics worn by women. Fashionable hairstyles and designer clothes are everywhere to be seen; just as French perfume and other personal luxuries are sought by the growing middle class. A few years ago mainlanders visiting fashion-conscious Hong Kong stuck out like the proverbial sore thumb; now they blend with the locals. For some years now karaoke has been a popular entertainment; McDonalds and KFC outlets cater to the taste for fast food alongside the more traditional Chinese restaurants. Nor is the tidal wave of bicycles the norm any more. In some cities they have even been banned from the city centre to make way for the ever-increasing population of cars. An efficient public transport system and taxis have replaced the humble bicycle. Private car ownership is growing, with many European and Japanese luxury makes now being manufactured in China. Even the prestigious Rolls Royce can be seen in major cities.

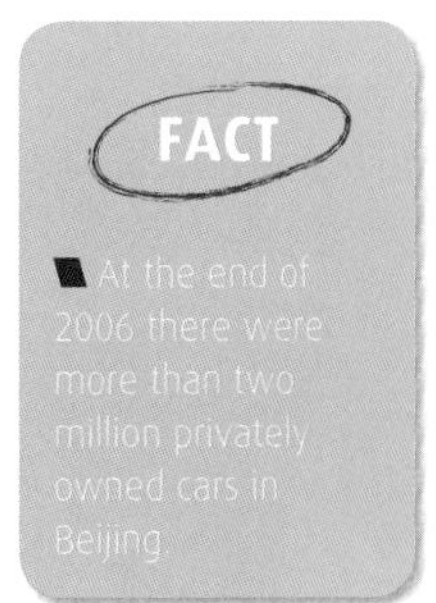

FACT
At the end of 2006 there were more than two million privately owned cars in Beijing.

Private schools and private hospitals are also making an appearance. Needless to say, in the major centres, foreigners no longer arouse the animated curiosity that they once did – as recently as 1978 visitors recall being followed, Pied Piper-esque, through the streets of the city of Jinan in Shandong province by an ever-growing crowd of excited locals who had never seen foreigners before.

There is a particular reason why Beijing is buzzing at the moment. Since 2001 when Beijing was chosen as the site of the 2008 Olympic games, the city proudly prepared for the arrival of over 10,500 international athletes and millions of visitors from all over the world for the summer series of sporting events.

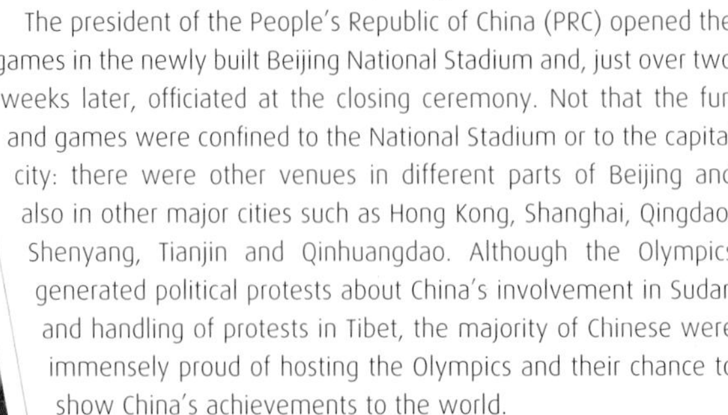

The president of the People's Republic of China (PRC) opened the games in the newly built Beijing National Stadium and, just over two weeks later, officiated at the closing ceremony. Not that the fun and games were confined to the National Stadium or to the capital city: there were other venues in different parts of Beijing and also in other major cities such as Hong Kong, Shanghai, Qingdao, Shenyang, Tianjin and Qinhuangdao. Although the Olympics generated political protests about China's involvement in Sudan and handling of protests in Tibet, the majority of Chinese were immensely proud of hosting the Olympics and their chance to show China's achievements to the world.

Economically, China has already overtaken Britain to become the world's fourth biggest economy. During 2008 it is set to overtake Germany and beat it to third place. Not only does China consume more grain, steel, aluminium, timber and iron ore than any other country in the world, it also buys more pianos than anyone else! As you stroll through a Chinese city on a summer's evening you can hear school children meticulously practising in nearby apartments. Its exports are phenomenal too. The safety scandals of 2007 apart, nearly every toy that you see in the west still has a 'made in China' label, as do the majority of television sets, computers, cameras and items of clothing. In 2005 China's share of world trade jumped to 6.4% from 1% in 1979. It has also become the world's third largest trading power after the USA and Germany, and in 2007 leapfrogged both the USA and Germany to become the largest exporter in the world.

As you will discover as you read through this book, China is a dynamic place to do business. It is also an extremely interesting and challenging place to take up work. You will be living in a country that is changing fast, that is reinventing itself yet again, and which represents both the vibrant world of the 21st century and the traditional world of ancient culture and customs.

It is now easier than ever to travel at leisure within China and you will have the chance to see the huge variation in terrain, from the jungles of sub-tropical Yunnan province (home to many of China's minority peoples) up through the extraordinary karst mountains around Guilin, all the way to the mountains of Tibet and the deserts of Xinjiang in the far west. You will also be able to marvel at the man-made wonders of the terracotta warriors in the ancient capital city of Chang'An (now Xian), the famed Great Wall, and the groundbreaking modern architecture going up almost overnight in Beijing and Shanghai. You will be able to delight in the range of Chinese cuisines: hot and spicy in the south-west; hearty and protein-packed in the north; delicate and subtle in the south; as well as sampling regional specialties from street stalls if you are adventurous, or from sophisticated up-market restaurants if you want to treat yourself. Whatever your food preferences, you'll be impressed by the freshness of the ingredients used and the ingenuity of the cooks. With a bit of practise you will soon learn how to master the use of chopsticks, if you can't already – after all any Chinese three-year-old can do it! By living and working in China you will obviously be able to familiarise yourself with its ways and wonders in far more depth than the inevitably whirlwind tourist. If and when you eventually return to your country of origin you will find that the experience has bitten deep and you will never forget it.

■ The Chinese national flag is bright red with five yellow stars. The big star represents the Chinese Communist Party and the four smaller stars are the people rallying around the Party. It was adopted in 1949 and chosen from among 3,000 designs submitted by all kinds of people.

PROS AND CONS OF LIVING IN CHINA

There are many great reasons for spending a few years living and working in China. As already mentioned, China is the world's fastest growing economy. It is one the few countries that has been almost completely unaffected by the ripples in the global economy in 2007. Many investors from Europe and the USA find this fast-growing market irresistible and have relocated or started up businesses in China. Since the late 1970s, the Chinese government has been putting in place

Why Live & Work in China?

policies to attract overseas investment. There are now a number of investment incentives for foreigners, and more and more cities have been opening up to foreign investment. China joined the World Trade Organisation in 2001, and since then many tariffs and quotas have been removed. Businessmen from the west are also attracted by the cheap cost and availability of land and labour. There are lots of employment opportunities for foreign experts and highly skilled personnel in a whole range of fields in this burgeoning economy.

By western standards, salaries in China are relatively low, but so is the cost of living. The general standard of living in China, although not as high as in western Europe or North America, is becoming quite attractive in some of China's major cities.

Pros:

- Low cost of living
- Cheap housing
- The fast-growing economy provides plenty of opportunities for investment and employment
- Many investment incentives available for foreign investors
- Easy acceptance for staying permanently as the country currently needs foreign experts

Cons:

- Low salaries
- The language difference
- Distance from home
- Serious pollution
- Heavy congestion in big cities
- Crowded, especially in coastal cities
- A complicated tax regime

There is, of course, a downside to such rapid development. An explosion in car ownership over the last decade has made congestion a real problem in many big cities. The roads simply cannot cope with the dramatic increase. Industrial development has caused serious air and water pollution in more than 40% of cities. There is also the problem of overcrowding in towns and cities along the southern and south-eastern coastline. For geographical, and climatic, as well as economic reasons, the western, northern and north-eastern regions attract far fewer foreigners.

Furthermore, for those coming from democratic western countries it is worth a reminder that despite a certain degree of relaxation of some of the more hard-line aspects of communism and a welcoming of some imports from the west, China is still not a country where freedom of speech is permitted. It is also worth preparing yourself for the possibility that, when you arrive having left your comfort zone, you have to allow for some feelings of culture shock as you react to everything around you seeming strange and different.

Finally, it's a really good idea for anyone who plans to live and work in China for a longer period and get to know the people and their culture to learn Chinese. Not many people in China speak fluent English, although many who come into contact

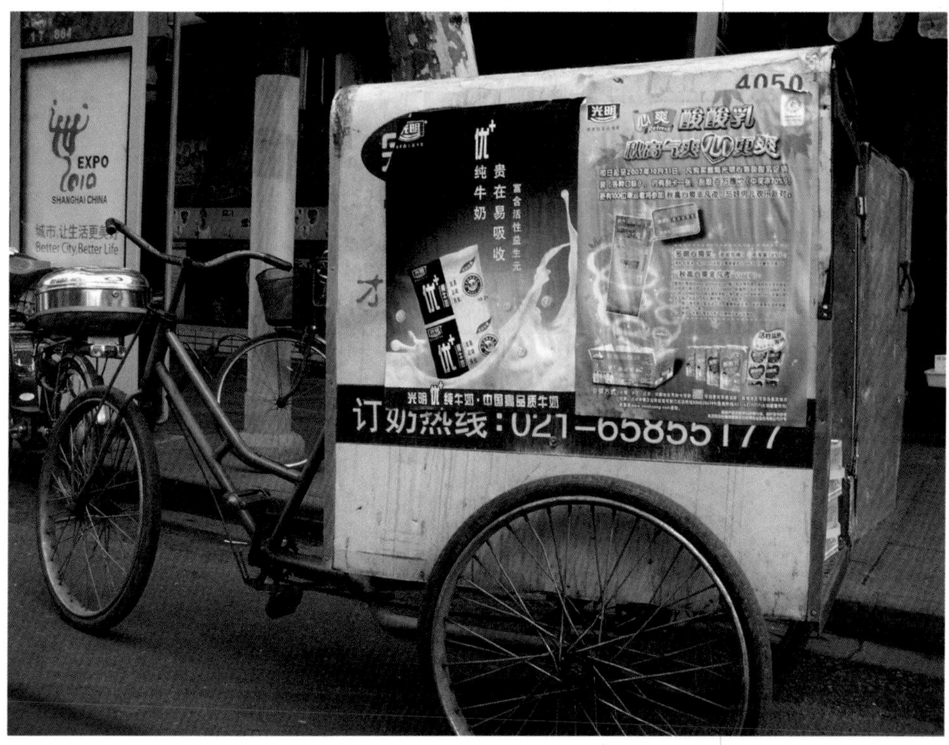

with foreigners, mostly those who live in the cities, tend to be able to express themselves adequately. There are many language courses you can sign up for and later on you may find a local person who would be keen to swap Chinese and English conversation for your mutual benefit. The advantages of being able to communicate in the language that is being spoken around you cannot be exaggerated. Learning simple characters is also practically very useful: how to identify public toilets, a restaurant or an internet café can save embarrassment and time.

PERSONAL CASE HISTORIES

Alex Thomson – businessman

How did you come to be living and working in China?

In 1988 I was re-examining my slightly eccentric life as a club manager/bartender and musician, thinking about how I could make a responsible shift into some new career opportunities. The economy in the USA was booming and there was a lot of optimism that you could do business in a non-corporate, creative way, so I thought I would go to school to get my MBA. The problem was that just getting an MBA was not really appealing to me at all, but I found a top-rated international MBA programme. The opportunity to study culture and language while getting a business degree made the transition much easier to accept. Basically, even though I was taking strides toward what I thought was the next stage in mature personal development, I knew I wanted to continue to make my life as unusual and interesting as possible. I truly believe, at least for myself, that a challenging environment is crucial for keeping the mind awake, so China seemed to be the best possible choice for my regional specialisation.

I've been in China for around three years. I first spent a couple months in Taiwan, at the time of the first inauguration of Chen Shui Bian. Then I started the language phase of my program in Hangzhou, stayed there for about six months, and then moved to Beijing in February 2001. After a semester of language and a six-month internship at a Chinese software company in Ya Yun Cun, I went back to the States to finish the MBA. Finally, I came back in September 2002 and have been in Beijing ever since.

What was your first impression of China?

I came over from Taiwan, so there was a bit of a transition period. What I remember about Taiwan were the pungent odours, conflictingly wonderful and disgusting at the same time: fresh and not-so-fresh fish, night markets, smog, musty humidity, temple incense. I loved it. Hangzhou had a similar sensory impact but I was already acclimatised a bit. The distinction was that the aroma of south-eastern China was permeated with dust and seemingly unbridled industrial exhaust.

I thought Taiwan was pretty chaotic, but when I stepped out of customs at the grimy architecturally functional international airport in Shanghai (Hongqiao Airport) and set out to find a way to Hangzhou, I knew that I was where I wanted to be. Taxi drivers were immediately telling me that the train station was closed and there were no buses to Hangzhou. I had *lao wai* (foreigner) written all across my forehead and no matter how hard I tried to present an image that I knew what I was doing I couldn't fake it. They were telling me that it would cost me ¥1,200 [£86/$171] to get there. I know now that you can rent a driver for an entire day including gas for 20% of that! My final deal was not too bad though. The shuttle bus is ¥80–¥100 and I paid something like ¥260 for the three-hour drive in a taxi because the driver was a local heading home, and wanted a last fare to bump up the day's take.

Of course, the drive was a teeth-clenching horror story, blazing through abandoned-looking industrial badlands and roadside villages where the chickens and the old folks seemed to instinctively get out of the cab's path at the last second. The driver augmented the effect by driving one-handed while screeching into his cell phone. I realised later that the Hangzhou language *Hua* only *sounds* like vicious arguing when the driver told me he had just asked his friend to meet him for beers and dinner after he dropped me off.

The secondary impression was that most people were nice, food was great, trying to get extra money out of foreigners was not cheating, but rather an institutionalised form of taking advantage of asymmetries in the marketplace, and that Hangzhou's West Lake was one of the most uniquely romantic places in the world.

What is your visa status? Was it difficult to get such a visa?

I have an F visa (business visa) now. It is not at all difficult to get one if you have a couple of thousand yuan. I just called one of the many 'visa consultants' and they paid a certain 'relationship fee' to the security bureau. They, in turn, send my visa to Guangzhou to be stamped and I'm all set for six more months. I don't even have to leave the country if my time has expired. Now that China is supposed to retaliate against the USA for visa restrictions and fingerprinting, however, I'm not sure how easy it will be in the future.

What sorts of places have you lived in? Was it easy to find accommodation?

In Hangzhou I lived in a foreigner dormitory apartment building. Three foreign students each had their own room and shared a living room and bathroom. It was a luxury apartment compared to the Chinese students who lived in bunks, eight to a room with no bathroom. We had a big fight with the administration because they told us we had to be back every night by 11pm. My schoolmates and I were graduate students in our late twenties and were dumbfounded that the people we were paying so much money to were telling us when we should go to bed. Their opinion was that we would cause unrest and instability among the regular college students if they knew we were trying to get away with disobeying policy. Ultimately a compromise was reached when we told the chief administrator that we would tell all future potential students from our schools that this school had a problem reconciling the rights of adults with its future revenue and marketing plans. The MBA was more useful than I thought it would be!

I have lived in varied conditions here in Beijing. I started with a new but overpriced apartment for foreign students at Beijing University of International Business and Economics (at least ¥4,800 a month). Then I moved to an apartment behind the east gate at a time when it was still supposedly illegal for foreigners to live in local housing communities. The rent for a really shabby two-bedroom apartment was about ¥2,800, definitely gauged under the auspices of the risk of housing foreign students.

I then lived in an apartment in Hua Jia Di Xi Li, which was rented by my former boss to my former girlfriend. He made a deal with her that, as a 'friend', he would rent a two-bedroom apartment of around 100 sq m to her for the same price plus one and a half hours of free English lessons a week. The market value for private teachers in the area at the time was about ¥160 per hour, so the total cost was ¥3,760 a month. Several months after I had inherited this deal, I realised that I had to talk to this person who said I was his 'close friend' every time he wanted me to translate something for him or help him with his IELTS (International English Language Testing System) studies. He was totally insulted when I suggested the arrangement was somewhat unfair. After a tremendous argument and the realisation that '*pengyou*' (friends), if someone actually has to say it out loud, is just another term for leverage in a business relationship, I moved out and never spoke with him again.

I now live in Wang Jing in a 90 sq m one-bedroom apartment for ¥2,700. It is modern and clean with relatively high-speed internet. The community is very clean, modern and convenient, and it has one of the largest South Korean populations in China.

I am actually looking for a larger apartment, hopefully with satellite TV and a bathtub. I've looked at quite a few this week and it's pretty good fun to watch the landlords factor in the extra charge for being a foreigner. There's a pause, their faces turn a little red, and their eyes turn to the upper right as they try to quickly calculate what can be added without seeming totally ridiculous. Sometimes they succeed and sometimes they don't.

The two-bedroom apartments I'm looking at here range from ¥3,300 for old-looking places with completely un-matching furniture, to ¥4,500–¥5,000 for something nice. That is just the offer price though. I will expect to bring it down to between ¥3,500–¥4,000, depending on the place.

What is the social life like? Was it easy to make a new group of local friends?

The nightlife scene is exploding in Beijing and it's very easy to make friends. Three years ago, there were a variety of clubs to go to, but you still didn't have a wide range of environments. Now you have at least the choices you would have in other large international cities, if not more. I like Beijing because it has become an international melting pot, while at the same time feeling intimate and relatively safe. This is very conducive to meeting people without having to worry about personal safety or similar concerns.

Most of the action takes place around Dong Zhi Men/San Li Tun, but places like Hou Hai (north of the Forbidden City) and some of the college areas like Wu Dao Kou and Bei Da (Peking University) have become well worth the visit.

The music scene is supposed to be the best in China, but I find that, although there are several clubs for live music, there is still not a lot of creativity beyond copying the music of western bands and then adding their own Chinese lyrics. Chinese rock for the most part totally missed out on Motown, and is mostly influenced by commercial and '80s rock.

Pretty much anyone with a pulse can make friends in Beijing. If you want to be with international people, there are parties and events almost every night of the week. If you have a hard time dealing with foreigners, there are droves of students and others who want to practice their English or just meet someone outside of their local paradigm.

What do you like best about China? What do you like least about China?

I must answer both questions at the same time because all I can give you is contradictions, contradictions, and more contradictions. I have heard this view from so many other people who have lived here for a while. People are friendly, but not. Everyone works hard, but doesn't get anything done. And often the best food leaves you with the worst side effects!

Well, of course I like the food! After a brutal Beijing winter, there is nothing better than going to an outside '*da pai dang*' (place to eat) having '*yang rou chuanr*' (roasted lamb) and drinking Yan Jing beer with friends. In all my travels in China, the night's meal and the potential to meet interesting people are always the highlights.

Of course there are a lot of friendly people who have taken me into their homes. However, I have found that when I am invited to a friendly dinner, there are often aspirations that as a foreigner I will bring some kind of opportunity to the table, eg someone wants me to teach their kids. This is a friendly way to do business, but it is not really friendship to me, and represents a grey area I have found to be frustrating at times.

On the other hand, on the occasions when there wasn't something to be gained, the environment was truly relaxing and endlessly giving. In the cases of teachers and students who became friends, the family of my girlfriend, or friends that were made outside of the so-called 'friendly' realms of dinners and karaoke, the true experience of friendships are very strong.

I think that people in cities in China are often not friendly toward each other unless they are from the same '*danwei*' (a working department), family or have other social connections. In a country of 1.3 billion people, there seems to be a kind of survival myopia, where in your everyday activities you just try to pretend like there's no one else in line, or on the road, or trying to buy things, etc. I can't tell you how many ladies and men, young and old, have looked me right in the eye and then pushed me out of the way to cut in a queue.

This ties into the other big problem I have which is not really traffic, per se, but the attitude to traffic. I have had a couple of great conversations with taxi drivers (who doesn't, I know) about the traffic situation. The Beijing taxi drivers are reeling at how many cars and new drivers have been added to the roads over the last two years. According to one taxi driver, driver training consists of something like knowing how to turn on the car, drive forward and pay a fee. It is not uncommon to see a woman with stuffed animals obscuring every inch of the left side, right side, and rear windows to the extent that the only unimpaired vision is directly to the front of the driver. I think this is symbolic in many ways of the myopia that I referred to above and the idea that most people on the streets are just looking out for number one. Concurrently, I am amazed at the amount of people who look truly dumfounded when they walk directly into a busy street without looking to find a screeching car sliding their way. Then they give an angry look to the driver as though he should not be in their path. It's like the tunnel vision of an individual who is working with a total lack of common sense, something that I still haven't really figured out yet.

The final contradiction is the contradiction between working and getting things done. I cannot diminish my respect for the people I see working hard everyday to make their lives better. This is the case all over China, and there is a tremendous amount of entrepreneurial spirit and dedication in the people I meet every day. At the same time, there seems to be a holdover from the Cultural Revolution, where common sense and the will to go the extra mile took some devastating blows. One friend of mine worked previously as an IT director for a large corporation in Shanghai, and now works for an international Chinese company. He says that his greatest problem is getting people to do something beyond the minimum required to keep the job and get a pay cheque.

According to him and others I have spoken with, if something is broken or there is a problem that would require creative thinking, everything shuts down and, most workers are likely to avoid it until management deals with the issue, even if it is inconvenient to them as well. Then, management must solve the problem because no one has memorised the solution during their time at university. I find this situation constantly in my everyday life as well, from the waitress who panics if I ask her to leave the cucumbers out of my *gong bao ji ding* (a chicken dish), to the police who will only file a report about my girlfriend's stolen cell phone because they will lose face in front of a foreigner if they don't.

What advice would you have for anyone thinking of coming to live and work in China?

I must make it clear after saying these few gripes that I truly love China. Everywhere there is the feeling that this is a culture that has survived history in an amazing way. People are fascinating. Places are unimaginably diverse. And this is truly a place where you can feel the remote past and the future of the human race grinding along together.

I see so many foreigners who refuse to learn a little Chinese. They live in totally isolated and self-contained communities, and represent everything that I was dissatisfied with in my own culture. They are here only to make a buck and it is obvious. They make the rounds from work to home to Starbucks. Many people like this that I have met seem to think that China is not much more than a flea market or a larger, cheaper Chinatown where you can find less expensive goods and housemaids, while living in a big house behind a wall. It completely feeds into stereotypes about foreigners and stereotypes about Chinese, and it plays no productive role in bringing our cultures closer together.

This is China. This is the country of the Chinese people and a rich Chinese culture. Don't come here if you don't want to participate.

Sean Williams – assistant director for a study programme

How did you come to be living and working in China?

I have lived in three parts of greater China: three years in Hong Kong, over a year in Taiwan, and four months in mainland China. I had a different reason for going to each place. In Hong Kong, where my dad lives, I went first to study the Chinese language and teach English and later to take a job as a paralegal in 1999, which alienated me so much that I decided to go back to school and get a second degree in Psychology at Hong Kong University. I went to Taiwan twice, once for eight months and once for six months, both times to teach English, first for a *bushiban* (cram school), and later for a Zen Buddhist temple. When I went to live in China, I went to act as an assistant director for a study abroad programme in Chongqing at Southwest China Normal University. I was supervising students who had come to visit China for the first time from a Benedictine university in Minnesota (College of St Benedict/St John's University).

What was your first impression of China?

The first time I saw China was in 1989, not long after the Beijing Massacre. I went to Guangzhou, which seemed drab and depressing and broken down at that time, and then to Guilin, which was beautiful and stirred some feeling of travelling excitement in me – though at the time I was a self-concerned teenager being taken there by my father, so I didn't pay as much attention to my surroundings as to my inner thoughts, obsessions, resentments, etc.

I really got to look at China with fresh eyes when I went by myself for the first time in 1995. I took a big backpack and about $500 and tried to get to as many places as I could in a month and a half. The impression I got from China from that trip was informed by journeys to Xiamen, Shanghai, Qingdao, Beijing, Wuhan, Wudang Mountain, and Yangshuo. Needless to say the impression was rather complex. I guess I saw the spiritual and the natural in tremendous tension with the man-made and material, with there being something to appreciate and to recoil at in each.

What sort of place did you live in? Was it easy to find accommodation?

When living a couple of hours out of Chongqing (in Bepei), I stayed in the 'foreign experts' quarters. I don't know how much my accommodation cost the university. For me it was part of my payment package. It was a decent-sized place, but pretty spartan. The carpeting and the wallpaper both looked several decades old. The bathtub did not have hot running water, so I had to heat up water on a stove and then pour it into the bath to wash. My window didn't have a view of, much other than the courtyard outside, where the students practiced t'ai chi, but it was pretty enough.

What was the social life like? Was it easy to make a new group of local friends?

The social life in Beipei was odd, but we did make a few friends, mostly through the university, and I met a couple of interesting characters in the little bars that they had there as well. On a Friday or Saturday night, you could go into one of these nightclubs and only about 30 people would be there, all dancing under a cheap revolving disco ball looking at themselves in front of a big mirror. There were karaokes as well, but I didn't feel so welcome there and they seemed more explicitly connected with prostitution. The local friends I got closest to were students or teachers at the university.

What do you like best about China?

I felt like China was another world, a fascinating and engaging but not a dangerous or threatening one, one that could teach me about who I was and who people are generally, without destroying me. Also, the mountains, the food, the trains, the friendly people, the $1 haircuts that come with a head wash and backrub, 25 cent beers in big cold bottles with *jiaozi* (Chinese dumplings), hot pot, singing Chinese communist-era songs in bars with strangers, the surprising diversity, the tolerance and openness, the intelligence, curiosity, humour, and optimism. And lest I be dishonest, I found the opposite sex even more charming and enticing than usual while in China, more so than in Hong Kong or Taiwan.

What do you like least about China?

The fear, the indifference to a stranger's suffering, the indifference to animal suffering, the pollution, the incivility in getting on a bus, the spitting, the greed-driven and face-driven dishonesty and corruption, the blaring of dogma, the potential oppression that hangs in the air even when it is not obviously expressed, the ugliness of most cityscapes, the spirit-robbing commercialisation of the most compelling and impactful aspects of Chinese landscape and culture.

What advice would you have for anyone thinking of coming to live and work in China?

Open yourself as wide as you can to new people, new landscapes and new experiences without losing sight of who you are, and who you've always wanted to be. Try to give back as much or more than you will inevitably take. Be prepared to learn what it means to have unaccountable power, even after a lifetime of feeling like a victim of unaccountable power yourself. The trouble you make for yourself will likely be easy to bear, easier than it might be at home, in fact probably too easy. That will not be the case for the trouble you make for others. Some of the people you will never see again will face things that you will never have to face.

Joey Roberts – businessman

Why have you spent a few years in China?

It was not planned at all. I was working in Hong Kong, and my company proposed that I should move to Shanghai. I accepted.

What was your first impression of China?

First impressions were biased by my excitement of discovering this mysterious country. I was amazed by the scale and speed of development in Shanghai. Then, over time, I realised the numerous shortcomings of living in a developing country without knowing the local language. I was amazed by the mix of people in Shanghai: well educated Chinese people living side by side with poor and ill educated people.

What is your visa status? Was it difficult to get such a visa?

My employer got me an employment visa (Z) with work and residence permit. It was not a problem to obtain.

What sort of place do/did you live in? Was it easy to find accommodation?

I lived in a town house within the ring road, $2,000 per month, in a Chinese community. Accommodation was very easy to find. We worked through one agent only and found one the second day of my visit.

What is the social life like? Was it easy to make a new group of local friends?

Being a non-Mandarin speaker, I only made local friends at work; none in the area I am living in. Social life in our Chinese community seems well developed. People share the alleyway together, especially in summer.

What do you like best about China?

The opportunity to learn about the challenges faced by the country and how the economy develops.

What do you like least about China?

The fact that some Chinese people – although a limited number – genuinely dislike foreigners.

What advice would you have for anyone thinking of coming to live and work in China?

Build up a reasonable level of Mandarin first; one that is sufficient to start interacting socially, in order to learn further through daily-life communication.

Ken Sherman – researcher

How did you come to be living in China?

To conduct fieldwork research for my PhD dissertation. I lived in Shanghai for two years.

What was your first impression about China?

Noisy and busy and exciting. It was difficult to get basic things done at first. People were friendly and helpful.

What was your visa status? Was it difficult to get such a visa?

I had an F visa for *fangwen*, essentially for a researcher. It was very easy for me to get, but I had already established institutional affiliation with a major academic institution in Shanghai. They took care of the necessary invitations and paperwork.

What sort of place did you live in? Was it easy to find accommodation?

In the '90s, westerners were still required to choose between living in dormitories or expensive housing designed for expatriates, with little in between. This has since changed. I rented a small apartment in the city centre (in the French Concession, near Huaihai Road). In 2000, the rent was ¥2,500 [£179/$357] per month. The apartment was about 20 years old and not at all luxurious, but very adequate for me. It had two large rooms, one of which I used as a lounge/study, the other as a bedroom, plus a small kitchen and bathroom. The apartment was unfurnished when I rented it, but the landlord furnished it well with my rent money, and after 18 months, decreased my rent to ¥2,000. The apartment did not have a washing machine, but I was able to make an arrangement with the landlord. They would have had to raise the rent a few hundred yuan per month to recover part of the cost of installing a new washing machine. Instead, they suggested I pay them ¥100 for them to pick up my clothes and wash them for me. Over the course of my stay we both came out ahead.

Friends with business salaries typically lived in nicer apartments, paying ¥5,000–¥6,000 per month.

I found the apartment through a real estate agent. I consulted many such agents, each showing me about three apartments before giving up on me. Most seemed quite tricky and played a lot of games – I only felt comfortable with two. I found the agents by simply walking around the neighbourhoods I hoped to live in, looking for realtors, and walking in. By law they were only allowed to receive a total commission worth one month's rent, but in practice they tried to receive one and a half to two months' commission by overcharging both parties. In my case I paid half a month, and the landlord paid a full month.

What was the social life like in your area? Was it easy to make a new group of local friends?

Shanghai is a very vibrant city with an exciting nightlife. It may take some time to begin with, but once you have made a few friends it is easy to meet a lot of people. I did make friends and establish long-term relationships, but perhaps not as close and not as easily as in other places. The Shanghainese can be very helpful and friendly, but have a reputation of being more inward looking, not as open to outsiders. I believe it is not as easy to make friends with local Shanghainese as it is in Beijing or Taibei. This is based on my own experience, and anecdotal evidence from friends who have lived in these cities.

What do you like best about China?

The people. It takes a long time and a lot of work to get to know people on their own terms, but I find it vastly rewarding. And the food. Where else can you eat such fabulous food on such a low budget?

What do you like least about China?

The difficulty in getting things done. For many things this gets easier with time, but it does take more work to live in China. Of course, this also becomes one of the rewarding things about living in China, but it can be difficult to see it that way at the beginning.

What advice would you have for anyone thinking of coming to live and work in China?

Patience. Everything will take longer, and seem more complicated, than it should. It is extremely worthwhile to work at getting to know China and the Chinese on their own terms, rather than expecting them to do all the work to understand you on your terms. When you are about to reach boiling point, short trips away are most advisable and productive. Rather than avoidance, such trips should be seen as part of the adaptation process. Keep your hobbies or develop new ones, eat good food, and make friends.

More practically, as soon as you arrive, get hold of some kind of weekly English-language newspaper or magazine advertising local events and the major western social and business organisations. Also, there are now many websites that offer up-to-the-minute information for people living in or moving to Shanghai – simply enter Shanghai into Google.

Alex Cribbin – student in Beijing for three months

How can you get to make friends with local people?

In the university setting there are many Chinese students who want to find language partners to exchange Chinese for a foreign language, mostly English, and this is quite a good platform to make friends with local Chinese. These exchanges are sometimes arranged through the university, but mainly you will find adverts for 'language exchanges' in all the cafés and restaurants on campus.

Other than this, young Chinese people tend to be pretty open, although you will need to know some Mandarin to converse with them.

What is the current attitude to young Chinese people having western boyfriend/girlfriends?

This is not frowned upon by any means, at least in my experience. Although you do have to be careful because evidently there are some young Chinese people who see westerners as a ticket out of China or to greater things and will therefore try to exploit a boyfriend/girlfriend relationship. I have had friends who have found themselves in tricky situations with their language partners who suddenly want more from them.

Is there anything that surprised you about Beijing that people thinking of going there should know about?

I think the thing that stood out for me the most, and was indeed quite surprising, was really how much of an alien you are when you first come to the country. Even though I knew that everyone spoke a different language and that I was in a foreign country, the feeling was still very intense. Much more so than places I've been in Europe and I think that's mainly because in Beijing it is really rare to find someone who speaks English.

Other than the obvious language barrier, the quality of the air definitely takes some getting used to, and also the road traffic is rather crazy – many of my friends from Europe were scared to cross the road!

How have you found travelling on public transport?

I don't think efficient is the first word that comes to mind when I think of Bejing public transport, but it isn't by any means difficult to get around. There are plenty of taxis around, which cost about ¥30–¥40 for a 20-minute cab ride. There are also a lot of 'black taxis', so if you're in a large group you can bargain a price to get into the city centre – no more than ¥10 per person.

There are currently three lines on the metro system: Line 1, Line 2 and Line 13. The first two are mainly in the city centre; Line 13 is often nicknamed the farmer line as it goes right out into the suburbs. Tickets on Line 13 are ¥5 flat rate and then another ¥3 flat rate for Line 1 or 2.

As for buses, I never quite got my head around the bus system. I think I only rode the bus once. I knew the bus number and exactly where I was going beforehand, but still managed to get off at the wrong place. The buses are always extremely crowded. I would not recommend them for getting around, but it's definitely worth trying for the experience!

What did you like about Beijing and what did you dislike?

I found Beijing quite an overwhelming place, although I have to say I liked this feeling. There was always the sense that something was going on, and I guess there is a sense of excitement living in a city that is really up-and-coming in terms of the future of the world. As for dislikes, I reckon they were the small day-to-day things that you only really think about when you're there.

Before You Go

VISAS, WORK PERMITS AND CITIZENSHIP

Luckily for you, the government of China has been trying to make entry easier for the increasing number of foreign visitors attracted to China. Usually it is not difficult to obtain a visa. There are eight different types and it takes roughly three to five days for the Chinese embassy or consulate-general to issue one. However, during the popular summer months, the embassy and consulate-general may apply more stringent standards for visa applications in order to limit the number of tourists.

Travelling to Tibet is more complicated. Special travel permits are required in addition to the Chinese visitor's visa; moreover, the regulations are continually changing and it is advisable to check the permit requirements before your trip.

- **The need for foreigners** With a population of 1.3 billion China has never been short of workers. However, China does need foreign investors and professionals. In 2005, around 380,000 foreigners registered to live and work in China. At the end of 2003 the government said it was prepared to grant permanent residence status to foreigners if they are professionals or investors. However, it remains fairly difficult for foreigners to obtain residence permits. Only those occupying senior company positions, who have lived and worked in China for several years, can have any realistic prospect of 'green-card' status.

The validity for a single or double-entry visa is 90 days from the date of issue. This means you have to enter China no later than 90 days after the visa has been issued. Often you will be permitted to stay for up to 30 days, which can be extended in some cases. Note that you should apply for your visa extension at the nearest Public Security Bureau (PSB). If you intend to stay for a year or more you are

required to have a health check and also an HIV test before entering the country. Some employers can insist you take an HIV test and chest scan at a clinic in China once you arrive in order to qualify for a work permit and work unit card.

Visas for Mainland China

Visit (L visa)

If you are going to China as a tourist, to visit family or for other personal reasons, you should apply for an L visa. This will grant you a 30-day stay, which can usually be extended twice – 30 additional days for each extension. If you are a frequent visitor to China you can apply for a double or a multiple-entry visa. Multiple-entry visas are valid for six months or 12 months. However, they are usually granted to those who have family members or who own real estate in China. Although it is not impossible for individual travellers to get multiple-entry visas, it is not very common. If you have family in China, you must submit proof of relationship or an invitation letter from your family along with your visa application. If you own property in China, you must submit both the original and a photocopy of the property ownership certificate (the original copy will be returned to you). Holders of L visas are not allowed to take up any employment in China during their stay.

Visiting Tibet

An L visa is required for entry to Tibet. Additionally, you must apply for a Tibet Tourism Permit (TTP). Foreigners are not officially allowed to travel independently in Tibet and the TTP is only available to those booked on a tour with an approved travel agency. Most agencies include the permit in a tour package and do not arrange permits separately. However, it is still possible to find agencies willing to arrange an inexpensive, 'single-person tour', which buy the right to enter Lhasa but provides little support thereafter. Applications can be made through independent travel agencies around China. Beijing, Shanghai and Chengdu remain the best places to organise paperwork and it usually takes about four working days to get a permit.

In theory, the TTP only grants you the right to travel around the Lhasa district. Those hoping to make more extensive tours of Tibet may find it more economical to arrange everything in advance. While it's easy to book onward tours from Lhasa, agencies will require you to hire a vehicle and a driver/guide, as well as obtain a separate Alien Travel Permit for any 'non-open' areas you may wish to visit. The result can be very expensive.

The PSB is ultimately responsible for vetting applicants and granting all permits and technically only deal with travel agencies and not individuals. However, once in Tibet it may be possible to make successful applications at local PSB offices. Many travellers have successfully got permits at the Shigatse PSB for access to Sakya, Everest Base Camp, Nangartse, Shalu, Gyantse and anywhere on the Friendship Highway. You will always need to provide copies of your visa and passport when making an application.

It is always advisable to check the permit requirements and the corresponding application methods as they change frequently.

Useful resources

China International Travel Services: *(head office)* 010 6608 7126; shuyu@cits.com.cn; www.cits.net; *(Los Angeles)* 626 568 8993; info@citsusa.com; www.citsusa.com

Tibet Travel Expert: 021 6431 1184; www.tibet-tour.com

Business (F visa)

This visa is for foreigners to come to China for business-related purposes or scientific-technological and cultural exchanges. Students who go to China for short-term (less than six months) advanced studies or internships must also apply for an F visa (not an X visa). For most F visas, you need to provide an invitation letter from the host company or organisation in China.

You can apply for a multiple-entry visa under the following circumstances:

- The organisation in China mainly responsible for your business visit specifies that you will need to enter China more than once in a short period. It should be stated in the application, in as much detail as possible, how many times you will need to enter and how long you will be staying each time.
- You have investments in China and need to enter the country to manage them from time to time.
- You are in a management position in a foreign company in China.

- You need to visit China frequently in order to execute contracts signed with Chinese companies.
- You have visited China with F visas twice in the last 12 months.

Multiple-entry visas for business purposes are available for six months and 12 months. You are required to provide proof, such as a business licence carrying your name and contracts signed with the business partners, to apply for a multiple-entry visa.

Those applying for an F-visa for China in Hong Kong will find things much easier. Hong Kong agencies are able to quickly and efficiently arrange business visas with minimum fuss. For this reason, many people who live in China but do not technically qualify for any of the other kinds of visa, routinely travel to Hong Kong to apply for a six-month F-visa.

Employment (Z visa)

It is necessary to get an employment (Z) visa before starting work in China. After obtaining a Work Permit for Aliens, issued by the Chinese Ministry of Labour, or a Foreign Expert's Licence, issued by the Chinese Foreign Expert Bureau, the authorised Chinese unit will provide you with a visa notification. You need this visa notification as well as your original copy of the Work Permit or Foreign Expert's Licence when applying for a Z visa. This visa is valid for one entry only with a duration of three months. You are required to go through residential formalities in the local public security bureau within 30 days of first entering China. You will then be issued with a Foreigner's Residence Certificate as proof of identity for living and working in China, though this will be valid only with an appropriate visa.

- **Changing your visa status** It is possible to change your visa status when you are in China, even though it is not encouraged by the Chinese government. If you are offered a job after arriving in China, your employer should apply to the Chinese Foreign Expert Bureau for a change of your visa status. You then have to go through all the formalities to get a Foreigner's Residence Certificate as mentioned above.

Dependents of the applicant should apply for the same visa if they are going to stay in China with the employed applicant. They will have to provide proof of kinship, such as marriage certificates and/or birth certificates, to identify their relationship with the employed.

Education (X visa)

Once you have received an offer from a university or college in China, you must apply for an X visa (but for study periods shorter than six months, you should apply for an F visa instead). An X visa is for those who intend to study or enrol in advanced studies or internships for six months or more. Apart from the Visa Application Form (Q1) you will need to submit Foreign Student Application Forms (JW201 or JW202), issued by the Ministry of Education and the enrolment letters from the educational organisation in China. If you intend to stay in China for over a year, you are required to have a medical check-up and attach the Physical Examination Certificate to the application. An X visa is a single-entry visa and you, as the holder, should go through residential formalities in the local PSB within 30 days of entry into China. Holders of X visas are prohibited from any employment during their stay.

Journalists (J-1 and J-2 visas)

In China, there are specific visas for visiting journalists. Foreign-resident journalists should apply for J-1 visas before entering China. Foreign journalists who are on temporary interview missions in China and will leave the country when the mission is completed should apply for J-2 visas. A letter from the Information Department of the Ministry of Foreign Affairs should be attached to the application. A journalist can also apply for such a letter from the Foreign Affairs Office in Shanghai or Guangdong. In addition, journalists must have a letter from their employer to confirm the purpose of the visit. In the run-up to the Beijing Olympics new laws were introduced giving foreign journalists new freedom to travel and interview without having to register movements and seek permission. The implementation and effectiveness of these rules was tested as the games approached.

Permanent residence (D visa)

A D visa is for someone who is going to reside permanently in China. It is only for people who have already got their application for residence approved by the government of China. You should present a permanent residence confirmation form for the municipality or county where you plan to live, along with your visa application form. You will have to apply for a Foreigner's Residence Certificate, which is the actual permit for staying in China for an unlimited time, from the local Public Security Bureau within 30 days of your arrival in China. You are required to submit your certificate to the PSB for examination once a year.

In the past, it was not easy to obtain permanent residence in China unless you were a close relative of a Chinese citizen. In 2001, the Chinese Ministry of Public Security launched a reform of the residence policy and mapped out the plan of a 'Green Card'-like system. Under this system, foreigners who do not intend to take up Chinese nationality, but who do plan to stay in China permanently are granted long-term residence (three years or more) and multiple entry visas to China. Under the revised immigration policy of 2003 and implemented in 2004, you are qualified to apply for permanent residence if you:

- Are invited as a senior advisor by provincial or ministerial level government institutions, or hi-tech professionals and senior managerial personnel who come to the country for scientific and technological cooperation projects, key project agreements or for professional personnel exchange programmes in China.
- Have an outstanding contribution to make to the city, or work for free-aid protocols for the city or for the central government.
- Are a scholar who is hired by universities or colleges at the provincial and ministerial level as an associate professor or above.
- Are hired as senior management staff or technicians, such as president, vice president, vice general manger etc, in a joint venture or foreign-invested company.

FACT

- In 2001, the Chinese Ministry of Public Security launched a reform of the residence policy and mapped out the plan of a 'Green Card'-like system.

- Have invested a minimum of $3 million (£1.5 million) in a Chinese city.
- Are granted important international awards, are distinguished foreign-born Chinese, and those who studied abroad but work in China for a senior rank management position. This is limited to Chinese people with foreign nationality.
- Are a dependent of a foreign expert, under the above conditions and who works in China in a senior position.

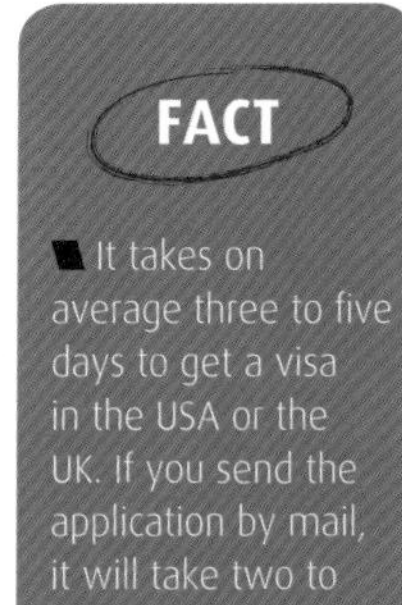

Application methods

The application method for all the different types of visa is basically the same. Apart from the specific documents mentioned in each section, there are a few documents that are required with the application for any of the visas. They include:

- Your valid passport (original) which has at least one blank page left. Your passport must be valid for at least a further six months at the time of your visa application.
- Visa Application Form (Q1). The same form is used to apply for any of the visas.
- Two passport photos. One should be attached to the application form.
- If an applicant was born in China but currently holds a foreign passport, he or she should also submit the original Chinese passport or the last foreign passport held with a Chinese visa in it.

It takes on average three to five days to get a visa in the USA or the UK. If you send the application by mail, it will take two to three weeks.

Note that the embassy and consulate-general of the People's Republic of China in the USA do not accept applications by mail. If you cannot apply for the visa in person, you have to entrust someone else to do it for you. You may choose to appoint a travel agency. Same-day and express processing services are available with additional charges. Payments must be settled either by cash or postal order. Personal cheques are not accepted. The embassy and consulate-general in the USA also accept money orders, cashier's cheques and company cheques. If you send your application to the embassy in the UK by mail, you should enclose a self-addressed envelope for the embassy to return your passport with your visa enclosed.

You can also apply for your visas to China in Hong Kong. You can apply to the Ministry of Foreign Affairs for your visa, which takes about two days to process. You can also apply through travel agencies such as China Travel Service (CTS) but note that these travel agencies only accept applications for travel visas.

Useful resources

Ministry of Foreign Affairs of the People's Republic of China, Hong Kong: Office of the Commissioner, 7th Floor, Lower Block, China Resources Building, 26 Harbour Road, Wanchai, Hong Kong; (+852) 3413 2300

UK Chinese embassy: 31 Portland Place, London W1B 1QD; 020 7631 1430; www.chinese-embassy.org.uk

US Chinese embassy: Visa Office, 2201 Wisconsin Avenue, NW, Room 110, Washington, DC 20007; 202 338 6688; chnvisa@bellatlantic.net; www.china-embassy.org

UK Chinese consulates-general:

Edinburgh: 55 Corstorphine Road, Edinburgh EH12 5QG; 0131 337 3220
Manchester: Denison House, 49 Denison Road, Rusholme, Manchester M14 5RX; 0161 224 8672
US Chinese consulates-general:
Houston: 3417 Montrose Boulevard, Houston, Texas 77006; 713 524 0780; visa@chinahouston.org; www.chinahouston.org
Los Angeles: 3rd Floor, 500 Shatto Place, Los Angeles, CA 90020; 213 807 8006; visa@chinaconsulatela.org; losangeles.china-consulate.org
New York: 520 12th Ave. New York, NY 10036; 212 868 2078; cnconsulate@yahoo.com; www.nyconsulate.prchina.org
San Francisco: 1450 Laguna Street, San Francisco CA 94115; 415 674 2940; www.chinaconsulatesf.org

Fees

Visa application fees are calculated on the number of entries rather than the type of visa you apply for. The following charges are for the Chinese Embassies in the USA and the UK. Note that the application fees for other nationalities in the embassies above are in general lower.

Fees for Visas

Type of visa	US$	GBP£
Single-entry visa	$100	£30
Double-entry visas	$100	£45
Multiple entry for six months	$100	£60
Multiple entry for 12 months	$100	£90
Express service (same day)	$30 extra	£15 extra
Express service (two day)	$20 extra	£25 extra
Mail service	N/a	£20

These fees are subject to change; for the latest information please contact the Chinese embassy or consulate in your area.

FACT

■ Students who are going to study in Macau are granted a one-year visa that must be renewed annually throughout their years of studying.

Visas for Macau

Short-term stay

Currently, citizens of 53 countries, including the USA, the UK and most European countries do not need a visa if they stay for less than 30 days. Citizens from the EU or members of the Treaty of Schengen are permitted to stay for up to 90 days without a visa. Other visitors should apply for a visa through the Chinese embassy or consulate-general before visiting Macau. Alternatively you can apply for the visa on the spot when you arrive in the city. The charge for obtaining a visa on the spot is MOP$100 (£6.40/$12.70). Extensions of visas should be made at least 10 days before the expiration and the maximum extended period is 90 days. Students who are going to study in Macau are granted a one-year visa that must be renewed annually throughout their years of studying.

Transit

If you are granted a visa-free stay from the Macau government, there is obviously no need to apply for a transit visa when you stop off in the city. Visitors who arrive in Macau through Macau International Airport are granted a five-day visa-free stay so long as they hold onward tickets and have booked seats with the airlines. If you enter Macau through other immigration ports, you can stay for two days without a visa.

Employment

Employers have to apply to the Labour and Employment Bureau in order to bring in employees from other countries. After the application is preliminarily approved, you, the employee, will be issued with an approval letter, which allows you to stay in Macau for 20 days while awaiting a formal approval. After receiving a formal approval, you will need to submit six passport photos and two photocopies of your passport in addition to the letter of approval to apply for an employment card (known as the 'blue card').

Labour and Employment Bureau: Rotunda de Carlos da Maia, Macao; (+853) 28564109; dsalinfo@dsal.gov.mo; www.dsal.gov.mo

Chinese Citizenship

Due to the difficulties and hassles that Chinese citizens continue to face in travelling internationally, it is virtually unimaginable for someone from Europe or North America to voluntarily swap their passport for a Chinese passport – regardless of their patriotism or politics. However, under the current law, it is technically possible

for foreign nationals or stateless persons to become 'naturalised' Chinese citizens if they are near relatives of Chinese nationals or if they have settled in China. A foreigner should apply to the Public Security Bureau for naturalisation.

In the past, most of the approved applicants were close relatives of Chinese nationals; not many foreigners were granted permanent residence for business or other reasons. However, in early 2003, the Chinese government first granted long-term residence permits and multi-entry visas to foreigners who had no relatives in China. The permit allows a foreigner to stay in the country for three to five years so there is no need to renew the permit annually.

FACT

If you wish to be naturalised and become a Chinese citizen, you should apply to the Ministry of Public Security attaching supporting documents, such as your marriage certificate (if applicable) and any business certificates.

If you wish to be naturalised and become a Chinese citizen, you should apply to the Ministry of Public Security attaching supporting documents, such as your marriage certificate (if applicable) and any business certificates. The Ministry will take several factors into consideration for each application. If you have close relatives in China, it is more likely that you will be granted citizenship. Moreover, if you have been an upstanding citizen in your home country and have also mastered the Chinese language, your chances of being granted citizenship are greatly increased.

The Chinese government does not allow dual nationality, except for citizens of Hong Kong and Macau who hold British national (overseas) passports and the Portuguese passport (MSAR). Naturalisation means that you will have to give up your original nationality.

Permanent residence in Macau

You are required to live in Macau for a continuous seven-year period in order to get permanent residence. The government issues a Temporary Residence Card (called the 'yellow card') to people who have near relatives who are Macau permanent residents and investors or professionals. Currently, successful applicants are initially granted a one-year or three-year permit. They can extend their stay but they have to do so at least 30 days before the expiration of their Temporary Residence Card. The government will grant another two years of stay if it is satisfied with the behaviour of the applicant during their initial stay. There is no limit to the number of extensions you can make. After a person has stayed in Macau continuously for seven years, he or she will be granted a Permanent Residence Card (called the 'white card').

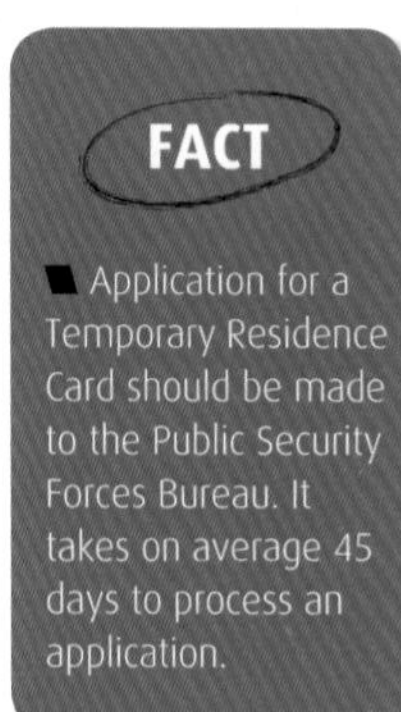

Useful resources

Identification Department: Avenida da Praia Grande, No 804, Edificia China plaza, 1st, 19th, 20th andar, Macau; (+853) 2837 0777; info@dsi.gov.mo; www.dsi.gov.mo

Ministry of Foreign Affairs: No 2, Chaoyangmen Nandajie, Chaoyang District, Beijing 100701; 010 6596 1114; www.fmprc.gov.cn/eng

Ministry of Public Security: No 14 East Chang'an Avenue, Beijing 100741; 010 6512 2831; www.psb.gov.cn

Public Security Forces Bureau: Calçada dos Quartéis, Quartel de S Francisco, Macao; (+853) 2855 9999; info@fsm.gov.mo; www.fsm.gov.mo

THE LANGUAGES

Although written Chinese was standardised over 2,000 years ago, many different dialects are still spoken in China. The written language is based on characters. Each character stands for one syllable that represents either a word or part of a word. There

Simplified *v.* traditional Chinese writing

In the 1950s, the Chinese communist government introduced the simplified writing system with the aim of achieving a higher literacy rate. Simplified characters have fewer strokes than traditional ones, which make them easier to write and to remember. Moreover, in the simplified writing system, there are fewer characters in total. However, simplified characters are not used in Hong Kong, Macau and Taiwan. In general, people who know one script can read the other, but it can be difficult. In the 1980s and 1990s, some people pressed for a return to the traditional writing system in the mainland. However, the simplified writing system is still the only official script and hardly any schools on the mainland teach students traditional writing.

are about 5,000 characters in daily use and they are the smallest linguistic units. The form of a character does not determine the pronunciation (although it can hint at it) and therefore the same words can be pronounced differently in different dialects.

Mandarin or *putonghua* is the official spoken language in China. It is the first language of 70% of the total population. Other dialects are:

- *Wu* (8.4%)

  Mainly spoken by people living in Zhejiang, Jiangsu and Anhui.
- Cantonese or *Yue* (5%)

  Spoken in Hong Kong, Guangdong, southern Guangxi Zhuang Autonomous Region, parts of Hainan, Macau, and also in many overseas settlements.
- *Xiang* also known as Hunanese (5%)

  The main language of people in Hunan and other south-central regions.
- *Hakka* (4%)

  Spoken in a wide range of areas including Guangdong, south-western Fujian, Jiangxi, Hunan, Yunnan, Guangxi, Guizhou, Sichuan, Hainan, Taiwan, Singapore, Malaysia, Indonesia, and amongst many overseas Chinese communities.
- *Min*(4.2%)

  Common in Fujian, large areas of Taiwan and Hainan, and also parts of eastern Guangdong.
- *Gan*(2.4%)

  Spoken by most people in Jiangxi, the eastern part of Hunan, and the south-eastern corner of Hubei.

Mandarin is the language of instruction in schools so that, even in regions where it is not the first language, you can still easily get by with it. When speaking to older

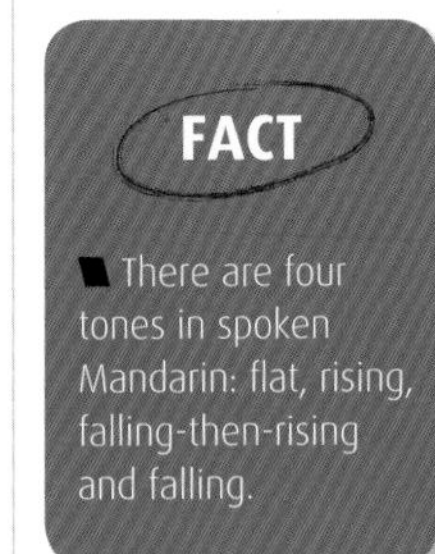
FACT
There are four tones in spoken Mandarin: flat, rising, falling-then-rising and falling.

generations, it is common for younger people to 'translate' from Mandarin. Even their own pronunciation of the standard Mandarin can be far from what is taught in the classrooms of Beijing.

Nowadays, the *Pinyin* system, using the Roman alphabet, is used to indicate the standard pronunciation of Chinese characters in Mandarin. It is the means by which most foreigners begin to learn Chinese and will feel fairly logical and phonetic for English speakers, except for a few letters such as 'q' (which is pronounced 'ch'). The grammar is quite straightforward but Chinese is a tonal language, making it tricky for many foreigners to pick up.

While some joke that mispronunciation of a character can cause great offence (the usual example is 'ma', which can mean both mother and horse, depending on the tone), in context most sentences can be deciphered correctly, so don't be put off by the complexity of individual tones.

It is possible to pick up simple characters quite quickly, and recognise them on signs, hoardings or instructions. This can be helpful when choosing the filling for dumplings in a restaurant, or identifying the ladies' from the men's toilets. There are plenty of books in city bookshops offering help and instruction on the written language, and of course there's no better way to learn than by getting out there and practising! Even if you only learn the words to recognise signs, it can be greatly rewarding and useful when navigating the area you choose to live in.

One useful site, *www.chinalanguage.com,* includes online dictionaries for Mandarin and some other dialects. It also allows you to input English, Korean and Japanese words to look for the corresponding Chinese characters.

BANKING

How to open a bank account

You do not have to be a permanent resident to open a bank account. Foreigners can open bank accounts with a tourist visa or a work visa. You can open it in Chinese or US currencies, and you need to put a small deposit into the account. If your bank at home has branches in China, it may be possible to open an account in advance. It is probably easier to arrange this in your home country. You can also transfer some money to your account in China before you go, reducing the risks entailed with carrying too much cash.

Banks

Banks, in general, are open seven days a week, 9am–5pm. However, some banks may close earlier, such as 4pm at weekends, or have rest hours in the middle of the day.

Online banking brings enormous flexibility to frequent travellers. Using this, you can transfer money, get your balance and check your transaction history. You can also use other services like stopping or reporting the loss of a cheque, requesting statements, ordering your chequebook, changing address and sending/receiving secured messages to/from the bank.

Banks in Macau

Despite its relatively small size, there are more then 20 different banks in Macau. There are two banks that issue banknotes: Banco Nacional Ultramarino (BNU) and the Bank of China (Macau Branch). Coins are issued by the Monetary Authority of Macau. Banks in Macau open 9am–4.30pm from Monday to Friday. They are closed at lunchtime and on Saturday.

Main Banks

Bank of China, Bejing: 010 6659 6688; www.bank-of-china.com
Bank of Communications, Shanghai: 021 5878 1234; enquiry@bankcomm.com.hk; www.bankcomm.com.hk
China Construction Bank, Beijing: 010 6360 3660; www.ccbhk.com
China Merchants Bank, Beijing: 010 6642 6868; www.mbchina.com
China Minsheng Bank; service@cmbc.com.cn; www.cmbc.com.cn
Hua Xia Bank, Beijing: 010 6615 1199; webmaster@hxb.cc; www.hxb.com.cn
Industrial and Commercial Bank of China, Beijing: webmaster@icbc.com.cn; www.icbc.com.cn

The People's Bank of China, Beijing: 010 6619 4114; master@pbc.gov.cn; www.pbc.gov.cn
Monetary Authority of Macau: www.amcm.gov.mo
Banco Nacional Ultramarino: www.bnu.com.mo/en
Bank of China, Macau: www.bocmacau.com/eng/index.htm

- **Withdrawing money** It's easy to withdraw local currency direct from cash points across China using your credit/debit card. No local charge is applied, though your own foreign bank will likely levy a service fee. ATM machines exist in all cities across China, and can even be found now is some very small towns and villages. If you want to use your Maestro/Mastercard/Visa card to withdraw money, this can sometimes depend on whether the ATM is connected to an international data line. In most airports and major shopping centres, this is not a problem; in other areas, look out for the Bank of China machines which are more likely to service international cards. Credit card payments are becoming more common in mainland China. However, China is effectively developing its own financial infrastructure and international cards are not always accepted. You can normally use a credit card in large hotels and department stores.
- The websites www.mastercard.com/atmlocator and www.international.visa.com/ps are useful if you are trying to locate an ATM machine in the city where you are staying.

Exchanging money and international transfers

Most foreign currencies (the US dollar, British pound and euro included) can be exchanged through the Bank of China, though hotels and exchange booths provide similar services (international airports and border crossings will generally have exchange booths). It will normally be more economical to exchange currency in China. This is a country hungry for foreign cash and banks and financial companies offer reasonable rates. In contrast, western banks rarely have a surplus Chinese currency and normally offer terrible value.

As recently as five years ago, it was common to see black-market currency traders loitering around bank entrances offering exchange rates for foreign currency. As the Chinese banking system has become more streamlined and networked, these traders are largely redundant, but you may see some if you head to more rural areas.

Money transfers can be made in banks and post offices. Making transfers through the internet will probably save time, so long as you already have the service set up.

Exchanging money in Macau

In Macau, there are licensed moneychangers for exchanging travellers' cheques. These moneychangers open seven days a week and some even open 24 hours a day. There is one in the basement of the Hotel Lisboa, and another is near the bottom of the steps leading up to São Paulo.

Currency

Renminbi (RMB) literally means 'people's money'. In speech, one renminbi is referred to as a *yuan* (¥), or – even more informally – *kuai*, which literally means 'piece'. You can sometimes see 'RMB' on price tags. One yuan is divided into 10 *jiao* (or 'mao') and one jiao can be further divided into 10 *fen* (though this division in virtually unheard of now). Notes are in the values of ¥1, ¥2, ¥5, ¥10, ¥20, ¥50 and ¥100; there are four different values of coins: ¥1, five jiao, one jiao and five fen.

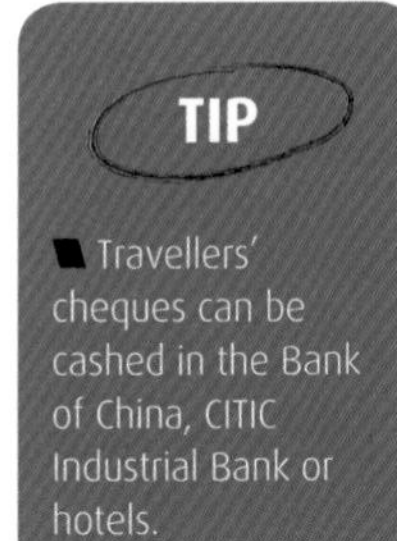

TIP

Travellers' cheques can be cashed in the Bank of China, CITIC Industrial Bank or hotels.

Macau's currency

Macau has used pataca since it was colonised by the Portuguese. Like Hong Kong, Macau uses the dollar as a unit. Prices are usually written as MOP$ or M$. There are five different denominations of bills: MOP$20, MOP$50, MOP$100, MOP$500 and MOP$1,000. Coins have the values of MOP$1, 50 cents, 20 cents and 10 cents. One Macau dollar is nearly equivalent to one Hong Kong dollar (HKD) and the Hong Kong dollar is widely accepted in all kinds of businesses.

The three currencies of greater China – the RMB, the MOP and the HKD – have been of roughly equal value for a long period of time. However, an important shift occurred in 2007 when the RMB, for the first time, became marginally more valuable than both the HKD and the MOP on the international money markets. It means the RMB is now often accepted in shops around Hong Kong.

i See *How to use this book* at the beginning of the book for currency conversions.

GETTING THERE

Plane

It is now very easy to fly to Beijing and Shanghai. In the past people tended to fly to Hong Kong, and then take another flight or train to mainland China. The Chinese government has been opening up its aviation market, and flying to Beijing or Shanghai now costs about the same as flying to Hong Kong. Flying from London to Beijing takes about 11 hours, and costs £400 plus for a return ticket in the low season. Flying to Shanghai takes one hour longer and the fare is more expensive. It is now possible to fly direct to many other Chinese cities (eg Qingdao), though with internal fares quite reasonably priced, check out both options before buying.

You can find companies advertising competitive fares in the travel pages of the Sunday newspapers and it's a good idea to check out what is on offer at flight comparison sites such as www.lowcost.com or travel sites such as www.expedia.com.

Flying from the USA may be easier and cheaper since Delta Airlines, which now has an office in Shanghai, gained approval to operate non-stop direct flights to Shanghai from its hub in Atlanta from March 2008. These flights will take just over 15 hours. Flights from New York currently start at about $850. It takes about 13 hours to Beijing from the east coast or 12 hours from the west coast. As with Europe, flying to Shanghai will take around one hour longer and may cost slightly more.

Airline and Useful Websites

Air Canada: www.aircanada.ca
Air France: www.airfrance.com
Air New Zealand: www.airnz.com.au
American Airlines: www.aa.com
Australia Airlines: www.australianairlines.com.au
British Airways: www.britishairways.com
Cathay Pacific Airway: www.cathaypacific.com
China Airlines: www.china-airlines.com
Delta Airlines: www.delta.com
Emirates Airlines: www.emirates.com
EVA Air: www.evaair.com
Finnair: www.finnair.com
Singapore Airlines: www.singaporeair.comwww.cheapflights.com
www.expedia.co.uk
www.onlinetravel.com
www.priceline.com
www.statravel.com
www.traveljungle.co.uk
www.travelsupermarket.com

The Trans-Siberian railway

Train

If you have time, an interesting alternative to flying is to travel from Europe to China by train. The famous Trans-Siberian railway connects China to Russia, Kazakhstan and Mongolia. From London, it takes about two weeks to get to Beijing, assuming that you do not stop over anywhere, and can be full of adventure. The service between Moscow and Beijing runs twice a week.

 The Man in Seat Sixty-one website (www.seat61.com) provides very useful details about travelling on the Siberian Railway, as well as other relevant information for travelling to China by ship.

FACT

For more information on how to import a car, see the *Cars and motoring* section in Daily life.

Ferry

Even though there are no ferry connections from western countries to China, you could fly to Japan and take the ferry to Shanghai. There are two ferry companies sailing all year round from Kobe and Osaka to Shanghai on a weekly basis. It costs about £100/$200 for a one-way economy ticket. Cabins with four berths and two berths are more expensive. You can book tickets via the Shanghai Ferry Company's website (www.shanghai-ferry.co.jp). You can also take the ferry between Kobe and Tianjin with China Express Line (www.celkobe.co.jp).

There are also ferry connections between South Korea and China. You can take a ferry to Yantai, Tianjin, Qingdao, Dalian, Shanghai or Dandong from the port of Incheon in South Korea. Ferries to most of the above cities operate two to three times a week and a one-way ticket costs about £57/ $113.

Ferry Companies

International Union Travel Agency: (+82) 02 777 6722
Jinchon Ferry Company: (+82) 02 517 8671
Taeya Travel: (+82) 02 514 6226. Sells ferry tickets to Tianjin.
Weidong Ferry Company: (+82) 02 3271 6710

Travel Services

China International Travel Service: (+86) 010 8522 7930; shuyu@cits.com.cn; www.cits.net
China Travel Service, Beijing: (+86) 010 6852 4860; bisc@chinats.com; www.chinats.com
China Youth Travel Service: (+86) 010 6513 3153
China Travel Service Hong Kong Ltd: (+852) 2789 5401; enquiry@chinatravel1.com; www.chinatravel1.com

PLANNING AN INTERNATIONAL MOVE

Removal and relocation companies

Even though it is probably cheaper to buy new furniture and electrical appliances for your new home in China, you may want to bring your beloved sofa or antiques with you. If you are moving from the UK, The British Association of Removers can provide a list of removers according to your current location. There are many removers in different parts of the USA and other countries as well. The cost depends greatly on the distance travelled and the weight/bulk of your possessions. Many companies also provide services for shipping vehicles. For more information on how to import a car, see the *Cars and motoring* section in Daily life.

Allied International: *(USA)* 800 323 1909; *(UK)* 020 8219 8000; *(Australia)* 3 9797 1600; *(Vancouver)* 800 795 2920; *(Toronto)* 866 267 9106; *www.alliedtoallied.com*
Allied Van Lines: 800 323 1909; insurance@alliedintl.com; www.alliedvan.com
The British Association of Removers: 020 8861 3331; www.removers.org.uk
Excess Baggage: 020 8324 2000; sales@excess-baggage.com; www.excess-baggage.com
Sterling Corporate Relocation: (London) 020 8841 7000; mail@sterlingrelocation.com; *(Paris)* 1 49 39 47 00; relocation@sterling-intl.fr; www.sterlingrelocation.com

Importing a car

The quota system for importing cars was completely abolished in January 2005, and in 2006 the tax on imported vehicles was reduced to only 25%. To import a car, you will usually need to pay a tax amounting to about 52% of the car's value although different ports charge different rates.

The current and future tax reductions have attracted many car manufacturers to enter this huge market. The quality of domestically manufactured vehicles has been improving and is now comparable to many foreign manufactured vehicles. Import tax, shipping fees and the higher basic price together make foreign cars much more expensive than domestic cars.

The Japanese Toyota Prius is now manufactured in China where it is an expensive car, costing from ¥288,000 (£18,770/$38,000); domestic Chinese brands cost less than half that amount.

Registration

You must register your vehicle in China before you can use it. The vehicle registration form can be obtained at the local offices of the Traffic Management Bureau. You are also required to supply the following documents: proof of the car owner's identity, proof of the origin of the car (receipt of purchase, import certificate, etc), certificate issued by the manufacturer proving the safety of the car (for locally manufactured vehicles), other import documents, receipts of tax paid and also photos of the car to be registered. Your car also has to be examined before registration. It usually takes three to five working days to issue the registration certificate. The fee is ¥10.

Useful resources

China Importing Car Trading Centre: zjqm@sina.com; www.chinaauto.com.cn
Ministry of Commerce: http://english.mofcom.gov.cn

Pets

If you want to bring your pets (cats and dogs only) with you to China, they will have to be quarantined for at least 15 days. Each person is only allowed to bring one pet in. You are not allowed to import birds. Apart from checking the regulations for importing pets in China, you also need to check the requirements for taking your pets out of your home country, especially if you want them to return with you some years later. In some cases, they are not allowed back once they have left the country. You should also check with the airline for the procedures and costs, if applicable, for bringing a pet with you on the flight.

FACT
More species of birds live in China than anywhere else in the world.

In general, two certificates are required for bringing pets into China: a vaccination certificate and a health certificate. You can ask a qualified veterinarian in your home country to issue a health certificate which should be issued within 30 days prior to departure. The vaccination certificate can be attached to the health certificate and all vaccinations should again be done within 30 days prior to departure. Copies of the certificate may be required when you leave your country and the airline staff may ask to look at it before allowing your pet to board the plane.

You should also check the regulations for importing pets with the local government authority as the rules vary. For instance, Shanghai is one of the few areas that would allow you to bring a cat into China. Chinese customs offices have the right to deport animals if the vaccination records are not authenticated and notarised by a state notary. Importation of exotic animals may be considered but you must obtain approval from the Chinese customs in advance. You should consider preparing Chinese-translated versions of the documents. This will probably help the customs officers to handle the matter and save your time at immigration. The Chinese embassy in your country should be able to translate the documents, or at least provide useful details about how to get certified documents in Chinese.

You will have to declare your pet at the customs department on arrival. Take your pet, fee and certificates to the customs and immigration plant and quarantine office at the airport, located before the customs exit. The certificates will be examined and customs officers will give you a stamped document allowing you to bring your pet in. You will have to pay a charge of ¥150 (£10.80/$21.50) for the examination and the stamped document. Note that there is a mandatory 15–30 days quarantine period, but you can usually keep your pet with you at home for this period. Quarantine officers will come and inspect your pet during the 30-day period, and a small fee will be charged. If visitors do not have their pets with them when entering China, they are advised to phone ahead before departure to ensure there will be staff at the airport office to meet their pets from the plane.

■ A dog must be registered with the local police station when you move into your apartment.

Cats and dogs

Cats must be vaccinated against Enteritis (E3) within 12 months of their arrival in China. You will need a certificate for feline panleucopenia and feline respiratory disease complex vaccinations. Keeping dogs is not encouraged by the Chinese government. Only one dog is permitted per family and in many cities there is a size limit for dogs. A dog must be registered with the local police station when you move into your apartment. All dogs, whether they are bought locally or imported from outside China, are required by law to be fully quarantined before they are licensed. In some cities, only local Chinese can register dogs and you will need a local resident to act on your behalf. However, many cities allow foreigners who hold a residence visa or a work permit to register their dogs. The cost for a dog licence is high and varies from area to area. Even within Shanghai, for example, the city is divided into two areas: the inner ring road and the outer ring road. People living in the inner ring road have to pay ¥2,000 to register a dog while people in the outer ring road pay ¥1,000.

To register a dog:

- Complete an application form and return it to the local Public Security Bureau
- Attach two photos of your dog (face and side)
- Attach a passport-sized photo of yourself to the application form

There are some companies that provide a service helping overseas visitors to bring their pets into China., including Pet Relocation, based in Beijing www.petrelocation.com.cn

Macanese regulations

In Macau, endangered animal species are banned from importation. A licence of import is required and the imported pet has to be filed with the appropriate Division of Hygiene and Sanidade (DHS) office. You could contact the Macao customs service for further information.

Useful resources

Animal and Plant Quarantine Bureau: (+86) 021 6586 3030; www.shanghaiguide.com

Customs General Administration (PRC): (+86) 010 6519 4114; www.customs.gov.cn

Hong Qiao Airport: (+86) 021 6268 8918

Macao Customs Service: (+853) 2855 9944; SA-info@fsm.gov.mo; www.sa.gov.mo

Ministry of Health: (+86) 010 68792114; manage@moh.gov.cn; www.moh.gov.cn

Pudong Airport: (+86) 021 3848 4500

世纪出版集团

Setting Up Home

A BACKGROUND TO ACCOMMODATION

China is currently undergoing huge social change, with tens of millions of people relocating to the big cities to enjoy improved living standards and better work opportunities. In 2007, the average household size was 2.9 people in most provinces in China and this is expected to decrease to 2.4 in the next 20 years. The average monthly income of migrant workers in cities, that is Chinese who have moved from one province to another, is ¥966 (£59/$120). However, the figures vary from province to province and the income in fast-developing provinces is usually a little higher. The average income of urban people is more than twice that of those who live in the countryside.

Eastern China is much more populated than the west. New national construction projects and the discovery of oil fields in the west mean that more people are seeking a future in the west. However, due to geographic and climatic factors, there is little prospect of western China ever matching eastern China for population density.

CHOOSING WHERE TO LIVE

House styles, prices and facilities vary from region to region. High-rise flats and houses with gardens are both available in big cities like Beijing, Shanghai, Guangdong and Tianjin. There are more parks and open spaces than might be expected in the big cities; it is intended that Beijing will eventually have green space on 50% of its area, though currently this still feels like a very distant dream. In major cities and the area surrounding them, houses and flats can fetch higher prices.

Macau

Macau comprises the peninsula of Macau and the two islands of Taipa and Coloane, which have been merged together in recent years due to land reclamation. Most people used to live on the peninsula of Macau, but thanks to the efficient transport linkage, more people now live on Taipa and Coloane. In 2006, Macau's population grew to over half a million. Its land area is just 28.2 sq km.

Useful resources

City Weekend: www.cityweekend.com.cn. A bi-weekly English guide to life in China that provides information on Shanghai and Beijing.

Ministry of Foreign Affairs: 010 6596 1114; webmaster@mfa.gov.cn; www.fmprc.gov.cn/eng

That's Magazine: *www.thatsmags.com.* Provides classified information on living in Shanghai, Beijing, Guangzhou and Shenzhen, including information on accommodation, employment and other services.

Macao Special Adminstrative Region of The People's Republic of China (MSAR): www.macau.gov.mo

Macao Trade and Investment Promotion Institute: www.ipim.gov.mo. Gives information on investment, residency, full contacts of official and business bodies.

NEIGHBOURHOODS OF SHANGHAI

Shanghai may be mainland China's most populous conurbation but it is a compact city, with most of the major tourist sights clustered together. Thanks largely to the commercial development of Pudong, business and office space is more spread out. Fortunately, in its elevated and subterranean metro system, Shanghai can boast the best urban public transport system in mainland China, albeit one that occasionally groans under the sheer weight of numbers.

The city is officially divided into 19 administrative districts, nine of which comprise most of the main 'city centre' area. However, there are two further methods of division that you should be aware of. One is a fairly simple east-west divide. 'Pudong' means, literally, 'east of the Huangpu River' and is a landscape of brashly modern buildings and wide boulevards, built from scratch since 1990 or so. To the west of the Huangpu is 'Puxi', the old city in all its cluttered, historic glory.

Due to Shanghai's colonial past and its modern-day influences, the former 'concession' zones are also still referred to. The French Concession, the most famous of these, officially straddles several districts, principally Luwan and Xuhui, but has an identity all of its own.

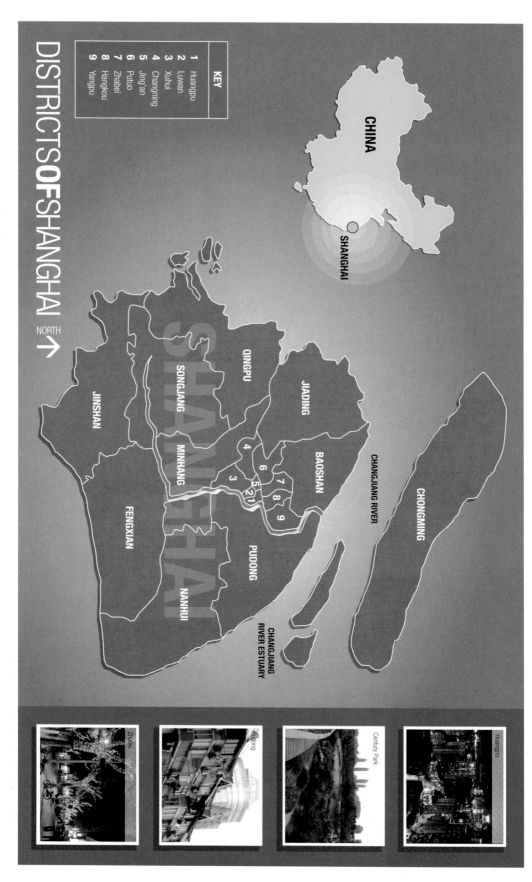

DISTRICTS OF SHANGHAI

NORTH

CHINA
SHANGHAI

CHONGMING
CHANGJIANG RIVER
BAOSHAN
JIADING
CHANGJIANG RIVER ESTUARY
PUDONG
QINGPU
SHANGHAI
SONGJANG
MINHANG
NANHUI
FENGXIAN
JINSHAN

KEY	
1	Huangpu
2	Luwan
3	Xuhui
4	Changning
5	Jing'an
6	Putuo
7	Zhabei
8	Hangkou
9	Yangpu

Huangpu

Century Park

Pudong

Zhabei

Shanghai is still overwhelmingly Chinese in character and expatriate residents tend to cluster in certain zones. Thanks to the fashionable dining and drinking scene, the French Concession is especially popular, particularly with younger foreign residents. Pudong has less character but offers pockets of luxury, where high gates encircle compounds of huge villas with large gardens and private pools. Shopping and entertainment facilities, meanwhile, are mainly concentrated in the central areas.

When choosing from the different areas, proximity to your work is an important thing to bear in mind – if there is any way you can avoid commuting during the rush hour, do so! The public transport system is comprehensive and runs efficiently. However, the sheer number of people attempting to make their way up and down elevators and onto trains can leave you, literally, fighting for breath.

Shanghai experienced China's first real property boom in the 1990s and hasn't looked back. However, despite what it costs to buy a new flat, it's possible to find pleasant, furnished apartments that are relatively inexpensive to rent, especially in relation to prices in London or New York. Even in expensive areas, it's possible to find cheapish accommodation thanks to Chinese reverence for new apartments. If you are willing to live in an old or slightly shabby looking apartment, costs can be slashed.

The number of agencies targeting foreigners has risen sharply in recent years. It's fair to say that you will likely pay a premium in order to deal with experienced staff who are fluent in English. If price is an issue, it almost always pays to have a Chinese person help you deal with a 'Chinese' estate agency.

Finally, the Shanghai Municipal Government is strict on foreign residents registering their stay in Shanghai. You must visit your nearest police station to fill out the necessary paperwork within 72 hours of signing a lease on a property.

All prices below are per month, and based (approximately) on a two-bedroom (80–120 sq m) property in a relatively new apartment complex. The price range will reflect several factors, including the exact size of the apartment, its age and general condition, views, location relative to metro stops and whether it comes with furniture and other amenities.

Currency conversion: ¥1,000 = £72/$143

Huangpu District

Huangpu is officially one administrative district but has quite distinct northern and southern sections. The northern half covers much of what was once the British Concession, later merged with American-claimed land in Hongkou to form the 'International Concession'. This is one of the most densely populated areas of the world, though few of the soaring apartment blocks recall the area's colonial past. It is also as close as Shanghai gets to a 'downtown' core. The area takes in People's Square, once home to a British-built racetrack and now home to major museums and theatres, and the Bund, a strip of neo-classical colonial buildings which line the western bank of the Huangpu. Many of Shanghai's best hotels are located here, as well as the major government administration buildings. It is also a notable commercial area, and takes in the shopping Mecca of Nanjing Road. In the southern part of Huangpu is the Old City where many indigenous Shanghainese still live in relatively low-rise *shikumen* dwellings. Few foreign residents would be willing to live in this kind of accommodation, owing to the poor facilities and cramped conditions. However, typical of Shanghai, next to this kind of crumbling neighbourhood, expect to see a soaring 40-storey apartment complex. The proximity to the central attractions means accommodation throughout the district is expensive.

Best for: Cosmopolitan lifestyle, shopping, theatre
Less good for: Congestion
Price factor: ¥3,000–¥8,000

Lujiazui

As the city's chief financial district, Lujiazui is Shanghai's equivalent of the City of London or Wall Street. The area has Pudong's entire grade-A office space and is, accordingly, rammed with major businesses and corporations. It is also home to at least three of Shanghai's monumental skyscrapers: the 88-story Jinmao Tower, the Christmas bauble-inspired Oriental Pearl TV Tower and the 101-storey Shanghai World Financial Centre, due to open in mid-late 2008. It is not an official district in itself and, located as it is just to the east of the Huangpu, comes under the wider area known as Pudong. Malls brimming with shops and restaurants have cropped up, particularly around Century Avenue, giving workers and residents here the option of avoiding a cross-town trip for their evening kicks. Despite the overhanging architecture, Lujiazui is quite spacious at ground level and free from much of the congestion on the opposite side of the river. That may change as construction here continues apace.

Best for: City workers
Less good for: Culture vultures
Price factor: ¥3,000–¥5,000

Century Park

Located in Pudong, Century Park is the largest park in Shanghai and is fringed by many new upscale apartment blocks. It's sandwiched between the Shanghai Science and Technology Museum, a favourite for families with kids, and Longyang Road where the Maglev (magnetic levitation) train begins its 431kmph dash out to Pudong International Airport. The Zhangjiang High-Tech Park, home to a series of major IT businesses, is a couple of stops away on line two of the metro. The area around Century Park is perhaps as green as suburban Shanghai gets. The modern buildings and excellent transport links are not necessarily reflected in the prices. The distance from Shanghai's 'city centre' means the area remains relatively inexpensive.

Best for: Nature-lovers, families
Less good for: Singles
Price factor: ¥3,000–¥5,000

Pudong District

The short, eight-minute ride on the Maglev train from Longyang Road to Shanghai's Pudong International Airport will reveal much about Pudong's character. This former swampland remains mostly drab and, compared to the forest of high-rises west of the Huangpu River, very flat. Much of the territory is filled with factories and warehouses. However, Pudong comprises a huge swathe of land and in amongst the industrial buildings lie real pockets of luxury. Being the only part of Shanghai where developers have had room to swing the wrecking ball, several sprawling compounds have sprung up where the Shanghai's wealthy elite can retreat with their families. Swimming pools, manicured lawns and security guards on the gate are the norm. Pudong is the best place if you would like to maintain the house-and-yard arrangement from back home. Shop around and the cheapest apartments in Shanghai can also be found. Transport, however, may be a problem if you aren't either willing or able to drive yourself.

Best for: Families, executives
Less good for: Young people, singles
Price factor: ¥2,000–¥5,000

Zhabei District

The southern part of Zhabei borders Huangpu and is only a short distance from People's Square and other central attractions. This tall, thin rectangular strip also boasts Shanghai's main railway station. Zhabei is a fairly undistinguished residential area that lacks the atmosphere of the French Concession or the vibrancy of Jing'an or Zhongshan Park. However, there are plenty of residential options, from cheap apartments in old residential blocks to new serviced apartments. There are a smattering of restaurants and bars, but most will tend to gravitate southward during their leisure time. The Suzhou Creek, a once-unpleasant waterway that has come in for serious urban regeneration recently, flows through the south of the district. Many of Zhabei's newer, classier apartment blocks line this route.

Best for: Budget conscious
Less good for: Glamour seekers
Price factor: ¥2,000–¥5,000

Hongkou District

Hongkou is home to one of Shanghai's two major stadiums. It hosts a variety of big-name concerts and sporting events, chiefly Shanghai Shenhua's home football matches. It is also one of Shanghai's more historic neighbourhoods. This is where the Americans first set up colonial shop in 1853. With port-access to the Huangpu, Hongkou was historically home to much industry and it remains a predominantly working-class area. During the Second World War, 20,000 Jewish refugees from Nazi-occupied Europe also lived in a notoriously overcrowded square-mile section of Hongkou known as the Shanghai ghetto. Hongkou is hardly Shanghai's prettiest quarter and it's one of the areas that will likely be dramatically changed ahead of the 2010 Shanghai World Expo. North Sichuan Road is Hongkou's main thoroughfare and is lined with several businesses and leisure venues.

Best for: History buffs, sports lovers
Less good for: Glamour seekers
Price factor: ¥2,000–¥4,000

Xujiahui

Xujiahui is the site of the oldest western settlement in Shanghai. Chinese Catholic Paul Xu started a Jesuit centre here in the early 17th century and invited foreign missionaries to stay. It is now home to the largest Catholic cathedral in China, the St Ignatius Cathedral, which was built in 1920 and holds daily mass. Xujiahui has also become a shopper's paradise, less glitzy than other shopping areas in the French Concession and Huangpu but no less frantic. It is home to the Shanghai Stadium and a variety of cinemas, sports complexes and other entertainment facilities. Most activity happens around the Xujiahui Metro Station itself, though the wider Xuhui District stretches much farther south, connecting central Shanghai with its more far-flung suburban areas. Just south of this area is Longhua Temple and, beside it, Shanghai's only urban pagoda. Prices for rented accommodation here may be cheaper than neighbourhoods nearer the river.

Best for: Catholics, shoppers
Less good for: Businesspeople
Price factor: ¥2,500–¥5,000

The French Concession

Definitely the most appealing part of central Shanghai, the French Concession retains much of its colonial charm thanks to its narrow, tree-lined avenues and well-preserved villas. It has, by and large, proved unfertile ground for the sky-bursting high-rises that dominate in other parts of the city. Moreover, it's the only place to stay if you're are a lover of fine dining and sophisticated drinking dens. The French Concession is packed with some of the city's best bars and restaurants, many housed in some of the large private concession-era houses. Huaihai Lu, which runs east to west, is the backbone to the French Concession and home to some of the best shopping in Shanghai. The French Concession also takes in Xintiandi, an uber-trendy leisure district in the east of the area. It's not the best place for apartments that feature all the mod cons, so families might struggle, but for atmosphere and charm, it is untouchable.

Best for: Foodies, young professionals
Less good for: Families
Price factor: ¥4,000–¥8,000

Jing'an District

Jing'an is arguably the top spot for upmarket shopping, thanks to the three goliath malls that have sprung up around West Nanjing Road. The Westgate mall, the CITIC Square mall and Plaza 66 are all temples to high fashion and expensive tastes. Nearby is the eponymous Jing'an Temple, a notable Buddhist landmark, though staid spirituality does not reflect the mood of this lively area. After the French Concession, Jing'an is next best for young and single foreign residents in Shanghai. In Tongren Lu it has one of the most lively bar strips in Shanghai. Jing'an has more than its fair share of upmarket apartment complexes. There is also a huge amount of office space and many major companies have their offices in this area.

Best for: Shoppers, singles
Less good for: Families
Price factor: ¥4,000–¥10,000

Zhongshan Park

The Zhongshan Park neighbourhood, in Changning District, was once rather sidelined, as it is way out west in Puxi. However, thanks to the building or extension of several metro lines in recent years, it is now the major transportation hub in the west of the city. The improved infrastructure has led to a number of major real estate investments, notably the mammoth Cloud Nine building which features a shopping mall, cinema, hotel and several restaurants. Like Gubei, Zhongshan Park is very convenient for Shanghai's second airport, Hongqiao, where many domestic

flights depart from. The park is also one of Shanghai's finest, with large lawns that – unusually in this ordered city – visitors are free to walk, lay or play upon. The restaurant scene is lively, but dominated by Chinese businesses; the international-flavoured French Concession is not far away.

Best for: Green spaces, transport links
Less good for: Major commercial areas
Price factor: ¥3,500–¥8,000

Hongqiao and Gubei

This area, also located within the Changning District, stretches from Zhongshan Park all the way out to Shanghai's second airport at Hongqiao. Gubei is a particularly popular neighbourhood with expat residents. Around Hongmei Road there is a cluster of bars and diners that cater to almost exclusively western tastes. Gubei has one of Shanghai's French-owned Carrefour supermarkets and caters to western tastes. However, it is not the most convenient area for transportation and, compared to the French Concession, lacks atmosphere. On the flip side, Gubei is quieter and perhaps more comfortable for those who find Shanghai too intense sometimes.

Best for: Families
Less good for: Transport
Price factor: ¥3,000–¥6,000

RENTING A PROPERTY

It is possible to rent a flat or a house without going through an estate agent but many people still prefer to do so. In most cases, estate agents do not ask for commission from tenants. It is advisable to go for a reputable real estate agent and make sure that you will not be charged commission. Before meeting your agent, ensure you have an idea of what you are looking for in terms of the size and number of rooms, how much rent you are prepared to pay and the ideal distance to public transport and your place of work. You should plan a site visit and take some photos of the place so as to have evidence of what is already inside and the condition of it, etc. When renting, tenants usually has to pay gas, water, electricity and telephone charges, even though it is possible to negotiate with the landlord about these charges.

Renting costs

> Some information on rental prices can be found at www.expatriates.com, though it is advisable to look for other websites of local estate agents for comparison.

Many foreigners prefer to live near to the business areas such as the Pudong area in Shanghai and the Chaoyang District in Beijing. It costs from around ¥3,000–¥6,000 ($396–$793/£195–£390) a month for a fully furbished flat with two to three bedrooms in these areas, though there is a wide range of choice available and costs can be kept down by sharing.

- **Renting in Beijing** In Beijing there are lots of listings on www.thatsbj.com and it's possible to find a small, clean, two-bedroom flat in a decent complex with fridge, stove, TV and reasonable bathroom for ¥3,600 a month. You can pay more than this, say ¥2,500–¥3,500 per person for a flat which is *'pretty wonderful, with nice furniture and lovely views over the city and lots of tacky paintings everywhere!'* as Pamela Hunt found who spent six months studying in Beijing in 2007.

> "I found the apartment through a real estate agent. I consulted many such agents, each showing me about three apartments before giving up on me. Most seemed quite tricky and played a lot of games – I only felt comfortable with two."
> **Ken Sherman**

Signing the lease

Before renting a house or flat in China, try to find someone to help you check the title document of the property to discover whether it is mortgaged or shared with other legal entities (documents will be in Chinese). Consent to lease has to be obtained if there is any other entity involved. The tenancy agreement should then be drawn up stating clearly the rent, payment date and frequency, the period of occupancy, and the rights and responsibilities of both parties. The tenancy agreement has to be registered at the property management body and this should be done by the landlord within 30 days of signing the agreement. A certificate of tenancy will then be issued within five days of paying an 'evidential fee', which is equal to 2.5% of the annual rental fee. This is shared equally by the landlord and the tenant.

You do not need a visa or any other identity document to rent an apartment, though you will need to get the landlord to register you with the local police and you will be asked to provide a copy of your passport at that point. This should be done

as soon as you move in, otherwise, you will be fined. You are usually required to rent a property for a period of six months or more. Many landlords are not keen on short-term tenancies and will ask for one to three months rent as a deposit.

You should ask for an ownership certificate if the property is government housing. The landlord must own the flat if it is government housing, otherwise complaints from neighbours may result in you getting thrown out. Make sure that there is a clause in the contract which ensures that you get your deposit and unused rent back if something like this happens.

FACT

In Macau, both the landlord and tenant must pay a commission fee which equals one month's rent from each party.

Estate Agents

Asiaxpat.com: www.asiaxpat.com. Contain adverts for accommodation in Shanghai, Beijing, Guangzhou and Hongkong.

Century 21: ; marketing@century21cn.com; www.century21cn.com

Expatriates.com: contact@expatriates.com; www.expatriates.com

Phoenix Property Agency: phoenix@shanghai-realty.com; www.shanghai-realty.net

BUYING A HOME

The Property Market

Still a communist country, the concept of private property is a slippery one for central government. All land is ultimately owned by the 'people' (ie the government) and, even now, people who 'own' their property technically only lease it from the government on a 70-year basis. However, this most troublesome of subjects has been discussed at recent Chinese Communist Party (CCP) congresses in Beijing and new legislation has strengthened property owners' rights. Nevertheless, this anomaly remains.

In urban areas, a high proportion of people own their houses or flats. This is largely due to housing benefits provided by the state or state-owned enterprises, before the country launched its opening-up and economic reform. Since then, the central government has been reforming the housing system. In the mid 1980s, tax reductions were given to developers who built more affordable houses.

If you are going to stay in China for a relatively short period, your company will probably provide you with accommodation as part of your expatriate remuneration package. It is not uncommon in China for companies to buy a whole storey of a housing complex to accommodate their staff.

Chinese people do not like to buy flats that have been lived in; they like to be the first occupants. Some Chinese say they do not like the idea that someone may have died in the flat.

China's economic boom has caused property prices to escalate several fold within a few years. In one recent case in Shanghai, 1,000 flats from a single housing complex were sold within a day. Beijing's hosting of the Olympic games in 2008 has attracted a lot of local as well as foreign investment in the real estate business. It is thought that the construction is far outstripping demand for such flats. Properties with good facilities, and those near the CBD (central business district) are the most popular. However, it goes without saying that if you are planning to invest in real estate it is essential to have a good understanding of how the market works.

Although property prices are expected to climb further, it has also been suggested that some factors like deflation and tighter control from the government may cool down the market. Moreover, the conveyancing procedure can be rather complicated and may vary in different provinces.

Types of property available

Since the merger of domestic and non-domestic commodity housing markets in 2002, foreigners are no longer limited to purchasing non-domestic housing. Recently introduced regulations insist that foreigners must have spent a year in China before they can buy a property.

If you are thinking of buying a property in China, there are many possibilities: flats in high-rise buildings (about 20 storeys); three to four-storey houses; serviced flats in hotels.

Newly built flats typically consist of a dining room, a living room, a bathroom, a kitchen and two or three bedrooms with one en suite. A typical urban flat is 90–110 sq m. Flats are usually sold without much furnishing. In fact, many are sold as shells with the owners expected to do even basic plastering and flooring themselves. That said, around 90% of newly sold flats have gas, electricity and water supplies installed. However, radiator/heating systems are only permitted north of the Yangtze River. In southern areas central heating is not allowed, although individuals can buy portable radiators.

The pre-owned property market is growing, though it is not yet as vibrant as the new property market.

How to find a house

The transaction processes are usually done through agents. Since not all real estate agencies are up to standard it is important to choose one with a good reputation and a good network throughout the country. Refer to the section on *Conveyancing* for more details.

Besides traditional marketing methods such as advertising in newspapers and on television, developers often hold property exhibitions in big cities like Beijing and Shanghai.

The *China Daily* newspaper's BizChina section (*www.chinadaily.com.cn/bizchina*) sometimes provides information on real estate exhibitions held in China.

Property prices

In areas of booming house prices the traditional Chinese greeting 'Have you eaten?' has been replaced by 'How much is your flat worth?'

As elsewhere in the world, the price of property varies a lot (some say it varies as much as regional cuisines and dialects) and depends on location, size and the facilities. In Shanghai, a property can range in price from around ¥15,000 (£1,076/$2,142) per sq m for a standard serviced flat to ¥27,000 per sq m for a flat with top facilities in a central location. Some properties in Zhejiang can be more expensive than those in Shanghai, though the average property price is lower. In general, it is more expensive to buy a house in the big cities or

the coastal areas, and the price goes down the further you go north and west, Beijing excepted.

Currently the Bohai Bay Area, which includes Beijing, Tianjin, Qingdao and Dalian, is the real estate 'hot spot'. This area also contributes 25% of China's GDP. In Beijing, residential sales prices rose from ¥8,000 per sq m at the beginning of 2006 to ¥10,000 at the end of the year. These prices may well be affected by the completion of all the housing units in time for the Olympics.

In Jinan and Qingdao, in Shandong Province, residential prices were around ¥2,300 per sq m in 2005. Since then prices have increased by 10.9% and by 5% in minor cities in Shandong.

In Guangzhou in May 2007 residential property cost around ¥11,300 per sq m.

Tianjin's real estate market was relatively stable in 2006 with average sales prices of ¥5,000 per sq m, representing an increase over the last few years of 17%. In Shenyang in 2006 residential property cost around ¥2,000–¥4,000 per sq m. Here, prices may well rise as disposable income increases. It is also likely that residential prices will fluctuate as national macroeconomic controls take effect.

Parking space may not necessarily come with your flat and sometimes there may not be enough parking space for all. If you can obtain a parking space, it will probably cost you a monthly rental fee of several hundred yuan. You will be provided with a parking certificate, which is a mandatory document for the annual inspection of the vehicle. You might be able to find cheaper parking if you shop

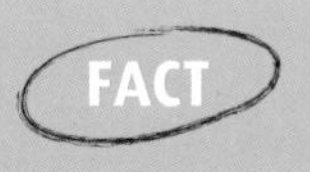

■ Many experts believe that statistics relating to economic facts in China are highly unreliable. This is partly because the situation there is changing so fast and partly because official figures may be setting things out in the most favourable light.

around, but paying slightly more may save you a lot of time and trouble. Indoor car parks sold on the market have to register with the real estate department. The title document will be issued either separately or together with the associated housing.

Prices in Macau

The Macau peninsula was once the most expensive part of Macau. Since transport has been improved and extended more and more people live in Taipa and adjoining Coloane nowadays, and property there can be as expensive as in the Macau peninsula. Like everywhere else in China, property prices have increased massively, doubling over the last five years. People normally prefer to use a real estate agent to purchase a pre-owned property. Note that 1% of the property price has to be paid, shared by the buyer and the seller, as commission. There are two kinds of government housing, namely, economic housing and social housing for lower income people. However, they are only for people who have lived in Macau for over five years.

Useful resources

DTZ Debenham Tie Leung: 010 6517 1280; www.dtz.com. The first wholly owned international real estate service provider in mainland China, providing property news, home searches and evaluation services.

Talking China: 021 6289 4299; talkingchina@talkingchina.com; www.talkingchina.com. This company provides real estate consultancy, mortgage advice, translation services.

Great International Property Agency, Macau: 238399; www.homemacau.com/eng

Kun Cheong Realty Company, Macau: 2884 0444; kchltd@macau.ctm.net; www.kuncheong.com.mo

Macau Housing Authority: 2859 4875; info@ihm.gov.mo; www.ihm.gov.mo

Furniture and household appliance businesses:
B&Q: www.bnq.com.cn
Ikea: www.ikea.com.cn
366f.com: www.365f.com/enindex.asp

Mortgages

Home mortgages in China are provided by banks. Usually developers will nominate at least two partnering banks for a particular project and buyers can choose between them. China Minsheng Banking Corporation Ltd is the first bank to launch mortgage services that allows borrowers to transfer their mortgages to another bank (non-specific mortgage services), which improves the flexibility to both buyers (borrowers) and the developers. However, at the time of writing, it is still a relatively new idea, which means most mortgages are fixed.

The three types of home mortgage are: a housing provident fund loan, a commercial housing loan and a portfolio loan.

- **A housing provident fund loan** This caters for staff with a provident (retirement/pension) fund account, which is the source of the loan. This must not exceed 80% of the property price and the maximum term is 30 years. For a pre-owned property, the maximum loan should not exceed 70% of the property price and the maximum term is 15 years.

- **A commercial housing loan** This is usually provided by designated banks chosen by the developers.
- **A portfolio loan** This is simply the application for both the housing provident und loan and the commercial housing loan.

In early 2007, the interest rate for a housing provident fund loan was 4.77%, while that of a commercial housing loan was somewhat higher depending on the term of the loan. The current fierce competition means that banks are constantly trying to design different types of mortgage products to suit the needs of individual clients. However interest rates have risen over the last two years in order to try to control rising house prices.

In general, it is quick and easy to apply for a home mortgage so long as you provide certain documents. First, submit an application and the relevant information to a bank. You will be required to provide proof of your account, your passport, work permit, marriage certificate, title document of the property, proof of income and receipt for the first installment you have paid for your property. If the application is approved, the bank will issue a letter of offer to you. After you sign the letter of offer, the bank will instruct its legal representatives to prepare a mortgage contract and notarisation. The contract has to be sent to government bodies for registration after you have signed it. Finally, the mortgage loan will be released.

Various fees are involved in the loan process and they vary from bank to bank. In most banks, you are required to pay an application fee, administration fees such as legal and valuation fees, a mortgage insurance fee and disbursements such as mortgage registration and stamp duty.

People applying for a mortgage in Beijing will need a credit rating report from the Beijing Personal Credit Service Centre. Those with a high rating will be entitled to lower interest rates and higher mortgage loan amounts. Basically, banks will seek ratings from the centre or check if you are on the 'black list'.

DTZ Debenham Tie Leung (www.dtz.com) provides information about credit rating reports, news on real estate property, legal amendments and new regulations relating to the real estate industry. Contact them on 010 6510 1388.

Mortgages in Macau

In Macau, various home mortgage products are offered by banks such as HSBC and Bank of China. Home mortgage loans can be up to 90% of the market or evaluated price of the property and repayment periods range from 20 to 30 years.

Bank Addresses

Bank of China: 010 6659 6688; www.bank-of-china.com

China Construction Bank: 021 6374 8585; www.ccb.com

China Minsheng Banking Corporation Ltd: service@cmbc.com.cn; www.cmbc.com.cn

The Hongkong and Shanghai Banking Corporation Ltd (HSBC): 021 6841 1888; online@hsbc.com.on; www.hsbc.com.cn

Standard Chartered Bank Macau: www.standardchartered.com

Purchasing Procedures

Buying a completed property

Every property which is approved for sale on the market must have a title document, which is also called the 'real estate ownership certificate'. The transaction will be void if the title document is missing. Therefore, it is important to ensure that the developers have obtained the title document before buying their properties. After you choose a property, an agreement will then be set up according to the rules pre-defined by the local real estate governing body. An application for registration of the transaction should be made to the local real estate transaction office within 30 days of the signing of the agreement. A receipt of application will then be issued to indicate that the process is completed and the documents are valid. You will be notified within 15 days if your application is successful. If the transaction is accepted, various fees such as the deed tax and transaction administration fee have to be paid according to the pre-agreed amount, and the new title document, indicating that you are the owner of the property, will be released. For non-local residents, after paying the deed tax and administration fees, a tax clearance document should be obtained and the title document will then be released.

Sometimes, developers make use of various gimmicks such as educational funds and free car-parking spaces which may add up to more than ¥10,000 (£717/$1,428), to attract customers. However, you should note that developers are not allowed to provide cash-back or other forms of benefits of over ¥5,000 to their customers. This is illegal and the promised benefits will not be valid.

In order to encourage foreigners to invest in property, tax incentives have been offered by the Chinese Government for several years. Expatriates who hold a DGM (deputy general manager) title or above in multinational corporations, such as banks, insurance companies, accountancy firms, investment companies, and research and development centres are eligible for tax incentives when purchasing cars and property. However, the total investments of the companies they belong to have to be $10 million or more. The incentives provided should not exceed 80% of the locally retained portion of their personal income tax paid in the previous year.

In addition to the legal and administration fees, the following fees will also apply when purchasing: stamp duty (equal to 0.05% of the purchase price); registration fee; fee for issuing a title document; deed duty (equal to 1.5% of the purchase price but 3% for flats and property in villages).

Legal documents for buying a property in Macau are in Chinese and Portuguese only. An English version may be available on request but this is not usual. You should consider employing a lawyer to handle the legal documents for you or, at least, find a translator.

Buying a property under construction

Developers in China are allowed to sell their properties before construction is completed. The property markets have now entered a new phase and it is not difficult for you to find 'pre-launch' or 'pre-sale' properties. However, the developers have to obtain a pre-launch certificate from government bodies before putting their uncompleted properties on the market. You should check the pre-launch certificate of the property you are interested in before making a decision. This can be done online at *http://www.xshouse.com/resoult.asp* or you can ask the developers to show you the certificate at their sales counter. Make sure the name of the developers the same as the one on the certificate.

The procedures for buying a property under construction are similar to those for buying a completed property. A pre-sale contract will be drawn up and sent to the real estate governing bodies for registration. This should be done within five working days of signing the pre-sale contract, and you will be given a copy of the registration. Payment is usually made by installments according to the progress of construction. Finally, the title document will be conveyed to you by the developer upon the completion of the project. Should there be any amendment to the pre-sale contract, both parties (developers and buyers) must consent in the form of supplementary contracts and these should be handed to the real estate governing bodies at the time of conveyance.

It used to be a problem in China that developers were not able to meet the promised date of completion, and the waiting could be never-ending. Even though this is less common now, it is advisable to do some research on the developers and make sure reasonable compensation is covered in the contract if the property cannot be completed on time. Interestingly, a new form of business has developed nowadays where constructors are targeting the building or re-building of the unfinished houses This has come about because of the high competition for land and the shorter time it takes to put these houses up for sale.

If you do not have permanent resident status in China, you have to go through normal buying property procedures such as setting up a contract and registering it with a government body. However, note that extra fees are payable before the sale. In addition, all translation has to be done by real estate governing bodies and you can employ your own lawyer or representative throughout the process.

The China Law Database (www.chinalaw.gov.cn/indexEN.jsp) provides information on legislation and property laws.

The conveyancer work

Owners intending to put their property on the market for resale are required to submit the original title document and a written sale and purchase agreement. They also have to register with the Land and Real Estate Bureau within 90 days of the transfer of ownership. Pre-sale transactions have to be registered within 30 days of signing the written Pre-sale Agreement, and the transfer has to be registered with the bureau within 15 days. Besides setting out clearer guidelines on how to settle discrepancies, the regulations represent a significant policy breakthrough by specifying the standard of service expected of government officials in handling property transfers and the associated liabilities for inadequate performance.

Useful resources

www.eastlaw.net: Contract law including conveyancing law in China can be found here.

TransAsia Lawyers: 010 6505 8188; Beijing@TransAsiaLawyers.com; www.transasialawyers.com

Property inheritance law

You can write a will to indicate one or more relatives as the lawful inheritors of your property. Alternatively, you can specify an organisation or private individuals as the lawful inheritors of your property in China instead of your relatives.

You can also draw up a will regarding your property in China according to the laws in your home country, but you are advised to consult a lawyer and make sure your will would be valid under the Chinese inheritance laws.

If a property owner dies having made no will, or if the will is invalid, the person recognised as the legal inheritor under the Chinese inheritance law will be the lawful recipient of the property. Under Chinese inheritance laws, primary and secondary inheritance rights are given to two groups of relatives. Relatives with primary rights include spouse, children (biological or adopted, born before or after marriage), parents (biological, adopted or step), and parents-in-law whose livelihood is supported by the deceased. The order as listed also reflects their priority to claim the inheritance. Relatives with secondary rights to inherit include siblings (biological or step), who take priority over grandparents. In addition, according to the inheritance laws in China, if the deceased is a foreigner, the succession of fixed assets has to follow the rules of the local government where the fixed assets are located. Movable assets follow the rules of the local government where the deceased lived.

FACT

If a property owner dies having made no will, or if the will is invalid, the person recognised as the legal inheritor under the Chinese inheritance law will be the lawful recipient of the property.

Masons, Shanghai: 021 6321 1166; www.masons.com. An international law firm and one of the first foreign law firms to be granted a licence to practise in China.

SERVICES AND UTILITIES

Property tax

Owners of property have to pay a tax only when they first make the purchase. The tax is calculated according to the value of the property. Taxable value is equal to 70%–90% of a property and the current tax rate is 1.2%. If the tax is levied on the rent and paid by the tenants, the tax levied is equal to 12% of the rent.

Urban real estate tax

This was set up in order to make better use of land and to reduce the differences in the incomes from land. The tax is levied annually and is calculated in terms of the area used by enterprises or individuals. The rate is higher in big cities and is ¥0.5–¥10 (£0.05–£0.70/$0.70–£1.43) per sq m. In middle-sized cities, the tax is ¥0.4–¥8 per sq m while that of small cities is ¥0.3–¥6 per sq m.

Energy

Several major – and sometimes controversial – projects have been launched to improve both electricity and gas supplies in China. Coping with the nation's growing energy demands ranks alongside environmental protection as the biggest challenge the Chinese government is currently facing.

The former State Power Corporation was broken down into 11 smaller companies in late 2002, and in 2003 the State Electricity Regulatory Commission (SERC), which acts as the watchdog of the industry, started operating. In the same year, China started experimenting with the idea of regional or provincial electricity markets in north-east China. More regional electricity markets are expected to be set up throughout the country due to the huge demand for electricity. When the regional electricity markets become mature and the pricing system is revised, they will be fully open to competition. Prices will become market driven instead of government driven.

Currency conversion: ¥1,000 = £72/$143

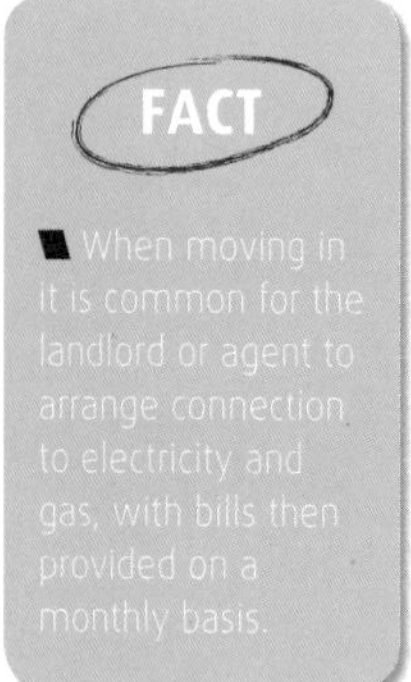
FACT
When moving in it is common for the landlord or agent to arrange connection to electricity and gas, with bills then provided on a monthly basis.

The electricity supply in China is 220 volts (50 Hz). Plugs come in a variety of shapes, and most sockets cater to at least two varieties: American-style plugs, with two flat parallel prongs and triangular plugs with three thin pins. Appliances with two round prongs may sometimes be used as well. You will need an adaptor for electrical appliances with large three-pin plugs, except in Hong Kong and Macau. Because of the voltage difference, you will need a converter to use your electrical appliances from the USA or most of Europe. Most laptop computers and some sophisticated appliances operate equally well on 220 or 110 volts. You are however advised to use a power surge protector for your computer. You may consider buying electrical appliances in China to save the trouble of bringing your own. These are in general cheaper than in the USA and Europe. In most parts of China the electricity supply is stable but, as mentioned before, the electricity network in the west of China is being improved.

When moving in it is common for the landlord or agent to arrange connection to electricity and gas, with bills then provided on a monthly basis. In some parts of the country you will find the utility bills are generally delivered in the form of a small piece of paper which is stuck to your apartment door.

Not all parts of China have central heating- this is centrally controlled by the government and is provided in the chilly north but not in the south. If there is central heating then it is run by the city and the cost is covered by the landlord, not the tenant. Heaters are turned on at the start of December and turned off at the end of March, regardless of the actual temperature. There are special boilers just for this winter heating.

Energy in Macau

Monthly bills for electricity and gas can be paid at banks, or you can set up direct debit services. In Macau, monthly bills can also be settled at ATMs or through online services.

Useful resources

State Grid Corporation of China: www.sgcc.com.cn/ywlm. One of the large power transmission enterprises in China, which consists of institutions and enterprises that were formerly state owned.

CEM-Companhia de Electricidade de Macau, SARL: www.cem-macau.com

Water

Water shortage is a serious problem that China aims to solve completely by the end of 2020. With that end in view a great deal of money and resources have been put into various projects aiming to solve the problem of the uneven distribution of natural water resources, by re-allocating water to areas of scarcity. These include the colossal south-to-north water diversion project, which will re-route water from the comparatively wet southern half of China to the rain-starved north via channels more than 1,000km long.

Foreign-invested companies are permitted to join the water supply market as a means of introducing competition. The three biggest water suppliers in the world, Vivendi Group, Thames Water and Suez Lyonnaise Des Eaux, have made China part of their global market.

It is not advisable to drink water straight from the tap: better to boil it first. The charge for water is about ¥2 (£0.14/$0.29) per cubic metre for residential use and ¥3 per cubic metre for business use. The monthly bills can be paid at a bank and your landlord or agent should organise connection for you when moving in.

Water in Macau

In Macau, water is provided by Macao Water, the fourth largest water supplier in China. First-time users with new meter connections have to register at the customer services counter of the company. You have to present identification and the title deeds to the property when applying for a meter connection for which you will have to pay a charge, in addition to a guarantee deposit and government stamp duty. Bi-monthly bills will be sent to your home address and can be settled by cash or cheque at post offices, banks, and service counters of Macao Water.

A joint portal provided by CEM (electricity provider) and Macao Water provides a variety of online services to enable their customers to view and pay electricity and water bills through electronic payments. Currently, you can only pay your bills online by using the e-banking service provided by two banks in Macau, namely BNU and Bank of China.

TIP
It is not advisable to drink water straight from the tap: better to boil it first.

Useful resources

The Ministry of Water Resources: 010 6320 2557; webmaster@mwr.gov.cn; www.mwr.gov.cn/english

China International Water & Electric Corp: 010 6238 1188; www.cwe.com.cn. State-owned company providing domestic and foreign consultancy services on water and electricity projects.

Macao Water Supply Company Ltd: 2822 0088; customer.info@macaowater.com; www.macaowater.com

Banco Nacional Ultramarino, Macao: 2833 5533; markt@bnu.com.mo; www.bnu.com.mo/en

Bank of China, Macau: www.bocmacau.com/eng/its

Telephones

The telecommunication industry has been reformed to an unprecedented degree by the Chinese government since 2002; the original state-owned China Telecom was split into northern and southern sectors in an attempt to break its monopoly and encourage competition. The northern sector inherited China Telecom's business in 10 provinces and municipalities, including Beijing, Tianjin, Hebei and Shandong and was merged with China Network, Jitong Network and Telecom, forming the new China Network Communication (known as China Netcom). The southern sector continued using the name China Telecom with the remaining 70% of the network and includes 21 provinces and municipalities in the southern and north-western regions.

Up to now, there have been four major telecommunication players in the industry: China Telecom, China Network Communication (CNC), China Mobile Communications Corporation (known as CMCC or China Mobile), and China United Telecommunications Corporation (China Unicom). China Telecom still enjoys the biggest share in the telecommunications market, followed by China Mobile. They are all monitored by the Ministry of Information Industries (MII) and provide services such as fixed-line telephones, mobile telephone networks, broadband and Virtual Private Network (VPN). Since China entered the World Trade Organisation, telecommunication services have been opened up to foreign companies.

Installing a telephone line

Most newly built houses will have a local fixed line already installed. To activate the service, you have to fill in a registration form and hand it to the local services provider. The initial installation fee is expensive, at about ¥800 (£50/$100). The average monthly phone bill for an expat making lots o f local calls is around ¥70 and rental fees are very modest – generally less than ¥30 per month. It is more expensive to install a telephone line in rural areas.

Phone bills can be paid at banks or at convenience stores. Alternatively you can set up a monthly direct debit service with the service provider.

Mobile phones

Competition is rife in the mobile phone market, especially in big cities like Shanghai. Mobile usage has exploded in recent years and an estimated half a billion Chinese – around 40% of the population – use a mobile, a figure which compares well with an average penetration of 60% in western countries. It is easy to subscribe to a mobile phone service in China but the network coverage still needs improvement, even in big cities. GSM and CDMA services are provided in China. Pay-as-you-go mobiles remain popular. The UK's biggest company, Vodafone, has already got a minority

Area Codes Of Major Cities			
City	**Area Code**	**City**	**Area Code**
Beijing	10	Lhasa	891
Changchun	431	Lijiang	888
Changsha	731	Luoyang	379
Chengdu	28	Nanchang	791
Chongqing	23	Nanjing	25
Datong	352	Qingdao	532
Dali	872	Shanghai	21
Dunhuang	937	Shantou	754
Foshan	757	Shenyang	24
Fuzhou	591	Shenzhen	755
Guangzhou	20	Shigatse	892
Guilin	773	Suzhou	512
Guiyang	851	Taiyuan	351
Hangzhou	571	Tianjin	22
Haerbin	451	Turpan	995
Haikou	898	Urumqi	991
Hohhot	471	Wuxi	510
Huangshan	559	Wuhan	27
Jilin	432	Xiamen	592
Jinan	531	Xian	29
Kashgar	998	Yangshuo	773
Kunming	871	Yangzhou	514
Lanzhou	931	Zhuhai	756

stake in China Mobile, one of the big mobile phone companies listed above. Nokia, Siemens and Ericsson have also set up manufacturing plants in China, competing with about 20 domestic makers.

If you bring a handset with you, you may need to get it unlocked in order to use another SIM card. There are hundreds of mobile phone shops in cities and towns who will be able to help. You can also buy a SIM card from these outlets. Check which card you are being offered; a local SIM can only be used within the city or province where you bought it; a country-wide SIM is more convenient if you make inter-city calls, but usually costs more.

- **Superstitious phone numbers** Different phone numbers can carry different prices. In the Chinese language, pronunciation of the number four is similar to the

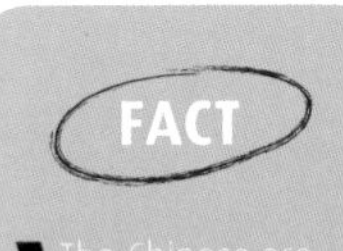

- The Chinese are superstitious about their phone numbers – different phone numbers can carry different prices.

word for death; and 914 sounds like the phrase 'just about to die'. Conversely, the number eight is considered lucky in Chinese culture. Consequently, phone numbers containing nines, ones and fours are often a lot cheaper than those containing eights.

Phone numbers

- Calling China The country code for China is 86 but note that Hong Kong and Macau have separate country codes (852 and 853 respectively). Local telephone numbers consist of eight digits (not including the area code). Apart from the two previously colonised cities, calling China from another country involves the following:

  86 + area code (omit the zero) + number

  You usually need to add 00 in front of 86 when making a call. It is the same to call other countries from China:

  00 + country code + area code (omit the zero) + number
- The country code for Macau is 853 and there are no area codes in the city. To make a call to Macau, dial 00 853 + number. Making an international call from Macau is similar to doing so in mainland China.

  Telephone booths are often hard to find, even in large cities. You cannot usually use them to make international calls, even though you can make domestic local or long-distance calls. A five-minute local call costs around ¥1 (£0.06/$0.12). It is also possible to find privately run phone 'shops' which use IP technology and have metered public booths that charge per minute.
- Emergency and useful numbers There are three emergency numbers for mainland China:

Police:	110
Ambulance:	120
Fire:	119

The emergency services number in Macau is 999.

- Other telephone numbers:

International assistance:	115
Local directory assistance:	114
Local long-distance call assistance:	113
Worldwide long-distance call assistance:	173/174
Macau local directory assistance:	185
Directory Enquiries, Macau:	181
International Telephone Enquiries, Macau:	101

International phone calls

The introduction of Internet Protocol (IP) phone services in late 1999 has significantly reduced the cost of making international calls. IP phone services allow you to make telephone calls along internet cables rather than conventional telephone wires. All of the four major Chinese telecom companies are now offering IP phone services and it is possible to cut the costs of calling overseas by two-thirds with IP services. For example, with the use of IP, calls from the USA to China drop from $0.59 (using fixed-line) to $0.21 a minute. Under the IP service, callers just need to dial five digits for the IP servers' access in front of the overseas number you wish to make the call to.

There are three main IP services available: IP phone cards (bought on a pre-paid basis), IP phone services (installed to your line) and PC-based internet phone services. IP cards are a simple and convenient way to make cheap calls both domestically and internationally, and can be used from any phone. They can be bought at hotels, post offices, department stores, convenience stores, telephone shops and small carts selling lottery tickets in big cities. The IP cards can be bought more cheaply when they are close to the expiry date, when you can save up to 60% of the printed price. Cards are available from ¥50 (£3/$6) to ¥500. You are advised to check the expiry date on the back of the card (usually valid for 12 months) when you buy one. It is also worthwhile to compare the different card rates for making calls to different countries and regions, as some cards are better value for certain countries. You can use IP phone cards on your mobile phone, but in general it is only possible if the card is from the same company as your mobile phone provider. The networks can sometimes get congested, so it is best to have a range of cards from different companies. A ¥100 card buys around 37 minutes call time to the USA and 27 minutes to Europe.

Arranging an IP phone service connection to your home can be a complicated process. It is probably not worth it if you are not a high-usage caller as the monthly fee can be far more than a normal fixed line. You are also required to have a residence visa and a local bank account to apply for the IP phone service. The calling fee is about ¥0.3 per minute for calling within mainland China. Calls to the USA and the UK are about ¥2.4 and ¥3.6 per minute respectively.

Internet phone services

This refers to the use of the internet, via a computer, to make telephone calls. All you need is a personal computer with an internet connection, speakers, and a microphone.

A headset or a microphone will cost you around ¥40 (£2.50/$5) at computer stores. There are a number of companies offering internet phone services, and you should compare the services and prices before choosing one. Skype, probably the fastest growing such company, provides a good service in China. The procedures for installing an internet phone are simple. You only need to download the software from the service provider and create an account for payment. If you access the internet through an office server, you may need to check whether your server has 'firewalls' which may prohibit you from using the internet telephone services. Your software downloading programmes will usually tell you if you have firewalls in place. You can dial from your PC to a normal telephone, or from your PC to another PC if the receiver has the same software. Rates for internet phone services are approximately 20% of IP phone rates, with a number of companies even offering free calls. The quality of China's broadband internet coverage is not yet at western standards and the sound quality of internet phone services can be a little patchy with slight delays. However, in general it is perfectly audible and great value.

Telephones in Macau

Telecommunication services in Macau have been developing considerably in recent years. The telecom business of Macau is largely controlled by Companhia de Telecommunicacoes de Macau SARL but the Macau Special Administrative Region Government has opened up the market in recent years and a number of new companies have entered the fold.

Making local calls from home is free. Local calls made from public phone booths cost MOP$1 (£0.07/$0.15) for every three minutes. You can also use the phones perched on little platforms in magazine and drinks kiosks, positioned at most crossroads in cities and towns. The kiosk owner will charge you when you hang up. The phones are usually red in colour and look like ordinary handsets found in homes.

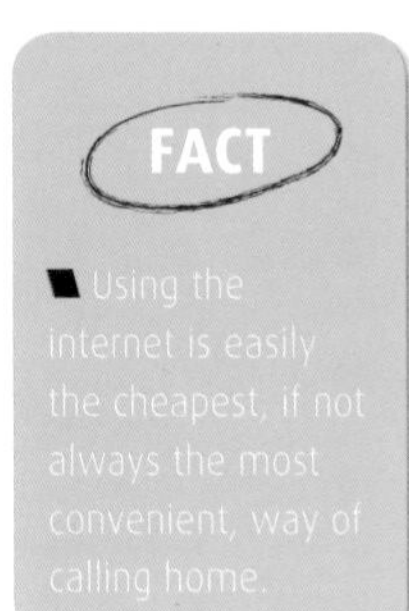

FACT
Using the internet is easily the cheapest, if not always the most convenient, way of calling home.

Telephones in Macau also offer international direct dialing, though in a hotel room, you may have to go through the hotel operator. It costs MOP $5.50 for a one-minute phone call to the USA during peak hours (Monday to Saturday, 6am to noon and 8pm to midnight) and MOP$4.50 on Sundays and off-peak hours. If you think you'll be making a lot of international telephone calls, purchase a prepaid phone card for MOP$50, MOP$100, or MOP$150 at Edificio CTM, Rua Pedro Coutinho, 25, which also has information regarding use of your own mobile phone in Macau.

For international directory assistance in Macau, dial 101; for local directory enquiries, dial 181.

Useful resources

China Mobile Communications Corporation (CMCC/China Mobile): www.chinamobile.com/english

China Network Communications Group Corporation (China Netcom): 010 6611 0006; www.chinanetcom.com.cn/en

China Telecom: 010 6602 7217; content@beijingnet.com; http://en.chinatelecom.com.cn

China United Telecommunications Corporation: www.chinaunicom.com.cn (Chinese language) or www.chinaunicom.com.hk (English)

CTM-Companhia de Telecomunicacoes, Macau: 6891 3822; www.ctm.net

IP Service Providers

Dialpad: www.dialpad.com

IconnectHere: www.iConnectHere.com (formerly deltathree)

Mediaring: www.mediaring.com

Net2phone: www.net2phone.com

Television

There is no TV licence requirement in China but there are advertisements between programmes on every station. For more on the television channels available in China, go to the *Media and Communications* section in Daily Life.
Competition between internet services is so fierce that prices are fairly low.

 MOVING IN

Furniture

When it comes to furnishing your flat, you can save yourself the expense and trouble of bringing your own furniture from abroad by buying what you need in China. Furniture and household appliances are much cheaper than they are in the USA and Europe. There are also many one-stop home decoration shops in China now and it is easy to obtain all the things you need in one place. The UK-based B&Q has more than 10 stores in major cities like Beijing, Shanghai and Guangzhou, and sells all sorts of materials and accessories for home decorating. The Beijing branch is even bigger than the largest branch in the UK. Chinese antiques are of course much sought after and popular amongst both locals and foreigners. But if you are not looking for Ming or Qing antiques you can get attractive Chinese-style furniture for less than western-style furniture.

Insurance

The insurance industry in China is still in its early stages, although it is growing very fast. Rising incomes and the arrival of foreign insurance companies have made people increasingly aware of the advantages of having a good insurance plan. This is particularly true in big cities. In 2002, AIA (American International Assurance), a leading insurance group from the USA, was the first group of foreign insurance companies to be granted a business licence in Beijing, where foreign insurance companies were prohibited prior to China's entry into the World Trade Organisation. You can now buy a range of insurance products, such as home, car, travel, life and accident insurance. Online applications are now possible on some insurance companies' websites.

■ You can save yourself the expense and trouble of bringing your own furniture from abroad by buying what you need in China. Furniture and household appliances are much cheaper than they are in the USA and Europe.

Useful resources

American International Group Inc, Shanghai: 021 6350 8180; ask.aiu@aig.com; www.aiush.com.cn/en

PICC Property and Casualty Company Ltd: 010 6315 6688; webmaster@piccnet.com.cn; www.picc.com.cn/en

AXA Asia Pacific Holdings Ltd, Beijing: 010 6500 7788 extension 7497; www.axa-chinaregion.com

Royal & Sun Alliance Insurance Ltd, Shanghai: 021 6841 1999; rsashang@uninet.com.cn; www.royalsunalliance.com.cn

PICC Property and Casualty Company Ltd, Beijing: 010 6315 6688; webmaster@piccnet.com.cn; www.picc.com.cn/en

ING General Insurance International Ltd, Dalian: 0411 2530 881; www.ing-cap.com.cn

New York Life Insurance Worldwide Ltd: 800 820 5882; p-r@haiernewyorklife.com.cn; www.haiernewyorklife.com.cn

加强社会主义
精神文明建设！
大的中国共产党万岁！

Daily Life

CULTURE SHOCK AND CUSTOMS

Some form of culture shock is almost bound to occur, particularly if you have not travelled widely or lived in a different culture before, and especially if you have gone to China on your own. It may not hit you immediately: you may be so excited by the mere fact of being in China, by all the fascinating sights, sounds and smells around you, that you may be on a high for a while. It may be that after the initial wonder has passed and you misinterpret a situation with a local person, or the heat gets to you, or the mosquitoes and monster cockroaches, or the noise, or your inability to speak and understand the language well, that you suddenly feel lost and unsure of yourself, and frankly homesick. Don't be hard on yourself; it's a natural feeling and you will most probably get over it. Spend some time with other people from your part of the world in the same boat, and try and find some home comforts – familiar food or activities. Bit by bit you will feel more at home and know more what to expect.

But be warned that culture shock can happen when you return home too. You realise you no longer know what it costs to send a letter. You may find that the place has changed somewhat, that you have moved on and now have experiences not shared by your old friends or your family. You may find, sadly, that they are not even very interested in hearing about your life in China.

Log on to http://edweb.sdsu.edu/people/CGuanipa/cultshok for some useful suggestions on how to handle culture shock.

Addressing people

In China, when addressing someone older than you, or senior to you, you should use their surname followed by their title, eg Wang Xiansheng, meaning Mr Wang. Chinese culture makes use of many more titles than is common in English-speaking cultures. There is barely a job or rank of any importance that doesn't have its own specific title eg Professor Liu, Officer Lin or Manager Song. Using 'Mr' is an acceptable alternative in most situations. You should address your Chinese business partners in a formal way, especially the first time you meet them. (See more on greeting a business associate in *Working culture and etiquette* in Working in China.)

> I am beginning to feel more aware of the dilemma of coming to a country for longer than a few weeks. People naturally want to immerse themselves in the culture but also tend to drift towards things that remind them of home. And, amongst foreign students at least, there is a really obvious sort-of snobbery some people have towards 'non-Chinese' things in China. Though I find it odd to define, for example, bars as 'non-Chinese' when they are full of Chinese as well as western people, and they are quite clearly in China. Lots of people refuse to go into Starbucks, I suspect not because of its link with globalisation etc, but because it's too 'western' (or worse – 'American'!).
>
> **Pamela Hunt**

The younger generation usually introduce themselves with their whole name and it is fine to call them by their first name.

Many foreigners are confused by Chinese names, as Chinese are by western names, and some may address you by your surname. The Chinese put their family names first and given names second. However, some Chinese will try to accommodate you by reversing them, thus making it really confusing! Most Chinese surnames are monosyllabic and the given names are more often bi-syllabic, so you can probably work it out. Shaking hands is very common, especially when you first meet someone. However, hugging and kissing are not common, and if you are male, do not initiate such gestures to a woman, unless you know her really well.

When addressing certain professions, it is polite to use certain forms of address. For taxi drivers, use *'shifu'*, meaning expert; for waiters and waitresses, use *'fuwuyuan'*, meaning server. Some years ago it was common to say *'xiaojie'* for waitresses, meaning 'Miss', but the term now has more negative connotations, so it's safer to stick to the more formal 'server'. Anyone who is in an educaitonal institution is generally addressed as *'laoshi'*, meaning teacher or 'revered older expert'. If you know them personally, place their surname before 'laoshi', eg Wang Laoshi.

It is becoming increasingly common for Chinese people involved in any kind of international context (working for a foreign company, studying English with other international students, having lived abroad and returned to China) to adopt English-sounding names. Those who have left China are likely to have used an English name abroad to make it simpler for people to address them; others choose names of famous Chinese pop stars (eg Britn); but many names are self-selected and are less than appropriate as a form of address. Buffet (after Warren Buffet), Penny (as a boy's name, after the British coin), Youth Forever (after their online screen name) and Rain or Sky (considered beautiful in Chinese) are not unheard of. You will often find names are given by older foreign teachers who spend their early retirement teaching English in China. Consquently, the names they give their students, which stay with them, can be old fashioned and out of sync with their western counterparts – for instance, 20-year-old Nancys and 25-year-old Berts. More recently, names have been lifted from blockbuster films. Rose and Jack, from the film *Titanic* (1997), were highly popular in the early 2000s.

Tips on greeting people

- Greetings are formal and the oldest person is always greeted first
- It is now common to shake hands with foreigners
- Many Chinese will look down when greeting someone
- Address the person by an honorific title and their surname. If they want to move to a more informal first-name basis, they will advise you which name you should use

Gift giving

Gift giving is a very important part of any culture. There are always rules attached to it. Gifts are given at Chinese New Year, weddings, births and in recent years, thanks largely to western influence, on birthdays.

There are a number of dos and don'ts:

- Always present and receive a gift with both hands
- Do not open a gift when it is given (it looks greedy)
- Do not give four of anything as the number four sounds like the word for death; but eight is lucky
- Clocks, flowers, handkerchiefs, straw sandals all have associations with funerals – so do not give them
- Knives, scissors etc are associated with cutting off relationships
- A basket of luxury food is a good gift
- Do not wrap a gift in paper that is blue, black or white
- Never send a Chinese person a green hat, especially to men, as 'wearing a green hat' means one's wife is committing adultery.
- Fruit is welcome on most occasions but no pears should be sent to couples who are getting married or are newly married as 'pears' sounds like 'separation'.
- In Cantonese, watermelon, melon, papaya or any other similar-shaped fruits and vegetables are all called *'gwa'*, which sounds the same as 'dying' in informal speech, so you should avoid sending them as gifts too.

The colour of the wrapping is important. Never wrap your gifts in black or white as both colours are related to death or funerals. Red is particularly good for weddings and Chinese New Year. Gold has also become popular for these situations. Even though red is generally welcome in all situations, you should never wear red clothes at a funeral as this means you are happy to see the person dead; black clothes, or more traditional white ones, have to be worn.

Take your shoes off when you arrive. Take a little something to the hostess.

Being entertained by Chinese hosts

Chinese people are more likely to take you to a restaurant than to their homes. It is a great honour to be invited home and if you can't make it it is polite to explain why. However do not make an assumption that you will be given a meal. The present writer was invited to the home of a family in Beijing for 7.30pm and expected dinner. It emerged shortly after her arrival that the family had had dinner at 5.30pm.

Otherwise follow the good manners of your own country – but eat with enthusiasm, praise the food, try everything and don't take the last piece of food on the dish in the middle of the table. It is usual for your host to drop choice pieces of food into your bowl. It is not appropriate for you to do the same for your host. Put bones on the table or in a special bowl, not in your own. It is usual for Chinese people to hold the bowl close to the mouth, to slurp food, speak with their mouths full, burp afterwards. See the next section, *Food and drink*, for more advice on eating etiquette.

FOOD AND DRINK

The Chinese are rightly proud of their food and eating will most probably be a major part of the delight of being in China for you, as indeed it is for the locals. Eating out is inexpensive in most places, and there is in most towns a range of restaurants from noodle stalls, where you sit on tables in the street, to more sophisticated eateries. It is usually possible to get something to eat at any time of day although restaurants tend to close early.

Chopsticks are the norm in most restaurants, except western restaurants and fast food shops. Do not worry if you do not know how to use them. Many places provide forks and spoons to foreigners. It will not take you long to learn how to use chopsticks. Ask your Chinese acquaintances and colleagues to show you how. It is well worth the effort and they will be pleased to help.

A Chinese meal normally consists of several dishes placed in the centre of the table and shared by everyone. At a family dinner, there is no separate starter and main course. All dishes are put on the table at the same time and you can help yourself to whatever you want, in whatever order. You can go back to the same dish as many times as you like. Usually Chinese people use their chopsticks to pick up a small piece from a dish, as there is not usually a serving spoon or chopsticks with the dishes. It is perfectly acceptable to hold your bowl in your hand and brush the rice or other food into your mouth directly from the bowl; in fact, leaving the bowl on the table all the time is considered juvenile and not good manners.

Eating ettiquette

Some have suggested that there are no table manners at a Chinese meal, but there are some things to remember to avoid offending your host. If a whole fish is served, the dish is always placed so that the head points to the most important guest. The eyes of a fish are considered the most delicious part, so if the head is pointing your way, and you are feeling brave, it will delight your hosts if you pick out the eyes first. When resting between courses, place your chopsticks across your bowl, or rest them on the chopstick stand next to your plate. Avoid leaving your chopsticks pointing at anyone, as this is considered rude. Similarly, don't stick them in your bowl so they stick up vertically; this reminds the Chinese of holding incense at a funeral and is not good manners. Tea is always drunk with a meal, and when filling your own cup, you should also fill your fellow diners. If they haven't touched their tea since the last fill-up, it is still polite to top it up further, to show they haven't been overlooked. When the teapot is empty, turn over the lid to indicate to the waiters that it needs to be refilled.

Newly arrived visitors to China are often treated to seemingly grand banquets with free flowing beer, rice wine and dozens of tantalising dishes. The trick is not to eat too much at a time, since as soon as one spread of plates is finished, more arrive. Graze on each dish but leave some space for what might come next. Traditionally, only poor people ate rice as a way of filling themselves up, as they never had enough meat or vegetables, so rice is usually served at the end of the meal, or not at all.

You are not expected to share the bill if you are invited to eat out at a restaurant, though these things are changing amongst the younger generation.

- **Vegetarians in China** Vegetarians often have a hard time in China, as the Chinese cannot understand why someone would choose not to eat meat. When asking for a dish without meat, it's not unusual to hear 'but there's not that much meat in it', or be served a vegetable dish sprinkled with pork. The Chinese have an extraordinary love of food: they will eat 'anything that flies that isn't a plane and anything with four legs that isn't a table'. Every part of every animal, bird and sea creature is used in cooking, so for many westerners, some of the dishes take some getting used to.

> After a brutal Beijing winter, there is nothing better than going to an outside 'da pai dang' place to eat having 'yang rou chuanr' (roasted lamb) and drinking Yan Jing beer with friends.
> **Alex Thompson**

Regional food

People roughly divide Chinese cuisine into four schools, according to the geographical location of the dishes' origins.

The south

The southern school mainly refers to the Guangdong or Cantonese style, where food is often stir-fried or steamed. There is a great variety of fresh ingredients available in southern China and the cooking methods often capitalise on this, emphasising freshness rather than strong flavours. Dim sum, which is very popular amongst locals and foreigners, are small dishes like steamed tapas, often consisting of meat or shrimp-filled dumplings and steamed meatballs. In the south, dim sum with tea is taken at breakfast or lunchtime. In the southern coastal cities, Chinese seafood is world famous in terms of variety and freshness. Rice is a supremely important element, particularly in the south, but also around the whole country; people rarely have a meal without rice, which is often cooked without any seasoning in order to leave room for the flavour of the dishes. The Chinese for 'to eat' literally means 'to eat rice'.

The north

In the north, which includes Beijing, Inner Mongolia, Shandong, and the three provinces of Dongbei (the area formerly known as Manchuria), the dishes are chunkier and oilier. Mutton is more common here since more farmers keep sheep as livestock. The north is too cold for much other livestock and poultry. Peking duck, however, is famously tasty. The crisp skin of the grilled duck is usually the most valued part. Mongolian barbecue and mutton hot pot are other famous dishes in the north of China. Northerners often eat dumplings or noodles instead of rice. The dumplings can be steamed, served in soups or deep-fried.

The east

The provinces of Jiangsu, Fujian and Zhejiang, as well as the cities of Shanghai and Hangzhou, are included in the broad and less-defined eastern school of Chinese cooking. These places are all along rivers and there is a great supply of freshwater fish and shrimps. Ingredients are usually fried, stir-fried or stewed. One of the most famous dishes in Hangzhou is '*longjing* shrimps', which is cooked with the famous longjing green tea leaves. Shanghai cuisine deserves a special mention and has its own distinct, often sugary, flavour.

The south-west

The cuisine of south-western China – the huge province of Sichuan in particular – is famous for its spiciness. Chilli dominates a great many of the dishes. There is also lots of bamboo in Sichuan and it is a very common ingredient. Every part of the bamboo can be used: bamboo shoots and the inner parts are for eating; bamboo leaves can be eaten or used as a spice; and the shell can be used to boil soup or to contain the rice when cooking it (so that the rice absorbs the flavour of bamboo). Pork, poultry, legumes and soybeans are also common ingredients in western-style dishes, along with chilli and bamboo.

FACT

Unlike in the old days, tipping is now quite usual in higher-end hotels and restaurants, especially with younger workers (older workers may find it insulting). A few coins is usually enough.

Macau

The Portuguese presence in Macau means there are a lot of Portuguese restaurants there. Many of them serve traditional Portuguese food and also Macanese food based on the cuisine of other parts of Asia and Africa that the Portuguese colonised. Portuguese wine available in such restaurants is very drinkable and not expensive. If you would like to have a lighter meal as a brunch or afternoon tea, you should try the '*zhupabao*' (pork sandwich), which is very famous in Macau. The desert 'ginger and milk' is worth trying as well.

Drinking

Not many Chinese people go out to drink at pubs but some like to drink alcohol with a meal. Wine is not very common yet, though its popularity is increasing, especially in the bigger cities; beer and Chinese rice wine are becoming more common. For more formal or festival dinners, sometimes brandy is drunk during a meal as well (by the tumblerful).

During a meal, you should always fill others' cups or glasses before your own, even if you are drinking something different.

The Chinese drink a lot of tea (some people believe that Chinese people drink more tea than plain water). There are many kinds of tea – 'black' or 'green' is only the start of describing the different varieties. Tea is drunk plain and never has milk or sugar added. Beer is also a relatively common drink at mealtimes. There are many good locally brewed beers; the best-known being Tsingtao, a German-style lager brewed in Qingdao, a former German concession.

SHOPPING

In most Chinese towns and cities there are department stores selling all the basic necessities of life quite cheaply. You can also get household goods, clothes and electrical equipment in these stores. In addition there are always markets where fresh produce can be bought. Freshness is a must for Chinese shoppers. However, in the last few years, western-style supermarkets have been coming to China: Wal-Mart, Carrefour, Metro and Tesco all have outlets in China. It is estimated that in 2005 supermarkets had captured 30%–40% of the urban food market, a proportion that is growing all the time. Supermarkets also carry imported foods and international brands such as Kellogg's. If you are in a reasonably sized city you will not have to do without your comfort foods.

Shopping for arts and crafts

If you are shopping for souvenirs and collectibles you will find that China has a fine range of beautiful handicrafts, works of art, antiques and locally made artefacts. The price ranges from ridiculously cheap to extraordinarily expensive. You can choose from a large and precious Qing vase to a cheap but delicate sandalwood fan.

Tea and tea utensils make very popular gifts. Good tea costs a few hundred yuan for 50g and there are many interesting varieties to choose from. The best-known one is *longjing*, best produced in Hangzhou. If you are keen to buy the best longjing tea, experts recommend *yuqian* (before rain), which is collected in early April. 'Silver needle tea' of Hengyang is another famous option. Yunnan tea may taste a bit different from that of other regions and smoked green tea called *tuocha* deserves at least a try. Good tea should go with good teapots, which are believed to enhance the flavour of the tea. In any case, Chinese teapots are often delicately crafted and really are works of art regardless of their functionality. The best-known teapots are from Yixing County in Jiangsu Province, where you can also find other tea utensils.

China has good antique markets such as Shanghai's Fangbang Lu antique market, Dongtai Lu antique market, Shanghai Antique and Curio Shop (in Duolun Lu). Apart from arts and handicrafts, antique posters are also worth collecting. Most so-called antiques are fakes – there are strict laws prohibiting the sale of genuine antiques – but replica pieces are well worth buying.

Regional specialties

- In Jiangsu, especially in Suzhou, you can find pretty embroidery, calligraphy, paintings and sandalwood fans.
- Silk is particularly famous in Suzhou and in the past, rich people travelled from other provinces to buy their cloth there. Ready-made articles like scarves, pillowcases and bed linen are more common nowadays but you can still buy fabric for tailor-made traditional clothes.
- Porcelain is the speciality of Jingdezhen in Jiangxi. Many porcelain factories are open for tourist visits.
- In Kunming and Dali (Yunnan Province), you can get good jade and marble.
- In Wuxi, you can buy freshwater pearls from nearby lake Taihu.
- In Guilin, you should try the chilli sauce, which is famously spicy and tasty.
- In Mongolia, inlaid knifes are beautiful souvenirs
- Religious paintings and embroidery are easy to find and a great variety of bamboo products are to be found in Sichuan.
- Macau sells excellent Portuguese olive oil, olives and wine. You can get these in most small grocery shops.

- Silk is particularly famous in Suzhou and in the past, rich people travelled from other provinces to buy their cloth there.

Books and bookshops

Very few bookstores in mainland China sell books in foreign languages. But in recent years, the book market has opened to foreign investors and you can now find English books in some bookstores in big cities. The chain Foreign Language Bookstore is one of the most popular with foreigners. A recent visitor to Beijing observed that the range of English-language books is improving rapidly and the price does not reflect very much of a mark up, but is almost the same as you would pay in the UK. You can also try the bookstores in big hotels and department stores such as Friendship Stores. Some of them do have a limited choice of English books and magazines. Check local listings for details of independent bookstores that may have opened up. Online bookstores may be more helpful if you are in a smaller city or you are looking for specific books. Amazon.com is an obvious online choice, but postage can be extortionate, given the import tax slapped on foreign publications.

Alternatively, you can order books from bookstores in Hong Kong, which might save you some shipping costs.

- Amazon.com is an obvious online choice, but postage can be extortionate, given the import tax slapped on foreign publications.

Bookstore Addresses

Foreign Language Bookstore: www.sbt.com.cn
Shanghai: 390 Fuzhou Road, Shanghai 200001; 021 6322 3200
Beijing: *(Wangfujing)* 235 Wangfujing Dajie, Beijing; 010 6512 6911; *(Xidan)*, Xidan Dajie, Beijing; *(Dongcheng)* 2 Xila Hutong, Dongcheng District, Beijing
Guangzhou: Beijing Lu, Guangzhou
Beijing International Bookstore: 31 Haidian street, Haidian District, Beijing; 010 6255 2499
Beijing Foreign Language Publications Ltd: 219 Wangfujing Street, Dongcheng District, Beijing; 010 6525 5140
Lufthansa Centre: 6/F, 50 Liangmaqiao Lu, Beijing; 010 6465 3388
Haidian Book City: 31 Haidiandajie, Haidian District, Beijing
Fengrusong Bookstore: 46, Haidian Lu (near south gate of Beijing University), Beijing.
Booksdirect.com.cn: China's first online bookshop. The prices are competitive and, based in Shanghai, there is free delivery to Shanghai, Hangzhou, Suzhou and Nanjing.

MEDIA AND COMMUNICATIONS

Newspapers

There are over 2,000 national and provincial newspapers in China, of which about 40 are for ethnic minorities. *People's Daily* is the national newspaper and is only published in Chinese, with English available on the website. *China Daily* is the only national English-language print newspaper, and has a comprehensive website. Both newspapers run the official government-approved version of the news, which can be transparently biased and pro-Party. *China Daily* is sometimes hard to find, even in big cities, though it's possible to subscribe from the post office. You may be able to find one or two in newspaper shops at five-star hotels, or in one of the government-run Friendship Stores. Shanghai has its own daily English newspaper, *Shanghai Daily*, which is often preferred by expat residents. *South China Morning Post* is a quality broadsheet based in Hong Kong, free from government censorship, and sold in select locations in the major cities. Five-star hotels and English-language bookshops are the best places to seek one out. Because the newspaper is still printed only in Hong Kong, it may not arrive until late in the afternoon. Newspapers like *Asian Wall Street Journal*, *Financial Times* and *International Herald-Tribune* may also be found in high-class hotels. Online newspapers are better options, if you have access to the internet.

Main Newspapers

Asian Wall Street Journal: (+852) 3105 2555; awsj.circulation@dowjones.com; www.wsj.com
China Daily: 010 6494 1107; www.chinadaily.com.cn
Financial Times, Hong Kong: (+852) 2905 5555; subseasia@ft.com;www.ftasia.net

The International Herald Tribune: (+852) 2922 1171; www.iht.com
People's Daily: 010 6536 8971; rmrb@peopledaily.com.cn; http://english.peopledaily.com.cn
South China Morning Post: (+852) 2565 2222; www.scmp.com

Magazines

English-language magazines are not especially easy to find in China. In big cities like Shanghai and Beijing, you may be able to find *Time, Newsweek, Far Eastern Economic Review* or *The Economist* in five-star hotels. English women's magazines such as *Cosmopolitan, Marie Claire* and *Elle* are very rare, in part because Chinese versions are available.

There is now an abundance of locally published English magazines which can be useful for expatriates and are, in the main, free. *That's Magazines* was the first on the scene and remains the best. It has separate monthly editions for Beijing, Shanghai and Guanzhou/Shenzhen and contains well-writen features on lifestyle, food, fashion, travel, as well as a comprehensive listings section where you can get information on property, cultural events etc. *City Weekend* is the next-best rival to *That's* but it is mainly for Beijing and Shanghai.

- English women's magazines such as *Cosmopolitan, Marie Claire* and *Elle* are very rare, in part because Chinese versions are available.

Magazine websites
That's Magazines: www.thatsmags.com
City Weekend: www.cityweekend.com.cn

Television

Central China Television (CCTV) is the only national television station in the whole of mainland China, and is government owned. CCTV has 11 channels, nine of which are broadcast in Chinese. CCTV9 and CCTV4 are the exceptions. CCTV9 is an international channel designed for foreigners and broadcasts mostly news bulletins containing government-controlled reports. In addition, there are cultural programmes, sports, business-related programmes, travel programmes, documentaries, and even sessions to teach basic Chinese. CCTV4 also sometimes broadcasts in English, but mainly shows news reports. CCTV8 and CCTV5 are for music and sports respectively, and you don't need to know much Chinese to enjoy watching these channels.

Hong Kong Star TV also provides broadcasting services for the mainland via satellite, which many people (Chinese and foreigners alike) find more entertaining than the often dry, traditional channels of CCTV. There are nine channels, including movies, sport, documentaries, news, etc. Those living in Guangdong can normally pick up the two English-language stations broadcast from Hong Kong – Pearl and ATV World – using their regular TV set.

Television stations
CCTV: cctv-international@mail.cctv.com; www.cctv.com
Star TV: star@newscorp.com.cn; www.startv.com

Websites

It is worth mentioning what is known the 'Great Firewall of China', or – more informally – the Chinese 'net nanny'. There is now an estimated 30,000-strong internet police force which, with the aid of western-provided technology, is dedicated to monitoring websites and emails. This means that on a technical level the five gateways that connect China to the global internet filter traffic coming into and going out of the country. Much of the keyword blocking technology is provided by western companies and is used to prevent people from accessing offending sites. Even China's 110,000 internet cafés are now highly regulated and state-licensed, and all are equipped with standard surveillance systems. The net nanny has famously blocked many important websites from being accessed in China, among them BBC News, Wikipedia, Flickr and YouTube (the latter three come and go, depending on the net nanny's mood swings). It's also common to encounter a time-out which will disable your internet connection for a set period of time should you make an undesirable Google search for, say, 'Falun Gong' or the 'Dalai Lama'.

- **Internet addiction** In the last few years internet addiction has become quite a problem for susceptible young men. Some of these attend a clinic (which also takes in alcoholics and drug addicts), for a special 'drying out' two-week programme. What will happen to them after the programme, as there is no aftercare given, is unknown. In Beijing, in any café (even one with only two tables), you can log on to wireless internet for free. Students are in the habit of going to one with a laptop, buying a cup of coffee, and staying there for three hours writing an essay.

Radio

Central People's Broadcasting Station (CPBS) is responsible for supervising all the radio stations in China. Most of these broadcast in Mandarin, and some in other Chinese dialects. China Radio International (CRI), a Chinese-run overseas radio service, broadcasts to other countries in about 40 languages including English, and it also provides online radio services. If you miss your home radio stations, a short-wave radio receiver enables you to receive some of the overseas channels such as the BBC World Service (www.bbc.co.uk/worldservice) and Voice of America (www.voa.gov). You can check the broadcasting frequency from their websites. It's also possible to get most radio stations through webcasts. The so-called Chinese 'net nanny', which sometimes blocks news content on the web for political reasons, generally does not block internet radio.

China Radio International (English service): 010 6889 1652; crieng@cri.com.cn; www.crienglish.com

POST

Post offices are usually on main streets, at railway stations, at airports and at major scenic spots. They open seven days a week. Normal opening hours are 9am–5pm, though some post offices open earlier or close later. Mail is delivered once a day but it can take longer for mail to arrive in rural areas and in the western regions. Look out for the green mailboxes, usually found in main streets and also railway stations.

Local mail within the same province costs ¥1.2 (£0.05/$0.09). Sending a letter to Hong Kong and Macau costs ¥2.5; the UK or the USA by airmail takes around 10 days and costs around ¥6, depending on weight. Express Mail Service (EMS) is available for mail that needs to be delivered in five to seven days (two to four days for the UK or the USA). The charges for EMS can be found at www.ems.com.cn. You can request someone from the post office to collect your parcel at home, by dialling the special number 185 for this service. EMS is also available for domestic mail and costs ¥20.

There is a fairly new service called PC-Letter. PC-Letter allows you to send your mail (in electronic form) to the nearest post office of the receiver and then the letter is printed out on a special printer, which seals your letter immediately after printing. The letter will then be posted through the normal procedure. You need to buy an electronic payment card from a post office to use this service. PC-Letter allows you to send your letter without leaving home and it is faster than normal mailing methods, as the letter can be sent directly to the nearest post office of the receiver rather than to your local post office first. There are limitations on the number of pages and the paper size for the letter. At the moment, only A4 and B5 paper sizes are accepted and you can only send a maximum of four pages. You also need special software to use the PC-Letter service. Still, this is a small revolution in letter writing and more details can be found from your local post office.

When sending a parcel, the post office worker will usually check the contents before posting it. You may be required to open your wrapped parcel for checking, so it is advisable to wrap it in the post office, after the staff have checked it and post offices have wrapping materials for this purpose. When claiming a parcel you need your identity document. It's often safest to bring your passport.

 The hotline for mailing enquiries is 11185.

Apart from normal mail services, post offices perform some of the functions of banks. You can open a savings account in a post office and you can also make a money transfers there.

Every year, different stamps are issued in China and you can order the forthcoming stamps in advance. The deadline for ordering next year's stamps is November of each year.

Macanese post offices

Post offices in Macau open 9am–5pm (or 6pm for some bigger post offices) from Monday to Friday, and 9am–1pm on Saturday. Two post offices, at the Macau Jetfoil Terminal and Macau International Airport, have extended opening hours from 10am–8pm Monday to Saturday. In case you cannot get to a post office during normal working hours, you can try these two but they are far from the city centre. Mailboxes in Macau are red and are on main streets. There are also some stamp vending machines on the main roads.

HEALTH

Health insurance

In mainland China, what medical insurance exists usually requires citizens to pay a substantial percentage of the costs of care themselves. Both employers and employees are required to contribute to medical insurance for employees. In general, employers have to contribute 6% of the salary of their employees while employees themselves contribute 2%. The contributions of employers are divided into two parts: one part is paid to the employees' personal insurance accounts and the other half is used to set up a fund for the general public. Every local government sets a minimum and a maximum level to be paid to the fund. When the contributions are below the minimum level, the amount is made up to the minimum level through the personal insurance accounts of the service users. The charges are paid mainly by the fund if they are within the minimum and maximum levels, while the service users pay a small part of it. The maximum amount the fund will pay is normally equal to four times the average annual salary of employees in the county.

Under the current legislation, employers and employees are required to contribute to government medical insurance. At the same time, the government encourages residents to have private health insurance as well. The government aims to have an 80% rate of private insurance coverage for the whole population by 2010. Currently, about 50% of people in urban areas are covered by private insurance but the rate is much lower in rural areas, often as low as 10%. You should seek advice from insurance companies before leaving your country, especially if you are going to stay for only a short period and are not going to buy any insurance within China. Some big insurance companies have branches in China and you can look for suitable insurance cover after you settle in.

Useful resources

American International Assurance Co Ltd: 800 820 3588; www.aigchina.com
AXA Asia Pacific Holdings Ltd: 010 6500 7393; www.axa-chinaregion.com
HTH Worldwide Inc, USA: 952 903 6418; studentinfo@hthworldwide.com; www.hthstudents.com. Special insurance for students.
ING General Insurance International Ltd: 0411 2530 881; www.ing-cap.com.cn
LAMP Insurance Co Ltd: www.lampinsurance.com. A newcomer to China.
Royal & Sun Alliance Insurance Ltd: 021 6841 1999; rsashang@uninet.com.cn; www.royalsunalliance.com.cn
New York Life Insurance Worldwide Ltd: 800 820 5882; r@haiernewyorklife.com.cn; www.haiernewyorklife.com.cn
PICC Property and Casualty Company Ltd: 010 6315 6688; webmaster@piccnet.com.cn; www.picc.com.cn/en

Hospitals

Almost all hospitals are owned and monitored by the government, even though there are many private hospitals created by joint ventures. Charges for medical treatments can vary, both from province to province and even hospital to hospital in the same city.

You are required to register at reception before seeing a doctor in a hospital. The charge for making a registration is around ¥1 (£0.07/$0.14) but you need to pay more if you want to consult a specific doctor. Some hospitals provide phone or online registration services but most of the websites are in Chinese. Consultation and medicines are charged separately. It is hard to predict the exact amount a person will need to pay as treatments and medicines are charged per item. You also need to pay before you receive any treatment, meaning often you must seek a diagnosis (for a small sum) and then pay for this before any action is taken. Hospitals usually ask for a deposit before providing services and patients or their family members will be asked to top up the deposit when the money is used up. The consultation fees vary and inpatient treatment costs are often based on the perceived amount that the patient can afford. Foreigners, by this logic, will often be asked for more than local Chinese.

There are ambulances for emergencies – but, unless requested, there will be no medical staff in the ambulance and the personnel present may have little or no medical training. Even more worryingly, traffic rarely makes much of an effort to part for an ambulance in its midst. It costs around ¥50 to call an ambulance and an extra ¥40 for requesting the presence of medical staff. Except in an emergency, foreigners are advised to go to a hospital in a big city as it is more likely the medical staff will speak English. Bear in mind that most hospitals do not accept credit card payments and you should have cash available if you or your family members need to go to hospital.

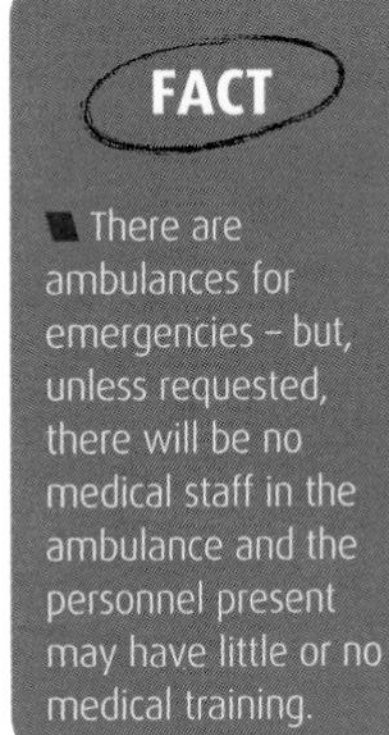

Due to the lack of consistent and reliable care in China's hospitals, most foreigners travelling to China with a company should expect to receive private health insurance as part of their 'expat' package. Any health issues that arise will be dealt with at one of the growing number of private hospitals where fees are high but patients can expect English-language information and overseas-trained doctors. It is also possible to visit these hospitals as a private customer, though expect to pay substantially more than you would at a local hospital.

Macanese hospitals

You are required to bring along your DH (Department of Health) computerised card when you use the services of hospitals or health centres in Macau. The card can be applied for from the administrative service at the hospitals or the health centres where you reside. You are asked to present your identity document and also proof of your address (eg water, telephone or electricity bill). The general consultation costs MOP$42 (£2.68/$5.32) for locals, MOP$60 for non-resident workers and MOP$120 for foreigners.

Traditional medicine

You could also try traditional Chinese medicine (TCM), which is gaining credibility among western medical practitioners. Many TCM doctors are also western trained. The idea behind it is that the body is a dynamic energy system. The aim of TCM is to maintain or restore harmony in the body and the balance of yin and yang. It uses acupuncture, herbal medicines, massage and the practice of *Qigong* (a system of exercises). While many Chinese now rely on western medicine, it is possible to find TCM clinics in some hospitals. In rural regions, you might be lucky enough to find a doctor sitting in his doorway. He'll spend time checking your pulse and examining your tongue and then prescribe either pills or bitter-tasting tea which he'll make up himself in his shop. While there are clear benefits to using this type of non-toxic medicine, it often takes longer to take effect. This is why many Chinese now turn to the more instant antibiotic treatments, administered by drip in a clinic. If you are taken ill and need treatment, don't be surprised if you are hooked up to a bag of antibiotics for a couple of hours before being sent on your way.

Useful resources

China Internet Information Centre: www.china.org.cn/english/travel/41850.htm. Gives addresses of all the hospitals in China.
Conde de S Januário Hospital, Macau: 6390 6016; info@ssm.gov.mo
Department of Health, Macau: www.ssm.gov.mo. Provides addresses and telephone numbers of hospitals and health centres.
Guangzhou International SOS Clinic: www.internationalsos.com
Ministry of Health: 010 6879 2114; manage@moh.gov.cn; www.moh.gov.cn

AIDS

The problem of AIDS in China has become severe. According to the Chinese government and UNAIDS, in January 2005 there were 650,000 people with HIV and 75,000 new cases of AIDS. Interestingly, this is lower than the 2003 figure of 800,000, though the government explains this in terms of improved data-colletion methods. The UN believes that the number of HIV carriers in China may increase to 10 million or more by the year 2010. In order to arrest the spread of AIDS, the Chinese government set up its first formal research centre in Shanghai in April 2004. In theory, anyone who is found guilty of covering up an outbreak of AIDS will be severely punished. However, some people have criticised public education on the issue and a survey released in 2003 reflected that one in four people in rural areas had never heard of AIDS and only 20% of the population knew HIV could be transmitted through sexual contact.

EDUCATION

As with the healthcare system, education in China can sometimes feel like something of a run-for-profit business. In the major cities – notably Beijing, Shanghai and Shenzhen – a raft of international schools have emerged over the past decade to cater for a growing middle class prepared to pay high prices for an international education. As expats start to settle in China, these schools are increasingly catering for their children too, offering a real alternative to the Chinese system. Fees are lower than sending a child back to the UK, and the best ones follow a national curriculum, keeping the child at a level equivalent to their home schools. Under Chinese law, it is only possible to 'opt out' of the Chinese school system if one or more of your parents is a non-Chinese citizen, so these international schools are a made up of students from very mixed backgrounds, often from Taiwan, Singapore, Hong Kong and other Asian countries as well as from Europe and America.

Following a curriculum that corresponds to your own country's system has huge advantages, not least when you return home and your child is at the same level

Private schools

It is thought that students that attend private schools are often children of hard-working parents who spoil them to compensate for the lack of time they can spend with them. These schools can be just as strict as the Chinese national schools, as discipline is seen as key to changing these 'little emperors' into useful members of society.

as his or her peer group. Move on to another country and the international schools there will pick up where your child left off. It has been difficult for overseas textbooks and learning aids to get through the Chinese importing system over the last decade, but it is now easier for schools to buy the resources they need, and your child will mostly be using the books they'll be familiar with from home. Some schools are turning to international curricula, such as the International Baccalaureate (IB), International General Certificate of Secondary Education (IGCSE) and International Primary Curriculum (IPC). These are designed to be more flexible approaches to the sometimes-rigid national curricula prescribed by European and American governments. They are also more aware of the international context, and so are deemed to be more relevant to large numbers of international students.

One of the biggest turn-offs for foreign parents in placing their children in China's national education system is the intensity and competitiveness of that system. Chinese children often study from dawn until well after dusk and endure a punishing schedule of exams that are continually assessing a child's rank amongst their peers, in any given subject. Learning is much more likely to be by rote.

If you would like your child to experience China's national education system, there are options outside the international English-medium schools. Private schools for Chinese are springing up all over China, mostly to cater for a growing middle class intent on spending as much as possible on ensuring their one and only child gets a foot up the ladder to university or a good job. These schools will often have an English-medium programme but doesn't always follow British or American curricula. There has been some concern for the survival of these schools, however, as they are funded exclusively by tuition fees, which can dry up, and force closure if enough students don't enrol.

Facilities at these schools may be comparable to those in the international sector, with often-excellent sporting equipment, swimming pools, IT rooms etc. Tuition fees are lower than at the international schools, but this may be false economy as private schools will levy extra charges for almost anything: school books, pencils, activities, education fund deposits. Check with parents of existing students for more information on how fees are charged.

The education system

China introduced a nine-year compulsory education system in 1986, however the policy does not yet apply all over China. In particular, some children in the western provinces are not able to access free government education. Nine-year compulsory education includes primary school education and junior high school education. Primary education starts at the age of six (seven for some areas) and lasts for six years. The children should then go to junior high schools, without having to take any examinations. Junior high school education lasts for three years and can be substituted by junior secondary vocational training, which is also open to those who have completed primary school. Although children are allocated to their closest junior or senior schools, there is often high competition to get into the best ones. Parents use their *'guanxi'*, or contacts, to get their child into the top-ranking schools, even if they aren't located nearby, which often leaves less well-connected families (and therefore less wealthy) to lose out.

Children take endless tests and exams throughout their school career, and often study after school until late into the night to achieve good grades. This often means that once children reach junior school, they drop their after-school activities, such as painting, singing and piano playing to focus on achieving the best marks in the class. This system is exacerbated by overly enthusiastic parents seeking to push their one and only child into university and a well-paid job. Unfortunately, suicide is not an uncommon occurrence in teenagers as a result of the double school and parental pressure to achieve.

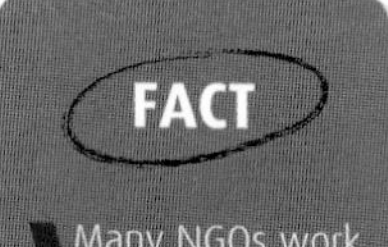

Many NGOs work hard to deliver rural education, especially to those in remote or minority areas, with a particular focus on getting girls to attend school.

- **The school year** If you are in China during the first week back at school in September, you may see dozens of school-age children parading around in military gear. This is part of the 'military training' each student undergoes at junior, middle and senior school to teach them discipline and humility. Children are expected to stand still for hours at a time and conduct exercises in the heat of the September weather for a week-long period. The school year continues in the form of two semesters, broken up by National Holiday week in October, the long Chinese New Year break in January/February, and May Holiday week around International Labour Day.

Useful resources

China education and Research Network: www.edu.cn
Ministry of Education (MoE): 010 6609 6114; emic@moe.edu.cn; www.moe.edu.cn
Education and Youth Affairs Bureau, Macau: 555533; webmaster@dsej.gov.mo; www.dsej.gov.mo

Basic education

Basic education in China includes pre-school education, primary school education and junior secondary school (high school) education, of which primary and junior secondary education is compulsory under the current system. At the moment, most schools are funded by the government and, in theory, are free of charge. In fact, local governments often impose various fees and taxes. School fees are not standardised and are decided by local governments. They range from 10 to ¥1,000–¥2,000 (up to £140/$240) a year. A 'single fee system' will be disseminated nationally in compulsory education within the next five years. Moreover the government plans to extend free schooling to 150 million rural schoolchildren. Many NGOs work hard to deliver rural education, especially to those in remote or minority areas, with a particular focus on getting girls to attend school.

Subjects taken in primary and junior secondary education are divided into state-arranged subjects and locally arranged subjects. Students are required to take end-of-term examinations or tests and they are also encouraged to take part in after-school activities. These activities include scientific, cultural and recreational activities and are usually organised by children's clubs, scientific and technological centres for teenagers, or other similar institutions.

Moral education plays a very important role in basic education in China. One main focus is the 'five loves': love of the motherland, love of the people, love of labour, love of science and love of socialism. Students need to study the cultural traditions and revolutionary history of the Chinese nation, the legal system, modern Chinese history, a general survey of China and policies on current events and to build up a scientific outlook of the world and life.

Students 30 years ago would have spent a substantial amount of time studying Marxism. Portraits of the great communist thinkers – Marx and Lenin foremost among them – can still be found hanging on classroom walls but their ideas are now given little more than lip-service.

Labour education and skills training are also included in primary and junior secondary education and students are encouraged to acquire some basic knowledge and skills related to productive labour. This represents one of the few reminders of China's status as a communist country. However, as China's economy changes, the importance of these classes has waned. The status of labourers may be higher in China than in other developing countries but in an increasingly materialistic and highly educated nation, Chinese workers are often regarded with little respect, as is anyone who has not excelled within the formal education system.

Macanese education

In Macau there is also basic compulsory education, but it is slightly different from that of the mainland. It also consists of six years' primary school education and three years' junior secondary school education, but one year's pre-primary education is also required. Basic education in Macau is free

- **School uniform** School children up to the age of 18 wear uniforms but there are different outfits for different days. Blue shorts or skirts, white shirts and a red toggled neckscarf are most common, but on sports days the pupils will wear nylon tracksuits emblazoned with their school's name. You'll see them boarding public buses to get to school although private buses are operated by international schools.

English in education

English may technically be just another subject, alongside physics, maths and sport, however, it has taken on huge importance for students and parents in China. Thirty years ago a pupil would have only begun learning Engish at age 15. These days students are learning from age eight or nine, and many parents send their children to kindergartens where they can learn to sing English-language rhymes. Proficiency in English is essential for students wanting to go to a top university, even if their chosen subject is not related to English. Students are often given homework tasks to speak to or start a conversation with a foreigner, so don't be alarmed if you are approached by a group of giggling teenagers eager to ask you a barrage of questions.

Top-down demands that China's children learn English from an earlier and earlier age has led to a lag in the standards in traditional teaching institutions. Students spend a large proportion of their time learning English but there remains a problem in actually using the language in an environment where there are few opportunities to practice, and where the teacher himself has probably never visited a native English-speaking country. This may partly explain the emergence of thousands of private schools across the nation. These cater to a huge demand for English learning among both children and adults. Only certain government-run schools are permitted to employ foreigners and many of the thousands of English teachers in China actually work unofficially in this tertiary education industry.

Macau

In Macau, most schools teach in Cantonese or English, though Mandarin teaching has gained importance in recent years. There are also a small number of schools that conduct lessons in Portuguese. Most students are required to wear school uniform on the mainland and Macau but it is still not very common in rural areas.

The structure of the education system

Pre-school education

Pre-school education is not compulsory in China and was not common before the 90s. The government reported that over 70% of children completed at least one year of pre-school education by the end of 1998. These days more and more parents send their children to kindergarten if they can afford it. Parents live in cities, far away from their own parents, so they can no longer rely on cheap babysitting and support, unless they bring them to the city to help out. For most Chinese families, who live in small apartments, this is not possible, so children are sent to pre-school to be taken care of during the day.

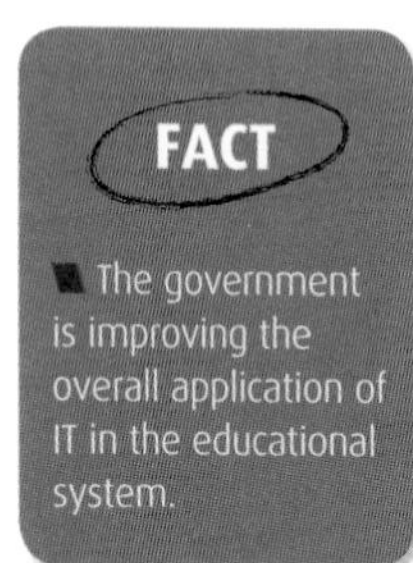

Children start kindergarten at the age of three or even younger and spend three years there. In some rural areas without kindergarten facilities, a year of pre-school classes for local children is often organised. Parents can choose to send a child to kindergarten for a whole day or half-day.

The main purpose of pre-school education is to provide physical, intellectual, aesthetic and moral training to prepare children for primary school education. They are also trained to express themselves. Games are an important part of pre-school education. Children start to learn Chinese and basic mathematics, and also have music lessons, art lessons and regular physical education. An added bonus is for proud parents to boast of their three-year-old's knowledge of English, painting, or computers. There is a strong rivalry between parents on how well their child is doing at school, and with competition tough later on in the school system, it is inevitable that children are starting to learn earlier and earlier to beat their peers later on.

Beijing schools

Beijing Oxford Little Professor Kindergarten: Asian Games Village North Gate, Building 308, Huizhong District, Beijing; 010 6493 6626

Beanstalk International School (Kindergarten): 1/F, B Building, 40 Liangmaqiao Road Chaoyang District, Beijing; 010 6466 9255; director@bibs.com.cn; www.bibs.com.cn

Eton International School: Room 701, 7F Lido Office Tower, Lido Place, Jichang Road, Jiang Tai Road, Chaoyang District, Beijing 100004; 010 6430 1590; info@etonkids.com; www.etonkids.com

The International Children's House, English Montessori Kindergarten: Beijing Lufthansa Center, Unit S 114, 50 Liangmaqiao Road, Chaoyang District, Beijing 100016; 010 6465 1305; China World Trade Center, North Lodge, 1 Jian Guo Men Wai Avenue, Beijing 100004; 010 6505 3869; info@montessoribeijing.com; www.montessoribeijing.com

JoJo English Academy, purple Jade Villas: 1 Purple Jade Dong Lu, Chaoyang District, Beijing; 010 8460 5671

Lido Kindergarten: Holiday Inn Lido Beijing, Jichang Road, Jiang Tai Road, Beijing; 010 6437 6688; sybil.wilson@lidoplace.com; www.lidoplace.com/schools/kinder.html

Shanghai schools

Children's Literature Kindergarten: East Kang Qiao Garden, Lane 2, Kangshi Lu, Shanghai; 021 6812 2658

KinderWorld International Kindergarten: F2, Somerset Grand Shanghai, 8 Jinan Road, Shanghai; 021 6386 7880; kinderworld@kinderworld.net; www.kinderworld.net

Shanghai Rainbow Bridge International Kindergarten: 2381 Hong Qiao Road, Shanghai 200335; 021 6268 3121; www.rbik.com

Shanghai Montessori Kindergarten: 1481 Haitian Garden, Huqing Ping Highway, Shanghai; 021 5988 5650

Tiny Tots International Pre-School and Kindergarten: 43 West Fuxing Road, Shanghai; 021 6431 3788

Other resources

The Australian International School: 35 Da Shu Yuan Xiang, Haishu District 315000, Ningbo Zhejiang Province; 0574 8730 6737; www.aussieschool-china.com

Sunflower International Kindergarten: 021 5030 3681; sunflowerm@online.sh.cn; www.sunmonte.com

Primary school

Most children start primary school at the age of six but in some rural areas entry is at seven. Primary school education is part of the nine-year compulsory education and usually takes six years. In general, a school year is divided into two semesters with 38 weeks of teaching, 13 weeks of holidays and an additional week in reserve. Chinese language and mathematics are compulsory subjects. Many primary schools now include English in the curriculum from grade three (age eight or nine) onwards. Other subjects include: physics, biology, chemistry, history, geography and politics. Unless it is an international school, lessons are conducted in Mandarin, except for English language lessons. After finishing primary school students can automatically go on to secondary school, though which school they go to will be decided by exams.

Secondary school

Secondary school education is divided into junior high school and senior high school. Junior high school refers to the first three years of secondary school education, which is part of the nine-year compulsory education. A school year consists of 39 weeks of teaching sessions, 12 weeks of holiday and an additional week in reserve. A school year is usually divided into two semesters. English language is a compulsory subject starting from junior high. Chinese language and mathematics are also compulsory.

Other subjects include: chemistry, physics, biology, history, geography and another foreign language. Physical education is not compulsory but is encouraged. Students who want to continue their studies in senior high school have to sit and pass locally organised entrance examinations.

Senior high school education lasts for three years and the curriculum is divided into subject courses and activities. Students have to choose their streams, either sciences or humanities, and subject courses are divided into compulsory ones and optional ones. Students are also required to take part in extra-curricular activities. There is one more teaching week in senior high school than junior high school. A school year therefore contains 10–11 weeks of holiday and another one or two weeks in reserve.

- **Class numbers** There are usually around 60 pupils per a class at primary and junior-middle school, with slightly fewer at high school. Schools are enormous by British standards, with as many as 2,000 students in a primary school. Classmate loyalty stays with the pupils for life, and it's not uncommon to hear of class reunions many decades after leaving school. Children often have a desk-mate, who they share a desk with the whole way through a stage of school.

Vocational education

Vocational education is divided into three different levels – junior secondary, senior secondary and tertiary – and consists of vocational schools and vocational training.

Junior secondary vocational education is for primary school graduates and is part of the nine-year compulsory education. The aim is to train workers, farmers and employees in other sectors with basic knowledge and certain professional skills.

Senior secondary vocational training is another choice for continuing studies for junior high school graduates who cannot continue their studies in senior high schools, or for those who are more interested in learning something different. It is not restricted to junior high school graduates: senior high school graduates can also apply to these vocational schools. Senior secondary vocational training can be offered by specialised secondary schools, skilled workers' schools or vocational high schools. It usually takes four years to complete the training. Some courses are open to senior high school graduates only and these, in general, last for two years. Students are expected to master the basic knowledge, theory and skills of their speciality after the training. As in senior high schools, cultural knowledge is also part of the studies.

Tertiary vocational training is for graduates from high schools and senior secondary vocational schools. Tertiary vocational training is divided into five categories:

- 30 higher vocational technology colleges
- 101 short-circle practical vocational universities
- Five-year higher vocational classes provided in regular specialised secondary schools
- Tertiary vocational education provided in some regular higher education institutions
- Reformed regular institutions offering two to three year higher education with emphasis on training technical talents in high-level professionals

Vocational training is mainly conducted and managed by the government. However, private enterprises are also encouraged to provide suitable training for their employees.

International schools

For the reasons given earlier in this section, most foreign children in China attend international schools. Lessons and textbooks will be largely in English, teachers will have received internationally accredited training and the teaching style generally prioritises personal development, creativity and independent thinking. However, international schools can only be found in big and affluent cities like Beijing, Shanghai, Guangzhou and Shenzhen. School fees can be extraordinarily expensive, in most cases over ¥164,000 (£10,000/$20,000) a year. Individual schools may make a point of following the curriculum of a particular western nation.

■ Lessons and textbooks will be largely in English, teachers will have received internationally accredited training and the teaching style generally prioritises personal development, creativity and independent thinking.

www.shambles.net is dedicated to international education and institutions of Asia, with a large section dedicated to China. You will find details of all schools eager to attract international students, contact details and a description of their curriculum and approach. It is well worth checking this site for up-to-date information on international schools in your region.

Beijing schools

Beijing BISS International School: No 17, Area 4, An Zhen Xi Li, Chaoyang District, Beijing 100029; 010 6443 3151; daren@biss.com.cn; www.biss.com.cn

Beijing World Youth Academy (WYA): 40 Liangmaqiao Lu, Chaoyang District 100016; 010 6461 7779; www.chinatefl.com/beijing/teach/beijingsq.htm

Beijing Yew Chung International School: Honglingjin Park, 5 Houbalizhuang, Chaoyang District, Beijing 100025; 010 8583 3731; www.ycef.com

Beijing Zongugnacun International School: 14 Taiyangyan, Dazhongsi, Haidian District, Beijing

International Academy of Beijing (IAB): Lido Office Tower 3, Lido Place Jichang Road, Jiangtai Road, Chaoyang District, Beijing 100004; 010 6430 1600

International School of Beijing: 10 An Hua Street, Shunyi District, Beijing 101300; 010 8149 2345 extension 1041; admissions@isb.bj.edu.cn; www.isb.bj.edu.cn. It also has a division for kindergarten students.

Spanish Educational Study Group: Heping Jie Beikou, Huixin Dongjie, Chaoyang District, Beijing

Swedish School: Legend Garden Villas, 89 Jichang Lu, Chaoyang District, Beijing 101300; 010 6456 0826; swedishschool@netchina.com.cn; www.swedishschool.org.cn

Western Academy of Beijing: PO Box 8547, 10 Lai Guang Ying Dong Lu, Chaoyang District 100103; 010 8456 4155; wabinfo@westernacademy.com; www.wab.edu

Shanghai schools

Shanghai American School: 258 Jin Feng Lu, Zhudi Town, Minhang District, Shanghai 201107; 021 6221 1445; info@saschina.org; www.saschina.org

Shanghai Community International Schools: 79, Lane 261, Jiangsu Road, Changning, Shanghai 200050; 021 6252 3688; info@scischina.org; www.scischina.org

Yew Chung International School: 11 Shui Cheng Road, Gubei Campus, 18 Rong Hua Xi Road, Shanghai; 021 6219 5910; ingridk@sis.ycef.com; www.ycef.com

Concordia International School: 999 Mingyue Road, Jinqiao, Pudong, Shanghai 201206; 021 589 90380; registrar@ciss.com.cn; www.ciss.com.cn

German School Shanghai: 437 Jinhui Lu, Shanghai 201103; 021 6405 9220; info@ds-shanghai.org.cn; www.ds-shanghai.org.cn

French School of Shanghai: 437 Jinhui Lu, Shanghai; 021 6405 9220; meunier@guomai.sh.cn

Japanese School: 3185 Hongmei Lu, Shanghai; 021 6406 8027; sjs10@uninet.com.cn; www.sjscn.com

Tianjin schools

Teda International School: 9 Xiao Yuan Street, Teda, Tianjin 300457; 022 252 90140; tjtis@starinfo.net.cn; www.tedainternationalschool.net

Tianjin International School: 1 Meiyuan Road, Huayuan Industrial Area, Nankai District, Tianjin 300384; 022 8371 0900 extension 100; tisadmissions@mtichina.com; www.tiseagles.com

Guangdong

American International School of Guangzhou: No 3, Yan Yu Street South, Er Sha Island, Dong Shan District, Guangzhou, Guangdong 510105; 020 8735 3393; info@aisgz.edu.cn; www.aisgz.edu.cn

Clifford School: Clifford Estates (Panyu) Ltd, Panyu, Guangdong 51149

Guangzhou Nanhu International School: 176 Yunxiang Road, Tonghe Street, Baiyun District, Guangzhou, Guangdong 510515; 020 8706 0862; www.GNISChina.com

Guangzhou International School: Building No 7, South Area, Zhongshan Dadao, Hua Jing New City, Guangzhou

QSI International School of Shekou: Villa 5, Guishan Villas, Shekou, Guangdong; 0755 2667 6031; shekou@qsi.org; www.qsi.org

Other schools

Hangzhou International School: 80 Dongxin Street, Binjiang District, Hangzhou 310053; 0571 8669 0045; dluebbe@scischina.org; www.scischina.org/hangzhou

QSI International School of Chengdu: 4th Floor, 17th Building, Area A, Phase 1, China Garden, Chengdu 610041; 028 851 98393; chengdu@qsi.org; www.qsi.org

QSI International School of Wuhan: Dong Shun Hua Yuan, Chang Qing Lu, Hankou, Wuhan, Hubei 430023; 027 8352 5597; jeffabare@qsi.org; www.qsi.org

QSI International School of Zhuhai: 2 Longxing Street, No 22 Gongbei Zhuhai 519020; 0756 815 6134; zhuhai@qsi.org; www.qsi.org

School of the Nations (Macau): Rua Louis G Gomes No 136, Edif Lei San, 4 Andar, Macau SAR; 2870 1759; sonmacau@macau.ctm.net; www.schoolofthenations.com

Xiamen International School: Jiu Tian Hu, Xinglin District, Xiamen, Fujian 361022; 0592 625 6581; askxis@hotmail.com; www.xischina.com

Universities

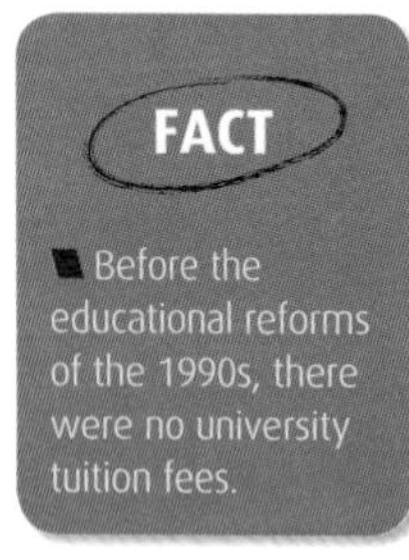
FACT
Before the educational reforms of the 1990s, there were no university tuition fees.

Before the educational reforms of the 1990s, there were no university tuition fees. However, students were not free to choose their jobs after graduation. Under the current system, students have to pay a tuition fee of around ¥5,000 (£360/$600) a semester. This may vary from university to university and from subject to subject. After graduation, most of the students select their jobs freely. There are loans available for students who have financial difficulties and there is also a part-time job system to help students support themselves. Scholarships are available to reward and help outstanding students.

According to government statistics, there are currently over 2,000 higher education institutes in China. Senior high school graduates have to sit a national examination to get an offer from a university. The competition for university places is extremely intense. For most subjects, it takes four years to get a bachelor's degree. A school year is usually divided into two semesters: from September to January and from February to July. Each semester consists of about 20 weeks. Students can choose their subjects from 12 disciplines including philosophy, economics, law, mathematics, education, literature, history, science, engineering, medicine, management and the military. Teaching is mainly conducted in Mandarin. Foreign students who want to study in universities in China have to pass a language test or study a Mandarin course before starting their studies.

The University of Nottingham opened a campus in Ningbo in Zhejiang province in 2004. It is the first joint-venture university in China and students graduate with a University of Nottingham degree, equivalent to that awarded in the UK. Teaching is in English and staff are recruited both locally and internationally. Many well-off middle-class Chinese like the idea of a British-style education and degree for their child and many other universities have begun to follow Nottingham's lead.

Macanese universities

It usually takes three to four years to get a bachelor's degree in Macau. Teaching is mainly conducted in English. However, courses of the law faculty are conducted in Cantonese and Portuguese, the official languages of Macau. Tuition fees for a bachelor's degree range from MOP$27,000–MOP$29,000 (£1,652–£1,775/$3,358–$3,606) a year. However, overseas students in general have to pay MOP$6,000–MOP$10,000 more.

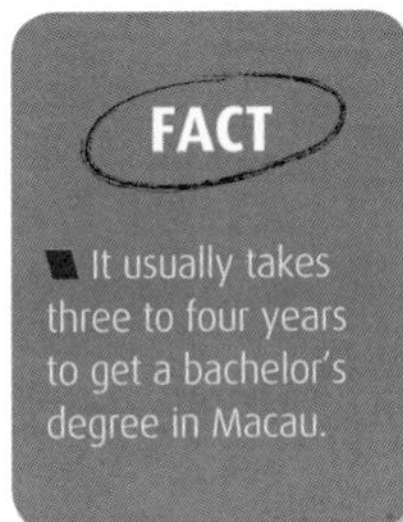

Major universities

Fudan University: 220 Handen Lu, Shanghai 200433; 021 6564 2222; webmaster@fudan.edu.cn; www.fudan.edu.cn

Macao Polytechnic Institute: Rua de Luis Gonzaga Gomes, Macau; 2857 8722; www.ipm.edu.mo

Macao University of Science and Technology: 2888 1122; registry@must.edu.mo; www.must.edu.mo

Nankai University: 94 Weijin Lu, Nankai District, Tianjin 300071; 022 2350 8825; admin@nankai.edu.cn; www.nankai.edu.cn

Peking University: Division of General Affairs, 2nd Floor, South Chamber (Nan Ge), Beijing 100871; 010 6275 1246; study@pku.edu.cn; www.pku.edu.cn

Renmin University of China: 59 Zhongguancun Dajie, Haidian District, Beijing 100872; 010 6251 1083; rmdxxb@ruc.edu.cn; www.ruc.edu.cn

Shanghai Jiaotong University: 1954 Huashan Road, Shanghai 200030; 021 6293 2414; icae@sjtu.edu.cn; www.sjtu.edu.cn

Sun Yat-sen University: Office of International Cooperation and Exchange, No 135 Xingang Xi Road, Guangzhou 510275; 020 8403 6465; adeao01@zsu.edu.cn; www.zsu.edu.cn

Tianjin University: 92 Weijin Lu, Nankai District, Tianjin 300072; 022 2740 6147; iso@tju.edu.cn; www.tju.edu.cn

Tsinghua University: Foreign Students Office, Tsinghua University 100084; 010 6278 4857; xn-fao@tsinghua.edu.cn; www.tsinghua.edu.cn

Tongji University: 1239 Siping Road, Shanghai; 021 6598 2200; xshchb@mail.tongji.edu.cn; www.tongji.edu.cn

University of Macau: Avenue Padre Tomás Pereira SJ, Taipa, Macao; (+853) 2883 1622; www.umac.mo

Wuhan University: The Office of The College of Foreign Students Education, Luojia Hill, Wuhan 430072; 027 8786 3154; fses@whu.edu.cn; www.whu.edu.cn
Xian Jiaotong University: Office of International Cooperation and Exchange, 28 Hanningxi Lu, Xian, Shannxi; 029 8266 8830; inte-cao@mail.xjtu.edu.cn; www.xjtu.edu.cn

Other resources

China Scholarship Council: webmaster@csc.edu.cn; www.csc.edu.cn
China education and Research Network: www.edu.cn
www.index-china.com: contains all links to the universities in China.

WOMEN'S ISSUES

Women have been regarded as inferior to men for most of Chinese history. In youth they were supposed to obey their fathers; in adulthood, their husbands; and in widowhood, their sons. This was institutionalised as the 'three obediences'. Once married (mostly by arrangement and regardless of their consent), they belonged to their husband's family, as did any children born to the marriage. Looking after her parents-in-law was one of a wife's prime duties. Until the 1950s in China, and 1971 in Hong Kong, a man was allowed to have as many wives as he wanted so long as he was able to support them. A man also had the right to sell his wife and children!

Even now, many parents prefer boys to girls as they still consider that daughters belong to other families after they get married.

Men and women have become much more equal nowadays, on account of many laws passed by the government and also educational and job opportunities. Nevertheless, women are still less favoured in many situations. Even now, many parents prefer boys to girls as they still consider that daughters belong to other families after they get married. Sons, on the other hand, are supposed to take care of their parents and continue the family business. Many parents will abort a pregnancy if they find out that the baby is a girl, because of the one-child policy. There are many stories of disappointed mothers of baby girls weeping in the hospital and of their parents-in-law refusing to speak to them or see the baby. In rural areas where children do not benefit from free compulsory education, parents prefer the sons to go to school if they cannot afford school fees for all the children.

Working women account for about 40% of the total workforce but many of them have reported discrimination and unfair treatment. Women also retire at the age of 55, five years earlier than men.

There is no tradition in China of men treating women with courtesy. Men go first and if there is one seat on a bus the husband will be likely to take it and leave his wife standing.

Although there is still unfairness between men and women, the gap is actually narrowing. In big cities, where people receive higher education, you will find fashionable, well-educated and financially independent women. Many of these women perceive their career as being as important as their family and do not want to be dependent on their husbands. Foreign influence has also changed the way Chinese people regard women. The recent series of Miss World contests, held on Hainan Island, was said to be a great breakthrough for the country. Beauty pageants were banned in China in the past, as they were regarded as displays of exploitation and decadence. People in general have viewed them as bad-taste events that focus only on outside beauty and ignore inner beauty, which counts for more in Chinese traditions. The tables now seem to have turned, with China embracing the pageant just as western media begins to turn its back on the event.

Western women in China

In general Chinese men have the idea that westerners, men and women alike, are more 'liberated' (to use the positive euphemism) than Chinese. Western women will usually find that, unlike in Arab or Mediterranean countries, they are not routinely ogled, whistled at or followed.

Precautions for your personal safety should be taken as in any foreign country, but China, as in many parts of East Asia, is considered to be a largely safe environment for women. Due to power shortages, streetlights in some areas are turned out early, or not used at all, so you can find yourself in areas with little lighting. However, you are rarely alone in China and will find yourself surrounded by people going shopping, teenagers walking arm in arm down the street or children playing in residential areas, even with the lights out. Keep a mobile phone with you at all times, and head towards shops or restaurants if you feel threatened.

In the business world, western businesswomen are treated with as much respect as their male counterparts; the wives of foreign businessmen are welcome to attend social functions and treated as being on a level with their husbands. There is no problem with foreign women drinking or smoking, even though it is still fairly unusual to see Chinese women doing so. For more on women in the work environment, see *Working culture and etiquette* in Working in China.

FACT

Precautions for your personal safety should be taken as in any foreign country, but China, as in many parts of East Asia, is considered to be a largely safe environment for women.

SOCIAL SECURITY AND BENEFITS

The ineffectiveness of China's social security system is evident in the sheer number of elderly or frail people who can be seen undertaking backbreaking labour or menial tasks. Despite its socialist underpinning, China is a society increasingly driven by free market economics and the state offers its citizens few guarantees. Most people must work to live. The sheer size of China's population is normally cited as the reason why European-style welfare provision would be impossible. Indeed, your family is regarded by most as the chief safety net in times of difficulty. Needless to say, foreigners living in China are not entitled to what few state benefits exist. However, an understanding of the limited benefits the state offers to its nationals can be useful when living within Chinese society. For information on employment-related social security, see *Aspects of employment* in Working in China.

Under current law, men aged 16–60 and women aged 16–55 are included in the working population. Anyone who is within the above range and is involuntarily not employed is classified as unemployed. Every employed person has to contribute 1% of his or her salary to unemployment insurance and is in return eligible for a monthly unemployment subsidy. However, the unemployed must have contributed to the unemployment insurance for at least one year, while employed, to be eligible for the subsidy. In addition, he or she has to register as unemployed and must be actively seeking work. The amount of unemployment pay provided depends on the length of time one has contributed to unemployment insurance during employment. The amount also varies from province to province but it must meet the lowest living standard of the province in which the unemployed person lives. Apart from the monthly cash subsidy, unemployed people can also apply for medical support, in case they need medical care during the period of unemployment. If someone dies while unemployed, the government will provide a sum of money to his or her family as financial help. The government encourages people to attend training during the period of unemployment in order to improve their chances of being employed again in the near future. See *Unemployment* in Working in China

CRIME

In general, foreigners are rarely the targets of violent or other serious crimes. However, pickpocketing is common enough in urban areas. Some cities are known to be more dangerous than others. The cities of Guangdong Province – Guangzhou, Dongguan and Shenzhen, in particular – have recently acquired a reputation for bag snatching and pickpocketing. Of the major cities in China, Shanghai and Beijing are by far the safest. Buses and trains are favourite spots for thieves, though they may work in quiet areas too.

Never exchange renminbi with locals on the street, even if the exchange rate sounds very attractive. Many foreigners, and even people from Hong Kong, have reported that the stack of money handed over to them is mainly paper with only a few real notes on the top and at the bottom. It may not sound like a very clever scam but it works well, with a few variations on the same theme.

Beggars are common at train stations and foreigners are particularly targeted as likely generous donors. They might even greet you in English. They can follow you for a long time even if you refuse to give them anything. Child beggars are especially common and they are usually controlled by adults. The money you give them actually goes into the pockets of these adults. Do not give money to any beggar. Once you do so, others may well flock around and follow you for miles until you give money to all of them.

Male travellers may come across another annoyance – prostitution. Prostitutes on the streets try to engage single male travellers in conversation or even grab their arms. Many brothels operate under the guise of hairdressing salons, so be careful if all you want is a haircut. It's safe to assume that if the lighting is pink, the salon isn't really a salon. Beware of 'nightclubs' as well, as in many regions of the country the word simply means brothels, rather than discos.

Police in mainland China are called *gong'an* and they are under the Public Security Bureau (PSB). Police wear a blue uniform with a blue or white hat. Apart from ensuring civil safety, the PSB is also responsible for affairs relating to foreigners, for example, extensions of visas. If your belongings are stolen, you should report to the foreign affairs branch of the PSB.

CARS AND MOTORING

Car ownership has been increasing in China. It was calculated in *The Economist* (March 2007) that by 2010 per capita car ownership will be 40 per 1,000, having leapt from four million in 2000 to 19 million in 2005. According to the National Bureau of Statistics in China, Beijing had the highest number of private cars in the country by 2002. The number of vehicles in the city further increased and by the end of 2005 was 1.54 million. As the infrastructure improves, districts that were once inaccessible are now attracting house builders. The occupants of new accommodation all want cars. Since China entered the World Trade Organisation, the reduction of import duties for foreign cars has encouraged European companies such as Audi, Rolls Royce and Mercedes Benz to open showrooms in China in response to the rising demand.

The potential for growth is enormous with just 6% car ownership at present, compared with 90% in the USA and 80% in Britain. There are almost three million automobiles in Beijing alone, of which two thirds are privately owned, and congestion is a very serious problem. The situation is the same in other big cities like Shanghai, Guangzhou and Chongqing. Riding a bicycle is probably faster than driving a car in Beijing during peak hours.

More and more roads are being built in the big cities and in between. There are frequent tolls and drivers have to stop and pay at every toll booth, meaning a journey in a private car is usually far more than a bus ticket, even before petrol and other overheads have been factored in. An average toll fee is ¥5–¥10 (£0.30–£0.60/$0.60–$1.20). Motorways apart, roads are divided into motorcar lanes and non-motorcar lanes and in some cases the boundary between the two is not clearly marked. Non-motorcars include bicycles, animal-towed carts and some electric cars that are under a certain size and run at a limited speed, including electric wheelchairs! Road signs are in Chinese, with the Mandarin pinyin (the Romanised written form of the sound) under the Chinese characters. English is rarely used, except for some tourist attractions. Parking can be a problem. There are never enough parking spaces in big cities and parking is prohibited in many areas. Many people prefer to risk a relatively small fine in addition to a more substantial towing fee and park on the streets or even the pavements rather than spend time looking for a car park.

China's car market grew 25% in 2006 and it has overtaken Japan as the second-largest car market in the world with sales of eight million vehicles, including light trucks and minivans.

Licence plates

You will need to go through the complicated process of obtaining a licence plate for a vehicle. Owing to overwhelming demand, city authorities hold auctions where a finite of plates become available once a month, usually at huge cost. Companies with a certain registered capital are entitled to one free licence plate and discounts are available if you can prove a vehicle is being used for business purposes only.

> I am amazed at the amount of people who look truly dumfounded when they walk directly into a busy street without looking to find a screeching car sliding their way. Then they give an angry look to the driver as though he should not be in their path.
>
> **Alex Thompson**

Driving licences

International driving licences carry no legal weight in China and only people with a Chinese licence are allowed on the road. Even with a licence, European and North Americans are limited to driving within a few designated cities, Beijing, Shanghai and Shenzhen among them.

Obtaining a driving licence in China is both expensive and difficult, and is a more realistic option if you are working with a major company who can help navigate the bureaucratic application process.

To obtain a licene, you should apply to the Traffic Management Bureau office in your city, which is part of the Public Security Bureau. You must have been living in China for at least a year before you can even consider getting a licence and you must have been in China for a continuous period of six months immediately before you make your application. You are also required to present your passport and your international driving licence. You may be asked to have your driving licence translated and stamped officially.

Everyone, foreigners included, applying for a driving licence needs to provide medical proof from a hospital that he or she is physically healthy and fit to drive. For a new application, you have to fill in the necessary paperwork and bring along the health proof and local identity card, or permit to stay for at least one year, to a recognised driving school. After passing the written driving test (which many find quite hard) and road test (which consists of a very easy bit of driving), a driving licence will be issued to you. Some people have found that the English in the written test is incomprehensible and the terms used are not the same as those in other countries. For example, learner drivers may be called 'practitioner drivers'. Questions are mainly in the form of multiple choice but there can be up to 100 questions in the test out of 750 which have to be memorised. You need to get 90% of them right.

The application fee for a driving licence is ¥50 and the charge for issuing a driving licence is ¥5. Residents often comment that the regulations and fees are in constant flux.

Government figures for road accidents are around 250 deaths a day all over China (the World Health Organisation (WHO) puts the figure at 680). The death rate per 10,000 cars is eight times higher than in the USA.

Driving regulations

A complicated written exam excepted, the practical standards for obtaining a driving licence in China are low to non-existent. Acccordingly, the only rule of the road is to expect the unexpected. It's common to see cars pulling out of junctions without looking or cyclists smiling serenely as they pedal across busy freeways. Unsurprisingly, China has an appalling road safety record. By the government's own admission, nearly 90,000 people were killed in accidents in 2006 alone. The WHO reckons there were far more.

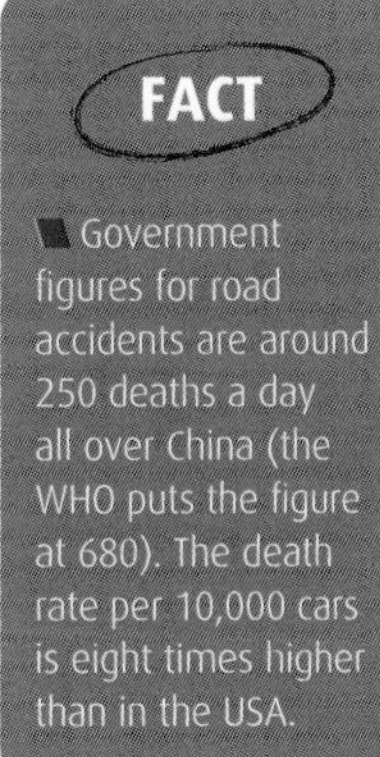
FACT
Government figures for road accidents are around 250 deaths a day all over China (the WHO puts the figure at 680). The death rate per 10,000 cars is eight times higher than in the USA.

In theory there is a cumulative points system for regulating driving behaviour. Points are accumulated, usually along with a fine, when a driver breaks particular rules. Drivers who accumulate 12 points will lose their driving licence and will need to attend a driving school again and sit a driving test in order to get their licence back. Those who accumulate no points within a year can renew their driving licences later than the normal period, as an incentive for good driving.

- The Chinese, like Americans and most Europeans, drive on the right.
- Pedestrians often don't cross at crossings, but walk in a determined way from lane to lane until they reach the other side. Cars, buses and lorries operate a swerving system to avoid hitting them, and this seems to work, albeit chaotically, well. If attempting this method, remember never to step backwards, as cars will be anticipating your moves, and will pass close behind you.
- Seatbelts are compulsory for car drivers and passengers, as are helmets for motorcycle drivers and passengers. However, this law is best seen as a

Traffic lights

Traffic lights consist of red, amber and green lights. As elsewhere, the red light means stop and a green light means go while amber is the signal for you to get ready. The lights turn from red to green directly, but there is a flashing amber light in between turning from green to red. Drivers can make a right-hand turn even when the light is red. In many cities, a useful second countdown is displayed above the traffic lights to show how long drivers must wait their turn for green.

commendable 'theory'. Don't be surprised if a driver interprets your desire to belt up as an affront to his driving skills.

- Using mobile phones or checking messages while driving is prohibited.
- You are not allowed to overtake a police car, fire engine or ambulance on urgent service.
- It is forbidden to overtake at crossroads, rail crossings, narrow bridges, on steep hills and in tunnels.
- You cannot stop if there is a yellow line at the side of the road.
- Motorcycles should keep to the right-hand lane.

Despite these rules, all of these things remain common sights in China.

Penalties for contravening traffic regulations can entail a verbal warning, a fine, withdrawal or cancellation of a driving licence and, in more serious cases, arrest. Pedestrians, passengers and non-motorcar drivers usually receive a verbal warning or a fine of between ¥5 and ¥50 (£0.30–£3/$0.60–$6) if they contravene road regulations. The offender will then receive a letter from the officer with details of the offence committed, the penalty, the date, time and location of the incident, and also the signature of the officer. Police officers may collect the fine immediately if the offender admits to the offence. After payment, he or she will receive an official receipt from the Ministry of Finance. The penalties for motorcars depend on what kind of regulation the driver breaks. The fine for illegal parking is ¥20–¥200, depending on where you park. If your car is towed away as well, you have to pay the towing fee. If the driver is at the wheel, police usually give a verbal warning and tell you to drive the car away immediately. The exact fine is decided by the local office but it must be within the range set by the central government.

Drink-driving

According to police statistics, most drink-driving cases in China happen between 8pm and 10pm, after the driver has dined out at a restaurant. The drinking limit for a driver is relatively low compared to the UK and the USA, though the offence has much less of a social stigma and police checks are rare. You are considered to be drink-driving if the blood alcohol level exceeds 30mg (per 100ml of blood). The limit in the UK and the USA is 80mg (per 100ml of blood). Police do very occasionally set up roadblocks and ask suspected drivers to take a breath test. Any driver with

Speed limits

The maximum speed on major roads is usually 120kmph and vehicles with a maximum speed of 70kmph or lower are prohibited. On roads with both motorcars and other traffic, the maximum speed is 70kmph if the two are clearly separated. Otherwise, it is 60kmph.

more than 100mg of alcohol in 100ml of blood will be sent to hospital for a blood test. A blood test will also be given to drivers who are unwilling or unable to give breath tests.

The penalties for drink-driving depend on the type of car (whether private, public or business) and also the blood alcohol level. A driver is regarded as technically drunk if the blood alcohol level exceeds 100mg (per 100ml of blood), and this is more serious than 'drink-driving'. Drunk drivers face 15 days' detention in addition to fines and suspension of driving licence. The penalty for a drunk private-car driver includes suspension of his driving licence for three to six months, a fine of ¥500–¥2,000 (£34–£133/\$66–\$264) and detention for 15 days. A drunk public or business-car driver faces the same period of detention, a fine of ¥2,000 and also a suspension of his driving licence for six months. A drink-driver of a private car will be suspended from driving for one to three months in addition to a fine of ¥200–¥500. For a public or business drink-driver there is a suspension of his driving licence for three months plus a fine of ¥500.

Anyone found guilty of drink-driving twice in a year, will have their driving licence cancelled and they will be prohibited from operating public or business vehicles for five years.

For information on how to import your car, see page 42.

Breakdowns and accidents

There are some government guidelines about what to do in case of a breakdown or accident on the road, though they are rarely followed. You must turn on the hazard lights. If possible, you should move your car to the side of the road; otherwise, try to put a sign at a certain distance behind your car to warn on-coming cars – you are advised to put a sign at least 150m behind your car if it breaks down on a motorway. It is advisable to carry the telephone numbers of companies that can provide towing and repair services.

You should also call the police if your car breaks down on a motorway. You are not required to call the police if there is an accident in which no one is hurt. The parties should try to settle the compensation between themselves. If they cannot agree about who is responsible, then they should call the police. Needless to say the police are called for the vast majority of accidents, even the most minor of prangs. Because of the contentious nature of most accidents, drivers will generally not move their car, even if it is blocking a highway, without the police having witnessed and photographed it first.

If someone is injured, you should call the police and an ambulance immediately. Hospitals are required to treat accident casualties immediately, even though they may not be able to pay for the treatment. The charges should be covered by the insurance of the car involved in the accident. If it cannot cover the whole amount, the government has an emergency fund set up specifically for accidents and this can be used to pay for the hospital charges if necessary. The party causing the accident is responsible for paying any treatment charges which exceed the third-party insurance cover and the government will tell the person responsible to pay the money back to the fund.

Telephone numbers for towing services
Dongdan Branch (Dongcheng, Beijing): 010 68399161
Highway Branch (Chaoyang, Beijing): 010 68398140
Xidan Branch (Xicheng, Beijing): 010 68399221

Buying a car

Buying a new car involves a number of procedures and you may consider paying a service fee to a car dealer to handle most of them for you. If you decide to handle it yourself, you need to do the following:

- First, purchase car insurance, as third-party liability insurance is compulsory in China. This should be completed before getting the licence.
- Since cars are classified as luxury goods in China, an additional fee of 10% of the nominal price of the car (before value-added tax) has to be paid to the transport department.
- You then have to show proof of ownership of a car parking space. (No proof of parking is needed if you buy the car via a company.)
- You are required to send your car for inspection and you will obtain a temporary licence five days after that. You have to wait for another 15 days (for domestic cars) or 30 days (for imported cars) to obtain a formal licence.

- You should present the temporary licence, a photo of your car, proof of payment of the road maintenance fee and registration information from the safety committee when you collect your formal licence.
- You are also required to pay the annual transport tax of ¥200 a year in order to complete the whole process.

If you are staying for only a short period, you may prefer to consider renting a chauffeured car from one of the major car rental companies like Avis.

Useful resources

0755car.com: www.0755car.com
General Motors: www.gmchina.com
National Bureau of Statistics of China: www.stats.gov.cn
Huation Auto Commerce Ltd: huation@vip.163.com; www.huation.com

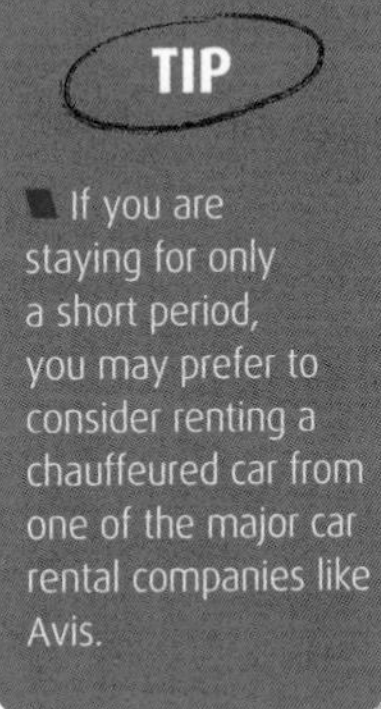
TIP
If you are staying for only a short period, you may prefer to consider renting a chauffeured car from one of the major car rental companies like Avis.

Car loans

At the time of writing, car loan regulation is undergoing consultation. Car mortgages can be divided into private car loans, commercial car loans and fleet loans. The loan for private use (either individual or fleet) should not exceed 80% of the market price of the vehicle, while that for commercial use should not exceed 70% of the vehicle's market value. Loans are provided by banks and the maximum loan term is five years. There is the possibility of extending the period once, but you have to negotiate with your bank. It is expected that more types of mortgages will be available for both domestic and imported vehicles.

In recent years, several foreign-invested companies have been allowed to set up car mortgage companies in China, including Toyota, GE Capital and Volkswagen. Credit systems were built to improve the quality of the car insurance industry.

SILK

Macau

Not all banks in Macau offer car loans but you can ask for help from the Bank of China, who offer car loans up to 80% of the market value of the vehicle. The maximum term of repayment is 60 months.

Useful resources

The People's Bank of China: 010 6619 4114; master@pbc.gov.cn; www.pbc.gov.cn
Industrial and Commercial Bank of China: webmaster@icbc.com.cn; www.icbc.com.cn
General Electric, Beijing: amy.zhou@geahk.ge.com; www.ge.com.cn
Volkswagen: service@volkswagen.com.cn; www.volkswagen.com.cn
Bank of China, Macau: www.bocmacau.com

OTHER TRANSPORT

Train

There is a well-established and efficient rail network in China which covers all provinces, Tibet included.

FACT

Pillows, sheets and blankets are provided as part of the price of the ticket and can generally be relied upon to be clean.

Ticket types

Tickets are not first and second-class but are hard seat, hard sleeper, soft seat and soft sleeper. Hard seats are the cheapest and most easily purchased ticket type, but with no reserved seating, you can sometimes find yourself sharing your seat with other people or, at times, animals! Although an interesting experience, it can be very tiring if your journey takes more than a few hours. Soft seats actually cost about the same as hard seats, but very few trains have them. These can be reserved, and it is possible to recline them if you need to sleep during the journey.

For long journeys, people usually prefer sleeper tickets. A hard sleeper ticket will buy you one of six bunks to a compartment, opening directly onto the corridor. The bunks are in two rows of three tiers and at the time of booking, you can request the top, middle or bottom. Each has its advantages and disadvantages: the bottom bunk allows you to sit down comfortably during the day and use the table next to the window. However, you may end up sharing your bed with those on higher bunks – which can either be intrusive, or an opportunity for socialising. Cracking sunflower

seeds and practicing your Chinese is an excellent way to pass the long journeys. The middle bunk allows you to escape your fellow passengers but is not tall enough to sit up comfortably. The top bunk allows you to really distance yourself from those around you, but with the least headroom, and proximity to the loudspeaker, is really the worst, and correspondingly, cheapest option. Pillows, sheets and blankets are provided as part of the price of the ticket and can generally be relied upon to be clean.

Soft-sleeper tickets cost about double the price of hard-sleeper tickets, and for the extra money, you get a well-decorated, closed compartment with only four bunks. This can be a good option if there are four of you traveling together, or if you want some privacy. If you are a woman traveling on her own, the hard-sleeper option can often feel safer as you are open to the rest of the carriage and can appeal to others for help, should you need it. Closed compartments can feel a little claustrophobic. Either way, the sleeper bunks can be surprisingly comfortable and one can get a good night's sleep after getting used to the rhythm of the train.

FACT

- Huge steel water heaters are stationed each end of the carriage which you can use to fill up your tea flask or instant noodle pots.

The journey

There is a guard for each carriage who is charged with checking tickets, sweeping the floor at regular intervals (usually of the many spilled sunflower seeds) and topping up the hot water flasks allocated to each six or four-berth compartment. They sleep in a small compartment at one end of the carriage, and you can contact them if you need help.

If you're traveling on a train that stops at stations along the way, you can often get out and buy snacks and drinks from platform vendors. Your carriage guard stands at the door and calls you back to the train before it's due to set off. Stops can last as long as 15 minutes at a time, so you usually have plenty of time to make your purchases. You'll see people handing money out of the window to vendors on the tracks, who aren't allowed to use the platform. These are mostly women who cook food and sell it for a few 'kuai' in polystyrene boxes. An alternative to these snacks is to visit the restaurant car. Here you can buy rather dull, standard and overpriced food or bottles of beer and sit at a table to eat.

As carriages are meant to be non-smoking, many people head for either the spaces between carriages, or the restaurant car to smoke, so this is often not the most pleasant environment to eat your dinner.

Early in the morning (at around 6:30am) music is pumped through the train into the carriages via loudspeaker and only ceases at lights-out, around 9:30pm. Initially this can feel highly intrusive, but after a while the music fades into the hustle and bustle of the carriage and you can ignore it. The restaurant car is a useful place to head to after the lights are switched off at 9:30pm, to read, chat or play cards with the off-duty guards.

Purchasing tickets

It is often quite difficult to get tickets for hard seats and hard sleepers. It is almost impossible to purchase a ticket on the day of travel, so it is advisable to book in advance. Sleeper tickets can be booked between three and seven days in advance depending on the route and (sometimes) the whim of the station. If you are prepared to pay more, soft-sleeper tickets are usually easier to get. Travel agents like China International Travel Service, China Travel and China Youth Travel Service may help you to get train tickets if you fail to get one at the train station. Four-star and five-star hotels also usually help customers to book train tickets, but usually charge for the service. However, given the hideous nature of the queues at railway stations, especially around holiday periods, this is generally money well spent.

If there is no direct route to your destination and you need to change trains, you will need to buy the ticket for the second leg of your journey at the second station. It is not possible to book a through ticket into different provinces, so be prepared for the possibility that you won't be able to relax during your transfer and may not even get your chosen seat on the train. In the event you need to kill time between trains, luggage storage is available in all stations for a small charge.

Staff in even large train stations are unlikely to speak English, though there may be ticket offices specifically for foreigners in larger stations such as Beijing. Have a friend write down your destination and desired ticket before you queue, or enlist the help of those around you. It will minimise confusion and may save you from buying the wrong ticket for the wrong destination.

Speed of trains

The first letter of the number of a train indicates the speed of the train:

- 'D' means bullet trains. These are the fastest, most comfortable and most expensive way to get between China's major cities.
- 'Z' are direct high-speed trains that operate non-stop between major cities.
- 'T' are express trains, and are likely to be the quickest way to get between two non-major cities.
- 'K' means fast.
- Those without any letter are trains traveling at normal speeds – these can be painfully slow.

If you are travelling from Hong Kong or Macau, China Travel will be able to help you book train tickets for travel in mainland China. Direct trains run from Hong Kong to Beijing, Shanghai and Guangzhou, as well as a handful of smaller Pearl River Delta cities.

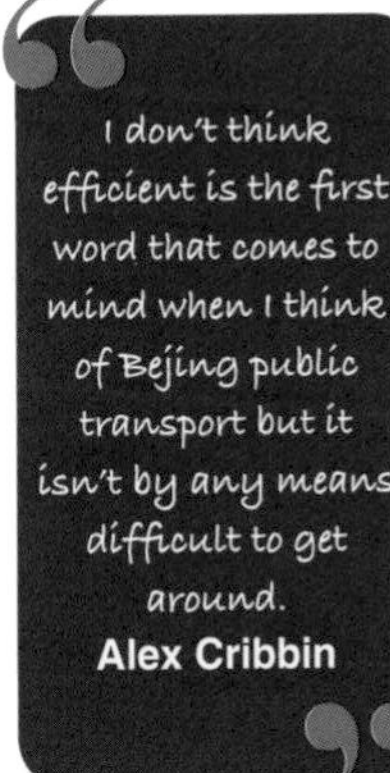

I don't think efficient is the first word that comes to mind when I think of Bejing public transport but it isn't by any means difficult to get around.
Alex Cribbin

Metro networks

An underground metro system has been running in Beijing since 1969. The original lines have the antiquated, creaking feel of European subway systems, though several new routes have opened up ahead of the Beijing Olympic Games and offer more modern facilities. Shanghai has the biggest underground and overground metro network in China, encompassing nine lines, most of which are brand new. Guangzhou, Chongqing and Shenzhen also have their own metro systems. The government also launched the CityRail trains in Beijing in early 2003. The CityRail connects the north-western suburb of Beijing to downtown (from Xizhimen to Dongzhimen) and you can transfer to other rail lines to go to other parts of Beijing. Fares range from ¥2 to ¥4 (£0.14–£0.28/$0.24–$0.48), depending on the distance. The west line, which goes from Xizhimen to Huilongguan, connects the Olympic village to the city centre.

There are currently three lines: two mainly in the city centre, one is a circle that follows the first ring road, and the other cuts across the middle, with stops at off tourist hotspots such as Tiananmen Square. The other is often nicknamed the 'farmer line' as it goes right out into the suburbs.

Useful resources

China Travel Net Hong Kong Ltd: Room A, 2F, Tak Bo Building, 62–74 Sai Yee Street, Mongkok, Hong Kong; (+852) 2789 5401; enquiry@chinatravel1.com; www.chinatravel1.com

China International Travel Service: 010 6522 2991; shuyu@cits.com.cn; www.cits.net

China Travel Service, Beijing: Zidutech Co Ltd, No 34 Fuwaidajie Avenue, Xicheng District, Beijing 100832; 010 6852 4860; bisc@chinats.com; www.chinats.com
China Youth Travel Service: 23C Dongjiaominxiang, Beijing 100006; 010 6513 3153
Metro and CityRail: www.ebeijing.gov.cn/Life/Transportation

Bus

Long-distance buses

Long-distance buses are another option for travelling around the country. Routes are extensive, often reaching rural areas that trains do not. Long-distance buses usually have regular stops for toilets and food and they cost about the same as hard-seat train tickets. Stopping every couple of hours for smokers to light up is very common, and knowing the Chinese love of food, most journeys include a stop at a roadside canteen where you may be treated to a meal as part of your ticket. You might end up sitting next to fellow travellers at typically large, round tables, and being served as you would be in a restaurant. The food is adequate and people eat quickly and usually in silence before heading back to the bus. Always remember to take your belongings with you. Although the driver will lock the bus, unscrupulous thieves will try their luck.

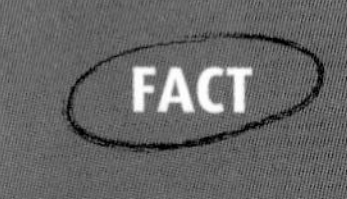

- Sleeper buses are available for long-distance travel but there is usually nowhere to lock your hand luggage and uneven roads can make sleeping difficult.

Sleeper buses are available for long-distance travel but there is usually nowhere to lock your hand luggage and uneven roads can make sleeping difficult. Seatbelts are rarely fitted, and with poor road safety outside cities, buses are not as safe as the train option. It is advisable to book bus tickets in advance at the bus stations or through hotels and travel agents, but even though there are timetabled departures, many coaches are privately run and will wait until they fill up before setting off. This can be frustrating if you have arrived on time, but it is very common and the Chinese rarely mind. Nowadays, many long-distance buses have TVs and DVD players fitted on board. You might be treated to a kung-fu movie with outlandish subtitles, or be forced to watch a dubbed Hollywood film at full volume for two or three hours. You will generally be treated to hot water or tea and a sweet snack during shorter journeys, which are included in the price.

Urban buses

Urban buses are cheap you buy your tickets from conductors or the driver. However, they are usually very crowded and it is very difficult to snag a seat, even outside rush hour. When buses are packed you must look out for pickpockets, and keep a close eye on your money and travel documents. Due to the serious travel congestion in some big cities like Beijing and Shanghai, travelling by bus can be a

> *I never quite got my head around the bus system. I think I only rode the bus once – I knew the bus number and exactly where I was going beforehand, but still managed to get off at the wrong place. The buses are always extremely crowded – I would not recommend them for getting around, but for the experience it's definitely worth trying it!*
> **Alex Cribbin**

very uncomfortable. Fares vary according the type of bus, so you can pay as little as ¥1 for a standard bus, or up to ¥3 for one with air conditioning.

Macau's buses

Buses are the main form of transport in Macau and they all travel in circular routes. The bus fare costs MOP$2.5–MOP$6 (£0.16–£0.38/$0.38–$0.76) and you have to have the exact change to put in the slot at the front of the bus when you get on. Bus route information is available at airports and ferry ports and all the stops are listed on the route maps. If you are planning to travel from Macau to the mainland, bus numbers three, five and nine can take you to the border gate and you can walk across to the gate to mainland China with your travel documents. You can also take bus number 26 to Zhuhai by crossing the new Lotus Bridge, but this is only open between 9am and 5pm.

www.apta.com/links/international/asia/china.cfm provides links to some bus companies.

Air

In recent years, the government has been improving airport facilities and inter-city air travel is now easy and comfortable. Shanghai, Beijing, Guangzhou and Hong Kong airports are China's international gateways and are also well connected to other Chinese cities. Other regional centres, including Kunming, Dalian, Harbin, Xiamen and Urumqi, have international flights with neighbouring countries. The Civil Aviation Administration of China (CAAC) is responsible for national civil aviation affairs. It publishes timetables for China's major airlines twice a year (usually in April and November) and these timetables can be purchased at Chinese airports. Beijing is the central connection for many cities. You can fly directly to almost all domestic airports from Beijing, including Shanghai, Hong Kong, Guangzhou, Qingdao, Dalian, Shenyang, Harbin, Hailar, Hohhot, Urumqi, Xining, Kunming, Lanzhou, Chengdu, Xian, Chongqing, Zhengzhou and Wuhan. The three major domestic airlines are Air China, China Eastern and China Southern. Spring Airlines, a relatively new budget carrier, operates flights from Shanghai to several domestic destinations. The majority of tickets are now issued as e-tickets and can be purchased directly from the airline or from one of several reliable online aggregators – Ctrip and Elong being the most reputable. Most plane tickets are calculated on one-way, single fares and prices generally reflect the distance travelled. A return journey is twice the price of a single.

Most plane tickets are calculated on one-way, single fares and prices generally reflect the distance travelled. A return journey is twice the price of a single.

Useful resources

Air China: master@mail.airchina.com.cn; www.airchina.com.cn
Air Macau: 6396 5555; airmacau@airmacau.com.mo; www.airmacau.com.mo
China Eastern: www.ce-air.com
China Southern: 020 8668 2000; webmaster@cs-air.com; www.cs-air.com
Civil Aviation Administration of China (CAAC): 010 6409 1114; www.caac.gov.cn
Ctrip: 21 3406 4888 extension 6 ; http://english.ctrip.com
Dragon Air: (+852) 2868 6777; www.dragonair.com
Elong: 10 6432 9999 extension 6 ; www.elong.net
Spring Airlines: 216 251 5777; www.china-sss.com

Ferries

The number of passenger ferry routes has dried up in recent years as China's road infrastructure has improved. Ferries in places like Chongqing, Guilin and Leshan are now run almost exclusively for tourists. The one major exception is the Pearl River Delta where there are a variety of long-distance routes from Hong Kong up into the Pearl River Delta, as well as Hainan. These are run by CKS (www.cksp.com.hk) who operate from the China Hong Kong ferry terminal in Tsim Sha Tsui.

Ferries in Macau

TurboJET, (www.turbojet.com.hk) based in Hong Kong, also provides ferry services across the mouth of the Pearl River to Macau and the short distance up to Shenzhen. The fare to Macau is MOP$138–MOP$172 (£8.80–£10.96/$17.50–$21.80) and MOP$200 to Shenzhen. They run regularly throughout the day. First Ferry operates between Hong Kong and Macau for MOP$123–MOP$131 one-way. However, there are only a limited number of ferries a day.

Taxis

FACT

■ Conversations involving simple words like English premiership football players can build up enough rapport with your driver to not be exploited.

Taxis are not expensive in China (about ¥2 per km). However, not all taxi drivers are honest, particularly with foreigners. The fare is based on the distance travelled but sometimes, especially in smaller cities and rural areas, the driver will propose a rate for the trip instead of following the meter. It is advisable to have the destination written down in both Chinese and English. If you accept the deal, probably after some bargaining, you should write the agreed fare down to avoid any 'misunderstanding' when you arrive at your destination. If you have picked up some Chinese, it is always worth chatting to the driver. Conversations involving simple words like English premiership football players can build up enough rapport with your driver to not be exploited.

You can either get in the front or the back of a taxi, which have bars or reinforced plastic surrounding the driver. Wearing your seatbelt is advisable, but be surreptitious about it, as some drivers will take your actions to mean you don't trust his driving skills. Picking up taxis is extremely easy in most cities and towns, and you can always ask for a receipt (*'piao*).

Taxis in Macau

Taxis in Macau are black or yellow and charge the same rates. The first 1.5km costs MOP$10 and MOP$1 for every additional 200m. There is an extra charge of MOP$5 for going to Taipa or Coloane from Macau Peninsula and MOP$2 for travelling between the two islands. It costs MOP$5 more if you take the taxi from the airport.

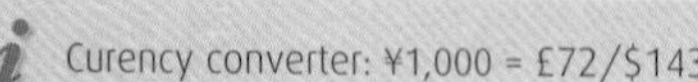

Curency converter: ¥1,000 = £72/$143

■ TAX

The Ministry of Finance (MoF) and State Administration of Taxation deal with all tax matters in China. The MoF is mainly responsible for making policies related to taxation and setting the rates for different kinds of taxes. The State Administration

of Taxation is involved in some of the policy making but it mainly deals with the administration of taxation like tax returns, tax refunds, etc.

 The tax year for mainland China is from 1 January to 31 December.

Individual income tax

Individual income tax (IIT) is charged according to the monthly income of an individual as well as the length of time he or she has been working in China. Foreign employees paid by foreign enterprises and staying in mainland China for fewer than 90 days are exempt from IIT. For those who stay from 90 days to one year, only their income derived in China is subject to IIT. However, directors, general managers or deputy managers of Chinese-based enterprises have to pay tax on foreign-sourced income for services performed outside China as well as income derived in China. Individuals who have been in China for more than one year, but less than five years, are taxed on both income derived in China and overseas. If you stay beyond five years, all worldwide income, no matter whether it is remitted to China or not, is taxable.

According to the State Administration of Taxation, in addition to wages and salaries, bonuses, cash allowances, personal tax paid by an employer and stock options are all taxable. Several allowances, including relocation allowance, child education allowance, business travel allowance, accommodation provided by an employer and company car expenses are exempt from tax. In July 2006 the monthly deductible allowances were increased to ¥1,600 (£114.82/$288.50) and ¥4,800 for

Individual Income Tax Rates	
Monthly taxable income	**Rate**
¥1–¥500	5%
¥501–¥2,000	10%
¥2,001–¥5,000	15%
¥5,001–¥20,000	20%
¥20,001–¥40,000	25%
¥40,001–¥60,000	30%
¥60,001–¥80,000	35%
¥80,001–¥100,000	40%
¥100,001+	45%

local and foreign IIT payers respectively. Tax rates range from 5% to 45%, according to monthly income. Income derived from personal services, royalties, interest and dividends is taxed at a flat rate of 20% if it exceeds ¥4,800, of which 20% is not taxable. If it is less than ¥4,800, the first ¥1,600 is not taxable, and the rest is taxed at a flat rate of 20%.

The tax year for Macau is the same as mainland China, from 1 January to 31 December. Tax returns should be filed no later than the end of February.

Tax in Macau

Income tax is called employment tax in Macau and taxable income includes wages, salary, bonus, dividends and commissions.

Other taxes

For business-related taxes including foreign-invested and foreign enterprise income tax, value-added tax (VAT), custom duties and consumption tax, see *Starting a Business* in Working in China.

For information on property tax and urban real estate taxes see *Services and utilities* in Setting up home.

Vehicle purchase tax

Owners of new vehicles are subject to vehicle purchase tax, regardless of whether the vehicles are purchased, imported, awarded or received as a gift. The tax is equal to the taxable value times the tax rate, which is 10% at the time of writing. Taxable value of a newly purchased vehicle is the sum of the selling price (excluding the VAT) plus any other additional charges of the purchase. If the vehicle is imported, the taxable value is equal to the selling price (including the VAT) plus the import tax and consumption tax. The taxable value of a vehicle will be calculated according to the market value of the same type of vehicles in the event that the vehicle is an award or a gift. The tax should be filed within 60 days of the purchase or import.

Tax Rates in Macau	
Annual taxable income	**Rate**
MOP$9,500 or less	Exempt
Next MOP$10,500	7%
Next MOP$20,000	8%
Next MOP$40,000	9%
Next MOP$80,000	10%
Next MOP$120,000	11%
Remainder	12%

This is a one-off tax and second-hand vehicles are exempted from the vehicle purchase tax. Where the value of a vehicle is calculated in another currency, it will be transferred to renminbi according to the exchange rate of the People's Bank of China on the day of filing.

Vehicle and vessel usage and tax

Users of vehicles and vessels are subject to this tax. For vessels and trucks, taxes levied are calculated according to tonnage. Otherwise, the amount of tax levied depends on the type of the vehicle. Tax is paid annually and the exact date for paying it is set by local government. Users of motor vessels have to pay ¥1.2–¥5 (£0.08–£0.36/$0.17–$0.71) per tonnage, while users of non-motor vessels pay ¥0.6–¥1.4 per tonnage. Trucks are subject to tax of ¥16–¥60 per ton and passenger cars are taxed ¥60–¥320 per car. Motorcycles are levied at ¥20–¥80. Users of non-motor vehicles also need to pay the tax, even if the amount is very small, at a rate of ¥1.2–¥4 per vehicle. Note that bicycles are included as non-motor vehicles and pay tax.

Stamp duty

This applies to contracts, documents for the transfer of property title, business account books, certificates and licences, or documents in the form of a contract. The tax rate varies according to the type of document to be taxed. Extra copies of the taxed documents are exempted from further tax.

Land transfer tax

When the ownership of land or property is transferred to another person, the new owner is subject to the land transfer tax. The transfer of ownership can be in the form of a sale, swap or gift. The current tax rate is from 3%–5%. The taxable value is equal to the selling price of the land or property, or the market price if the ownership is transferred as a gift. In case of a swap of ownerships between two parties, the tax is levied on the difference in values in the two pieces of land or the properties. The new owner should file the tax within 10 days of the transfer of ownership.

Useful resources

State Administration of Taxation: webmaster@chinatax.gov.cn;www.chinatax.gov.cn
Finance Service Department, Macau: 2833 6886; www.dsf.gov.mo

20

Working in China

FINDING A JOB

A guide to the market

The government has been trying to rein in the fastest growing economy in the world for many years, without a great deal of success. The Asian Development Outlook (ADO) 2005 (the annual publication that forecasts economic trends in the region) predicted that the growth rate of exports will slow because of easing demand in industrial nations and higher costs for Chinese exporters. It also said that manufacturing and construction, hampered by bottlenecks in energy and transportation, land constraints, and reduced levels of investment will also slow.

The industry sector was forecast to expand by 9.3%–10.2% over three years to 2008. Agriculture will grow by 3%–4.6% a year in this period, reflecting the government's efforts to support rural production and farmers' incomes. As more domestic service industries open to the outside world, an average 8% growth in the services sector is expected for 2005–2007. In addition to guiding its economy to a more sustainable growth path, the People's Republic of China is working to fulfill commitments it made when joining the World Trade Organisation (WTO) in 2001. In this regard, the PRC has reached its goal of cutting trade tariffs, with the general tariff level lowered from 15.6% in 2001 to 10.1% in early 2005, according to ADO.

In services such as banking, insurance and securities, the PRC has met its WTO commitments on time. Over the past three years, more than 2,300 national laws and regulations that ran counter to WTO rules have been revised. Some of these are laws related to intellectual property rights protection, and included trademarks, patents, copyright and protection of computer software. However, it is still proving difficult to enforce these laws, as the abundance of pirated DVD vendors testify.

China continues to be a favoured destination for foreign investment. In the first half of 2007 it was up 12% on the previous year. It appears that investors come partly for unskilled labor, which is about 4% of the cost that it is in the USA and one third of the cost in Malaysia. In addition, the country's infrastructure continues to strengthen, and its business environment has improved significantly since it joined the World Trade Organisation (WTO).

Despite the forecast of a soft landing for the economy, significant challenges remain. Risks to the outlook include a possible return to extraordinarily high growth rates of investment, which could spark further overheating. At the time of writing there has been little success in macroeconomic efforts to cool growth. Economic growth in 2007, for example, topped a phenomenal 11%.

The soft-landing scenario could further be disrupted by potential problems that cause growth to slow more sharply than planned. The country must maintain rural income growth, stimulate development of small and medium-sized enterprises and speed up banking reforms.

Although tertiary industries have been developing rapidly in the last two decades, the Chinese economy is currently mainly supported by secondary industries and agriculture.

Unfortunately, a large percentage of the Chinese workforce still lacks the knowledge and skills to develop the tertiary industries such as banking and finance, telecommunications and information technology. Thus, the Chinese government is encouraging more foreign experts and high-skilled workers to come to China. As a result, many big multinational manufacturing companies, biochemical businesses, and high-quality technology companies come to the coastal areas to start their businesses. There is no doubt that skilled professionals in these high-intellectual and technological industries are in great demand in the current Chinese market. The demand for skilled labour in Shanghai is particularly great.

The market is badly in need of people who are trained as computerised machine operators, jewellery designers, IT programmers, multi-media programmers and other high-level professionals. As a result, the salaries offered can be very attractive, especially if you take into account the low living costs in China.

Macau's employment market

Macau is one of the two duty-free ports in China, which means goods, capital, foreign exchange and people flow freely in and out of the city. It is integrated with the world economy and, due to its historical background, it also has special economic ties with the European Union. The government has planned and launched a series of projects after the hand-over to China in 1999. Macau's airport, which cost $11.8 billion to build, was completed in 1995. Western businessmen and travellers can now avoid the trouble of travelling to Macau through Hong Kong, which has increased Macau's competitiveness as a business centre. Apart from the airport, projects such as the Lotus Bridge project (the construction of a deep-water port on the north-eastern side of Coloane Island), the land-reclamation projects along the Praia Grande (Macau's historic waterfront) and the Docas (docks) areas, have also has helped to turn Macau into a business centre and speed up its economic growth. The liberalisation of Macau's casino industry has also fuelled an economic boom. Currently, tourism and gambling are two of the most important industries in Macau.

Skills and qualifications

It is difficult to generalise on the skills and qualifications needed to work in China; it varies from industry to industry. As mentioned above, if you possess a certain special skill or are an expert in a particular industry, in general it will not be difficult to find a job in China. A university degree may not be the most important qualification for selection, except for certain academic or teaching posts, but you may get a higher salary if you do have one.

English speakers have a definite advantage, as the supply of fluent English speakers in the current labour market is limited but the amount of foreign trade is increasing. A knowledge of Mandarin is also an advantage as you will probably need to work with local clients or suppliers, and also the local government.

China has become one of the world's most 'wired' nations in a very short time and most companies in big cities will require their employees to possess basic computer skills.

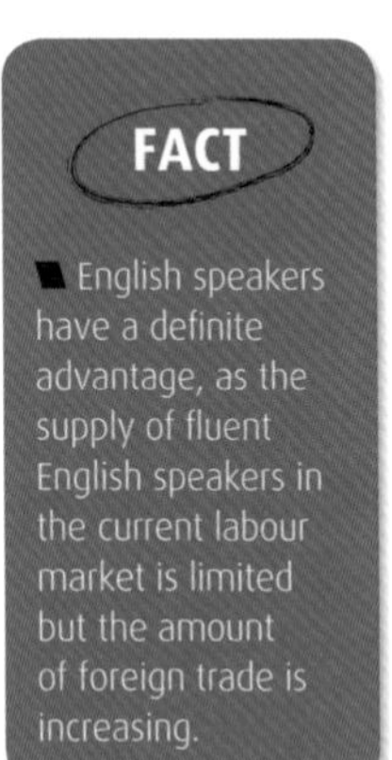
FACT
English speakers have a definite advantage, as the supply of fluent English speakers in the current labour market is limited but the amount of foreign trade is increasing.

Salary guide

China's economic and industrial growth in recent years has driven an increase in the country's salaries. In particular, salaries of middle to high-ranking staff working in foreign enterprises have been rising far more rapidly than the consumer price index. According to the National Bureau of Statistics, the average income for people working in the state sector rose by 16% year-on-year to reach ¥5,000 (£359/$713) for the first quarter of 2006 (or ¥20,000 per annum).

Meanwhile, the average income for the sector including employees working in governments, public-funded institutions and all companies (both private and state-owned) rose by 15% year-on-year to reach ¥4,700 for the first three months of 2006.

For collective enterprises, which are often set up with both private and public cash, the average income for the three-month period rose by 15% to ¥2,800. Income growth averaged about 13% in other sectors.

There can be a big difference in the average salary between different areas in China. The western and central parts of China are less developed but there are major development projects being carried out by the central government. However, average salaries in the west and central parts are still much lower than that in the more developed coastal cities. In Shanghai and Beijing, the average annual salaries of employees in 2006 were ¥24,000 (£1,561/$3,167) and ¥22,000 (£1,431/$2,903) – more than double that of central and western regions like Guizhou and Shanxi, where employees earned only about ¥9,000 in the same year. Shanghai, Beijing, Zhejiang, Guangdong and Tianjin were the top five provinces and municipalities paying the highest salaries. The average salary for top executives in the big cities is around ¥162,800.

White-collar workers

The average salary for university graduates in 2006 was relatively low. In 2003, there were more than 2.4 million university graduates and by 2006 this number had more than doubled to 4.95 million. The current supply of university graduates

exceeds the available jobs at the appropriate level, which keeps the monthly salaries of graduates low as they are competing for jobs. It was estimated in 2005 that 65% of new graduates earn between ¥1,000 and ¥2,000 per month. New graduates also find that it is difficult to get employment without experience – a common lament across the world, but one that is particularly acute in China where competition is so fierce.

Educational qualifications are important if you want to negotiate a higher salary. The higher the education level you have obtained, the higher the salary you will probably receive. The average annual salary for university graduates within the state sector is about ¥42,830 (£3,060/$5,220). However, if you have an MBA qualification, you will receive an average annual salary of about ¥74,250 (£5,300/$9,050). This reflects the fact that China is urgently in need of experts who are graduates of higher education to fill senior managerial positions.

Blue-collar workers

In general, blue-collar workers' salaries are lower than those of white-collar workers. It goes without saying that, in a nation of 1.3 billion, foreign workers from a blue-collar background will find it extremely tough to compete in the Chinese marketplace without accepting a salary that would pale in comparison to what they could get in their home country. In recent years, blue-collar workers' salaries have been rising considerably, due to the high demand for 'skilled' or 'advanced-skilled' workers. However, it is estimated that only 3.7% of the 70 million blue-collar workers are classified as 'advanced skilled workforce'. The supply of skilled workers, although limited, boosts the average salary of the whole group.

There is a big gap between the salaries of low-skilled and high-skilled workers. Over 70% of Chinese workers are unskilled and have a low educational background. An unskilled labourer in China earns about ¥750–¥1,000 per month (£48–£65/$99–$132), which is less than one-fifth of the monthly salary of skilled workers.

Salaries are usually paid monthly, either by cash, cheque or direct to the employees' accounts. Some companies may pay their employees, especially temporary or daily waged workers, through a middleman. However, you should avoid getting your wages through this method as there have been complaints that they take the money and disappear. Some companies include an extra monthly payment to employees as a bonus but it depends on the practice of the companies and the profit made that year.

Regulations on minimum wages to protect workers from being exploited came into effect in March 2004. Each local government has its own minimum wage but overtime payments, allowances and any extra payments such as working night shifts or in a dangerous environment are excluded from the minimum wage.

Macau

As with Hong Kong, there is no minimum wage in Macau. Wages are set according to the qualifications and experience of employees. There is a great discrepancy between the salaries of different industries. Banking, finance and transport sectors in general enjoy higher salaries when compared to other industries. The average salary of employees in banking and finance is about MOP$12,000 (£733/$1,489) per month while that in transport is about MOP$9,000 per month. However, employees in the manufacturing industry, on average, earn only MOP$4,000–MOP$5,000 a month.

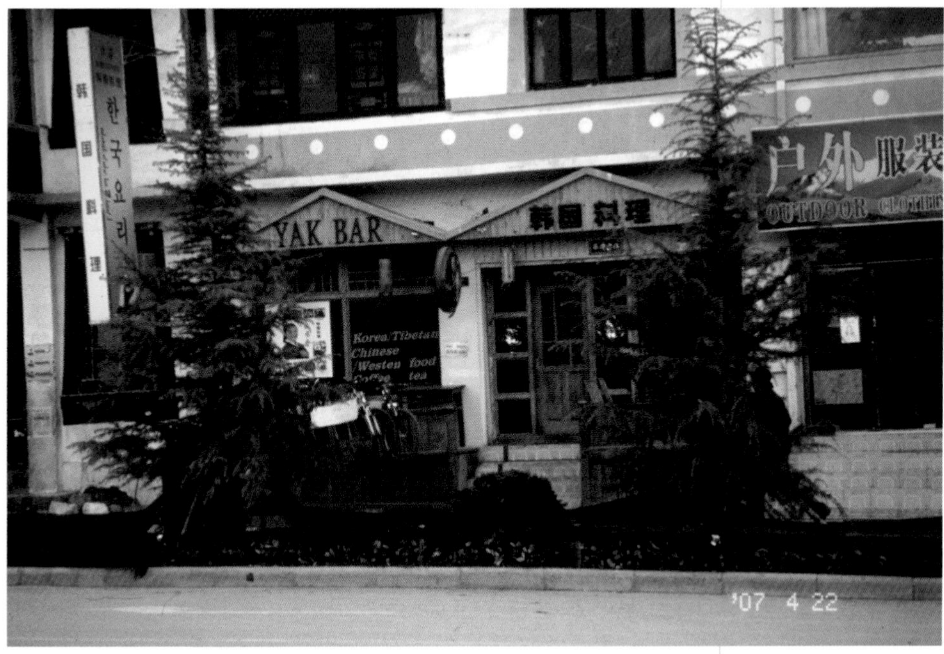

Even though tourism is an important industry in Macau, the average income of travel agents, restaurant and hotel staff is quite low, just slightly better than those of manufacturing workers. Salaries are usually paid directly to the employees' bank accounts. Even though some companies may still pay their employees by cheque or cash, it is not usual.

Job search resources

There are only a limited number of English newspapers in China and this may be a problem when you are looking for jobs. Moreover, since companies have to get permission before they can place advertisements in the media, many companies prefer to use other recruitment methods. Overseas publications such as *The Economist*, the *Financial Times* and the *Guardian* may include some vacancies in Chinese companies but the number of jobs you can find there is very limited.

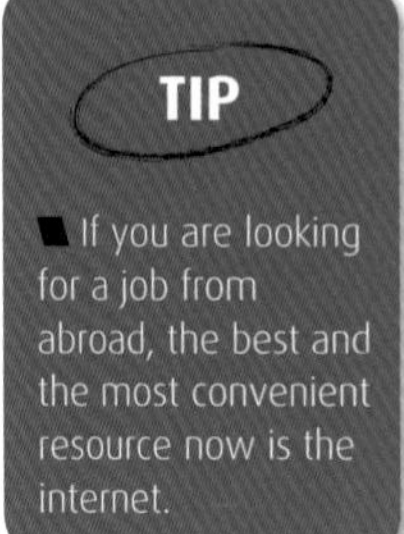
TIP
If you are looking for a job from abroad, the best and the most convenient resource now is the internet.

If you are looking for a job from abroad, the best and the most convenient resource now is the internet. There are many online newspapers and websites for companies to post recruitment advertisements. There are also a variety of online recruitment agencies, all of which advertise and update the list of vacancies frequently. Most of these websites provide registration services. The services are normally free of charge but some of the agencies ask for a membership fee. You can also lodge an inquiry with these recruitment agencies stating your interests and expectations and they will then search and match the job that is the most suitable for you.

From time to time, there are also job fairs held in China. Many cities, especially the bigger ones, hold annual job fairs around the time of university graduations. You can also try writing directly to the company you are interested in working for. Of course there is no guarantee that there are vacancies, but some students have reported that they have gained intern opportunities through this method.

- **Finding a teaching job** If you are looking for a teaching job, you can put your enquiries to a Chinese embassy abroad. Every year, the Ministry of Foreign Affairs of the People's Republic of China recruits foreign teachers (FTs) and foreign experts (FEs) through the embassies to teach English in different regions. These jobs are not publicised in the media, probably because there is a plentiful supply of teachers and it is believed that genuinely interested people will discover the opportunities themselves. More details about FTs and FEs can be found in the *Long-term employment* section later in this chapter.

Recruitment Websites

Abroad China: www.abroadchina.org. This is the largest database of language jobs in China, with positions and information on salaries, incentives and workload.

China Exchange: www.chinaexchange.org. This is an exchange programme offering opportunities for recent college graduates and seasoned teachers. The programme will subsidise the travel expenses of successful candidates in China during the employment period.

China Net for International Talent: www.chinajob.com. This features the latest expert and professional vacancies in teaching, engineering and many highly demanding high-technology jobs, and the latest news of professional jobs in China as well as opportunities for foreign exchanges.

International Manpower Service: www.chinesemanpower.com. This is the largest manpower service in the world. It focuses on recruiting and employing qualified associates in all fields and at all levels for employers. This agency covers most of the core industries in China, including automobiles, technology and chemistry.
JobChina: www.jobchina.net. This is a bulletin board both for employers to post their advertisements and for job seekers to lodge their CV. This website specialises in IT professional jobs and MBA jobs in China.
Portfolio International Recruitment: www.portfoliointernational.com. An agency specialising in recruitment for hotel, catering, and leisure industries.
Sinoculture: www.sinoculture.com. This website features English-teaching opportunities in schools and universities throughout China.
Talent Consulting Corporation: www.excellent-job.com. A private agency ratified by the Beijing Personnel Bureau, engaged in talent exchange and consultation. You can fill in an application form to apply for a job through this website.
Teach in China: www.teach-in-asia.net/china. This website will redirect you to another 11 websites for ESL (English as a second language) or EFL (English as a foreign language) teaching jobs in various parts in China.
Wang and Li Asia Resources: www.wang-li.com. This private agency focuses on business and professional management jobs in China, and provides consultation and guidance for individuals to develop and to identify their talents in order to meet the capabilities and qualities that leading multinational companies in China value most.
Zhaopin.com: http://english.zhaopin.com. In the 'citychannel' area, you will be redirected to jobs in some popular regions in China including, Beijing, Xian, Dalian, Wuhan and Nanjing. Zhaopin is the mainland's leading recruitment job listing and classified website. It offers thousands of jobs from entry level to senior management positions throughout China in multinational, joint venture and local Chinese companies in all industries and job functions.

Recruitment Agencies

Bole Associates: bej@bo-le.com; www.bo-le.com. Recruits for five core practices: internet, financial services, consumer products, pharmaceutical and industrial appointments.
Euro-group: szhang@euro-group.com; www.euro-group.com
Futurestep Corporate: info@futurestep.com.hk; www.futurestep.com.hk
Futurestep: info@futurestep.co.uk; www.futurestep.com.hk
Hudson: www.hudson.com
Lynton John & Associates, Beijing: lja@ljaconsult.com; www.ljaconsult.com
PricewaterhouseCoopers: www.pwcglobal.com
Stanton Chase International: info@stantonchase.com; www.stantonchase.com

Macau Recruitment Agencies

Agencia Emprego Hong Fu: 2821 6679
Agencia Emprego Son Hou: 2835 3628
Chong Ou Technical Services Ltd: 2871 5335
Firma Au Traders: 2859 1314
Fu Cheong: http://starschool.uhome.net/fucheong
Guang Dong Hoc Shing Labour Managing Group: 2843 9316
Sociedade Apoio Empresas: 2833 6936
Successful Consultants Ltd: www.sclimited.com
Weng Lei International Company: www.wenglei.com.mo

Online Newspapers and Magazines

China Daily: www.chinadaily.com.cn

China News Digest: http://my.cnd.org. A weekly internet news journal with a job advertisement section.

China Economic Review: www.chinaeconomicreview.com. A leading English-language business journal about China.

Classified Post: www.classifiedpost.com. This is a supplement of Hong Kong's *South China Morning Post* which advertises lots of jobs within Hong Kong itself. There are also increasing numbers of good-quality jobs in China advertised there too. The hardcopy of the supplement comes with every Saturday edition of the newspaper.

Financial Times: www.ft.com

The Global and Mail: www.globeandmail.ca. Canada's national newspaper.

The Guardian: www.guardian.co.uk

The Independent: www.independent.co.uk

JobsDB.com and CJOL.com: www.jobsdb.com.cn

Journal Ou Mun (Macau Daily News): www.macaodaily.com

Jornal Tribuna Macau: www.jtm.com.mo

Kidon Media-Link: www.kidon.com/media-link. An independent site providing a complete directory of newspapers and news resources on the internet. This covers the major news and newspaper directories for many parts of China.

The National Post, Canada: www.canada.com/national/nationalpost

New York Times: www.nytimes.com

Recruit: www.recruit.com.hk. This is a career portal for a wide range of fields from general positions to highly qualified positions for working professionals. Hardcopies can be found every Tuesday and Thursday in all MTR stations.

Semanario Desprtv Macau: www.macausports.com.mo

That's Magazine: www.thatsmags.com. This is an online English magazine providing the latest news and vacancies in Beijing, Shanghai, Guangzhou and Shenzhen.

The Times: www.the-times.co.uk

USA Today: www.usatoday.com

The Wall Street Journal: www.wsj.com

Other useful resources

British Chamber of Commerce in China: 010 6593 2150; www.britaininchina.com

British Council China Initiative: (+44) 020 7930 8466; www.britishcouncil.org.cbiet

British Council: (+44) 020 7930 8466; www.britishcouncil.org

China-Britain Business Council: (+44) 020 7828 5176; www.cbbc.org

Global Chinese Resource: www.jia-bin.com. This provides Chinese resources for business, company, travel, job, college, magazine, book and other links.

Crimson Publishing: www.crimsonpublishing.co.uk. Publishes a series of books about working abroad, including hints for looking for jobs and directories for companies in different sectors. Titles including *Summer Jobs Worldwide* (Crimson Publishing, 2007), *Work Your Way Around the World* (Susan Griffith, Crimson Publishing 2007) and *The Directory of Jobs and Careers Abroad* (Guy Hobbs, Vacation Work 2006) provide information for short-term employment, voluntary work and careers abroad.

Macau Business Assocation: Macau's Chammer of Commerce, 175 Rua de Xangai, Macau; 576 833

Macau Trade and Investement Promotion Institute: 4th and 5th Floors, World Trade Centre, 918 Avenida da Amizade, Macau; 710 528

World Trade Centre Macau: 17th Floor, World Trade Centre, 918 Avenida da Amizda, Macau; 727 666. This centre offers trade information services and arranges conferences and exhibitions.

JOB IDEAS

One reason why China continues to open its markets is that it provides a chance for industries to absorb the experience and acquire the skills of foreign experts to

> **FACT**
>
> ■ Since China adopted the opening-up policy in the late 1970s, it has altogether introduced over two and a half million foreign experts in the fields of agriculture, education, manufacturing and news reporting.

further speed up economic growth. In general, almost all foreign experts working in China can be categorised as either economic and technological experts, or cultural and educational experts. The economic and technological experts are those working in commerce, finance, industry and foreign enterprises. The cultural and educational experts are those working in higher education, the press and publishing, scientific research and art institutions. The State Statistics Bureau believes foreign experts play a very important role in promoting China's social and economic construction. According to the National Statistics Bureau, every year China introduces more than 240,000 foreign experts. Since China adopted the opening-up policy in the late 1970s, it has altogether introduced over two and a half million foreign experts in the fields of agriculture, education, manufacturing and news reporting.

The table below shows some of the major fields in China that recently employed foreign experts.

Foreign Experts in China

Types of jobs	Number of foreign experts (approximately)
Manufacturing	250,000
Social services	180,000
Culture/education/arts/media	26,500
Commerce	26,000
Scientific research and general technical services	23,000
Real estate	14,000
Communication and telecommunications	11,000
Construction	6,000
Agriculture	4,500
Public utilities	3,000
Public health/sports/social welfare	2,000
Mining	1,500
Finance/insurance	1,250
Prospecting	1,000
Other organisations	75,000

In 2004 the Chinese Nation Labour Officials announced the urgency of importing more foreign hi-tech and management professionals so as to sharpen the competitiveness of the country in global markets. At the end of 2006, it was reported that there were 180,000 foreigners from some 90 countries, registered as foreign workers. Most of these foreign employees come from Japan, the USA, South Korea and Singapore, and some are from Hong Kong, Macau and Taiwan. Some estimates approximate that there are about 50,000 and 30,000 foreign workers in Beijing and Shanghai respectively. However *China Daily* recently reported a figure of 500,000 in

Shanghai. As always in China, it pays to be sceptical about statistics. However, there is no doubt that both Beijing and Shanghai are home to more and more foreigners every year.

Although the figures might look impressive, the job market for expatriates is actually shrinking. At the moment, a number of foreign experts in China employed as managers, diplomats, and embassy staff are either on hefty salaries or in very easy jobs. Apart from these, expatriates face increasing competition in the job market from Chinese students educated in the UK or US, who are often favoured by multi-national companies for their combination of both local and international experience, and language skills..

Manpower Inc, a world leader in the employment services industry, launched its first international partnership office in China in Shanghai in May 2005. This initiative is the first in a series of public-private partnerships designed to introduce and adapt international employment best practices to support China's rapidly expanding economy.

> *This is an unprecedented partnership program between a governmental institution in China and a global employment services corporation on employment, vocational training and employment services. This is the first time a governmental institution in China has partnered with an outside entity on a project of this magnitude.*
>
> **David Arkless, senior vice president of corporate affairs for Manpower Inc**

EMPLOYMENT REGULATIONS

Work permits

According to the Ministry of Public Security, more than 1.9 million foreigners come to China for business and for conferences; 119,900 people come for employment; and 10,900 people recently came for permanent residence.

In order to work in China, you must hold an appropriate type of temporary or permanent residence visa. Visas are issued to foreigners according to the purposes of their visit. For more details about entry regulations and types of visa applications for mainland China, see *Visas, work permits and citizenship* in Moving to China: Before You Go.

Working in Macau

You will need a work permit to work in Macau. Your employer should arrange it for you before you arrive in the city. If you need to renew your permit, you should go to the Macau immigration office in person.

> *Macau Immigration Office*: Ground Floor, Travessa da Amizade (opposite to the Palace Floating Casino near the Macau Ferry terminal), Macau; 2872 5448

RECRUITMENT PROCEDURES

Once you have found a job you are interested in, applying for it is a pretty straightforward process. You should attach your CV to your application form or letter. Your CV should be concise and should pinpoint your relevant strengths such as language ability and computer skills. You should also include details of your education, work experience and contact addresses of referees. You should make it easy to read with suitable headings and neat formatting.

You may be asked to fill in your gender, age, nationality or even weight and height sometimes. Despite the equal opportunity laws that exist, the Chinese seem to accept prejudicial employment practices as an inevitable part of life. There certainly isn't the same pretence at non-discrimination as in the west. Some companies may require a passport-size photo. In general foreigners need not worry that they will be discriminated against due to their religion or gender, though racial discrimination may be encountered, especially outside the increasingly cosmopolitan big cities. The Equal Opportunity Employment laws, which have been in effect since January 1995, technically prohibit all the above discriminations, though the lack of transparency in employment decisions means the local labour bureau is unlikely to be able to act. Don't be surprised to see an employment ad requesting an employee of a specific age, height and gender.

TIP

- Don't be surprised to see an employment ad requesting an employee of a specific age, height and gender.

- **Interview research** It is really important to do some research on working culture and etiquette (see the section later in this chapter) before an interview. Even when working in multinational organisations, knowing traditional Chinese values and influences will be helpful as they remain the dominant beliefs of the society as a whole. It helps to show that you are genuinely interested in the job and have a commitment to China.

Recruitment procedures for FIEs

A foreign-invested enterprise (FIE) is a joint venture formed by a foreign and a Chinese partner. Compared to ordinary foreign enterprises (businesses owned solely by foreign investors) FIEs enjoy less flexibility when recruiting employees. Even though foreign enterprises are required to seek permission before posting advertisements in the media in China, the government does not overtly interfere in how they select employees. However, the government has specific rules on recruitment for FIEs. FIEs are required to give priority to candidates from the same province in which the company is located. Also, the Chinese partners in joint ventures are given more authority than the foreign partner when selecting employees. The local labour bureau prefers to have the Chinese partners taking the responsibility for recruiting employees. Only if no suitable candidates are found in the local province can the company recruit people from outside the province, which would include foreigners.

Recruitment of Chinese nationals by FIEs are usually done through designated agencies such as the Foreign Enterprises Service Corporation (Fesco) and China International Intellectech Corporation (CIIC). Employers will file the job positions and the requirements to these 'employment centres'. These centres are under the control of labour and social security departments as well as the personnel departments of the government. They keep files of candidates who are looking for jobs. When there is a job vacancy, an employment centre will choose the most suitable candidates for interview. In the past, vacancies were 'appointed' by these government-monitored employment centres and enterprises rarely rejected the candidate appointed. However, the selection process is changing and employers nowadays usually give their opinions on the candidates to the employment centre before someone is finally selected.

ASPECTS OF EMPLOYMENT

Types of contracts

In China, a written employment contract between the employer and the employee is either in the form of a collective contract or an individual contract. A collective contract is a binding contract between the employer and a trade union, which represents the employees. An individual contract is a binding contract between an individual employee and the employer and there is no need to have a trade union as middleman.

According to Chinese labour law, collective contracts must be sent to the relevant labour authorities for approval but this is optional for individual contracts. Though it is not compulsory, it is a common practice for the enterprise to submit a draft copy of their employment contract to the local authority for pre-approval. A contract is not valid until it receives certification by the provincial, municipal or autonomous people's government within one month of its execution.

Employers are obliged to address the following issues in the employment contract:

- Job nature
- Term of probationary period and employment period, if any
- Dispute resolution
- Disciplinary action
- Dismissal and employee resignation
- Working hours, annual leave and holidays (optional)
- Employee benefits (optional)
- Special training (optional)
- Confidentiality requirement (optional)
- Tort liability (optional)
- Severance pay (optional)

In addition to the employment contract, foreign-invested enterprises (FIEs) are required to keep a record for each employee. This record should include the following information about the employee:

- Name, ID number, marital/family status and home address
- Employment commencement date
- Probationary period
- Job title
- Wages plus bonuses
- Leave entitlement (annual, sick, holiday and maternity)
- Notice period
- Date of termination

The FIEs are also required to give the employee a handbook which clearly outlines the benefits provisions the employee will enjoy and which serves as the employee's code of conduct.

Contracts in Macau

In Macau, an employer should clearly define the job nature and requirements as well as stating the position, length of contract and salary in the employment contract. The contract should also include holidays and benefits that the employee is entitled to. The probation period, overtime payments, procedures and compensation for ending the contract and bonus (if any) are normally included as well. You should ask your employer to include all these if they are missing in the contract. After signing the contract, your employer should give you a copy of it for reference.

Termination of employment

The labour bureau is very concerned about the laying-off of employees. As a result, the local bureau may sometimes exert pressure on a company not to dismiss their employees unless necessary. The most common method of termination is to give 30 days advance notice to the employee. However, the exact period of notice should be in accordance with the details of the employment contract. The employer also needs to report the dismissal to the local labour bureau.

Employees who are dismissed for disciplinary violations will normally have the opportunity to defend themselves in front of the management of the company. If their defence fails to change the decision, they can appeal against the termination to the labour arbitration commission or before the People's Court if they have strong reasons.

The employer must inform the local bureau of pending dismissals due to redundancy or bankruptcy. Companies must seek the support and approval of the labour bureau to terminate a contract with an employee who has not committed any disciplinary violation.

In China, revocation of a contract is permitted under the following conditions:

- Both the employer and employee agree to the termination
- An employee is found not up to the requirements during a probationary period
- An employee seriously violates the rules or labour discipline
- An employee causes serious financial loss through dereliction of duty
- An employee is investigated for criminal acts
- An employee does not turn up to work after an illness
- An employee remains unqualified for a post after training
- Changes in the 'objective conditions' on which the contract was founded
- The employer is on the brink of bankruptcy

If the contract is terminated for any of the above reasons, the severance pay is equal to one-month's salary. If the contract is terminated for other reasons, it must be by mutual consent and further payments could be sought.

You should note that an employer cannot terminate a contract with an employee if: the employee has been disabled in an industrial accident or by occupational disease; a woman is on maternity or nursing leave; the employee is on non-work-related sick leave within a certain statutorily defined period.

Probationary period

The probationary period in China varies according to the regulations of each city. It also depends on the length of the contract. If the contract is for up to six months, the maximum probationary period is 15 days. If it is more than six months but less than one year, the maximum probationary period is one month. For more than one year but less than two years, two months is the maximum probationary period. If your contract is more than two years but less than three years, the probationary period can be up to three months. Otherwise, the maximum probationary period is six months. It should be noted that not all contracts make provision for a probationary period, particularly contracts with state-owned enterprises.

FACT

- Workers in China are flexible in terms of working hours and are prepared to work extra hours if necessary. Indeed, this is one of China's great competitive advantages in the global market and the laws in place to guarantee workers' rights and safety are often flouted with impunity.

The severance pay should be an 'economical compensation' based on the labour law and other regulations. On top of this 'economical compensation', the employee has the right to a further severance pay of three to six months if his or her contract is ended because of non-work-related injury.

Macanese regulations

In Macau, an employer has to provide prior notice to an employee if he or she wants to end the contract before it expires, and vice versa. An employee who has served the company for three months or more should be given prior notice for ending a contract at least 15 days before the effective date. On the other hand, an employee should tell the employer at least seven days before leaving. Employers have to pay compensation to employees for terminating contracts. The amount of compensation varies from seven to 20 days' salary, depending on the period of service.

Working hours and overtime

According to current Chinese law, excluding meal times, the maximum working hours should not be more than 40 hours a week. For most jobs, you can expect to work for approximately eight hours a day, although some industries like hospitals, post offices and banks are usually open seven days a week and you are required to have greater flexibility if working in these fields. Business hours for many companies are 9am–5pm Monday to Friday and some companies may open on Saturday morning as well. Most the government offices are open on weekdays only until 5pm.

Workers in China are flexible in terms of working hours and are prepared to work extra hours if necessary. Indeed, this is one of China's great competitive advantages in the global market and the laws in place to guarantee workers' rights and safety are often flouted with impunity.

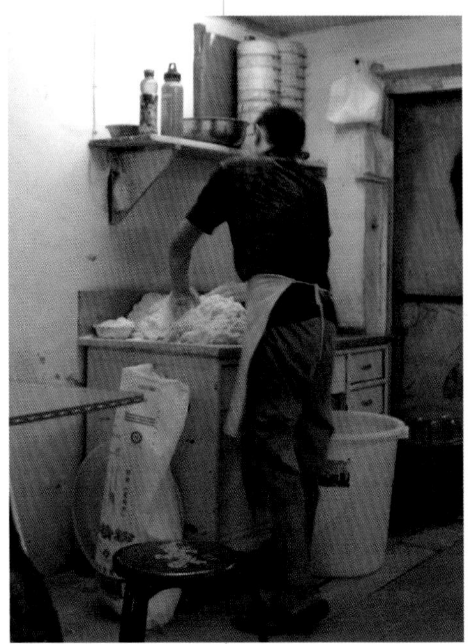

The Chinese government set up a labour standard system in 2001 to protect the rights of both employers and employees. This stated that employers must not extend the working hours of employees without first consulting the trade union or the workers. In addition, the extra period of work should not exceed one hour per day. In very special cases, overtime work may be three hours a day, or 36 hours in a month. The employer should ensure that all workers have at least one day off per week as well as other legal holidays. More importantly, if you are required to work overtime, under the current labour standard system, you should be paid at 150% of the normal salary for the extra hours. If you are required to work weekends or on legal holidays, you should be paid two or three times your normal pay rate respectively.

Macau's working hours

Under the labour law in Macau, the working hours of an employee should be within eight hours a day and 48 hours a week. Employers are required to provide at least 30 minutes' break for their employees every day. Employees are entitled to a rest day in every seven days, apart from the 10 legal holidays. There is no standard overtime rate, but it should be according to the contract between employer and employee. However, if an employee is asked to work on a rest day, the employer has to pay double the normal salary as well as providing the employee another rest day within 30 days.

Holidays

Apart from days off and legal holidays, employees are also entitled to at least five days of paid annual leave. Chinese companies and industries are also required to increase the days of annual leave for employees who serve their companies for a long period. Employees who serve their companies for 15–24 years, are entitled to 10 days of paid annual leave. Those who serve 25 years or more will receive 14 days of paid leave a year.

Employees can enjoy full pay (monthly base pay, not including bonus or social subsidies) while they have statutory holidays, rest days, annual leave, sick leave, marriage and bereavement leave, unless stated otherwise.

The legal holidays include:

- New Year's Day
- Chinese New Year (seven days' holiday, usually in mid-January to early February)
- International Labour Day (1 May)
- Qingming Festival (5 April)
- Mid-Autumn Festival (September or October)
- National Day (seven days' holiday, 1 October to 7 October)

In reality, there are only 10 days of genuine holiday in amongst these dates. China's two week-long holidays – at New Year (January/February) and National Day (October) – are dubbed 'golden weeks'. The intention is to give every worker seven consecutive days off work (thus allowing migrant workers time to return home). However, only three of these seven days are genuine holidays. The remaining four days are comprised of the surrounding weekends. Staff will always be required to work the weekend that precedes or follows the 'golden week' in order to make up the time.

Most observers would tend to agree that, were all of these employment rules effectively enforced, the Chinese economy would be substantially less robust than it currently is. While wanting to provide a fair deal for workers, the government also knows that its economy has been built around the ready supply of cheap labour. It is – as always – more pragmatic than dogmatic when it comes to interpreting the letter of the law.

Holidays in Macau

In Macau, every employee is entitled to at least five days' paid leave a year. Some companies will offer extra annual leave to employees who serve the company for a longer period. If employees do not take all their annual leave before the employment is terminated, employers have to pay for the rest of the annual leave as compensation.

There are 10 legal holidays in Macau including:

- New Year's Day
- Chinese New Year (three days holiday, usually in mid-January to early February)
- Qingming Festival (5 April)
- Labour Holiday (1 May)
- The day after the Mid-Autumn Festival (usually in mid-September to early October)
- National Day (1 October)
- Chung Yang Festival (in October)
- Macau Special Administrative Region Establishment Day (20 December)

Medical leave and sick pay

The Chinese system of paid medical leave is similar to the system of annual leave. The longer you serve in the company, the longer medical leave you can take. According to the current system, medical leave is divided into seven levels, ranging from three months per year to 24 months in a 30-month period.

Apart from medical leave, employees will also receive sick-leave payments. If an employee has to be off for up to six months and he has been working in the company for up to two years, then he will receive 60% of his normal salary. If he has been in the company for eight years or more, he is entitled to 100% of his normal salary. Otherwise, if an employee has to be off for more than six months, and he has been in the company for only two years or less, then he will receive 40% of his normal salary, or 60% of normal salary if he has been working for three years or more in the same company.

Length of Medical Leave	
Condition of service	**Length of medical leave**
Up to 10 years of total working experience and serving in the present company for up to five years	Three months continuous or within any six-month period
Up to 10 years of total working experience and serving in the present company for more than five years	Six months medical leave within any 12-month period
10 years or more total working experience and serving in the present company for up to five years	Six months medical leave within any 12-month period
10 years or more total working experience and serving in the present company for six to 10 years	Nine months medical leave within any 15-month period
10 years or more total working experience and serving in the present company for 11–15 years	12 months medical leave within 18-month period
Serving in the present company for 16–20 years	18 months medical leave within any 24-months period
Serving in the present company for more than 20 years	24 months medical leave within any 30-month period

Work-related injury

In the case of work-related injury, the employer is also responsible for all medical expenses. Compensation for taking care of the injured is provided every month until the end of the leave. The amount of compensation is equal to the average monthly salary in the 12 months before the injury. The injured employee is also entitled to a disability allowance, which is a single payment of six to 24 months' salary according to the degree of disability. Length of leave due to injury at work is from one month to two years though some seriously injured employees can extend leave up to three years.

If an employee dies in the course of work, family members receive compensation from the local government every month. The spouse is eligible to receive 40% of the average salary of the county and each of the other family members receives 30% of that average salary. Moreover, a one-off compensation of 48–60 months' average salary will also be provided to the family members.

Maternity leave

Every female employee is entitled to 90 days maternity leave, of which 15 days are before confinement and 75 days are after it. At the same time, a child-bearing subsidy is provided to pregnant employees for not less than 90 days. Pregnant employees may also use hospital services free of charge as long as their needs are directly related to their pregnancies.

Social insurance

There are five main kinds of social insurance. Both employers and employees are required to contribute to three of them: unemployment insurance, the provident fund and medical insurance. The remaining two are the sole responsibility of the employer.

Unemployment Insurance

Both employers and employees are required to contribute to unemployment insurance. Employers have to pay around 2% of the total payroll of the company while employees have to pay about 1% of their wages. However, the actual rate of contribution varies from place to place.

Provident fund (pension)

As in many other countries, China has a provident fund system for employees. Every employer must register with a local provident fund management centre within 30 days of the establishment of a company. Both employers and employees are required to contribute to the fund. The rate of contribution is set by local government and varies from place to place but the amount paid by employers will not exceed 20% of the total payroll of the enterprise. Employees have to contribute about 6%–8% of their wages to the provident fund.

Medical insurance

Both employers and employees are required to contribute to medical insurance. An employer has to contribute around 6% of an employee's salary for medical insurance while the employee pays 2%, however, there are slight differences between cities.

Work injury insurance

The occupational safety section of the labour law highlights the importance of providing employees with safe work conditions. The employer should provide the employee with at least the minimum safety and hygiene standards based on the national and local regulations. Apart from that, employers are also required to contribute to work injury insurance. There are three levels of insurance for injury at work, according to the perceived risk, and employers are required to contribute from 0.5% to 2% of an employee's total salary. The exact amount of contribution, similar to other insurances, is based on the local regulations but in general, employers pay approximately 1% of an employee's salary. All compensation, treatment charges and disability allowance costs an employer incurs will be paid for by the insurance.

Child-bearing insurance

Female employees are entitled to child-bearing insurance, which ensures that they receive maternal leave, child-bearing subsidy and other medical care related to their pregnancy. Employers have to contribute about 1% of the employee's salary to this insurance. Since child-bearing insurance is not yet universal in the whole of China, for those regions in which the insurance is not available, employers are responsible for paying the child-bearing subsidy for a period of 90 days. The subsidy is a single payment of ¥400–¥1,000 (£29–£72/$57–$143).

Trade unions

Many foreigners living and working in China will have little or no contact with trade unions, however the section below will provide information about the role and power of trade unions in China that may be useful in business dealings.

All trade unions in China must come under the umbrella stewardship of the All-China Federation of Trade Unions (ACFTU). ACFTU is a voluntary organisation of workers and currently has about 102 million members. The goal of the ACFTU is to safeguard the rights and interests of the workers and it represents them in discussions on different matters related to work with the employers.

One of the major functions of trade unions is to assist workers to sign suitable employment contracts with employers. China's trade union law was set up in 1992 and it granted trade unions the authority to sign collective agreements with companies on behalf of the workers. Trade unions act as a representative party to negotiate with the employer on matters relating to remuneration, working hours, vacations, occupational safety and health, insurance and welfare. When trade unions are involved, foreign-invested enterprises normally sign collective contracts instead of individual contracts with their employees.

A trade union can also interfere with punishments handed out by employers on workers if the punishments are considered improper or the reasons are not sound. In such cases, an employer has to provide a satisfactory explanation to prevent the trade union from taking the case to court. Trade unions also participate in the investigation of work-related accidents and may ask for compensation on behalf of the injured or deceased. In the case of disputes at work, trade unions will present the demands and opinions of the workers to the employer and negotiate for the benefit of employees.

A basic-level trade union, ie one set up within a company, should include at least 25 members. Otherwise, a trade union can be set up jointly with two or more units. Workers who are members of trade unions are required to contribute 0.5% of their monthly salary into the trade union's fund. Enterprises have to contribute 2% of workers' monthly salaries to the fund as well. All wage earners in companies, institutions and state organs within China are eligible to join trade unions, regardless of their nationality, race, sex, occupation, religion or educational background.

It should be noted that, not being a truly independent organisation, the ACFTU has been fairly ineffective in protecting some serious abuses of workers' rights in China, particularly given the links that exist between business leaders and senior figures in local government. As a developing country, perhaps it's not hugely surprising that most officials place greater emphasis on protecting the interests of business. Independent trade unions remain illegal.

All-China Federation of Trade Unions: 010 6859 2730; acftuild@public3.bta.net.cn; www.acftu.org.cn

All wage earners in companies, institutions and state organs within China are eligible to join trade unions, regardless of their nationality, race, sex, occupation, religion or educational background.

Macau

Every employee in Macau is free to join or not to join a trade union and it is illegal for an employer to prohibit employees from joining, or to force them to join a particular one. Trade unions in Macau are responsible for protecting the rights of employees as well as being their representative in the case of employment disputes. However, some people have reported that trade unions in the city do not have strong bargaining powers and employers may not take the opinions of the trade unions very seriously.

WORKING CULTURE AND ETIQUETTE

Significant cultural differences exist between China and the west; between China and other parts of Asia; and even, in fact, between different parts of China. Research suggests that the Chinese are generally more at ease working in an environment where what is expected in their job description is clearly set out, and where the relationship between senior staff and subordinates is formal and distant. The first names used in a western office are not the norm in China.

www.china-labour.org.hk includes current debates on labour rights and labour unions and information on other issues relating to labour and employment. It helps to facilitate workers' collaborative actions and to settle legal and administrative disputes.

It is a cliché that Chinese think of themselves more in terms of the group they belong to rather than in terms of individual status and achievement. It is also still the case that parents often influence the important life decisions of their grown up children – such as what to study, what career to follow, where to live (preferably near the parents if not actually with them) and choice of marriage partner. Parents expect to have a say. Young people may like to wear jeans and eat hamburgers at McDonald's but deep down, Chinese values still apply.

However in a business context, although some generalisations about Chinese culture should be kept in mind, there is great diversity, just as in the west. Chinese personalities vary enormously. It is important to appreciate this tremendous diversity, as family background, education, work experience, and lots of other factors play their part.

When people first come to China, for example, they immediately notice the difference between people who work in state-owned companies and those who work in the semi-private sector. Attitudes toward work also vary a lot according to age, and despite more than half a century of communism, multinational companies are still able to find young managers keen to work for firms that reward an individual's achievements rather than seniority and loyalty. There seem to be the same portion of budding entrepreneurs and innovators in China as in any other country. It helps that China's enduring family set-up can act as a safety net if a new business fails.

If you are employed in a multinational company where the Chinese staff have become familiar with a western management style, you may find the way of working is not unlike what you are used to. In such companies, especially if they have been established in China for a while, you can generally fit in without having to adapt.

For others, working in an entirely Chinese environment can be a really difficult challenge. Many state enterprises or Chinese companies may have a work culture reminiscent of the 'iron rice bowl' days of the 1960s and 1970s. 'Asleep on their arms' was one observer's comment on the work ethic of people serving in state-owned shops. If you go to work with a Chinese company or a joint-venture company, there are significant working and cultural issues that you will need to face. Depending on

the industry, the history, the culture and management, working with Chinese people can be a pleasure or a trial.

Office culture

The typical Chinese office

In China the typical office layout is open-plan. Factory offices are open-plan and similar to British ones, but jobs are broken down to the basic level, so that staff deal with a lot of repetitive work similar to actual production methods.

The office hierarchy

Chinese people in general take business hierarchy seriously, and a typical Chinese office is much more hierarchical than a western office. People in higher positions expect to earn more and they are usually more experienced, which means they are typically older too. Many Chinese who are in higher positions expect to keep their distance from their subordinates and may not like being called by their first names. There is a feeling that use of a first name will lessen respect.

Sometimes employees will not have the courage to point out the mistakes of their bosses because it will upset the hierarchy to do so. Many find that the way to move up the career ladder is to agree with your elders and seniors, and not to rock the boat or question your seniors' strategy and authority. If you were to convey your opinions to your seniors, it is likely they would not be respected, however insightful they may be. An employee's position in society (whether they

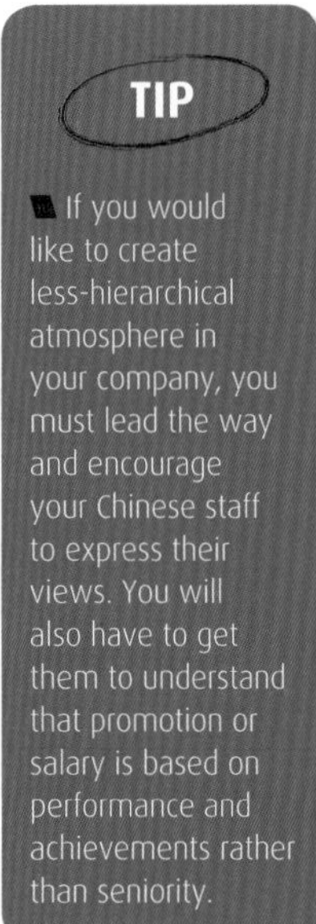

TIP

If you would like to create less-hierarchical atmosphere in your company, you must lead the way and encourage your Chinese staff to express their views. You will also have to get them to understand that promotion or salary is based on performance and achievements rather than seniority.

Office life in Beijing

There is an interesting blog by Geoffrey Fowler, a Wall Street Journal reporter about office life in Beijing. He writes: 'When American lawyer Jennifer Gallo moved to Beijing a few months ago, she had to go from her own office in San Francisco – "my little haven", she called it – into a shared room with another lawyer. After one day of polite silence in the new office, Ms Gallo's Chinese office mate cried out, "Jennifer Gallo, you are incorrigible!"

Her co-worker's problem: too much quiet. "My Chinese colleagues seem to thrive on noise and community", says Ms Gallo, 30. She's surrounded, she says, by loud talk, buzzing gadgets and a "concert of ring tones". Her office mate's phone blasts Work It by Missy Elliott.

But the lack of personal space goes beyond noise, she says. "It goes to the very heart of this American idea that certain things are better left unsaid." In recent months, Ms Gallo has been given assessments of her wardrobe ('very nice, could be European'), muscle tone ('flabby', a translation settled on after consultation with a group of English speakers) and childbearing prospects ('certain to have many boys').' You can read the whole article on www.collegejournal.com.

are head of a household or in a political organisation) can still impact on their importance at work. This hierarchical atmosphere can also facilitate bullying in the workplace.

Working relationships

The concept of 'face' is very important in China and it is not usual for Chinese people to point out other's mistakes bluntly, especially in front of other people. They will expect you to behave the same way. An employer should give advice to an employee individually, especially if he or she is not performing very well. Business partners, also, do not comment on the performance of their companies in social situations, especially when their employees are present. Advice is more easily accepted when expressed in a private conversation, and a healthy dose of 'beating around the bush' may help sometimes.

If you would like to create less-hierarchical atmosphere in your company, you must lead the way and encourage your Chinese staff to express their views. You will also have to get them to understand that promotion or salary is based on performance and achievements rather than seniority.

When you send gifts to staff in a company, you should take into account that people in higher positions expect to receive nicer (and more expensive) presents than their subordinates. It is normal for bosses to take staff for meals at lunchtime and issue invitations to restaurants, bars and clubs, to facilitate office networking.

Business culture

If you are in China to do business, you will certainly have to acquaint yourself with Chinese business culture. Don't forget that China has been a closed economy for a long time and while it has certainly taken on the world economy for some years now, there are still significant and major business cultural differences. It is certainly important to learn about Chinese business culture before landing in China.

The China-British Business Council (CBBC) has several recommendations. You should prepare in advance, read up about the country, and if you invest time and effort, it will be possible to make money. You should know who you are meeting, take an interest in the cultural and social factors that influence the thinking in China and the making of business decisions. The CBBC, along with everyone else who writes about business in China, highlights the importance of *guanxi* or 'connections'. They emphasise that you have to meet the right people, develop long-term relationships and make sure that you see to it that favours and generosity are reciprocated. This is the single most important asset.

A major problem in China is the relatively young framework of laws and the inexperience of the people who put them into practice, as well as the traditional bureaucracy. The only way to deal with this is through a network of reliable local people who know their way around – such as consultants, agents, employers and lawyers.

To get more business tips from the CBBC, contact: enquiries@cbbc.org.

In additions the business culture in China, is dependent on the industry, company or even the part of China where the company is based. For example, in the north, business is seldom discussed until you have shared a meal together at a restaurant; while in the south, business may come before social interaction.

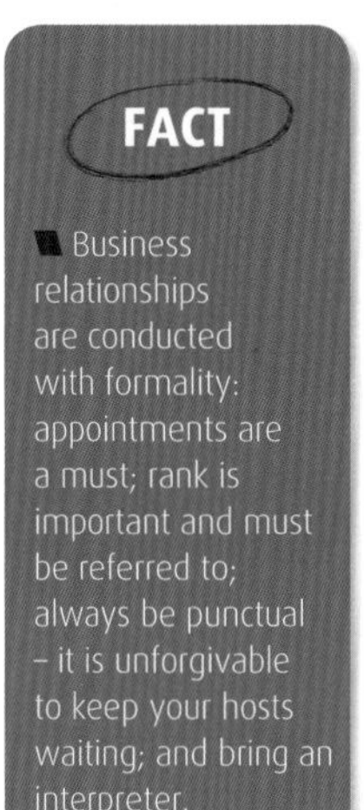
FACT
Business relationships are conducted with formality: appointments are a must; rank is important and must be referred to; always be punctual – it is unforgivable to keep your hosts waiting; and bring an interpreter.

Overall, the business culture of China is more to do with human interaction than anything else. There must be a fair amount of socialising before real business discussions of any kind can get going. Do not insist on a serious discussion on your very first meeting as developing a social or friendly bond is considered extremely important as far as Chinese businessmen and business culture are concerned.

Business hours are long and can be as long as 7am–9pm, although they are officially 9am to around 6pm.

Business etiquette

The Chinese, who are used to family businesses, are not so comfortable doing business with companies who are strangers to them. Therefore you need a go-between, who can introduce you and give you and your company a character reference. Before you arrive in China it is a good idea to send ahead fairly detailed information about your company and its products or services.

Business relationships are conducted with formality: appointments are a must; rank is important and must be referred to; always be punctual – it is unforgivable to keep your hosts waiting; and bring an interpreter.

You are expected to reciprocate when someone invites you for dinner or sends you an expensive gift. You should return a meal or a gift of some kind. If you have invited business associates to a restaurant, ask your guests what they would like for dinner before suggesting anything from the menu. In the end, they will usually let you make the decision anyway!

It is not considered good form to conduct business discussions during meals and social occasions. There is a dividing line between business and pleasure in China, so try to be careful not to confuse what should be separate.

Business meetings

It is important to be punctual and properly dressed. Gone are the days when Chinese hosts wore badly cut suits with open-necked shirts and sneakers. Men should wear conservative, dark-coloured suits, shirts and ties and formal footwear; women should wear neutral-coloured suits or dresses with a high neckline and shoes should have low heels – nothing provocative or attention grabbing.

Address men as 'Mr' or 'director', women by their job title (executive director, section manager) or as 'madame'.

Business cards

- Business cards are essential and are exchanged when you are introduced to someone. Your title should be on the card plus information about the company that would impress people. One side of your card should be in Chinese (simplified characters). As with a gift, present and receive the card with both hands, Chinese side up. When you are given a card, look at it carefully before you put it away or put it on the table beside you. Don't write anything on the card unless the giver tells you to. You will receive many cards at a meeting and it is a good idea to arrange them in front of you in the order in which the givers are sitting. That way it will be a bit easier to remember who is who and what their status is.

Have lots of business cards with you and be ready to give them out.

TIP
Have lots of business cards with you and be ready to give them out.

Have your key points firmly in mind and try to anticipate having to be persuasive but absolutely without being aggressive.

Refreshments at business meetings are usually green tea. You will get a cup which will be periodically refilled.

In general, remember not to cause your Chinese hosts or associates to 'lose face' – a much more serious issue than among westerners. So do not openly criticise, or show your counterpart to be wrong. It is also important to be modest about yourself, as the Chinese are. It's better to err on the side of caution and politeness.

Bear in mind the following points about Chinese culture:

- Well over half of Chinese live in rural areas. This agrarian culture emphasises cooperation, harmony, and obedience to familial hierarchy.
- Keeping to hierarchical relationships yields social harmony. Taoism – seeking 'the way' between yin (passive) and yang (active) forces – encourages compromise in business and allows both sides to maintain valid positions. The best compromises result from the ritual back-and-forth of haggling.
- Some people think that because Chinese words are based on pictures rather than sequences of lètters, Chinese thought tends toward more holistic processing of information and emphasises the bigger picture over the details.
- Hundreds of years of external and internal strife and war have resulted in a mistrust of strangers and cynicism about rules.

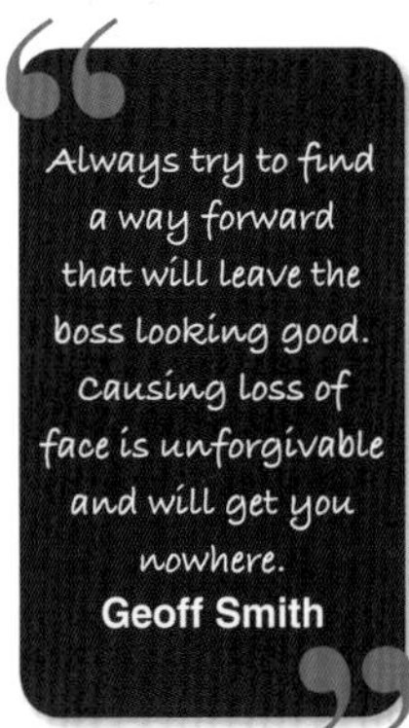
Always try to find a way forward that will leave the boss looking good. Causing loss of face is unforgivable and will get you nowhere.
Geoff Smith

Negotiating practices and taboos

The Chinese are tough, skilled negotiators. An intermediary is essential during meetings with strangers. This trusted business associate connects you with his trusted associate, creating a personal link to your target organisation or executive. Intermediaries interpret the moods, body language, and facial expressions of the negotiators. It is the intermediary – not the negotiators – who should first raise business issues for discussion, and often settle differences.

Chinese businesspeople value relationships among friends, relatives, and close associates. Favours are always remembered and returned, though not necessarily immediately. It is very bad news not to return a favour, hospitality or a gift and will seriously prejudice your relationship.

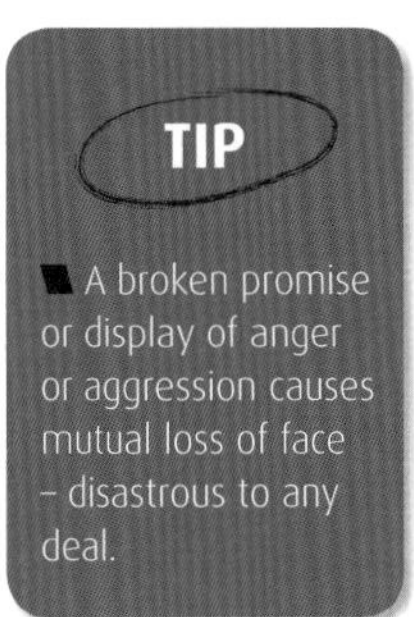

Casualness about social status doesn't work with people who value obedience and deference to superiors. Sending a low-level representative to a high-level negotiation can mean the end of the deal.

Relationships of equals are cemented through friendships and good feelings, generated during months of home visits and long dinners. Any attempt to do business without first establishing harmony is impolite.

Chinese businesspeople will often discuss all issues at the same time in apparently random order – looking at the whole package rather than the details. Nothing is settled until everything is settled. This holistic thinking contrasts with the linear approach adopted by westerners and creates the greatest areas of tension between negotiating teams.

The Chinese bargain intensely over price, making offers with room to manoeuvre. Their tactics are often silence and patience. Both sides are expected to make concessions but it often takes weeks of haggling. A broken promise or display of anger or aggression causes mutual loss of face – disastrous to any deal.

The Chinese prize relentless hard work. They prepare diligently for negotiations and expect long bargaining sessions. Demonstrate your endurance by asking lots of questions, doing thorough research, and showing patience.

Conversational taboos

- If you want to keep on the right side of your Chinese hosts and colleagues there are some topics that you would do well not to raise:
- Taiwan is considered a province of China so you must not refer to Taiwan as an independent country, either explicitly or by suggestion.
- You must be careful when praising the Japanese too highly. The Chinese have not forgotten the atrocities of the 1930s and 1940s.
- It may be acceptable to gently criticise General Mao Zedong, though he is still revered in certain quarters in China. However, Deng Xiaoping is regarded by most as a visionary leader beyond reproach.
- You should be careful about praising Shanghai too much in front of natives of Beijing, and similarly vice versa.
- The situation in Tibet is also very sensitive. Most Chinese regard Tibet as an inalienable part of China and any suggestion otherwise may cause problems.

Business correspondence

These days it is completely the norm to send emails. But employ common sense by always backing up important messages with a hard copy just in case there is a problem with the technology.

A few dos and don'ts from businessman Geoff Smith:

- Do show respect to senior management.
- Don't dress down for a first meeting (whatever the Chinese might be wearing).
- Have plenty of business cards (in Chinese and English) and give one to everyone if you can't work out who is the senior one of a group.
- Don't be late for meetings.
- Don't criticise the boss in front of juniors.
- When negotiating, always try and find a way forward that will leave the boss looking good. Loss-of-face is unforgivable and will get you nowhere.
- Don't assume the person who does the meeting-and-greeting and all the talking at a meeting is the most influential. It could be that the silent person

in the corner is the decision maker. Some Chinese businessmen still pretend they can't speak/understand English even though they are perfectly competent (this gives them more time to think, but is also a hangover from the old days).

- Do assume that you have to build up a relationship first before you will do any business. You may have to listen to a lot of 'introductory material' which you already know, but the Chinese consider this is all part of the build up to the main point of a meeting.
- Do be prepared to host dinners. Leave it up to the Chinese side to tell you who should be invited to work dinners/lunches. They might also like to advise you where they would like to eat, and make the booking.
- Do make an effort to eat a bit of all the dishes offered (whether you are paying or not), and certainly join in all the toasts. Be prepared to initiate your own toasts. Food and drink is such an important part of Chinese social life, it doesn't go down well if you don't look as if you are enjoying it.
- There is not much socialising after work – lunches and dinners between Chinese and foreign business partners are counted as work.
- *Guanxi*, literally 'relationship', is still the most important feature of doing business in China. Foreigners are amateurs at this compared with the Chinese!

WOMEN IN WORK

In the old pre-Mao China, the status of women was low and they mainly worked as housewives and took care of their children and parents-in-law. Nowadays, many women have their own career and are financially independent. Currently, female workers make up about 37% of the total workforce. In the old days, women rarely went out to work after they married, especially after they had children. However, nowadays many married women work and return to work after they have a child.

Given that the male/female population ratio is 1.2:1, this means that about 50% of the female population is contributing directly to the economic development of the country.

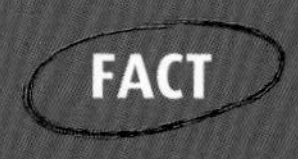

- Given that the male/female population ratio is 1.2:1, this means that about 50% of the female population is contributing directly to the economic development of the country.

Nevertheless, it is harder for women than men to find work. Over 50% of the female population is looking for a job, but only about half of the whole female population is employed. Even though the status of women is rising, sexual inequality at work, and for wages and job opportunities still exists. It is not only less-skilled female workers who face unemployment; the situation is the same for highly educated females as well. According to an article in *China Daily*, many female college graduates nowadays attach revealing photographs, such as photos in a mini skirt or even in a bikini, to their CVs in order to increase their chance of getting a job. Some of them also emphasise their ability to sing, dance and drink to show that they are qualified for public relations positions. Some employers do not deny that they prefer male employees to female employees, as women need to take maternity leave and nursing leave. Many employers prefer not to recruit fresh female university graduates as they believe these mid-to-late-20s women will get married and then pregnant soon after they start work. Even though the labour law clearly states that men and women should be treated equally in the job market, many people believe that there is more to be done to make these regulations effective. Many working-women also

Percentage of Female Workers in Different Sectors	
Item (by sector)	**National total in percentage (%)**
Farming, forestry, animal husbandry and fishery	37.1
Mining and quarrying	25.3
Manufacturing	43.0
Production and supply of electricity, gas and water	31.6
Construction	17.1
Geological prospecting and water conservancy	27.0
Transport, storage, post and telecommunication service	28.3
Wholesale, retail trade and catering services	44.9
Finance and insurance	45.9
Real estate	34.2
Social services	41.7
Healthcare, sports and social welfare	58.0
Education, culture and arts, radio, film and television	45.5
Scientific research and polytechnic services	33.5
Government agencies, party agencies, and social organisations	25.2
Others	36.2

complain that different retirement ages for men and women discriminates against women, and they are fighting for the same retirement age as men.

Sexual harassment, sad to say, is quite common in mainland China. According to a national survey about 79% of female workers, as opposed to 22% of male workers, reported that they had experienced sexual harassment at least once. Verbal harassment and physical touching are common, especially from male superiors. However, most of the harassed women do not report these cases. The first court case on sexual harassment in Beijing was not heard until April 2003. Since then, more women have complained about being sexually harassed. In 2005 the standing committee for national people's congress outlawed sexual harassment and domestic violence. If you are sexually harassed, you should report it to the local labour bureau.

Maternity leave and nursing leave

According to the Female Worker Labour Protection Provisions, pregnant employees are entitled to 90 days of maternity leave, of which 15 days are before confinement and 75 days are after it. Some cities provide paternity leave as well but the length of leave varies from city to city. Maternity leave can be extended if there are difficulties arising from birth such as miscarriage or multiple offspring. For every extra child born, an extra 15 days maternity leave are granted. For employees who miscarry, 15–42 days are granted. Employers are also required to provide a nursing period for their employees during workdays so that they can feed their babies.

Maternity benefits

Even though it is not yet a universal policy, some cities require employers to contribute to a local maternity insurance fund. The contribution rate of the fund ranges from 0.5% to 1% of an individual employee's salary. A pregnant employee is expected to receive maternity leave with full pay from her employer. She can also benefit from her local maternity social insurance fund, which covers all expenses that are associated with her pre and post-natal care. Hospitalisation, medical expenses and delivery are also covered by the fund in some cities. Moreover, a child-bearing subsidy is provided to pregnant employees for not less than 90 days. The calculation of this subsidy is based on the average salary of the individual employee in the previous year. Employers in regions that do not have the maternity insurance fund still have to pay the maternal subsidy to their pregnant employees, even though they are not required to pay monthly contributions.

TEMPORARY WORK

In recent years, the short-term or periodic employment pattern has become a new trend in some parts of China. The Beijing municipal government has introduced short-term and contractual employment to create more job opportunities. Instead of signing a 10-year contract with a new employee as in the past, many companies and government institutions prefer short-term contracts, for three to five years, or even periodical contracts. Under this latest employment pattern, many job-seekers prefer to leave their files with employment agencies to search for a better job even during their period of employment. Jumping from one job to another is more frequent than before.

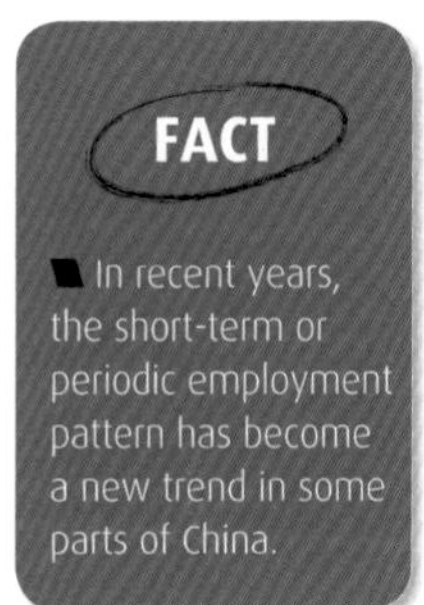
FACT
In recent years, the short-term or periodic employment pattern has become a new trend in some parts of China.

Summer training programmes and camps

Many local and foreign organisations arrange for foreigners to go to China to lead summer programmes or participate as assistants. Most of these are English-learning programmes for secondary school students or for English teachers in China. The China Education Association for International Exchange (CEAIE) organises such summer programmes every year and invites foreigners to teach participants English. The programme for secondary teachers lasts for six weeks while an English camp for students is two weeks shorter. There are many organisations that recruit volunteers to teach in China.

Educational Services International (ESI), a US Christian group, also organises summer programmes in China, but it only recruits English speakers who are Christians. Two weeks of training will be provided before you go to China and the whole programme lasts for about six weeks. You can make your application at any time of year but you have to pay about a fee to join the programme.

WorldTeach is a non-profit organisation based at the centre for international development at Harvard University. They recruit English speakers to teach in summer camps in China every year as volunteers. The whole programme lasts for about two months (from late June to late August) and every volunteer participates in two to three camps in different areas in China.

Colorado China Council (CCC) includes a great deal of sightseeing out of the teaching time and it sometimes organises additional trips after the programme, which you can join by paying extra. You need to hold at least a bachelor degree to join the programmes of CCC. As with ESI and WorldTeach, participants need to pay to join the programme.

Useful resources

Educational Services International, USA: 800 895 7955 (toll free in USA and Canada); teach@esimail.org; www.teachoverseas.org
WorldTeach, USA: 617 495 5527; info@worldteach.org; www.worldteach.org
Colorado China Council, USA: 303 443 1108; alice@asiacouncil.org; www.asiacouncil.org

Hotels

Work in cafés in tourist areas can sometimes be taken on without a work visa, but you are usually paid at a low rate. Hotels very often employ foreigners to teach their staff English, to write or translate menus, or as receptionists. You can approach a hotel directly – preferably in a tourist area – to ask about job possibilities. Portfolio International (*www.portfoliointernational.com*) are professional recruitment experts specialising in the hotel and catering industries. Positions are categorised into hotel general managers, hotel operations, leisure and golf, sales and marketing, corporate, food, drink, entertainment and chefs.

Internships

China joined IAESTE (International Association for the Exchange of Students with Technical Experience) in February 2000. IAESTE offers paid course-related work placements for students in science, engineering and technology to provide them with practical experience as well as theoretical knowledge. These placements normally last for 12 weeks in summer but longer placements can be arranged at other times of the year (www.iaeste.org).

The internship is open to students attending courses at universities, institutes of technology and similar institutions of higher education in science, engineering and technology. You must be studying at a university at the time of the internship, which means you cannot join the programme either before your first school term starts in the university, or after you finish your studies. Exceptions can be made for fresh graduates doing their practical training immediately after final examinations. Post-doctorate trainees will normally not be accepted.

You must apply to the IAESTE office in your home country. The application period usually lasts from September to early or mid-January and you are required to pay an application fee. You will then be provided with a list of details of all international internships and you have to submit an application update, CV, transcripts, etc. Successful candidates will be notified by mid-March but the placement has to be confirmed by the employer.

Abroad China, based in the USA, organises both exchange studies and placements for university students. It helps to arrange placements in many fields, including accounting, design, business administration, management, communications, computer science, consulting, education, English as a second language, finance, human resources, information systems, international relations, marketing, advertising, public relations, public policy, government, social work, law, hotel/restaurant hospitality and tourism. Short-term interns are usually unpaid but people staying with the organisation for more than six months usually receive a stipend. Abroad China will arrange accommodation, usually in universities or with host families, for participants.

Useful resources

IAESTE, USA: 410 997 3069; iaeste@aipt.org; www.iaeste.org
Abroad China Inc, USA: 703 834 1118; info@abroadchina.net; www.abroadchina.net
Intern Abroad: www.internabroad.com/china

Voluntary Work

Many local and overseas charitable organisations recruit volunteers to help people in need in China every year. China Charity Federation (CCF) is the largest China-based charitable organisation and it has a wide range of programmes to help victims of natural disasters, the elderly, orphanages, etc. Christian Salvation Service, a US-based group, currently operates an after-school study centre for elementary school children in Anhui Province and recruits volunteers to help with homework. Many Hong Kong and overseas charitable organisations send volunteers to mainland China to help people in need, as well as raising funds overseas. There are also some overseas organisations, such as the Red Cross and the Rotary Club, which have branches in China; you can contact them directly for voluntary work.

Since pollution is a serious problem in China, many environmental protection groups conduct projects or surveys, with the aim of arousing people's concern. These non-profit organisations such as Earthwatch, World Wide Fund for Nature in Hong Kong, and Asia Soil Conservation Network (ASOCON), require many volunteers to carry out these projects and surveys in different parts of China and they welcome your participation.

The website www.volunteerabroad.com is currently asking for volunteers to help rebuild the Great Wall in the parts where it needs repair.

PERMANENT WORK

Teaching

Though only a certain number of schools are permitted to employ foreign teachers, the demand for English teachers in Chinese schools is very high in both public and private institutions. It's not difficult to find work, either officially or informally. Very often, just being a native English speaker is enough.

As mentioned previously, the ministry of foreign affairs of the Chinese government recruits foreign teachers (FTs) and foreign experts (FEs) through Chinese embassies every year. You need to hold a master's degree or above in the relevant areas, such as English and linguistics, to be an FE. Moreover, you are also required to have

some teaching experience at tertiary level. FTs are mainly university graduates and are not required to have teaching experience. FTs are placed in secondary schools or sometimes primary schools while FEs can choose to work in university-level institutes. You should make your application to the Chinese embassy in your home country. You should attach a covering letter, a CV, a copy of your passport (the page with your personal details), a copy of your education certificate and a passport-size photo. There are also different short-term and long-term programmes held by the China Education Association for International Exchange (CEAIE) for foreigners.

There are plenty of other channels for foreigners to find a teaching position in China and one of the best routes is to join a work programme, such as Professional Placement in Chinese Schools, organised by China Services International (CSI). CSI only arranges for foreign teachers or experts to go to schools that are assessed by local governments and have fulfilled all criteria. In other words, CSI works closely with local provincial authorities and local schools in order to assure a positive placement experience for potential foreign teachers. International applicants who participate in the CSI teaching placement programme will receive a monthly salary based on contractual agreement.

- **Teaching salaries** Salaries for teaching jobs in China range from ¥2,500 to ¥5,000 per month (from around £160/$335), depending on where in the country you are teaching and what kind of school is employing you. An interesting point to note is that the salary is open for negotiation and you may ask for a higher salary. Educational level and teaching experience are important factors to determine your salary. The salary of a foreign teacher who has a BA is legally not less than ¥2,500 per month; a master's degree holder with five years' teaching experience will earn ¥3,500 or more per month; and

- the monthly salary of a doctorate degree holder or an associate professor from an overseas institution will be ¥4,600 or above.
- At the end of each academic semester, many (though not every) foreign teachers will receive ¥1,000 as their end-of-term bonus. Other benefits include fully paid furnished accommodation during the contractual period, and a return international travel ticket to your resident country, or an equivalent sum of money in yuan.

You should only apply to schools which have obtained provincial authorisation to hire foreign teachers. Otherwise, you may find that the school cannot afford to provide the above salary payments and benefits.

The Council on International Educational Exchange (CIEE) organises a very similar programme to that of CSI.

The British Council also runs a programme for university graduates to work as English-teaching assistants in Chinese secondary schools. Successful candidates will stay in China for about 10 months and they are provided with free accommodation in addition to a salary between ¥2,500 and ¥3,500. The closing date for this programme is around March every year and you should make your application directly to the British Council. It will cost you £48. More details can be found at www.languageassistant.co.uk.

You can find teaching jobs in China through a number of recruitment websites, such as the China TEFL Network, the Zhejiang Foreign Experts Service and China Education. There are more and more private institutes looking for foreigners to teach English and it is easy to find a huge number of these institutes through a google search. There are several placement organisations, such as CIEE, who have links with these foreign language institutes and they will be able to arrange a teaching job in China for you.

Teaching English Abroad (Susan Griffith, Crimson Publishing 2008) is a very handy directory and provides useful details on teaching English in China. Also take a look at www.china-recruitment.co.uk.

TIP

- You should only apply to schools which have obtained provincial authorisation to hire foreign teachers. Otherwise, you may find that the school cannot afford to provide the above salary payments and benefits.

Useful resources

The British Council, UK: 020 7389 4596; assistants@britishcouncil.org; www.languageassistant.co.uk

China Education: www.chinatoday.com. This provides information of vacancies in universities in China.

China Education Association for International Exchange (CEAIE): 010 6641 6582; ceaie@ceaie.edu.cn; www.ceaie.edu.cn

China Services International (CSI): www.chinajob.com

China TEFL network: www.chinatefl.com. A China-teaching job-listing site.

Council on International Educational Exchange (CIEE), UK: 020 7478 2020; infoUK@councilexchanges.org.uk; www.councilexchanges.org.uk

GAP (UK): 0118 959 4914; volunteer@gap.org.uk; www.gap.org.uk. A placement organisation arranging teaching jobs for school leavers.

Language Link, UK: 020 7225 1065; info@languagelink.co.uk; www.languagelink.co.uk

Zhejiang Foreign Experts Service: www.teach-in-zhejiang.com. Provides the latest ESL/EFL vacancies in schools in China.

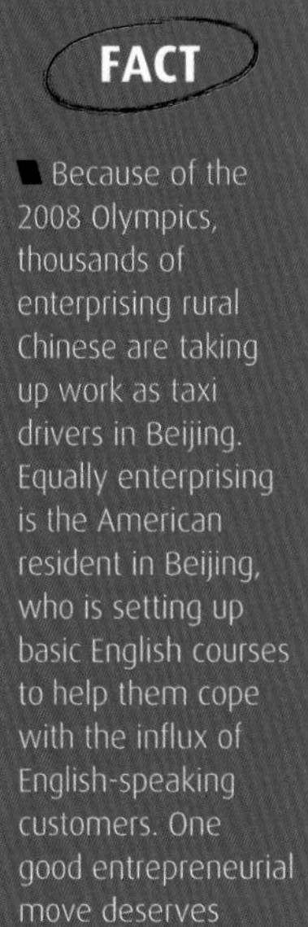

- **Preparation for teaching English in China** There is a special course for those wanting to teach English in China run by the Boland School TEFL Training Center (Suzhou, Jiangsu Province, China; katie@boland-china.com; www.boland-china.com). The course leads to an International TEFL Diploma teaching qualification for teaching English as a foreign language worldwide. The Boland School's China program is designed to prepare those interested in teaching English to live and work in China, Hong Kong, Taiwan, or elsewhere in Asia. In addition to the standard internationally recognised diploma, it includes 20 hours of survival language lessons plus coverage of cultural background, etiquette, history, education, and an introduction to Chinese students and language learning difficulties. The courses are held monthly and consist of a 148-hour graded programme over four and a half weeks. The maximum student/teacher ratio is 8:1 and there are 10 hours of peer teaching and a minimum of eight hours observed classroom teaching per trainee. There are also comprehensive job placement services and job fairs on-site every month. A job guarantee and flight-reimbursement guarantee are included. The curriculum includes the optional TEFL-China Certificate. The costs are $1,395, not including accommodation, or $1,595 with single-room accommodation.

Media

The China Watch Forecasting Services predicts a brighter future for this industry in the coming years as a result of the decision to allow greater foreign participation, especially in television production, to boost the revenue of the industry. Currently, foreign media experts are urgently needed to input new ideas into the industry. As the State Administration for Radio, Film, and Television (SARFT) admits, most of the current premium content is foreign-made. SARFT also acknowledges the need for deals to exchange content with foreign producers, and then to re-sell them to local cable companies. SARFT's approval for foreign participation and investment in the Chinese entertainment media industry triggers a sudden emergence of multi-national media companies and therefore creates a huge number of jobs in this field.

Besides television productions, there is greater foreign participation in the cinema industry. There is also a major effort to protect intellectual property and more local incentives are offered to attract foreign investments. There are an increasing number of joint ventures in film production, and a foreign partner can own up to 49% of a joint venture. In addition, more cinemas and production houses in China welcome foreign experts, such as movie producers, to create better prospects and greater profits in the industry. For details of the large media companies, see the *Directory of major employers* later in this chapter.

Banking and finance

The Chinese government wants to make Shanghai a major financial centre in Asia, and the world. This makes banking and finance crucial in Chinese economic development. Foreign banking consultants and financial experts should not find it difficult to find a job in China, especially in Shanghai. Moreover, banks have been extending the scope of their services. Apart from account management and mortgages, many banks provide credit card services, travel insurance and also online banking services. There are also more foreign enterprises using the services of local banks. The expansion of banking business not only creates more job opportunities but actually requires more foreign experts to support the increasing demand in services from foreign enterprises. For leading companies in this sector, see the *Directory of major employers* later in this chapter.

Executives

Foreign investment has been increasing at a rate of 20% in recent years and more and more foreign enterprises are tempted to establish branches in China. In the first half of 2007 foreign direct investment was up 12% on the previous year. These enterprises look for experienced executives, especially in human resource management, financial management and marketing, to put the business on the right track and manage the business in this fast-changing economy. Foreign-invested enterprises have to give priority to local candidates under government regulations and you may find it more difficult to get employment with one. However, foreign enterprises are not bound by these regulations and some of them are particularly interested in candidates from abroad, as their business partners are mainly outside China.

INDUSTRY OVERVIEW

Information technology

This is one of the fastest-growing industries in China. Yet spending on IT as a percentage of Chinese GDP is far below that of other major economies, though it is growing, from $23.6 billion in 2003 to an estimated $34.8 billion in 2006.

There are enormous business opportunities for IT vendors. Banks and insurance companies in particular look for foreign IT vendors as these foreign experts usually provide all the intellectual solutions, while domestic vendors are mainly responsible for providing hardware and software. Moreover, the education and medical industries, as well as banks and insurance companies, will also demand more IT products in the coming years. Highly skilled and experienced workers in IT businesses will be very welcome to work in China for the next five to 10 years. There is also a demand for product designers to increase the competitiveness of products and to increase the market share.

The increase in demand for advanced technology products also stimulates the production of semiconductors, digital household appliances, medical equipment, etc. In the past, these products were mainly imported from other countries but more domestic products can now be found as the technology and skills for local production are getting better and better. Many locals nowadays actually prefer to buy cheaper homegrown products instead of imports as the quality of the two is similar.

According to *The Economist* (March 2007), China has recently recorded huge growth in hi-tech exports, especially computers, DVD players and mobile phones.

Between 1998 and 2004 American imports of Chinese laptops went from $5 million to $7.7 billion and computer monitors from $860,000 to $4.9 billion.

FACT
Between 1998 and 2004 American imports of Chinese laptops went from $5 million to $7.7 billion and computer monitors from $860,000 to $4.9 billion.

Production of computer hardware

In order to attain the World Trade Organisation (WTO) requirements, China has signed the Information Technology Agreement (ITA), outlawing quotas for chips, computers and other high-technology projects. It also agreed to reduce tariffs on these products to zero by 2005. In the past few years, local computer makers have improved in many ways and they are now very competitive in the market. The number of imported computer products has fallen significantly and local products now occupy a larger market share.

Semiconductors

In recent years, foreign investment in the semiconductor industry has been increasing. Many multinational companies not only invest in computers but also in consumer electronics. Foreign and multinational investments are still the leaders in the semiconductor industry. Local companies are facing more difficulties, such as infrastructure constraints and lack of clean water, in developing the industry. The lack of technological research has also limited the development of the industry. For these reasons, local companies often have to seek foreign advice and investment to further develop their business. The National Labour Department encourages more foreign-technology experts to come to China to conduct research and to provide advice and professional training for local companies.

Manufacturing

Manufacturing has always been the key industrial backbone in China and makes up 35% of GDP. Major manufacturing products include steel, automobiles, machinery, petrochemicals, home electrical appliances and computers. At the moment, 50% of the world's best-known companies have set up joint ventures or foreign enterprises in China. Since China entered the WTO in 2001, the manufacturing industry has continued to flourish and China is expected to become a major manufacturing centre within five to 10 years. In the past, manufacturers focused more on the practical aspect of their products, and the designs might not have been as attractive as those of other countries. Manufacturers nowadays are beginning to understand the importance of design.

The automobile industry

The automobile industry in China is looking good. Production of joint ventures accounts for 65% of the whole industry. Many of these joint ventures are formed by world-famous automobile companies. Some famous Chinese brands include: Santana, Jetta, Auti, Polo (partly owned by Volkswagen), Buick, Sail (partly owned by GM), Fukang (partly owned by Sitielong), Accord (partly owned by Honda) and Bluebird (partly owned by Nissan). Wholly domestically developed automobiles account for 25% of automobile production in China while imported automobiles account for only 10% of the market.

The number of China's privately owned sedans soared 33.5% year-on-year to 11.49 million at the end of 2006, according to the latest data released by the National Bureau of Statistics (NBS). By the end of 2007, the number of private automobiles had increased even more to 35.34 million,. The country sold more than seven million automobiles in 2006, including 3.8 million sedans, according to figures from the China Automobile Industry Association, with sales predicted to reach over 10 million a year by 2010.

The number of privately owned vehicles has been on the rise since the country's accession to the WTO in 2001, when 43% of the country's civilian vehicles were

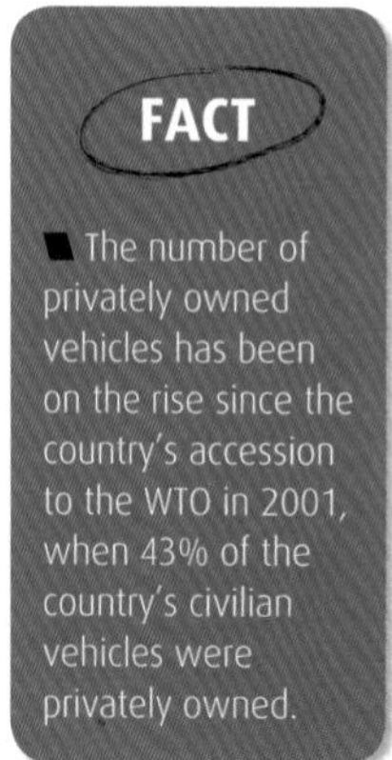
FACT
The number of privately owned vehicles has been on the rise since the country's accession to the WTO in 2001, when 43% of the country's civilian vehicles were privately owned.

privately owned. China, once known as the kingdom of bicycles, has overtaken Japan to become the world's second largest auto market after the USA.

As the automobile market is looking so strong, it is believed that more prominent manufacturers will set up joint ventures in China. The scale of local automobile manufacturing will grow quickly and domestically made automobiles will be exported to other countries in the near future. In other words, manufacturing industries in China will no longer be restricted to the domestic market but will also penetrate the international market.

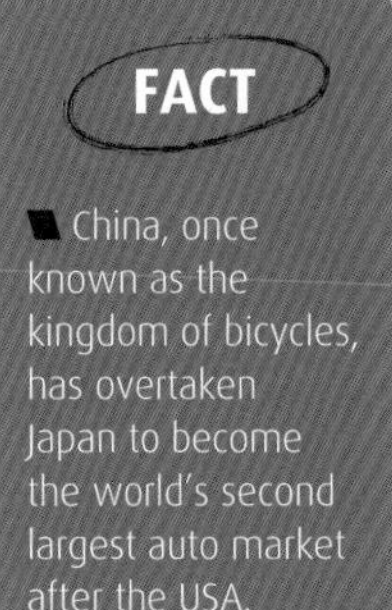
FACT
China, once known as the kingdom of bicycles, has overtaken Japan to become the world's second largest auto market after the USA.

Electronic parts in vehicles

In 1980, the electronic parts used in vehicles in the global market was worth only $4 billion. China sold over three million cars and became the fastest expanding market in 2003. It was also the fifth largest automobile manufacturer in the world, competing with industry giants such as Ford, General Motors and Volkswagen. In 2006, directly driven by the fast-growing automotive industry, China's automotive electronics market continued to maintain its growth momentum. For the whole year, automotive electronics sales revenues reached ¥86.76 billion, up by almost 40% year-on-year.

Machinery

Much lower-level and middle-level machinery and machine tools are produced in China. Domestic production of machinery accounts for 30% of the output of the industry while machine tools, manufactured by both domestic enterprises and joint ventures, was about 25%. Imported tools have a market share of 25% in the industry. More sophisticated machines are mainly imported from abroad and account for 20% of the market. In the next few years, Chinese enterprises will focus on the development of middle-level to high-level machinery. There will be more middle-level machines exported overseas whereas the export and production of low-level machines will be reduced.

Transport

As the country develops rapidly and more foreign traders visit China, the Chinese government has been improving the quality of existing airports as well as opening up its airways to more foreign airlines, and candidates who can speak fluent English will have an advantage in getting a job in this new international area.

The Yantai-Dalian Railway Ferry Project is due to be in service by the end of 2007. It is only one of a series of new sea-transport routes in China and some of the routes, such as the Yuehai Railway Ferry that links South China's Guangdong province and the island of Hainan, are already in service. The Chinese government is also extending its rail services and aims to cover more regions in the west of China.

'Go West' has been a major development project since the late 1990s. In order to attract more investors to start businesses in the west, it is important to improve the transportation connections from east to west. Apart from railways, many highways are being built or will be built to make the transport of materials and finished goods easier. Some existing ones will be extended to provide better connections between cities. About 45,000km of expressways have been or are being built at the time of writing. More details about transportation development are covered in the *Regional guide* in About China later in the book.

Communications and telecom

A few years ago there was an imbalance between supply and demand for many telecom products, and it was expected that the growth in consumption would slow down. However, the expenditure on telecommunication products and digital cameras is now accelerating. China has the largest telecom market in the world. The Ministry of Information Industry reported there were 798 million telephone users in July 2006. It is predicted that the fixed-line telephone market will continue to expand and the growth will extend to the use of broadband services. Broadband customers will expand from big cities into the less wealthy north-west regions. The goal of the State's telecom development is to merge all national operators into Chinese Satellite, which holds satellite and internet licences. Currently, apart from Chinese Satellite, China Telecom, China Netcom, China Mobile and China Unicom are the four multi-functional operators.

There are now more than half a billion mobile phone users in China. Motorola and Nokia are still the leaders in the handset market. However, a serious oversupply problem will lead to sluggish growth in the sales of traditional handsets and will trigger a technological change in the market. The introduction of new cellular technology, for example, the third generation mobile, is likely to be the future direction in China. The $2.8 billion partnership agreement between the British giant, Vodafone, and China Mobile is an example of building a strategic partnership in this competitive market. The foreign partner contributes more advanced technology while the Chinese partner helps it to expand the business inside China. In order to secure their market share in this large market, many foreign companies are looking for strategic planners and it is believed that they will play an important role in the Chinese telecom industry.

Digital TV

It is believed that digitalisation of TV broadcasting will be the main trend throughout the world's broadcasting business. This trend will boost a rapid development of relevant software and information industries. The China Centre for Information Industry Development estimates that this will generate a growth of over ¥1,000 billion in the broadcasting industry and will become a major money-spinner in China's future economy.

Import/export

Imports and exports have been an important part of industry since the early 1980s and they have further flourished since China entered the WTO in 2001. According to Customs statistics, China's foreign trade in the first seven months of 2005 rose 22.8% over the same period of the previous year. Exports surged 32%, and imports climbed 13.8%, 18.2 percentage points slower than the growth of exports. Japan, the USA and the EU are the three major trading partners of China. Apart from these three, Hong Kong, the Republic of Korea, ASEAN (Association of South-East Asian Nations), Taiwan, Russia, Australia and Canada are also major trading partners.

Machinery and electronic products are major export items. They alone accounted for 51.9% of the total exports of the country and achieved 64.3% growth in 2003. In 2007 the government planned to give these exports a boost. Other export items include garments and accessories, textile yarn, fabrics and textile products, plastic products, shoes, furniture and toys. The import of primary goods showed a significant growth of 47.7% in the same year. Major imported items include iron ore, crude oil, soyabean, timber, machinery and equipment, chemical and chemical-related products, steel and motor vehicles.

In late 2006, China's trade surplus reached $10 billion, compared with $10.55 billion in July of that year and $4.52 billion a year earlier. Exports in August surged 32.1% to a record $67.8 billion and imports increased 23.4%, also reaching an all-time high.

Farming and horticulture

It is impossible to overestimate how important agriculture is in China. Even though many cities are transforming themselves into industrial and financial bases, China is still a major supplier of food to many countries. If you want to experience life in rural areas and are interested in farming and horticulture, the International Farm Experience Programme can arrange a three-month placement on the outskirts of Beijing.

Working in China

Farmers in China are usually very poor but if you are prepared to be a volunteer, you could approach the local farmers directly if you speak some Mandarin, or get someone to help.

International Farm Experience Programme, UK: Young Farmers Centre, National Agriculture Centre, Stoneleigh, Warwickshire CV8 2LG; 02476 857204

Useful resources

China Charity Federation (CCF): 010 6601 2629; www.chinacharityfederation.com
Christian Salvation Service, USA: 314 535 5919
Red Cross China: 010 8402 5890; redcross@chineseredcross.org.cn; www.chineseredcross.org.cn
China Environmental Protection Foundation: 010 6494 7722 ext. 5111; cepfpound@public3.bta.net.cn; www.cepf.org.cn
Rotary Club of Shanghai: shanghai@rotary3450.org; www.rotaryshanghai.org
Earth Watch International, USA: 978 461 0081; info@earthwatch.org; www.earthwatch.org
Asia Soil Conservation Network (ASOCON): 010 6320 2840; www.asocon.org
Friends of the Earth: (+852) 2528 5588; www.foe.org.hk
Green Power: (+852) 23142662; info@greenpower.org.hk; www.greenpower.org.hk
HOPE Worldwide Hong Kong: (+852) 2588 1291; enquiry@hopeww.org.hk; hk.hopeworldwide.org
Medecins Sans Frontieres: (+852) 2338 8277; office@msf.org.hk; www.msf.org.hk

Oxfam, 17/F: (+852) 2520 2525; info@oxfam.org.hk; www.oxfam.org.hk
The Community Chest of Hong Kong: (+852) 2599 6111; chest@commchest.org; www.commchest.org
WWF Hong Kong: (+852) 2526 1011; wwf@wwf.org.hk; www.wwf.org.hk

DIRECTORY OF MAJOR EMPLOYERS

Accounting

Ernst & Young: *(Beijing)* 010 6524 6688; *(Shanghai)* 021 6219 1219; *(Guangzhou)* 020 8331 2788; *(Chengdu)* 028 8660 6111; www.ey.com
KPMG: (Beijing) 010 8518 5000; *(Shanghai)* 021 5359 4666; *(Guangzhou)* 020 8732 2832; *(Shenzhen)* 0755 8246 3398; *(Macau)* 781 092; www.kpmg.com.cn
PricewaterhouseCoopers: *(Beijing)* 010 6561 2233; *(Shanghai)* 021 6386 3388; *(Tianjin)* 022 2330 6789; *(Macau)* 7995 111; www.pwccn.com
Deloitte: 010 6528 1599; www.deloitte.com

Airlines

Air China: master@mail.airchina.com.cn; www.airchina.com.cn
China Eastern: www.cea.online.sh.cn
China Southern: 020 8668 2000; webmaster@cs-air.com; www.cs-air.com
Civil Aviation Administration of China (CAAC): 010 6409 1114; www.caac.gov.cn
Dragon Air Ticketing Office (Hong Kong): 2868 6777; www.dragonair.com
Air Macau: 6396 5555; airmacau@airmacau.com.mo; www.airmacau.com.mo

Banks

Bank of China: 010 6659 6688; www.bank-of-china.com
The People's Bank of China: 010 6619 4114; master@pbc.gov.cn; www.pbc.gov.cn
Bank of Communications: 021 5878 1234; enquiry@bankcomm.com.hk; www.bankcomm.com.hk
China Minsheng Bank: 95568; service@cmbc.com.cn; www.cmbc.com.cn
China Construction Bank: 010 6360 3660; www.ccbhk.com
Hua Xia Bank: 010 6615 1199; webmaster@hxb.cc; www.hxb.com.cn
China Merchants Bank: 010 6642 6868; www.cmbchina.com
Industrial and Commercial Bank of China: 95588; webmaster@icbc.com.cn; www.icbc.com.cn

Construction

ARUP: *(Beijing)* 010 6597 3788; *(Shanghai)* 021 5396 6633; *(Shenzhen)* 0755 519 8187; webmail@arup.com; www.arup.com
Atkins Faithful & Gould Ltd: *(Shanghai)* 021 6249 1498; barry.piper@fgould.com.hk; *(Beijing)* 010 6567 7933; beijing@atkins.com.cn; *(Shenzhen)* 0755 8246 2109; shenzhen@atkins.com.cn

Industrial Consultancy Services

McKinsey: www.mckinsey.com/locations/greaterchina
Watson Wyatt: *(Beijing)* 010 8529 9071; david.cheng@watsonwyatt.com; *(Shanghai)* 021 5298 6888; michele.lee@watsonwyatt.com; *(Shenzhen)*, 0755 8236 4888; michele.lee@watsonwyatt.com; www.watsonwyatt.com

Information Technology

Dell: www.dell.com
HP: www.jobs.hp.com
IBM: www-07.ibm.com/employment/cn/en

Insurance

American International Assurance Co Ltd: 021 6321 6698; www.aigchina.com
AXA Asia Pacific Holdings Ltd: 010 6500 7393; www.axa-chinaregion.com
ING General Insurance International Ltd: *0411 2530 881; www.ing-cap.com.cn*
New York Life Insurance Worldwide Ltd: *800 820 5882; p-r@haiernewyorklife.com.cn; www.haiernewyorklife.com.cn*
Royal & Sun Alliance Insurance Ltd, Shanghai: 021 6841 1999; rsashang@uninet.com.cn; www.royalsunalliance.com.cn

Law

Allen & Overy: *(Beijing)* 010 6505 8800; *(Shanghai)* 021 6288 3099; www.allenovery.com
Baker & McKenzie: 010 6505 0591; www.bakernet.com
Barlow Lyde & Gilbert, Hong Kong: 2840 2618; hdonegan@blg.com.hk; www.blg.co.uk
Cameron McKenna: 010 6289 6363; www.law-now.com
Claydon Gescher Associates: 010 6500 6552; cgaltd@public.bta.net.cn; www.cgaprc.com
Clifford Chance: 010 6505 9018; www.cliffordchance.com

Freshfields Bruckhaus Deringer: 010 6505 3448; www.freshfields.com
Herbert Smith: 010 6505 6512; www.herbertsmith.com
Lovell White Durrant: 010 8518 4000; www.lovells.com
Simmons & Simmons: 021 6249 0700; www.simmons-simmons.com

Manufacturing

China Display Company Ltd: 021 6484 9898; chinadisplay@online.sh.cn; www.cn-display.com
Shanghai Apollo-Fudan High-Tech Industry Co Ltd: 021 6564 8661; www.apollo-fudan.com
Texas Instruments China Inc: www.ti.com.cn/job

Media

BBDO CNUAC, Beijing: 010 6526 3961; www.bbdo.com
CCTV: cctv-international@mail.cctv.com; www.cctv.com
China Radio International (English service): 010 6889 1652; crieng@cri.com.cn; www.crienglish.com
China Star International Advertising Company Ltd: 010 5100 1451; cstar@chinastaradv.com
Creative Interface: *(Beijing)* 010 6416 9388; production@creativeinterface.com; *(Shanghai)* 021 6437 0376; sally@creativeinterface.com; www.creativeinterface.com
Optimum Media Direction: *(Beijing)* 010 8529 9088; *(Shanghai)* 021 6375 8885
Star TV: 010 8518 8500; star@newscorp.com.cn; www.startv.com

Oil Companies

China National Petrolum Company: 010 6209 4114; master@hq.cnpc.com.cn; www.cnpc.com.cn
Shell: (HR department) 010 6505 4501; www.shell.com

Pharmaceutical

Dow Chemical Ltd: *(Beijing)* 020 8752 0380; *(Guangzhou)* 020 8752 0380
Glaxosmithkline: 010 8529 6868
Johnson & Johnson: www.jnj.com/careers
Procter & Gamble Ltd: www.pg.com.cn/job

Telecommunications

Motorola China Electronics Ltd: 010 6564 2288; www.motorola.com.cn
Siemens Ltd: 010 6472 1888; www.siemens.com

Unless you have a specific company in mind, the best source of jobs is on the internet. There are many sites that specialise in jobs in China. You can also pick up English-language expatriate magazines that are available in many four or five-star hotels in big cities and look at the job opportunities listed there. Many of these magazines also have a website where you can place your CV.

Websites

www.corporate.globalsources.com
www.learn4good.com
www.jobsabroad.com
www.made-in-china.com
www.rileyguide.com
www.Wang-Li.com

REGIONAL EMPLOYMENT GUIDE

Southern China

Southern China refers to four areas: Guangdong, Fujian, Hainan Provinces and Guangxi autonomous region. Since these regions are along the coastline, easy transportation is an advantage for trading with foreign partners. Moreover, the government has set up many Special Economical Zones (SEZs), particularly in Guangdong province, to further boost the economic development of this area. The southern part is, on average, richer than other areas of China.

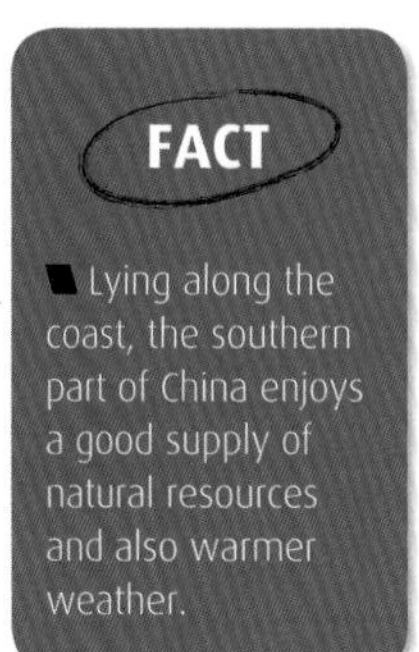

Lying along the coast, the southern part of China enjoys a good supply of natural resources and also warmer weather. In this region, petrochemical, electronics and machinery industries (apart from imports and exports) contribute a great deal to economic development. In Fujian, apart from the above-mentioned industries, construction, forestry, fisheries and aquiculture and textiles are also pillar industries. The Guangxi government focuses on the development of heavy industries such as hydropower, metal and building materials. In recent years, the Hainan government, in contrast, has focused more on light industry such as electronics and information technology. It has also become a popular tourist destination in the last decade, especially among Asians.

Guangdong

Guangdong is one of the most important business areas in China. Economic development in Guangdong mainly depends on the SEZs, which include Shantou, Zhuhai, and Shenzhen, the largest of the three. The Guangdong area benefits from its geographical proximity to the Pearl River Delta, which is an important connection to Hong Kong and Macau. In past decades, the development of this region has relied heavily on imports and exports, which account for 74% of the total GDP in this area. However, the Guangdong region has been slightly overshadowed by the eastern coastal regions, especially Shanghai in the early 2000s.

Many foreign investors have started their businesses in Shanghai or moved their base there in the last decade. Those sourcing manufactured goods from China are looking for cheaper suppliers than those in Guangdong and are finding that labour costs, and therefore prices of goods, are cheaper further north in areas such as Shanghai or Shandong. In order to encourage more foreign investors to develop their business to maintain an impressive economic growth in Guangdong, the Chinese government offers more investment incentives to promote the development of small and medium-sized enterprises. These now significantly help to support the economy in the Guangdong area. According to statistics from the local industrial and commercial department, there has been a significant increase in the number of privately owned enterprises since 2002.

The GDP in Guangdong scored over ¥1 trillion (£71 billion/$122 billion) in 2003, increasing by 13.6% when compared to that of 2002, and was the highest in the last eight years. The Guangdong area is once again attracting a lot of foreign investment, in particular in the industrial sector, which contributed 61.7% to the GDP of the province. Many factories, both locally or foreign owned, have grown rapidly since China joined the WTO in 2001.

ECONOMIC ZONES OF CHINA

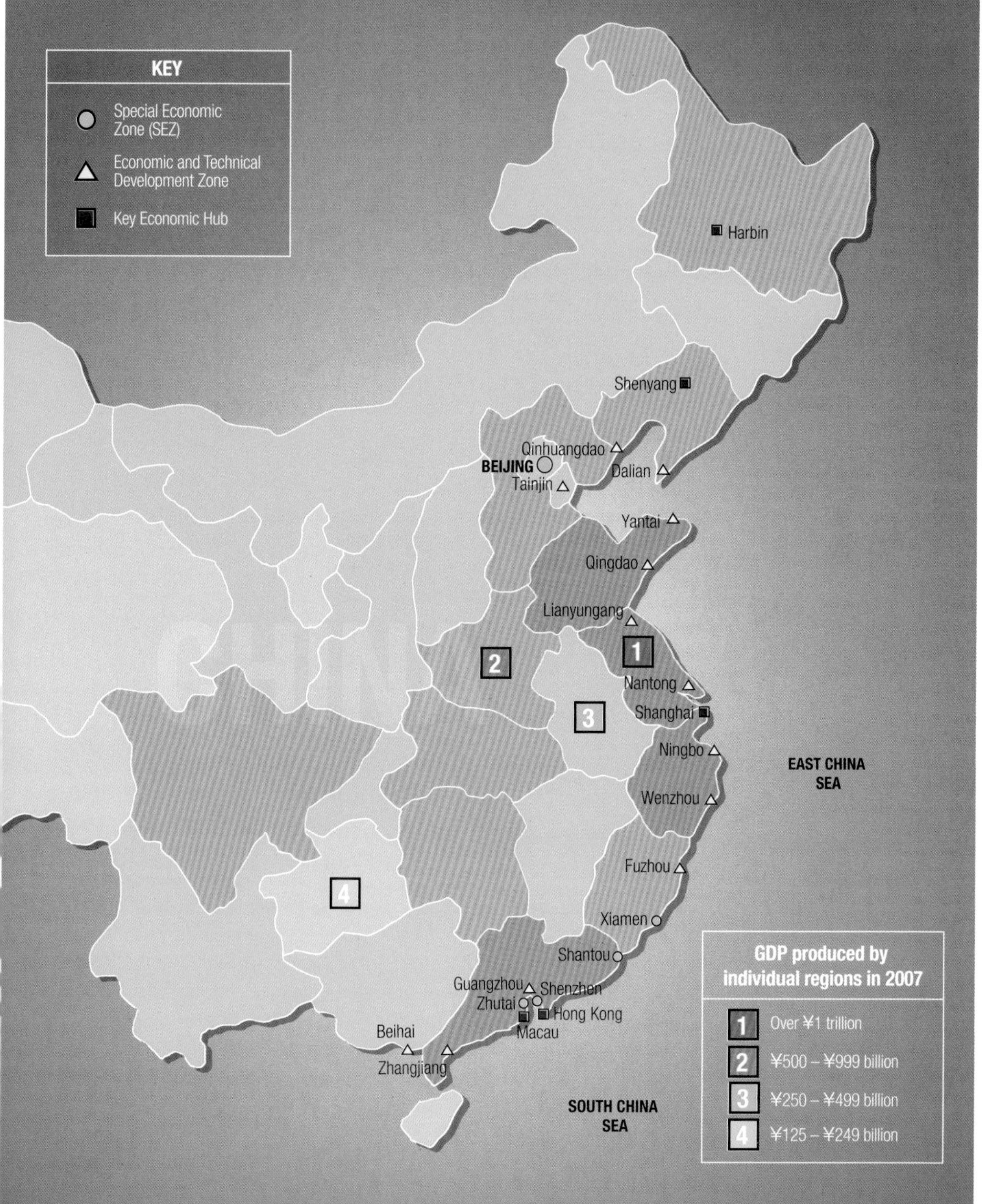

Ya Ming Pearl Tower, Shanghai

Beijing

Lujiazui, Shanghai

Hong Kong

Currently, skilled people who specialise in high-technology management, software development, electronic, chemical, pharmacy, trade, textile, audio-visual products and toys are highly sought after in this area.

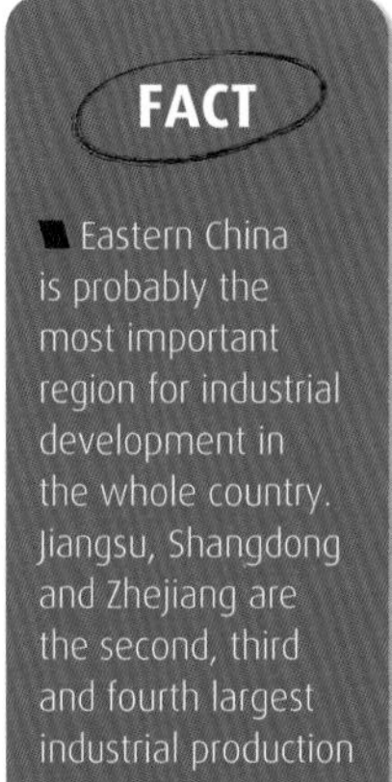

Eastern China is probably the most important region for industrial development in the whole country. Jiangsu, Shangdong and Zhejiang are the second, third and fourth largest industrial production bases in China in after Guangdong.

> www.job168.com provides the latest information on job vacancies in the Guangdong area. Some of the jobs offered are with big companies such as Coca-Cola, Philips, Nokia, Media, Mattel and Newell Rubbermaid. It also specialises in searching senior management vacancies for their clients.

Eastern China

Eastern China has developed rapidly in the last two decades. Cities along the Yangtze River delta, including Nanjing, Ningbo and Shanghai, are important for the economic development of China. The Chinese government provides a number of investment incentives in order to attract more foreign companies to these areas. As with the southern part, eastern China is particularly desirable for trading because it is along the coastline and has many ports, which make it a convenient trading centre.

Eastern China is probably the most important region for industrial development in the whole country. Jiangsu, Shangdong and Zhejiang are the second, third and fourth largest industrial production bases in China in after Guangdong.

Eastern China was mainly engaged in light industries in the 1980s and early 1990s. However, heavy industries such as automobiles, machinery, petroleum and chemical industries have started to dominate the market and have become a major support for the local economies. They were estimated to account for 60% of the total income of the region. Foreign investment in these regions has greatly increased: Jiangsu is particularly favoured by Taiwanese investors while many Hong Kong investors set up their businesses in Zhejiang.

The regions have become important IT, telecommunication and electronics manufacturing bases in recent years. Kunshan and Wujiang in Jiangsu and the Hangzhou Bay area in Zhejiang are major manufacturing areas for these industries. These areas are near to Shanghai but the labour costs are comparatively lower. Eastern China is also famous for beautiful scenery. Cities such as Hangzhou, Suzhou, Jinan and Qingdao are popular destinations for tourists. Income from tourism and souvenirs, such as handicrafts and silk, is also important to local economic development.

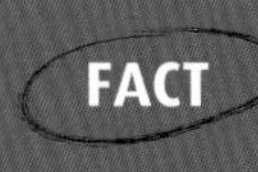

Currently, over 80 of the world's top 500 companies such as Motorola, Microsoft, Compaq, Itochu and Wal-Mart have already invested or decided to invest in western China.

Western China

Western China includes Yunnan, Guizhou, Sichuan, Shaanxi, Gansu and Qinghai Provinces as well as three autonomous regions, Tibet, Xinjiang and Ningxia. The implementation of the 'Go West' policy by the Chinese government at the beginning of the 21st century underlines the intensification of its efforts to accelerate the development of the western part of China. Under this strategic development, an increase of capital investment in infrastructure, the provision of favourable investment incentives, widened scope for foreign investment and investment in human capital (labour) are being adopted to create a more conducive investment environment in western cities, such as Urumqi, Chengdu and Xian. Currently, over 80 of the world's top 500 companies such as Motorola, Microsoft, Compaq, Itochu and Wal-Mart have already invested or decided to invest in western China.

The region is rich in energy and mineral resources that are the backbone of industrial development. Sichuan, Shaanxi and Xinjiang have the three largest natural gas fields in China, amounting to 61% of the country's total. The west also has abundant hydropower resources to generate electricity to support domestic consumption as well as satisfying the demands of the coastal areas. The 'west-to-east' natural gas transmission and the 'west-to-east' electricity transmission are two major projects being carried out now and will provide major income for the west in the coming decades.

The exploration and development of the western region, apart from economic benefits to the country itself, also implies more employment opportunities in the region. There will be more important positions for foreign technological experts to provide advice and support for the western development projects.

Transport links

The building of major roads is one of the biggest projects sponsored by the Chinese government in the region. The highway network will connect the west with major cities in the east: 47 roads and bridges will be built in or around Chongqing involving a total investment of ¥200 billion (£14 billion/$24 billion). The construction of a complete new highway network will connect Chongqing to Guizhou, Chongqing to Changsha, Chongqing to Wanzhou, Changshou to Fuling, and Chongqing to Hechuan. At the same time, a new 1,700km-long highway will be constructed in Shaanxi, which will connect Baotou to Beihai, Xian to Hefei, and Yinchuan to Wuhan National Trunks. In addition to the above two projects, the current Sichuan highway will be extended from 1,000km to 2,000km by 2009. It is estimated that the total cost for the highway network project will be around ¥700–¥800 billion.

Apart from the highway network project, rail transportation also plays an important role in the development of the west. Since 1999 the Chinese government has completed two huge feats of railway engineering, laying tracks across the deserts of Xinjiang to connect Kashgar, close to the Pakistan border, with Urumqi, and creating the highest railway in world across the Tibet-Qinghai Plateau to connect Lhasa, Tibet's provincial capital, with Golmud and, by extension, the cities of eastern China. The Chinese government is currently improving the connections between the western regions and improving technology on tracks in the eastern regions to enable faster travel. Rail engineers who are specialised in modernizing rail networks and high-speed rail are very much in demand.

Other projects

Apart from government projects, there is also a considerable increase in private projects in the west. Many of these private projects are connected to agriculture, medicine and environmental protection, and employment opportunities in these areas are wide open.

Tourism is going to be another important industry in western China. The State Development Planning Commission, National Tourism Administration and Western Region Development Office of the State Council have decided to explore and to develop several plans in north-western and south-western China. Areas such as Shaanxi, Qinghai, Gansu, Inner Mongolia, Ningxia, and Xinjiang will benefit from this. Key areas to be developed are around the Silk Road. Some of the potential routes are:

- The north and the south flanks of the Silk Road
- The Tianshui–Lanzhou–Wuwei–Zhangye route
- The Hulun Buri–Heilongjiang–Jilian route and Zhangjiakou–Chengde–Chifeng–Hohhot route
- The Urumqi–Korla–Kashgar route
- The Baoji–Pingliang–Liupanshan–Yinchuan route

Apart from the areas around the Silk Road, the south-west is another key region to benefit from the current government and private enterprise projects for tourism. Seven projects are currently under development. They include:

- The Shangri-la route covering Yunnan, Sichuan and Tibet
- The Chongqing–Sichuan–Guizhou triangle
- The south-eastern Guizhou–northern Guilin
- The Guilin–Yangshuo–Wuzhou–Zhaoqing–Guangzhou route
- The Lancang–Mekong River route

As tourism develops in the region, many job opportunities related to hotel management and catering are created. Moreover, better daily catering facilities will be required on long train journeys between the west and the east and will provide opportunities for chefs as well as serving staff. Besides, to maintain the sustainable development of the tourist industry in China, more experts in marketing, management and administration will be required, especially in large tourist agencies.

Shaanxi

Shaanxi benefits from its abundant reserves of natural resources including coal, natural gas and oil. It is an important energy production base and accounts for 20.4% of the total output. Shaanxi is also a base for heavy industry, which accounts for 60% of the area's total industrial output. Nonetheless, light industries such as food and beverages, electronics, telecommunications and pharmaceuticals have become more and more important in recent years. The central government has also developed economic and industrial zones that offer special tax incentives to encourage foreign investment. Famous companies with businesses in the region include Xian-Janssen Pharmaceutical Ltd, Xian Aircraft Co, Xian-Volvo Automobiles, Shaanxi Changling Refrigeration, Metro (from Germany) and Carrefour (from France).

Sichuan

Sichuan is considered to have the strongest economy in western China. It has the most established industrial sector in the western region, and is also the major agricultural production base for rice, wheat, rapeseed, citrus fruit, peaches, sugar cane and sweet potatoes. Moreover, it is famous for its natural scenery and is a popular destination for tourism. The major industries in Sichuan are machinery and metallurgy, pharmaceuticals, food and beverages, electronics and information technology and power generation. Of all the industries, electronics and telecommunications have recorded the quickest growth at over 27.8%.

The province has successfully attracted international investors such as Microsoft, Onsun, Sony, Cisco, Intel, IBM, Fuji, Siemens and Motorola to establish research and development centres. Intel Chipset Plant invested $375 million in the province at the end of 2003 and became the biggest investor in Chengdu.

Yunnan

Tourism is the most important industry in Yunnan, as it is one of the most popular tourist centres in western China. There are many hotels with a good reputation and the gross income of the tourist industry has reached 13% of the province's total GDP. Tobacco is an important crop in Yunnan, and recently accounted for 36.7% of the province's total output.

Tibet Autonomous Region

The strong cultural and religious atmosphere has made Tibet into a popular destination for domestic tourists in China, although restrictions are placed on foreign tourists. The total income from tourism reached ¥636.24 million in 2006, up 78.65% on the previous year. In order to strengthen tourism in Tibet, some new routes and destinations will be opened to tourists. These new destinations include six different parts of Tibet and five neighbouring provinces in Nepal. There will also be three overland circular routes, namely the Lhasa-Nyingchi-Shannon-Lhasa circuit, the Lhasa-Ngari-Nagqu-Lhasa circuit and the Lhasa-Nagqu-Qamdo-Nyingchi-Lhasa circuit. Apart from tourism, Tibetan medicine, biological products and health food, farm and animal produce processing and traditional handicrafts, mining and building materials are other important industries.

Xinjiang Uygur Autonomous Region

Similar to Shaanxi, Xinjiang is also rich in energy resources. It has the largest reserves of oil, natural gas and coal in the country. Its coal reserves reach 27 million tons (40% of the country's total) and its oil reserves reach 30 billion tons. Crude oil output reached 20.2 million tons in 2002 which was the third highest in the country. Tarim, Junggar, and Turpan-Hami basins are the major sources for oil and gas supplies.

Oil and petrochemicals, food and beverages, textiles, metallurgy, building materials, and electric power are the six pillar industries of Xinjiang, which account for 85.2% of the total output of the region with the petroleum industry alone accounting for 63.9%. Light industries, such as textiles and garments (especially wool and cashmere), leather processing, papermaking, sugar refining and carpet weaving, are getting more popular. As stated in the 10th five-year plan, the Xinjiang government will accelerate the development of information, biotechnology, energy and environmental protection industries in the coming years. Foreign investors are encouraged to participate in the development of agriculture, food processing, textiles, petrochemicals, mining, building materials and environmental protection.

Central China

Central China includes Shanxi, Henan, Hebei, Anhui, Hunan and Hubei Provinces. This region borders the Yellow and Yangtze Rivers, both famous for their rich cultural heritage. The central part, when compared to other regions of China, has less investment incentives and it is not usually the first choice for investors to start their business in.

This region actually has many social-economic advantages making it a desirable development area. The area is rich in natural resources, which is good for agriculture and industrial development. Moreover, being centrally located, it is well connected to all other areas giving it logistic advantages. The large population of the area also provides enough manpower and low wages. However, since workers, in general, receive very little or even no education, they do not have the knowledge and experience to qualify for important management roles. Consequently, expertise in management, finance and marketing will be major advantages when looking for jobs in this area. On the downside, foreigners living in these regions may have to expect to do without some of the comforts of home.

www.chinacareer.com offers a job-listing database in both Chinese and English.

North-east and the north

The north-east region comprises Heilongjiang, Jilin and Liaoning Provinces and the north region consists of the autonomous region of Inner Mongolia. In north-east China, half of the region is covered by forest and the timber industry is the backbone of the local economy. It is said that there are 'three treasures' in north-east China – milk, pilose deer antlers and ginseng – and they also play important roles in the local economies. There has been large-scale logging in this region and in order to avoid further excessive exploitation, the Chinese government plans to revitalise the region and build up an 'eco-economy'. The idea of 'eco-economy' is to satisfy current demand without threatening the supplies of future generations. It is no longer permitted to cut large amounts of timber and forestry and timber companies are asked to shift their sources of timber regularly to provide time for the trees to regenerate.

Apart from timber, the north-east region is also rich in coal, iron ore, boron, magnesite, diamonds and jade. Primary industry accounts for about 10% of the total income of the region. As with many other regions, secondary industry is the major source of income. Petrochemics, metallurgics, machinery and electronics are the chief industries in the region, particularly in Liaoning Province. Tobacco processing has recorded a rapid growth of over 15% in recent years. Other industries such as beverages, garments and textiles, furniture, smelting and pressing of ferrous metals, transport equipment, have also grown well in recent years.

Inner Mongolia

This autonomous region is located in the north of China and is reported to be among the poorest in the country. However, the secondary and tertiary industries in Inner Mongolia are actually growing. There was a 66% growth in foreign investment in 2001 and the annual GDP growth was about 10% in the last few years. Farm and dairy production and processing, electricity, animal husbandry, and metallurgy and chemicals are the major industries that support the local economy.

Municipalities

The four municipalities – Shanghai, Beijing, Tianjin and Chongqing – are directly under the control of the central government and enjoy privileges in economic development that may not be found in other provinces. The idea of setting up municipalities is to help these regions grow rapidly and hence stimulate the development of the surrounding areas and improve the economic development of the whole country.

Shanghai

Population: 18 million
Area: 6,340 sq km

Shanghai has probably been the fastest-growing region over the last decade, especially in commercial development. It remains the most entrepreneurial city in China and is full of start-up companies led by both Chinese and foreign residents. Foreign investment in Shanghai increased rapidly in the last decade as investors were enticed by tax incentives, especially in the New Pudong Area. Even though tertiary industry accounts for about half of the GDP, industry still plays an important part of the economic development. Major industries in Shanghai include automobiles, petrochemicals and fine chemicals, fine steel and iron, equipment complexes, biomedicine, and electronic information, in which automobiles, equipment complexes and electronic information are growing at rapid rates. They will dominate the GDP in a few years time.

In Shanghai, expertise in finance, management and marketing will give advantages when looking for jobs. Many companies also seek native English speakers to improve the English standards of staff. It is also not difficult to get a teaching job in the area.

Useful resources

Government Office of Shanghai Municipality: 021 6321 2810; www.shanghai.gov.cn
Pudong Human Resources: www.pdhr.com
Shanghai Human Resources Market: www.hr.net.cn
Shanghai Job Bank: www.shanghaijob.com
Talent Shanghai Co.Ltd: www.talentshanghai.com. This website specialises in the recruitment of middle to high-ranking managerial officers in fields of consumer goods, IT, telecommunications, high-technology, manufacturing, logistics, finance and insurance, construction and real estate.

Beijing

Population: 13.8 million
Area: 16,800 sq km

Being the capital of the country, Beijing has always been first choice for investment. Its tertiary sector is the largest in the whole country and accounts for more than 60% of the GDP. It is believed that the tertiary sector will further expand in the future as many international enterprises in finance, IT and telecommunication show their interest in expanding their businesses in Beijing – especially after it was named as the host for the Olympic Games 2008. In recent years, Beijing has undergone a series of reconstructions and developments in preparation for the 2008 event and the improvements, such as better transport, make it a more desirable place for doing business; a significant increase in foreign investment has been recorded.

Industry also contributes a great deal to the economy. Heavy industries dominate and account for over 70% in the secondary sector and major industries in Beijing include electronics and telecommunications equipment, chemicals, automobiles, machinery, metallurgy and food making. The future focus of development in this area is on hi-tech industries such as electronics, information technology, biological engineering, pharmaceuticals and new materials. Currently, Beijing's gross output value in the technical market makes up nearly 15% of the national total. Retailing is developing fast in Beijing with many international enterprises such as B&Q, Wal-Mart, Ikea, Metro and 7-Eleven setting up branches in the area. The B&Q in Beijing is even bigger than the largest branch in the UK, its home country.

The presence of heavy industry is one factor that explains why Beijing is one of the most polluted cities in China, with the appalling air quality being a perennial complaint among foreign residents.

Useful resources

Government Office of Beijing Municipality: 010 6519 2233; szfbgt@bjgov.gov.cn; www.beijing.gov.cn

Tianjin

Population: 10.4 million
Area: 11,300 sq km

Tianjin is the biggest mobile phone manufacturing base in China. It has been estimated that four in 10 cell phones used in the country are manufactured in Tianjin. This has been the result of investment by large international telecommunication enterprises such as Motorola, Samsung and Sanyo.

Apart from telecommunications, Tianjin is also a popular centre for industrial development. Its gross industrial output, of State-owned enterprises and private enterprises together, contributed ¥332 billion in 2002, the third largest among all provincial capitals and other cities, after Shanghai and Shenzhen. The four major industries include electronics, automobiles, metallurgy and petrochemicals.

Its tertiary sector is expanding rapidly as well. Transportation and storage, trades and catering services, banking and insurance, and real estate are the four fastest growing service industries. Exports from Tianjin were declining over the last few years, which is unusual in China. However, imports grew at a rate of 37% in the same period. In the first few years of the millenium, imports from Korea, Taiwan, Germany and France have had the fastest growth.

Useful resources

Government Office of Tianjin Municipality: 022 2330 5555; webmaster@tianjin.gov.cn; www.tianjin.gov.cn

Chongqing

Population: 32.5 million
Area: 82,400 sq km

Chongqing is the youngest but also the largest of the four municipalities. It is one of the most important industrial bases in China, especially in the automobile industry. Other major industries include iron and steel, military production, transport equipment, metallurgical products and chemicals, of which transport equipment accounts for more than 37% of the total industrial output. Many international companies have set up their businesses in Chongqing in recent years. Big names include Nokia, Ericsson, American Standard, Honda, Suzuki, Isuzu, Yamaha, Mobil, Hutchison Whampao and Samsung. Unlike the other three municipalities, where the tertiary sector is the main focus for development, the government plans to further boost Chongqing's secondary development as well as encouraging steady growth in the tertiary sector. The government aims to attract more foreign investment in automobiles, hydropower stations and construction and real estate in the next few years.

www.china.org.cn includes a brief introduction to each province, autonomous region and municipality (go to 'Province Wide').

Useful resources

Government Office of Chongqing Municipality: 023 6385 4444; cqgov@cq.gov.cn; www.cq.gov.cn

- **Chinese place-names** All Chinese place-names have a meaning which is obvious in modern Chinese. Hence, Beijing means 'northern capital', Nanjing means 'southern capital', Henan means 'south of the Yellow River', Hebei means 'north of the Yellow River', Yunnan means 'south of the clouds' etc. They are mostly pretty common words so as you learn some Chinese you should come across them in other contexts.

STARTING A BUSINESS

There are good reasons why many foreign investors are keen to start a business in China. Some business experts believe that by as early as 2030, the economy of this country of 1.3 billion people will be equal to that of the USA. While the world growth rate was only 3% in 2006, and many countries experienced an economic downturn, there was over 10% growth in China. It is safe to say that China is, at the moment, the fastest-growing economy in the world and the rapid increase in foreign investment contributes to this phenomenal growth rate.

Apart from the huge market, cheap labour and raw materials are other reasons for foreign investment in China. The government is also actively attracting more foreign investors to start their business in China by offering various investment incentives.

The tax arrangements are especially attractive for investors who want to start businesses in the western and central regions.

There is no export tariff on most commodities. The average import tariff was lowered to 9.9% in 2005. As a member of the World Trade Organisation, China also provides preferential tariffs or quota removals to other WTO members.

- The tax arrangements are especially attractive for investors who want to start businesses in the western and central regions.

Investment incentives

The Chinese market was opened to foreign investment in the late 1970s and since then, it has grown steadily. In the last decade, the government has been actively seeking foreign investment by developing many new policies, and this is a major reason for the recent phenomenal growth in the sector.

Tax reduction used to be granted to foreign-invested enterprises (joint ventures) and foreign enterprises (wholly foreign-owned enterprises) if they start their businesses with establishments or venues in a special economic zone such as Shenzhen, Zhuhai, Shantou, Xiamen and Hainan. The corporate income tax in the special economic zones was 15% rather than 33% for Chinese companies, but from the beginning of 2008 there was be a new blanket 25% rate for all firms. There will be transitional tax rates given to those companies who have operated in China under the preferential tax rate in the past. However, within five years the government will force all companies to pay the same standard 25% rate.

In order to attract enterprises for developing long-term projects in China, some enterprises are granted exemption from income tax for the first few profit-making years. Foreign-invested enterprises with an operation in production for over 10 years are exempt from corporate income tax in the first two profit-making years. Sino-foreign joint ventures engaged in port and wharf construction and with an operation period of over 15 years can apply for corporate income tax exemption in the first five profit-making years as well. They are also granted a 50% reduction of tax in the following five years. The same is offered to infrastructure projects which are to be carried out for 15 or more years and are related to airports, ports, wharfs, railways, highways, power stations, coal mines, water conservancy facilities and agricultural development in Hainan Special Economic Zone and also Pudong New Area.

Owners of foreign-invested enterprises are eligible for a 40% tax refund if they re-invest the profit they obtained in the same enterprises or establish other enterprises locally. If the foreign investor re-invests profits directly in establishing or expanding an export-oriented or hi-tech enterprise in China, they can even get a 100% refund for the amount of tax levied on the re-invested amount.

The development of central and western regions is one of the highest priorities of the Chinese government. Foreign-invested enterprises that develop their businesses in these regions can enjoy tax exemption for two years and a 50% tax reduction in the following three years. They are also offered a reduced tax rate of 15% for another three years after the above tax reduction expires. Hi-tech or export-oriented enterprises are offered a 50% reduction in corporate income tax for three years, if exports account for 70% or more of their annual output value.

Do not be disappointed if your enterprise does not fit into any of the above categories. The government updates these investment incentives from time to time.

For more information, the Hong Kong Trade and Development Council has a very good webpage in English: www.tdctrade.com/chinaguide

How to start a new business in China

Preparation

As always when investing in another country, you need to do some research before you start. In particular, you should find out about the laws and regulations concerning operating a business in China. Books and websites about doing business in China will give a rough idea about the business environment and the prospects for different businesses. Although costly, contacting consultant companies may save you time in the end.

Suffice to say that the Chinese business environment is nowhere near as transparent as it professes to be. Undoubtedly, there is great opportunity here, but there's also great risk, particularly for those who do not understand the country or its idiosyncratic way of doing things. China's previously planned economy is still in the process of casting off the shackles of socialism and, in many situations, politicians still have the power to make or break a company. Developing connections with local officials remains an essential part of doing any kind of business in China.

Business regulations, and also investment incentives offered by the government, differ across regions and this may affect where you choose to set up your business. Sometimes substantial amounts can be saved with tax concessions. China has also delineated some development zones; companies are usually offered benefits if they establish their businesses in these areas.

Many people find it easier to start a joint venture with a local partner. If there is someone you know and trust, it may well save you a lot of time and heartache in the long run. However, joint ventures come with their own difficulties and will require the foreign partner to develop an understanding of the sometimes-unfathomable Chinese mindset.

Useful resources

China-Britain Business Council, UK: 020 7828 5176; bernadette.rosario@cbbc.org; www.cbbc.org

China Council for the Promotion of International Trade (CCPIT): 010 6802 0229; info@ccpit.org; www.ccpit.org

China Online Inc, USA: 312 664 8880; cxu@chinaonline.com; www.chinaonline.com

Hong Kong Trade Development Council: (852) 2584 4333; hktdc@tdc.org.hk; www.tdctrade.com

Ministry of Commerce of the People's Republic of China (MOFCOM): 010 6512 1919; http://english.mofcom.gov.cn

Ministry of Foreign Trade and Economic Cooperation (MOFTEC): 010 6519 8114; moftec@moftec.gov.cn; http://english.mofcom.gov.cn

US Commercial Service: 010 8529 6655; beijing.office.box@mail.doc.gov; www.buyusa.gov/china/en

Business consultants

Acorn Greater China Market Research Co Ltd, Shanghai: 021 5407 1566; china@acornasia.com; www.acornasia.com

BR Cohen & Associates, USA: 877 810 1574; info@brcohen.com; www.brcohen.com

China Strategy, Shanghai: 021 6279 7330; Parker@chinastrategic.com; www.chinastrategic.com

East Asia Business, UK: 020 8361 5152; info@east-asia-business.com; www.east-asia-business.com

Synovate: *(USA)* 703 790 9099 extension 104; dc.us@synovate.com; *(UK)* 020 7017 2400; uk@synovate.com; www.synovate.com

Useful websites

China Update: www.chinaupdate.net

China Expat: www.chinaexpat.com

The Internationalist: www.internationalist.com

US Commercial Service: tic@ita.doc.gov; www.export.gov

Accountants

Apart from auditing, many accounting companies also provide business advice and help their clients with business research. Some big accounting companies have regular publications on various issues concerning doing business in China. Accounting firms are familiar with the laws and regulations, which can be very helpful if you are new to the Chinese environment. They can also provide you with the most up-to-date information and professional opinions, which are useful for reducing the risks in this competitive market.

Useful resources

Contact the individual companies for branch information.

Deloitte Touche Tohmatsu, Beijing : 010 6528 1599; www.deloitte.com
Dezan Shira & Associates Ltd, Beijing: 010 8519 2001; chris@dezshire.com
Ernst & Young, Beijing: 010 6524 6688; www.ey.com
KPMG, Beijing: 010 8518 5000; jane.yang@kpmg.com.cn; www.kpmg.com
PricewaterhouseCoopers, Beijing: 010 6561 2233; www.pwchk.com

Choosing an area

Your choice of location will depend on what kind of business you are starting, who your target customers are and your budget. Most of the financial businesses are based in Shanghai, Beijing or Guangdong Province. Many industrial enterprises have set up in interior areas such as Sichuan or Shaanxi Provinces, where land and labour are cheaper than in the coastal cities. The government had attracted foreign investment by offering a 15% corporate tax rate for setting up a company in a special economic zone, a high-technology development zone or the Pudong New Area in Shanghai. However, from 1 January 2008, all companies now pay a standard 25% tax on income. Enterprises are eligible for a tax refund if they re-invest their profits in China. In addition, the government and provinces usually provide more help in the development zones. Some other provinces are also keen to attract particular groups of investors.

Currently, the government is putting a lot of effort into developing the western and central areas of the country. It is improving the transport system, electricity supply etc, to make these areas more accessible and suitable for business. Many investment incentives are available for foreign investment in regions like Gansu, Sichuan, Yunnan, Guizhou, Shanxi, Ningxia, Qinghai, etc. The Hong Kong Trade and Development Council has a complete illustration of the development of the western and central regions, which includes the most updated preferential policies launched by the government. Go to www.tdctrade.com

- **Factors to consider** Depending on the type of business, other factors to consider when choosing your area include the buying power of the local market, which can vary a lot across regions. Even if you are not aiming to sell products to the local market, the standard of living of a region also predicts the quality of staff you can hire locally and their salaries. In the inner parts of China, it is more difficult to find local employees who can speak fluent English or who are university graduates, but the labour costs will be much lower compared to coastal cities. Transport and the energy supply are also important considerations, especially for factories.

- The Hong Kong Trade and Development Council has a complete illustration of the development of the western and central regions, which includes the most updated preferential policies launched by the government. Go to www.tdctrade.com

A useful journal is published by the China-Britain Business Council: *China-Britain Business Review*. It can be found at www.CBBC.org

Useful resources

Chinese government website: www.chinainvest.gov.cn. Provides details about investment news and recent projects.
Hong Kong Trade and Industry Department: www.tid.gov.hk

Business structures

Foreign investors starting a business in China can either start an enterprise independently or form a joint venture with a Chinese partner.

■ Wholly foreign-owned enterprises (WFOE)

Wholly foreign-owned enterprises are limited liability companies solely owned by foreign investors. They have to be primarily engaged in the export business, and China should not be their primary market. If you intend to sell your products to the local market, the government will generally recommend that you start a joint venture with a local partner instead. According to Chinese law, WFOEs are obliged to employ some local labour and they may also have to recruit staff through government employment agencies. Even though it is not clearly stated what the appropriate ratio of capital contribution for machinery to cash investment should be, business consultancies usually suggest the cash investment should constitute 30% or more of the total investment.

WFOEs are subject to a lesser degree of interference from the government compared to joint ventures. However, they are also excluded from some business concessions that joint ventures enjoy. Before starting a WFOE, you will need to consult agencies that are familiar with the business environment and also check the regulations.

■ Joint ventures

A joint venture refers to a business formed by two or more parties who are from different regions or countries. At least one party must be local to the area of business. The parties have to come up with an agreement on the details, such as how to run the business, share of responsibilities, profits and capital contributions, etc. The major advantage of forming a joint venture is that you will share costs, risks and responsibilities. It is also the easiest and officially recommended way to access the Chinese market, since there is a local party who is familiar with the market and the regulations.

There are two types of joint venture in mainland China:

- *Equity joint venture*
- *Contractual joint venture*

In a contractual joint venture, there is no restriction on how much the foreign investor has to contribute. But in an equity joint venture, the foreign investor has to contribute at least 25% of the total capital. Investors can contribute to the enterprise in cash, buildings, equipment, materials, intellectual property rights and land use rights. For contractual joint ventures, labour, resources and services are also accepted forms of contribution.

One other distinctive difference between the two forms of joint ventures is whether investors can withdraw registered capital or not. Investors in equity joint ventures are restricted from withdrawing the registered capital during the term of the contract but those of contractual joint ventures are not prohibited from doing so. Contractual joint ventures also enjoy greater flexibility in management but they are required to have a trade union. Profit and risk sharing in equity joint ventures are proportionate to the capital contributions of the parties while they are decided by contractual terms in contractual joint ventures. Long-term businesses typically take the form of equity joint ventures, whereas contractual joint ventures are more common in small and medium enterprises. For more information on joint ventures see www.cbbc.org

Raising finance

Personal savings and contributions from business partners should probably be your primary financial sources, but it is also common for investors to seek help from banks. If possible, you should try the banks in your own country first. Since you have transaction records there, it is easier for the bank to assess your ability to pay back the loan. Many Chinese banks do lend money to foreign investors, and interestingly it is sometimes easier for a foreigner than for a local investor to borrow money from them. The terms and interest rates vary from bank to bank so you should contact different banks before making a decision. Some banks only provide loans to established enterprises and not to individuals who are new to the market. Since a few months' local transaction records would be necessary, this means it would not be very easy to borrow money after you enter the country. In addition to that, you have to present documents such as business licences, tax registration certificates and maybe financial statements as well. You may also consider banks in Hong Kong when you look for loans, as many provide loans for investors to start businesses in China.

- **Business plans** You have to prepare a business plan to outline the details of the business you want to start and how are you going to run the business. In the business plan, you should include the market research you have done and your vision for the development of the business. A detailed financial plan is also a very important part of your business plan. You should set out the start-up cost, daily running cost, salaries, cash flow plan, expected income and when the expected profit can be generated. It would be good to have your CV and that of your business partners in your business plan as well. Before you present your business plan you should also be familiar with the laws and regulations of running a business in China.

There are many government investment incentives available for foreign investment but most of the mare tax concessions rather than cash loans. However, do familiarise yourself with these as it will help you to estimate the size of loan you need.

Useful resources

Agricultural Bank of China: ebmaster@abchina.com
Bank of China: 010 6659 6688; www.bank-of-china.com
The Bank of East Asia Ltd, Hong Kong: 2842 3200; www.hkbea.com
China Construction Bank, Beijing: 010 6360 3660; www.ccbhk.com
China Merchants Bank: 0755 8319 8888
China Everbright Bank: 010 6856 0469
China Construction Bank: www.ccb.cn
Citibank, Hong Kong: 2868 8888: www.citibank.com.hk
Hang Seng Bank Ltd, Hong Kong: 2198 1111; www.hangseng.com
The Hongkong and Shanghai Banking Corporation Ltd, Hong Kong: 2822 1111; www.hsbc.com.hk
Hua Xia Bank: 010 6615 1199; webmaster@hxb.cc
Industrial and Commercial Bank of China: webmaster@icbc.com.cn; www.icbc.com.cn; *(USA)* 212 838 7799; icbcusa@yahoo.com; *(UK)* 020 7397 8888
Standard Chartered Bank, Hong Kong: 2820 3333; www.standardchartered.com.hk

Registering your business

Unfortunately setting up a business in mainland China can be complicated. An application has to go through several different departments at different levels for approval. It usually takes months to get all the necessary approvals.

A joint venture with a Chinese partner

This might be one way to speed up the process. In this case, the Chinese party (ie your partner) will be responsible for most of the application procedures.

For a new application, the Chinese party has to submit the project proposal to the local development planning commission or economic and trade commission. The business partners then work together to compile a feasibility study report to the commissions stated above for approval after the project proposal is approved. The parties can only sign the contract, the articles of association and other relevant legal documents after the feasibility study is approved. The Chinese party should then submit the documents to the local foreign trade and economic cooperation department where the joint venture is located for examination and approval. After all these are approved, the Chinese party is responsible for applying for an approval certificate from the provincial or municipal foreign trade and economic cooperation department. The department will then issue an approval certificate and you then apply within 30 days for a business licence for the joint venture from the provincial or municipal administration for industry and commerce.

After registration, the joint venture still has to go through some other procedures. These include applying for an official seal and enterprise code, opening a bank account, and registering for tax payment and customs declaration with the local public security. Technical supervision, taxation, customs, finance, foreign exchange administration, banking, insurance and commodity inspection departments will also need to be approached.

On a personal and cultural level you should bear in mind the advice given in the *Working culture and etiquette* section about doing business with Chinese people. This time you will both be on the same side, more or less, rather than negotiating with each other. However there will still be ample room for misunderstandings unless you are careful.

See www.cbbc.org for more useful information on joint ventures.

Foreign enterprises

To set up a foreign enterprise, a foreign investor has to first submit a preliminary application, by submitting a report to the foreign and economic cooperation department at county level or above at the place where the proposed enterprise is located. The report should include details of business objectives, business scope, scale of operation and products to be produced. In addition, it should include details of technology and equipment to be used, land area required, conditions and quantities of water, electricity, gas and other forms of energy resources required, and requirements for public facilities.

After receiving a written reply from the relevant government authorities, the investor should then hand in a formal application along with all the required documents to the local foreign trade and economic cooperation department at county, municipal or provincial level. The investor has to apply for an approval certificate to the foreign trade and economic cooperation department after getting the approval for the formal application. Finally, you must apply for a business licence from the provincial or municipal administration for industry and commerce within 30 days of the collection of the approval certificate. Similarly with a joint venture, after registration a foreign enterprise must go through other procedures such as applying for an official seal and enterprise code, before running the business.

Foreign-invested enterprises are also required to make financial registration with the financial authority within 30 days of submitting the applications for business registrations.

Useful resources

Hong Kong Trade and Development Council, Hong Kong: 1830 668; hktdc@tdc.org.hk; www.tdctrade.com

Ministry of Commerce of the People's Republic of China (MOFCOM): 010 6512 1919; http://english.mofcom.gov.cn

Ministry of Finance (MOF): 010 6855 1114; webmaster@mof.gov.cn; www.mof.gov.cn

Ministry of Foreign Trade and Economic Cooperation (MOFTEC): 010 6519 8114; moftec@moftec.gov.cn; http://english.mofcom.gov.cn

UK Chinese Embassy: 020 7723 8923; press@chinese-embassy.org.uk; www.chinese-embassy.org.uk

US Chinese Embassy: 202 625 3350; chinaembassy-us@fmprc.gov.cn; www.china-embassy.org

Trademark registration

There are several departments that are responsible for handling trademarks, and there may be confusion over their responsibilities. All the departments relating to trademarks are under the supervision of the State Administration for Industry and Commerce (SAIC). The departments are:

- Trademark Office: the government authority for the registration of trademarks in China.
- Trademark Management Office: the administrative unit for managing all trademark-related matters.
- Trademark Affairs Offices: trademark agents set up by the state, located in major cities.
- The Trademark Review and Adjudication Board: responsible for handling disputes relating to trademarks.
- Enterprises should make their applications to the Trademark Office for the registration of trademarks. Foreign-invested enterprises may apply directly to the Trademark Office or through trademark agents. However, foreign enterprises have to appoint trademark agents to do so. Note that an application for trademark registration and the supporting documents should be in Chinese; if any of the documents is in a foreign language you should also provide a translated version. If you have registered your trademark in another country within the previous three months, you will be given priority for your registration.
- Under the regulations of SAIC, it is only possible for someone to post an objection to the use of a trademark within the first three months from the date of publication. If this happens, the Trademark Office will make a decision

based on the reasons for objection. If there is no opposition or the opposition is not justified, a trademark will be granted a formal approval, and a certificate of registration will then be issued. A registered trademark is valid for 10 years and it will be granted validity for another 10 years each time it is renewed.

Useful resources

State Administration for Industry and Commerce (SAIC):
010 6803 2233; www.saic.gov.cn
State Intellectual Property Office of PRC: www.cpo.cn.net
Trademark Office (CTMO): 010 6802 7820; www.ctmo.gov.cn

Import/export permission

Enterprises or individuals need to obtain permission for the right to import or export in advance if they want to engage in the import/export business. Almost all commodities are open to import and export rights, except 16 crucial ones that are currently under state monopoly. Most commodities are subject to import tariffs. The government lowered the average import tariff to 9.9% at the beginning of 2005. Tariffs for raw materials and industrial supplies are less than 20% in most cases. Tariffs for consumer goods range from 20% to 50%, except for a few selected luxury items like pearls and tobacco, which will be taxed at 100% or more. All commodities are also subjected to Value-Added Tax (VAT), which is calculated on top of the import tariffs. The average VAT rate is 17% at the moment with a reduced rate of 13% for books and some types of oils. Small businesses pay 6%. There is no export tariff on most commodities. However, licences may be required for some of them. You should note that some countries might impose 'safeguard' tariffs on Chinese exports, which is permitted under the terms of China's accession to the WTO and is valid until 2014.

Useful resources

General Administration of Customs of the PRC: 010 6519 4114;
http://www.customs.gov.cn
Ministry of Commerce of the People's Republic of China (MOFCOM):
010 6512 1919; http://english.mofcom.gov.cn
State Import and Export Commodities Inspection Bureau: 010 6599 4600
State Intellectual Property Office of PRC: www.sipo.gov.cn

Ideas for a new business

Import/export

Import and export businesses have been among the most important industries in China, and are probably the most common business for foreign investors. If you check the place of manufacture of everyday products, you will find that many of the things you bought in the USA or Europe are made in China. These include both semi-finished products and completed products. The USA is one of many countries that import a great deal of Chinese products. China's trade surplus with America was $114.7 billion in 2005. Raw materials and labour in China are cheap, and this is one of the reasons the export business flourishes. In addition, there is no export tariff on most of the goods produced. After entering the World Trade Organisation in 2001, China has been on tariff agreements with other members of the WTO and thus import tariffs are reducing. At the same time, many of the import and export quotas have been removed. This makes it cheaper to import goods from other WTO countries to China and vice-versa.

Cars

China's has been the fastest-expanding automotive market in the world in the last few years. It is now the second largest vehicle market in the world, second only to the USA. The 70% increase in production of vehicles in 2003 is predicted to increase to six million vehicles by 2010. Since the technology in car making has been improving, many of the American and European automotive manufacturers have set up joint ventures with Chinese partners to produce cars in China. The low production cost allows the vehicles to be sold at a lower price and this stimulates sales in the western markets as well as in the local market. However, experts are warning of a danger of overproduction.

Home improvement stores

The concept of 'home' is an important one for the Chinese, and many of them are keen to have their own property. According to government statistics, the home ownership rate is increasing throughout the entire country. In some big cities, the increase in the home ownership rate is up 75%. Moreover, many Hong Kong people are going to the mainland to buy houses due to the difference in land prices. Several years ago, the home of even a relatively middle-class family would only have consisted of whitewashed walls, basic furniture and a simple gas burner in the kitchen. Now, people are spending large amounts of money on fitted kitchens, matching furniture and elaborate bathrooms. Electric goods are cheap and readily available, so enormous televisions and hi-tech DVD players are the features of many living rooms in affluent areas. Many new home owners are willing to spend money on kitting out their home with stylish and modern decor. Western home designs and furniture are popular. B&Q and Ikea are two successful examples of home improvement stores.

Travel agencies

The number of Chinese tourists travelling outside Asia has been increasing. Most of them are fairly well-off and do not mind spending money abroad. Some young people enjoy travelling by themselves but most people prefer to join guided tours and travel packages. There may be an opportunity to set up an agency that organises trips to Europe or the USA. Local tours in China are mainly organised by Chinese travel agents, but tours conducted in English should be able to attract foreign visitors.

English-learning centres

Since the Chinese written language is not based on an alphabet, and spoken Chinese and English are so different, it is not surprising that many Chinese people have a hard time learning English. As international business becomes more and more important, learning English is high up on many job seekers' priority lists. Many find spoken English is particularly difficult to learn from books or local Chinese teachers. There are many native English speakers who are willing to go to China for a gap year, so setting up a business to organise teaching could be very successful. The government also gives great support to importing foreign English teachers; it is easy to get work permits for your teachers.

Restaurants and pubs

Most of the many good restaurants in China serve Chinese cuisine. As the number of foreign visitors keeps rising and Chinese citizens increasingly travel abroad, the demand for different kinds of restaurants is likely to increase. In cities, young locals are keen to try anything new, so you should not worry too much about being authentic. To avoid head-on price competition with small family run restaurants, you should probably target the high-income groups and business visitors looking for a posh night out. Fast food restaurants might be an alternative. Although the traditional food culture is strong in China, hostility towards western fast food outlets is unheard of. Young people see fast food as an interesting and cheap alternative to traditional meals. Similarly, many youngsters in big cities like Shanghai and Beijing are fascinated by the idea of western pubs and clubs.

Setting up a subsidiary

There can be very few major foreign companies who have not already set up a subsidiary in China or are considering doing so. The major car manufacturing companies are among the most obvious, as well as some well-known cafeterias and telephone companies. Foreigners from whatever country are bound by the same regulations, have to face the same approval procedures, and are treated in the same way.

As there are a number of legal and business restrictions on foreign companies wanting to conduct business in China, setting up a subsidiary is a good idea for those who have long-term business interests in China. Establishing a subsidiary works well for a company that wants to make direct investment in China, hire local staff, conduct research and development and market products and services directly to China. It also helps to overcome some of the restrictions faced by foreign companies.

A subsidiary – often referred to as a foreign-invested enterprise (FIE) – has to have a minimum of 25% of equity shares held by foreigners. But if all the shareholders are Chinese-registered companies or Chinese citizens then the company should be a domestic company.

When it comes to subsidiary approval, most can be approved and registered at the provincial or city level, quicker than by the central approval authority, sometimes even within a month. Since China has been a member of the WTO it has become more flexible about the number of industries that can have foreign investment.

FACT
Since China has been a member of the WTO it has become more flexible about the number of industries that can have foreign investment.

The company then has to register with the State Administration for Industry and Commerce or the equivalent at the city or provincial level. The subsidiary will then be issued with its business licence from which time it will be considered legally established and incorporated. You must pay the registration fee and the announcement fee, which are collected by the registration authority and based on the amount of capital registered in the company. These costs normally amount to ¥7,001–¥21,033 (£514–£1,543 $1,000–$3,000). The biggest cost therefore will be the 'registered capital'.

By Chinese law shareholders have to put real money into the enterprise. All shareholders of the subsidiary must subscribe the registered capital to the company according to their respective ownership percentage. This has to be paid in full within a specified time period of the setting up of the subsidiary. The first contribution to the registered capital is to be no less than 15% of the registered capital to be made within 90 days of the business licence being issued. However, different local governments have different policies on the minimum registered capital so it is necessary to check in the area where you plan to set up the subsidiary.

An important question is of course where to locate the subsidiary? There are now hi-tech parks and industrial parks in many cities and regions of China. There may be tax benefits too. The major taxes are regulated at the national level but there are also some local taxes and charges. When choosing a location it is important to bear in mind the following:

- The presence of a qualified pool of employees, so possibly near a university
- '*Guanxi*', which in this case refers to the potential for developing a good relationship with local government officials and local enterprises.
- Local support for your subsidiary
- The transport system
- The general infrastructure

The subsidiary's highest authority is its board of directors who are appointed by the shareholders. Arrangements about controlling the subsidiary can also be made between it and the parent company. In some cases the parent company owns the critical intellectual property and will license it to the subsidiary. Another common arrangement is that the subsidiary's products can only be marketed, distributed and sold through the parent company.

Whereas a domestic company can carry out any legal business, a foreign invested subsidiary receives a licence only for a specific business.

It should also be remembered that a foreign invested subsidiary's earnings in foreign exchange, apart from a maximum amount that it is permitted to keep in its bank account, have to be converted into renminbi. This is because China does not allow foreign currency to circulate freely within its territory.

There are some authorised agencies that are able to help foreigners to get through the whole incorporation process smoothly, but it is not always necessary to resort to their help, as many local governments are very keen to attract foreign investment.

With a good understanding of the rules and regulations and the constraints on doing business in China it is possible to do well.

For more detailed information about how to go about opening a subsidiary see www.fenwick.com/docstore/publication. This company has published a guide to opening a subsidiary in China.

RUNNING A BUSINESS

Employing staff

Unlike many other countries, finding employees through government employment agencies is the main way of employing staff in mainland China. These employment agencies are usually called 'employment centres' or 'human resources markets', and they are under the control of labour and social security departments, as well as personnel departments. Apart from the recruitment of staff, employment agencies also provide services like file management and handle matters related to social insurance. In fact, in some situations, you may not be allowed to employ staff on your own, for example, when employing a person who currently works for a state-owned enterprise (SOE). In this case, you will need an employment agency to negotiate with the SOE to get the employee released, and also to recover the employee's personnel file. If you want to post an advertisement in the mass media (newspapers, magazines, television or radio), you must apply for prior approval from the local labour and social security department. 'Head-hunters' or recruitment consultants are becoming increasingly popular, especially amongst foreign enterprises and foreign-invested enterprises.

Before engaging an employment agency, you should ask them for proof of legal status, ie the approval certificate issued by the labour department. You should have a clear idea about the scope of services, charges, names and telephone numbers of its supervisory authorities before entering into any commitment. Employment agencies, at the same time, will ask you for documents about your enterprise. You should present a letter of introduction, a copy of the business licence and other proof of registration as a legal entity. You should also provide an identification document for the person who is in charge of the recruitment process. You should prepare a profile for recruitment requirements and the employment agency will find the right person for you according to that profile. In the profile, you should include: an introduction to the enterprise; the number of staff to be recruited; the nature of the job, terms of employment and the remuneration of each position; fringe benefits; and labour protection.

Check the validity of the documents provided before signing a contract with any proposed employees. The Labour Law requires that there is a contract between an employer and an employee. You should refer to the Labour Handbook for making

TIP

- If you want to post an advertisement in the mass media (newspapers, magazines, television or radio), you must apply for prior approval from the local labour and social security department.

Early-morning exercises - a great way to get employees ready for the day!

mandatory terms and conditions to be included in a contract. After being signed, the contract has to be sent to the labour administrative department for examination for authentication within 30 days of the employee starting work. You should consider appointing a service agency specialising in human resources employment to manage personal files of your Chinese staff. These service agencies provide services including verification of the identity of staff, salary track record and political reports. They also provide services like preparing assessments of technical qualifications, contract authentication and matters related to social insurance.

Employers are required to contribute to social insurance for their employees. There are five types of social insurance including provident funds (pension), medical, unemployment, work-related injury and child-bearing insurances. Both employers and employees have to contribute to the first three, and the last two are the sole responsibility of employers. The rate of contribution varies with the type of risk and type of injury. Refer to the *Aspects of employment* section earlier in this chapter for more information on social insurance.

Important points to bear in mind when recruiting staff:

- Do not rely too much on 'personal recommendations' as the recommender may favour his or her relatives or close friends instead of a really suitable candidate.
- Avoid paying wages through employment agencies or middlemen. There have been complaints that employees have not actually received wages from such agencies.
- Try to provide good fringe benefits to attract the best candidates.
- Consider providing training (for instance, language skills) for your staff.
- Note that discrimination against age or gender is illegal.
- Consider employing a reliable personal assistant to deal with recruitment, especially if you do not speak Chinese.

Useful resources

Centre for International Exchanges: 010 8421 6690; yujingjing@mail.molss.gov.cn
China Employment Training Technical Instruction Center: 010 8463 1199 master@osta.org.cn; www.osta.org.cn
Ministry of Labour and Social Securities: 010 8420 1114; webmaster@mail.molss.gov.cn; www.molss.gov.cn

Taxation

Foreign-invested enterprises and foreign enterprises are liable for the following taxes:

Foreign-invested enterprise and foreign-enterprise income tax

Foreign enterprises used to receive preferential tax treatment in China but recent reforms unify the income tax of domestic and foreign enterprises. As from 1 January 2008, both domestic and foreign-funded enterprises are subject to a 25% statutory rate.

There are two tax rates for foreign-enterprise income tax, depending on whether an enterprise has establishments or venues within mainland China. Foreign enterprises with establishments in China are subject to the same tax system as a foreign-invested enterprise. They are liable for 25% corporation tax, which is calculated on the income derived both inside and outside China. For foreign enterprises with no establishments in China, or no proof that the income generated is effectively connected with the establishments, the tax rate is 20% and it is only levied on income derived inside China.

For both foreign-invested enterprises and foreign enterprises, the income tax is levied on an annual basis and paid in advance in quarterly instalments. The owners have to file an annual tax return along with final account statements within four months of the end of a tax year and the tax should be paid within five months, from the end of the tax year. Profit tax in Macau is currently 2%–15%, depending on the level of net income.

FACT

- Profit tax in Macau is currently 2%–15%, depending on the level of net income.

Value Added Tax (VAT)

All enterprises and individuals engaged in the sale or import of goods or the provision of processing, repair or maintenance services in China have to pay VAT. Taxpayers are divided into two groups: small-scale taxpayers and general taxpayers. Enterprises or individuals whose taxable value of sales is below ¥1 million (£66,197/$130,787) for production of goods or services and ¥1.8 million for those engaged in wholesaling or retailing are classified as small-scale taxpayers. General taxpayers are those who do not fall into the category of small-scale taxpayer. There is no VAT on exported goods.

The following are taxed at the rate of 13%:

- Grains
- Edible vegetable oil
- Drinking water
- Heating
- Air-conditioning
- Hot water
- Coal gas
- Liquefied petroleum gas
- Natural gas
- Methane
- Coal products for domestic use
- Books
- Newspapers and magazines
- Feedstuffs
- Chemical fertilisers
- Pesticides
- Agricultural machinery
- Agricultural plastic sheeting
- Other commodities as specified by the state

Other than these commodities, the VAT on imports is 17%.

Customs duties

There are two tariff rates for customs duties in China: the general tariff rate and the preferential tariff rate. Some countries and regions have signed a reciprocal tariff agreement with China. Goods from these countries and regions are taxed at the preferential tariff, which is lower. Goods from other countries and regions will be taxed at the general tariff rate instead. The average import tariff rate is 9.9% while the export tariff rates are between 20% and 50%.

Consumption tax

Consumption tax applies to 11 categories of goods, including cigarettes, alcoholic drinks and alcohol, cosmetics, skin-care and hair-care products, fine jewellery and precious stones, firecrackers and fireworks, gasoline, diesel oil, motor vehicle tyres, motorcycles, and small motor cars. If your enterprise engages in the production, subcontracted processing or importation of any of the above goods, it is subject to consumption tax. Consumption tax is levied on top of VAT and the tax rates vary from 3% to 45%. With the exception of yellow spirits, beer, gasoline and diesel oil, which are taxed by volume, other goods are taxed by value at the production stage.

Useful resources

State Administration of Taxation: 010 6513 3585; dongcheng@bjsat.gov.cn; www.bjsat.gov.cn

Macau Trade and Investment Promotion Institute: 2871 0300; ipim@ipim.gov.mo; www.ipim.gov.mo

RETIREMENT IN CHINA

Few readers of this book are likely to be interested in retiring in China, but a brief note on the subject may be of interest. In China, the retirement age is 60 for men and 55 for women. However, non-professional female workers are often asked to retire when they reach 50. Since many female workers, especially professionals, prefer to work beyond 55, the government may allow them to extend their retirement age to 60 if they are in good health. Pension schemes were not introduced before the mid-1990s. Employees who started working before the launch of the pension scheme have to contribute to the provident fund for 10 years to enjoy full benefits. Those who started working after the launch of the scheme are required to contribute to the fund for at least 15 years to enjoy the same benefits. Employers are also required to contribute to the fund but their contributions will go to the central government provident fund rather than an employee's individual account.

Time Off

PUBLIC HOLIDAYS

1 January	*New Year's Day*
January/February	*Chinese New Year – week-long holiday**
8 March	*International Women's Day (half day off for women)*
1–7 May	*One week's holiday for International Labour Day**
1 June	*International Children's Day (half day off for those aged 13 or under)*
1 July	*Birthday of the Chinese Communist Party*
1 August	*Anniversary of the founding of the PLA (People's Liberation Army, for all armed forces personnel)*
1–7 October	*Week's holiday for National Day**

Some public holidays are based on the Chinese lunar calendar and therefore do not have a simple fixed date in the western calendar, such as the Chinese New Year in late January/February, a week-long holiday.

*China's three week-long holidays – at New Year (January/February), Labour Day (May) and National Day (October) – are dubbed 'Golden Weeks'. The intention is to give every worker seven consecutive days off work (thus allowing migrant workers time to return home). However, only three of these seven days are genuine holidays. The remaining four days are comprised of the surrounding weekends. Staff will always be required to work the weekend that precedes or follows the 'Golden Week' in order to make up the time.

SOCIALISING

Making friends

As soon as you arrive, get hold of some kind of weekly English-language newspaper or magazine advertising local events and the major western social and business organisations.
Ken Sherman

Chinese people are in general friendly and any shyness is quite often easily explained by the huge language difference. It is not too common for the Chinese to start a conversation with a foreigner, unless they are keen to practise their English, which means that an ability to speak Chinese is a definite plus.

Unlike in North America, it is unusual for anyone to start a conversation with a stranger in China. Therefore, it is much easier to build up your social network through friends and colleagues whom you already know. Universities are among the easiest places to make local friends, as young people are eager to make the acquaintance of people from different cultures. Joining special-interest classes is also a good way to make friends with Chinese people.

Given the size of the country, regional cultural differences are very noticeable. The traditional stereotypes have it that the southerners are talkative and witty; northerners sincere and honest; and westerners stubborn and dedicated. However, demographic factors dominate these days, and thus you are more likely to find young, well-educated middle class people who are eager to make foreign friends in coastal cities, and maybe more sincere and authentic friendships in the rural regions.

Relationships

Away from big cities, a Chinese girl and western man walking hand-in-hand might raise a few eyebrows. However, social acceptance of mixed-race relationships has increased markedly as China has opened up to the outside world.

Generally speaking, the Chinese regard westerners as prone to having uncommitted sexual relationships. Accordingly, they will be wary of relationships between the two groups. At the same time western men, in particular, need to be cautious and ensure that a Chinese girl or woman is not mainly interested in him for the sake of a foreign passport.

Marriage

If you are marrying a Chinese citizen, you have to make a Statutory Declaration either in front of a registered solicitor or to a Notary Public. In the declaration you have to state your name, sex, date of birth, nationality, passport or ID card number, occupation, address and marital status. This declaration then needs to be sent to the embassy or consulate-general of the People's Republic of China for authentication. If the document is accepted, your declaration will be legalised. The legalisation is valid for six months. After entering China, you and your fiancée or fiancé must go to the local government office to submit your marriage application. You must also present the legalised declaration you made earlier. You will be required to have your health checked by a designated hospital. You and your partner will go through a marriage registration after the application is approved and the marriage certificate will then be issued to you.

There is a minimum legal age for marriage in China, which is older than in western countries. For males it is 22 and for females 20. Bigamy is illegal.

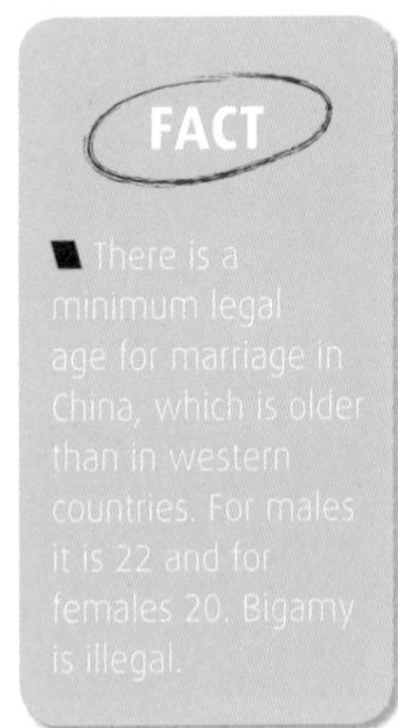

Homosexuality

Homosexuality is still a sensitive topic to many Chinese and is regarded as a social disgrace by many Chinese. Perceived as a mental illness, it was only removed from the list of psychiatric disorders in 2001. Needless to say, gay marriage is still banned in China. Some homosexuals are brave enough to be open but more prefer to hide. A hotline for homosexuals daily receives many calls for counselling and support and many callers claim they find it difficult to make friends. As the country opens up and it is easier to access the internet, more people, especially the more educated, have started to accept gays and lesbians. There are now more bars and meeting places for homosexuals, and even university courses about homosexuality. Homosexuality is becoming more accepted in major cities like Beijing, Shanghai and Guangzhou. Online listings for the major cities will contain details of local events and club nights.

ENTERTAINMENT AND CULTURE

Cinemas

Although there are usually cinemas in the cities, they are rare in rural areas. Most of the movies shown in China will be in Mandarin. English movies are not common. In fact, the government sets quotas on the number of foreign films that can be shown on general release in any one calendar year. Even when an English or American movie is shown, the dialogue may be dubbed into Mandarin. Some foreign movies are shown in Beijing and Shanghai but the choices are limited. The cinemas that regularly provide films with English subtitles are Cherry Lane Movies (in Beijing) and Studio City (in Shanghai). There is one French cinema in Beijing specialising in French movies. IMAX has a cinema in Shanghai that frequently shows foreign movies.

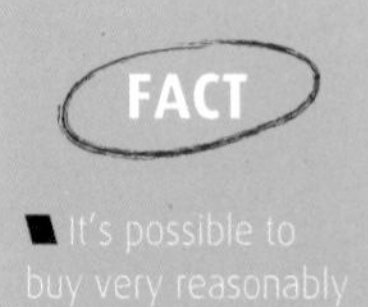

It's possible to buy very reasonably priced DVD players in China for as little as ¥300.

You can find DVDs in department stores but pirate discs are sold cheaply 'on every street corner', as a recent visitor to China reported. The Chinese are more likely to watch DVDs at home than go out to the cinema. The speed at which blockbuster movies are copied and distributed (Hollywood, western or Asian) makes for more up-to-date viewing than waiting for the cinema release. You can generally pick up the latest blockbuster films from people selling DVDs in underpasses, bars or markets, but there is a surprisingly wide range available in the little shops that pop up here and there before the local authorities close them down periodically. Hong Kong and Korean films are very popular with the Chinese as they tend to be more

expressive and emotionally explicit than Chinese counterparts. French, German, Spanish and independent British films can all be found among the Hollywood and Jackie Chan collections.

DVDs can cost as little as ¥7 (£0.50/$1) in some cities, though you'll pay up to ¥40–¥50 in department stores. In the past it was important to buy Zone 9 DVDs for them to work on western players, but with more sophisticated machines nowadays, this distinction seems less important.

It's possible to buy very reasonably priced DVD players in China for as little as ¥300.

When flying home, remember to put your DVD collection in a single pouch or holder to minimise the risk of confiscation. If you are carrying large numbers of fake DVDs in their sleeves, it might look as if you intend to sell them on.

Useful resources

Cherry Lane Movies: Sino-Japanese Youth Exchange Centre, 40 Liangmaqiao Lu, Beijing; 010 6461 5318; www.cherrylanemovies.com.cn. Movies with English substitles.

Da Guang Ming Cinema: 290 Xizang Zhong Lu, Shanghai 200001; www.shdgm.com

Lycee Francais de Pekin: 13 Dongsi Jie, Beijing; 010 6532 3498

Studio City: Westgate Mall, 10th Floor, 1038 Nanjing Xilu, Shanghai; 021 6218 2173

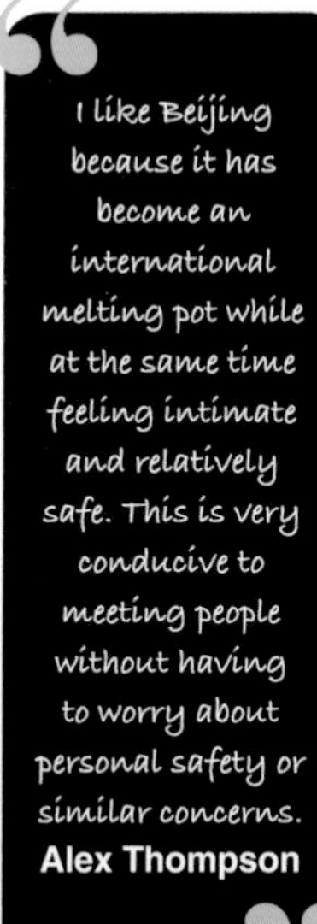

I like Beijing because it has become an international melting pot while at the same time feeling intimate and relatively safe. This is very conducive to meeting people without having to worry about personal safety or similar concerns.
Alex Thompson

Entertainment

Chinese cities famously stay awake until late. Even in small towns and cities you are likely to find restaurants, bars, karaoke parlours and discos plying their trade into the

small hours. Information about local events and club nights can be found on online listings for major cities.

Karaoke bars are extremely popular with groups of young people and recognisable by the acronym 'KTV', literally karaoke television, literally pronounced *ka la ok*. Private booths are hired out by the hour for a maximum number of participants (often up to 20) containing a television, a number of microphones and a huge list of songs to choose from, although mostly in Chinese. Drinks are available to order from passing waitresses.

There are concerts of Chinese and western music from time to time, and theatrical events. Recently Broadway and West End musicals have appeared on tour in Beijing and Shanghai, with *Les Miserables* going down very well.

- Information about local events and club nights can be found on online listings for major cities.

Chinese opera in all its many regional forms is also a popular form of entertainment, but can be an acquired taste for the untrained ear. You will sometimes find impromptu performances in corners of parks by older citizens, singing songs from famous operas.

Another popular pastime for the older generation is group exercising in parks and open spaces. Someone will wheel out a stereo with loudspeakers and the dancing begins. This could be simple clapping in a circle to ballroom dancing or gentle aerobics, but all accompanied by often-incongruous Europop or indistinguishable 'musak'. In parks, you'll find intriguing exercise equipment that emulates gym machines like the treadmill. Exercise is considered very important for the older generation to keep mind and body in good condition. Walking backwards is meant to be good for your heart, so don't be surprised to see groups of older friends chatting while slowly moving backwards.

You can find details of cultural events on various websites:
www.chinadaily.com.cn/entertainment
www.wcities.com
www.thatsbj.com/blog

Gambling in Macau

Despite Macau's small size, its gambling business has become world famous in recent years. Thanks to the liberalisation of the gambling industry and the associated influx of international gambling kings, Macau's casinos turn over more money than those in Las Vegas. Casinos, large and small, are the landmarks of Macau. Historically, the most famous and visually dominant was the Lisboa Casino. The Lisboa hotel is one of the most expensive in Macau and also holds nightly dance shows in the casino. However, recent developments have dwarfed the Lisboa. The Macau Jockey Club organises horse racing every Wednesday and Sunday. This usually attracts a lot of Hong Kong people, especially in the summer, when horse racing in Hong Kong is out of season. There is also greyhound racing managed by Canidrome, which is the biggest greyhound-racing venue in Asia.

Part of the reason for Macau's success is that gambling is, officially, illegal in mainland China. With movement restrictions being relaxed, mainlanders are now streaming in by their millions to try their hand at the blackjack tables.

Casinos

Canidrome: 2833 3399; www.macaudog.com

Lisboa Casino: 2–4 Avenida de Lisboa, Macau Penisula, Macau; 2837 7666; (hotel reservations) 2837 5811; www.casinocity.com/mo/macau/maclisbo

The Macau Jockey Club: Est Gov Albano da Oliveira, Taipa, Macau; 2882 1188; www.macauhorse.com

Art and museums

There are over 1,800 museums in China, although not all are worth a lengthy visit, thanks to uninspired presentation and poor or non-existent English translations. Almost all provinces have a museum about the history of the area. Some musems are housed in well-preserved, spectacular historic buildings. In and around Beijing, for example, are the Forbidden City, the Summer Palace and the Old Summer Palace. These are a must. They give you a vivid picture of the life of the Imperial family in the old days. Western visitors note with irony the official sponsor of the Forbidden City's information boards and signposts is American Express, and until recently the only café inside its walls was a Starbucks. After pressure from Chinese groups, this has now closed, but the signposting is likely to make Mao turn in his grave (or in his case, his mausoleum).

Other interesting museums in the capital include the History Museum, Museum of the Chinese Revolution, the Military Museum of the Chinese People's Revolution and the China Opium War Museum.

There are also a great number of art galleries, for example The China Art Gallery. For more specialised topics, there are the China Aviation Museum, the China Geological Museum,

The Terracotta Warriors in Xian

the China Coin Museum, the China Printing Museum, etc. The birthplaces of Chinese leaders such as Mao Zedong and Deng Xiaoping and Sun Yat-sen, are also very popular.

Outside the capital, the Shanghai Museum and the Shanxi History Museum, in Xian, are the genuine must-sees.

Most of the museums charge an entry fee, which is usually less than ¥10 (£0.70/$1.42). Some of them prohibit photography so you should always ask before taking pictures. Signs are often not translated professionally into English, but it's still possible to make out the meaning. Chinese museums and exhibitions focus greatly on size, length, age and values, and not as much on descriptions of context, daily life or feelings. Much of the information can therefore feel a little dry and sparse for those used to more detailed and thoroughly researched exhibits elsewhere.

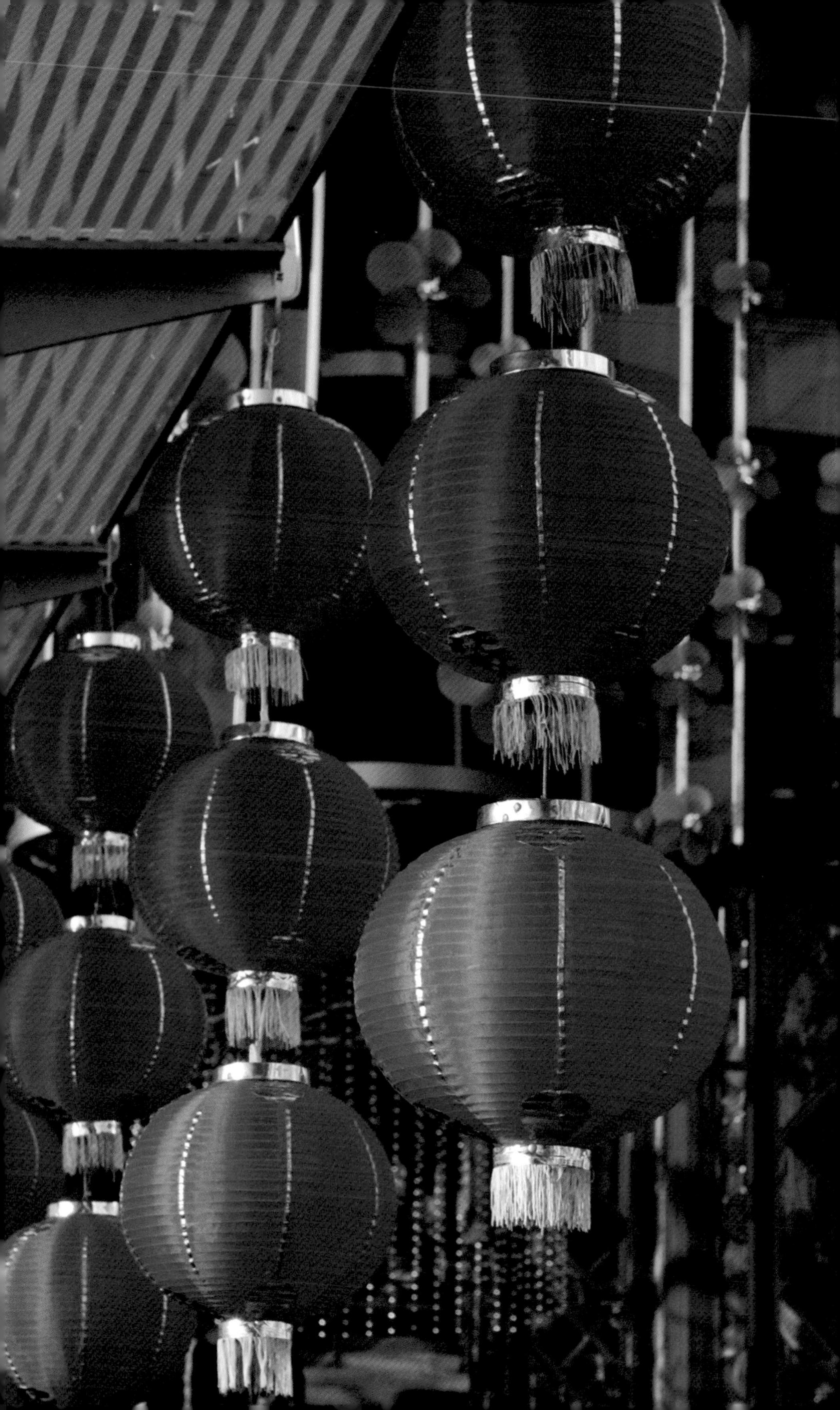

About China

THE PEOPLE

For many hundreds of years Chinese people were very cut off from the rest of the world. In Chinese, the word 'China' translates as 'middle kingdom' and the people did indeed think that they were in the middle of the world and that their culture and history were superior to those of the surrounding countries. Certainly, with such a huge and varied terrain, China was very self-sufficient and did not need of much anything from other lands. So the Chinese became very proud of being Chinese and often very unwilling to let foreigners in or to let them get to know Chinese people and the culture. One western woman in China in the 19th century described the country as being surrounded by walls. This is probably some of what lies behind the old stereotype of Chinese people being 'inscrutable'.

The Chinese were pretty shocked in the 19th century when western nations, because of their superior military strength and introduction of opium, forced themselves on to Chinese soil and demanded trading rights and special concessions. Chinese pride took a big knock from which, in some ways, it is still recovering.

The social system

In the last hundred years the social system has also changed dramatically like in many other places. Traditionally there were four classes in Chinese society. Top of the pile were the scholars and government officials who had studied and passed the official examinations. Next came farmers in recognition of their important role in providing food for the population, then artisans and craftsmen, and last in the pecking order were merchants. It has been argued that because the merchant class was despised, the capitalist middle class, which helped to propel the development of democracy in the west, never developed and flourished as it did in parts of Europe. Successful wealthy merchants would make sure that their sons studied and became government officials. In theory the government exams were open to all men (except for actors and beggars) but of course you needed to be pretty well off to spend time studying for the gruelling exams.

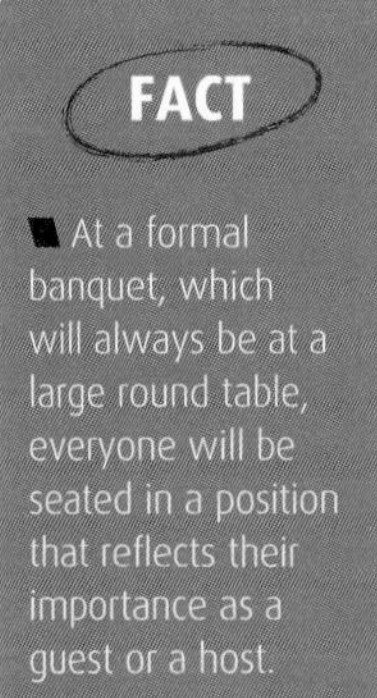

FACT
At a formal banquet, which will always be at a large round table, everyone will be seated in a position that reflects their importance as a guest or a host.

The exam system was abolished at the beginning of the twentieth century, and in theory, so was the class system, but Chinese society remains fairly authoritarian and hierarchical. Given this strict social structure, the student challenge to the government in 1989, seemed astonishing. Students, labour activists and intellectuals demonstrated against the government's authoritarian rule & strict ecomic policies, leading to a heavy-handed military reaction that left hundreds, if not thousands dead. However, these demonstrations reflected the traditional power of scholars to challenge the status quo; one that has been exercised previously throughout Chinese history.

Although nowadays there is still a lot of respect for scholars and teachers, the middle class is growing fast in China, as is their disposable income. As elsewhere, the term refers to people with stable incomes who aspire to buying cars and a house and who can afford to pay for education and to go on holiday. If the middle class continues to grow at the present rate it is estimated that by 2020 middle class people will account for 40% of the total population.

The family

In China, where most people traditionally live off the land, the family is the most important unit. It is also true to say that the males are the constant parts of that unit whereas the females come and go. This means that a family is made up of a man, who in theory has been born and brought up in the village where he lives, and his wife who has been brought in from another family and probably another village, their sons, their sons' wives and children. The daughters, once of marriageable age, will have been married to men from other villages and have moved away to become part of their husband's family. That is one reason that sons are to this day favoured over daughters. Daughters have been popularly described as 'goods on which one loses money'.

It was the son's duty to look after their parents in old age, to worship their souls after they died and to continue the family line by having children themselves. These values have been around since the mists of time, when it was thought ideal to have five sons and two daughters. Of course real families were often much smaller but it was – and still is – very important to have sons. Stories of the disappointment felt by parents and especially grandparents at the birth of a daughter are not uncommon.

Instead of staying with their parents in a big family house, as was the ideal in the old days, young married couples now usually move away from their families and quite often the parents will help them buy a new house.

One-child policy

As a result of the one-child policy, implemented in 1979, Chinese families are typically small these days.

According to the statistics conducted by the Chinese Bureau of Statistics in 2005, the male-female ratio is currently an artificially disparate 51.52% to 48.48%, which is mainly the result of the official one-child policy.

The preference for sons runs very deep in Chinese culture and the one-child policy has been very difficult for people who were disappointed to have a daughter. Some parents choose to abort if they find out that the foetus is female. It is also thought that there are parents who do not register the birth of a daughter in order to try again for a son.

The one-child policy still applies in China and is widely accepted, mostly in cities. In rural areas, it is possible to have a second child if the first-born is female or disabled. This is meant to give the family the chance to have a boy to help practically with farming, but reinforces the inequity of women (and indeed disabled people) in society. Minority peoples are given even more favourable rights in regard to their children, in an attempt to redress the balance of their persecution during the harsh days of the 1960s and 1970s, and to promote the importance of the minorities in Chinese society. As a result, some are allowed to have up to three children. Even for those breaking the one-child rule, *guanxi* (contacts) and money speaks volumes. With the right contacts and the ability to pay fines, families can and do have more than one child.

Nowadays with only one child per couple the family set up is rather differently. There are no longer big families with uncles and aunts and cousins. Instead there is one child with two doting parents and two sets of grandparents all focusing their attention on him or her. In some ways the direction of filial respect has reversed and it is the parents who answer to the child's whim. No wonder many are referred to as 'little emperors'.

As a result of the one-child policy, westerners can observe a different kind of friendship amongst schoolchildren – something more akin to siblings than school friends. Best friends, and any cousins they may have, take on a more important role in childrens' lives.

- **Movement of people** To Chinese people their birthplace, or 'ancestral village', is an important part of their identity. Chinese people will generally return to their original homes during events like Spring Festival (Chinese New Year).

  Nowadays more and more people are migrating to the cities. It is estimated that around 56% of the population still live in rural areas but the move to the cities is projected to continue as country people aspire to the comforts of city life.

HISTORY

Pre-history to Qing Dynasty

Human activity in China possibly dates back 500,000 or 600,000 years. Excavations show signs of early habitation, and the fossils of Peking Man (discovered in 1923–1927 in Choukoutien) further demonstrate the existence of early human beginnings.

Excavations have shown that the imperial period started in the Xia Dynasty. The first form of writing was found dating back to the Shang Dynasty, as were the first textual records. The following table is a brief summary of past dynasties:

The Dynasties of China		
Dynasty	**Period**	**Remarks**
Xia	2200–1700BC	No written record found but there is archaeological evidence for the dynasty.
Shang	1700–1027BC	The first dynasty with textual records. Ancient writing found on tortoise shells.
Zhou	1027–2211BC	
Western Zhou	1027–771BC	
Eastern Zhou	770–221BC	Confucius gained influence among the emperors. Laozi wrote the *Tao Te Ching* and Taoism first took root.
Qin	221–207BC	China was unified for the first time by Qin Shi Huang. There is also unification of the writing system, measuring units and currency. Qin Shi Huang built a huge underground mausoleum, filled with thousands of Terracotta Warriors, to protect him into the afterlife. It remained undiscovered until the 1970s. The first parts of the Great Wall were built to prevent incursions by 'barbarians'. 'Burning of books and burying of scholars' (213BC): many valuable books of history, literature and medicine were destroyed in an attempt to unify thoughts and political opinion.
Han	206BC–AD220	
Western Han	206BC–AD9	*Wuxing,* a cosmological system built around the Five Elements (metal, wood, water, fire and earth) is developed. It allegedly can predict the rise and fall of dynasties and is used by early feng shui practitioners. Sima Qian wrote the first Chinese history: *Record of the Grand Historian* (*Shi Ji*).
Xin	AD9–24	
Eastern Han	AD25–220	Buddhism first introduced into China. Records of contacts with other countries including Japan, India, Persia and Rome have been found. The Silk Road became an important route for trade between east and west.
Three Kingdoms	AD220–280	The history of this period was the basis of the novel *The Romance of Three Kingdoms* (Luo Guanzhong), one of the so-called 'Four Classics'.
Wei	AD220–265	
Shu	AD221–263	Liu Bei invited Zhuge Kongming to be prime minister.
Wu	AD229–280	
Jin	AD265–420	
Western Jin	AD265–317	
Eastern Jin	AD317–420	
Southern and Northern Dynasties	AD420–589	
Southern Dynasties	AD420–589	
Song	AD420–479	

(continued)

Dynasty	Period	Remarks
Qi	AD479–502	
Liang	AD502–557	
Chen	AD557–589	
Northern Dynasties	AD386–581	
Northern Wei	AD386–534	
Eastern Wei	AD534–550	
Northern Qi	AD550–577	
Western Wei	AD535–556	
Northern Zhou	AD557–581	
Sui	AD581–618	The Grand Canal was built. The Great Wall was reconstructed.
Tang	AD618–907	Some of China's most enduring poetry was written. The best 300 poems were later collected into a book known as *The Three Hundred Tang Poems* (*Tang Shi San Bai Shou*), and made popular among the public. Revival of Confucianism. Queen Wu became the first female emperor in China. Foreign trade was particularly active during her rule. All Buddhist temples were destroyed and monks and nuns were forced to leave in AD845.
Five Dynasties and Ten Kingdoms	AD907–960	
Later Liang	AD907–923	
Later Tang	AD923–936	
Later Jin	AD936–947	
Later Han	AD947–950	
Later Zhou	AD951–960	
Ten Kingdoms	AD907–979	
Liao	AD907–1125	
Song	AD960–1279	The weakest of the major dynasties in history with the smallest territory. Economic and cultural developments flourished, including *Song Ci* (poetry), astronomy, geography, painting, calligraphy, ceramics and philosophy. Zhu Xi established Neo-Confucianism.
Northern Song	AD960–1127	
Southern Song	AD1127–1279	
Jin	AD1115–1234	
Yuan	AD1206–1368	Founded by Genghis Khan's grandson, Kublai Khan. China became part of the Mongol Empire. Beijing became the capital for first time. Marco Polo visited China. Classification of the population into four groups: Mongolians were at the top of the pile and Han-Chinese at the bottom.

Dynasty	Period	Remarks
Ming	AD1368–1644	Zheng He explored 'The Western Ocean' with his fleet at least seven times. Visited South-East Asia, Sumatra, Java, Ceylon, India, Persia, the Persian Gulf, Arabia, the Red Sea as far north as Egypt, and Africa as far south as the Mozambique Channel. The Great Wall was made 600 miles longer. In 1557 the Portuguese established a permanent settlement in Macau. It only became a colony in the 19th century.
Qing	AD1644–1911	Further expanded territory. The State Examination System re-introduced. Men forced to wear their hair the Manchurian way (shaved forehead and top and a plait at the back). In the west this became a trademark for the Chinese. Hong Kong was ceded to the British in 1842 after China lost the First Opium War. In June 1858, the Tianjin Treaty was signed. Eleven more ports were opened to western trade, in addition to the first five Treaty Ports. Empress Dowager Cixi was the real powerholder, ruling the country for 40 years (1856–1908).
Republic of China	AD1911–1949	(see below)
People's Republic of China	AD1949–present	(see below)

The Chinese people have long called themselves 'Han ren' or 'Tang ren' ('ren' means people) because the Han and the Tang Dynasties were the most powerful dynasties ruled by the Chinese. Although the Yuan and the early Qing Dynasties may have wielded more power, they were ruled by ethnic minorities who came from the northern part of China. Han Chinese and minority peoples have never mixed very well and marriages between the groups are uncommon.

The fall of the Qing Empire

By the mid-19th century the weak Qing Dynasty had become unable to resist the western powers' demands for trade rights. Parts of the territory were leased or ceded to foreign countries leading to popular unrest. This unrest plus the weakness of the government gave rise to political movements and Sun Yat-sen was among those who grew to prominence at this time. On 10 October 1911, after the fall of the Qing Dynasty, the Republic of China was founded. Sun Yat-sen was elected as provisional President in December. In 1921, after continuing political turmoil, Sun Yat-sen was elected president of a self-proclaimed national government in Guangzhou city. He delivered his famous speech 'Three Principles of the People' (*San Min Zhuyi*) in 1923. These are nationalism, democracy and socialism and are the foundation of the country.

By the 1920s the nationalists (Guomindang) were the dominant political party in eastern China. In 1921 the Chinese Communist Party was founded through the influence of the Comintern (the Soviet Communist International). The threat of Japanese invasion in 1924 caused a brief alliance of the Chinese Communist Party and the Guomindang. But after Sun Yat-sen died in 1925, the two groups diverged and there was a 20-year-long civil war. Only when the Japanese invaded and occupied China in 1937–1945, did the two parties agree to join forces against the enemy. Almost as soon as the Second World War ended in 1945 fighting broke out again between the Guomindang (led by Chiang Kaishek), and the Communist party (led by Mao Zedong). Mao defeated Chiang's troops in 1949 and proclaimed the People's Republic of China on 1 October with him self as leader.

Chiang fled to Taiwan with his remaining army and proclaimed it the Republic of China, as it is officially called to this day.

People's Republic of China (PRC)

The chaotic aftermath of years of war and financial weakness dogged the early years of the PRC. With the Soviet Union as a model, economic and social reforms were introduced and after inflation was halted in 1953 as the country developed rapidly.

Despite the success of the first five-year plan, Mao's belief in mass cooperation led him in 1958 to introduce the Great Leap Forward, which aimed at rapid growth in industrial and agricultural production. Premier Zhou Enlai and other government members favoured agricultural incentives but Mao believed that the Great Leap Forward would make China into a major steel producer and insisted on putting most of the resources into the steel industry.

As we know now, the Great Leap Forward was a disaster. The supply of iron ore in China was limited, so farm tools and other iron household necessities were melted in people's backyard furnaces. The steel produced was poor and of no market value. The three years of the Great Leap Forward not only impoverished the country but also caused up to 40 million people to die of starvation, according to some historians.

In 1950, the Soviet Union and the PRC had signed a mutual defence agreement but their relationship began to deteriorate after 1958. In 1959, the Soviet Union restricted the flow of scientific and technological information to China and in 1960 withdrew all Soviet professionals. The two countries began to have open disputes in international forums.

After the failure of the Great Leap Forward, Mao resigned as head of state and Liu Shaoqi became president of the PRC. But Mao was still the leader of the Chinese Communist Party and retained de facto power.

Liu Shaoqi and Deng Xiaoping reformed government policies and focused on agricultural incentives and economic development. Liu and Deng received increasing support from party members and the general public. Mao's reaction was to attack Liu and Deng, criticising them for restoring capitalism and introducing social classifications.

The Gang of Four (Yao Wenyuan, Wang Hongwen, Zhang Chunqiao and Mao's wife, Jiang Qing) supported Mao and initiated the Cultural Revolution, which was formally launched in May 1966. PRC officials and members of the government were criticised. Criticism spread, as the notorious Red Guards were encouraged to get rid of intellectuals and any opponents of Mao. Chaos reigned in China as thousands of artists, writers and teachers were physically abused and sent to re-education camps. Schools were shut down, temples and churches were burnt. Books, history records and works of art were destroyed. The Cultural Revolution did not completely end until Mao died in 1976. It was also not until Mao's death that Deng Xiaoping returned to the position of vice-premier and vice-chairman of the party. Deng, intent on economic development, introduced the 'Four Modernisations' (agriculture, industry, defence, and science) and the 'Open Door' policy. Since then, the PRC has developed rapidly.

POLITICS AND ECONOMY

Government

The Chinese government is basically divided into central administration and local administration. The central government formulates laws, regulations, and policy directions, and manages the budget and personnel changes. Local governments implement these policies and laws. The primary bodies of the government include the National People's Congress, the State Council and the President.

National People's Congress (NPC)

This is the highest authority of the People's Republic of China (PRC). The NPC general meeting is held once every five years. The central committee of the NPC consists of 300 delegates, all elected by the provincial people's congresses for a term of five years. They meet for two weeks every year to produce work reports for the current year and to approve proposals for the coming year.

The NPC elects the President, and also has the power to impeach or replace a president. The proposals of the State Council have to be approved by the NPC before they are carried out. The NPC selects the central committees for the Politburo (political bureau) Standing Committee and they, in turn, select about 500 members of the NPC to form the Standing Committee.

The current Politburo Standing Committee includes nine members, with President Hu Jintao and Premier Wen Jiabao on the committee. The Standing Committee has the constitutional authority to modify legislation within limits set by the NPC and it also has the power to interpret the laws of the PRC.

President

The President of the state is elected by the NPC. In practice, the top leaders of the Chinese Communist Party (CCP) nominate a candidate to the NPC and the delegates vote on the nomination in the general NPC meeting. The President also serves as the general secretary of the CCP. The Premier and other members of the State Council are nominated by the President and approved by the NPC. Hu Jintao has been President of the PRC since March 2003 and was elected for a second five-year term in October 2007.

State Council

The State Council is chaired by the Premier, currently Wen Jiabao, and is the central administrative body. The State Council Standing Committee consists of the Premier, four vice-premiers, five state councillors, and the secretary-general. Other members include the heads of each governmental department and agency – about 50 people in total. The State Council holds monthly meetings, while the Standing Committee meets twice a week. Members serve a term of five years, up to two consecutive terms. The State Council formulates and implements laws, drafts and submits proposals to the NPC, formulates the tasks and responsibilities of ministries and commissions of the State Council, prepares the state budget and administers civil and public affairs. The Premier is nominated by the President and approved by the NPC. Other members in the State Council are nominated by the Premier, and must be approved by the NPC. Although the President is not included in the State Council, he has the power to remove any member from it.

Local administrations

There are several categories and levels of local administration. They can be separated into two-level, three-level and four-level administrations (central government is not counted as one of the levels).

The delegation of authority to local governments aims to implement the laws and regulations of the State more effectively. Since each province, city or town faces different economic and environmental advantages and disadvantages, contingency adjustments have to be made to ensure these laws and regulations run smoothly in different regions. Moreover, provinces, cities and towns may deal with local issues for which the central government does not normally provide guidance.

Local legislation must:

- Be set up according to the local economy, politics, legal system, culture, customs, and conditions of the people and be appropriate for the local situation.
- Specifically solve the obvious issues not covered in the legislation and regulations of the central government, or issues that it is not appropriate for the central authorities to settle.

Political parties

The biggest political party is the Chinese Communist Party (CCP) with an estimated membership of 70 million, about 5% of the population. As a rule, the President of the government is also the general-secretary of the CCP. There are eight legally registered non-communist parties in China. Rather than acting as opposition parties, they coexist with the CCP, engaging in mutual supervision. Members of non-communist parties, as well as some other non-party bodies, are called to the Chinese People's Political Consultative Conference (CPPCC) for consultations. The eight non-communist parties include.

The Revolutionary Committee of the Chinese Guomindang

- Founded in 1948 and composed mainly of former Guomindang members or those who have historical connections with them, many of whom now live in Taiwan.

The China Democratic League

- Established in 1941 by intellectuals at more senior levels.

The China Democratic National Construction Association

- Formed in 1945 – members are mainly businessmen and academic specialists.

The China Association for Promoting Democracy

- Founded in 1945 by intellectuals in cultural, education (primary and secondary schools), scientific and publishing fields.

The Chinese Peasants and Workers' Democratic Party

- Set up in 1930 – composed of people who work in public health, culture, education, and science and technology.

The China Zhi Gong Dang

- Founded in 1925 – members are mainly overseas Chinese, relatives of overseas Chinese and specialists or scholars with overseas connections.

The Jiusan Society

- Founded in 1945 – members are dominated by college or university professors working in science and technology, culture and education or public health.

The Taiwan Democratic Self-Government League

- Formed in 1947 – consists of people born or with family roots in Taiwan but who are currently living on the mainland.

Economy

The Chinese economy began to recover when Deng Xiaoping regained his position, and introduced the 'Four Modernisations'. Between 1978 and 1994, China's GDP recorded 9% growth on average, making China one of the fastest-growing economies in the world. Industrial reform took place in the 1980s and many (TVEs) Township and Village Enterprises were set up in rural areas, becoming one of the driving forces for national economic development. Unlike state-owned enterprises TVEs are run by local authorities in the mode of a private business. Thus the local authorities are responsible for losses and have to face competition, but any profits go to the local government instead of the central government. Deng also set up several Special Economic Zones (SEZs) where foreign investors are provided with extra incentives to start businesses. Shenzhen, Zhuhai, Shantou, Xiamen and the island province of Hainan are all SEZs.

In addition, from the late 1980s to early 1990s the government established 15 free trade zones, 32 state-level economic and technological development zones, and 53 new and hi-tech industrial development zones. The establishment of the Shanghai Pudong New Zone has further stimulated the economy by turning Shanghai into a major centre for banking and finance. Through the 1980s and 1990s, China's average growth rose to 9.7%. Foreign direct investment (FDI) has increased by more than 20% since China joined the WTO in 2001. The growth rate in 2003 was actually about four times the world average for that year. In 2005 the economy grew by 9.3%, became fourth biggest economy in the world in 2006, and is forecast to grow a further 11% or so by the end of 2007. With Beijing host to the 2008 Olympic games there is no end in sight to the huge levels of foreign investment.

The middle class It is estimated that about one-fifth of the population is considered middle class. The figure only increased by 4% between 1999 and 2003 but is now rising rapidly. These people on average possess assets that are worth $9,250–18,500 $18,000–$36,000. The increase of the middle class has changed the consumption pattern and many companies have now chosen to target this sector of society. The increase in sales of vehicles, properties, travel, etc, has stimulated economic growth and many middle-class households have also started to run their own businesses. Recently, new laws have been implemented to provide legal protection for private property, due to the rapid increase in home ownership.

The Chinese government also aims to increase the number of middle-class households by cutting the taxes of the poor and allowing more people from rural areas to work in cities. It is believed that the increase in the average income of households, and the low living costs will result in a middle-class society that is beneficial for the economy. It is expected that around 40% of the population will be categorised as middle class by the year 2020.

RELIGION

Religion in China that was swept away at the time of the communist revolution has made something of a comeback since the 1980s. In the old days religion was pluralistic: there was Buddhism, Taoism and ancestor worship, but there were often no clear distinctions between them. A given temple was not always definitively Buddhist or Taoist and the priest in charge, if asked, would not be able to reply for it was simply not a relevant question. There has always been a great degree of religious tolerance.

In many ways the most important religious practice was that of ancestor worship. If you did not worship your ancestors by treating them with respect and giving them food offerings and so forth, they could exact revenge. But if any of the plethora of gods who were worshipped did not respond to your requests you could simply stop worshipping them without fear of the consequences. To be forgotten and neglected was the fate of many gods.

A recent BBC news report told of the re-opening of a Buddhist pagoda in eastern China. The temple complex, which dates back to the Tang dynasty, had been destroyed and rebuilt several times over the last 1,350 years.

A Shanghai University survey conducted in February 2007 suggested that around 300 million people in China follow a religion. The survey found that Buddhism, Taoism, Catholicism, Christianity and Islam are the five major religions – Chinese people talk about Catholicism as separate to Christianity, which includes Protestant churches. In spite of a now more tolerant atmosphere, believers are only permitted to go to government-approved churches, mosques and temples. This includes the selection by the state of both the successor to the Dalai Lama and the head of the Catholic church, both of which have been strongly disputed by the current Dalai Lama and the Pope.

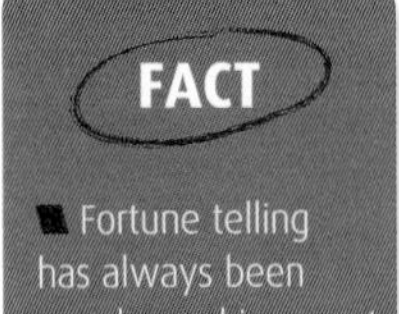

FACT

- Fortune telling has always been popular and in recent years it has been possible to read your own fortune with a computer programme.

GEOGRAPHICAL INFORMATION

Area

China is the third largest country in the world after Russia and Canada. At 9.6 million sq kms it is about the same sze as the USA. Russia is to the north-east of China and there are train connections between the two countries. Mongolia is to the north. The western province of Xinjiang borders Pakistan, Tajikistan, Kyrgyzstan, Kazakhstan, Russia and Mongolia. Vietnam, Laos and Myanmar (Burma) are to the south of

Yunnan Province. North Korea shares a border with Jilin and Liaoning. Tibet is separated from Nepal and India by the Himalayan mountains.

China has a huge coastline, stretching down most of the eastern side and along the southern fringe of the country. There are deserts in the north and west, while the mountains that are spread throughout the country reach their highest peaks in the south-west.

The western terrain mainly consists of highlands. The average altitude of the Tibet-Qinghai Plateau ('the roof of the world') is 4,500m above sea level. The Himalayan peaks are on average 6,000m above sea level. The world's highest peak, Everest or Zhumulangma Feng, straddling the border of Tibet and Nepal, is a lofty 8,848m above sea level.

The densely populated central and south-eastern regions of China are mostly farmed lowland and provide the main supply of food for the whole country.

Rivers flow from the mountains in the west eastwards across China and into the Pacific Ocean. The two major rivers, the Yangtze River (Chang Jiang) and the Yellow River (Huang He), link the west and the east of China and provide the country's major water supply. The Yangtze River (6,300km), also known as the 'lifeline of China', is the world's third longest river, and flows from Qinghai to Shanghai. The Yellow River (5,460km) also has its source in Qinghai and flows northwards to Shandong. It is named after the colour of the water, which comes from the very fertile loess or silt carried by it. It is the second-longest river in China and is also where Chinese civilisation is believed to have originated. Unfortunately, the Yellow River still causes serious flooding, as it always has, when the silt blocks the mouths of tributaries. One of the most serious recent floods was in 1998. It caused more than 3,000 deaths and 14 million people were made homeless.

Regional divisions

China is made up of 22 provinces (23 if Taiwan is included), five autonomous regions, four municipalities and two special administrative regions – each with its own capital city and local government. The local governments act independently when handling local affairs and are allowed to refine the laws of the State within certain limits.

Municipalities

The four municipalities are Beijing, Shanghai, Tianjin and Chongqing. Beijing, in, north-eastern China, has been the capital of China for nearly 800 years and has many well-preserved imperial buildings. Shanghai, on the east coast, is probably the fastest-growing economic region. It is predicted that within the next 50 years Shanghai will replace Hong Kong as China's – perhaps even Asia's – most important financial centre. Chongqing and Tianjin are major industrial centres. Chongqing, in the centre of the country, is the largest motorcycle producer in China; the coastal municipality of Tianjin is famous for its watches car manufacturing.

Provinces

Along the eastern and south-eastern coastlines are the affluent provinces of Jiangsu, Zhejiang, Fujian, Shandong, Guangdong and Hainan. All are rich in natural resources. Many of the cities (Zhejiang's Hangzhou, Jiangsu's Nanjing and Hainan's Sanya in particular) are popular tourist destinations.

The main agricultural provinces are inland: Anhui, Jiangxi, Hunan, Hubei, Henan and Shanxi. Here, the population density is quite high – though lower than the coastal provinces.

Heilongjiang, Jilin, Liaoning and Hebei are in China's north-east and comprise the area formerly known as Manchuria.

Located inland, Shaanxi, Gansu and Guizhou are relatively poor provinces due to a lack of natural resources.

Sichuan and Yunnan are two huge provinces in the south-west and attract many domestic and international tourists. Qinghai is in the west.

Autonomous regions

Over 90% of the population are Han Chinese, most of whom live along the coast or in the central regions, but there are also 55 ethnic minorities dotted throughout the country. Differences in culture and lifestyle prompted the Chinese government to set up autonomous regions for provinces with a high ratio of minorities to the Han Chinese.

In the Guangxi Zhuang Autonomous Region in the south of China about 75% of the population is non-Han. There are over 15 million *Zhuang* (the major group) in the province. There is also a sizeable population of *Miao* and *Yao* living in the hilly regions. Ningxia Hui Autonomous Region is in the north-west of China and in the middle section of the Yellow River. More than one-third of the population are *Hui* – Muslims descended from Arab and Iranian traders of the Tang dynasty.

In the far north is the Inner Mongolia Autonomous Region, 15% of whose population is *Mongolian,* the rest being Han with a comparative handful of Hui and *Manchu*. Mongolia (the country, which is not part of China) lies to the north and Russia to the north-west. The Mongolia Autonomous Region province contains China's biggest area of grassland.

The Tibet Autonomous Region has become a popular destination for both domestic and foreign travellers in recent years. Its position at the base of the Himalayas and its strongly traditional culture are the reasons for its popularity. Government tax breaks have also encouraged a large number of Han economic migrants from easterly provinces in recent years. There are about 2.5 million people in Tibet, over 90% of whom are Tibetans, but there are now more Han than Tibetans in Lhasa. Tibetans also live in Qinghai, Sichuan, Gansu and Yunnan Provinces, as well as Xinjiang.

The Xinjiang Uygur Autonomous Region is the largest region of China. About 19 million people live in the region, around 60% of whom are non-Han. *Uygurs* form the major ethnic group but there are also 19 other minorities in this region.

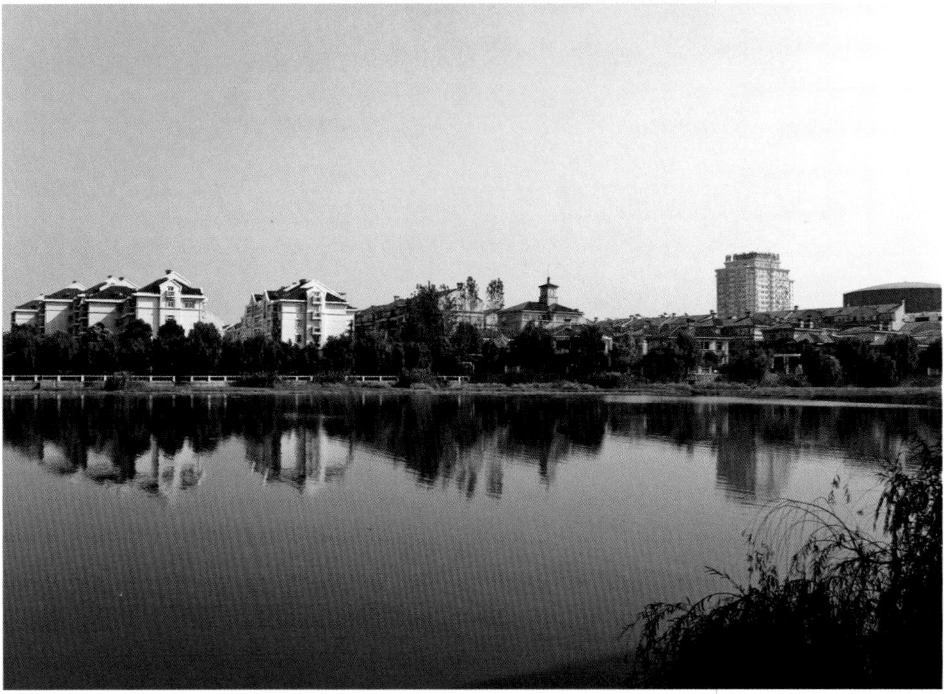

Special Administrative Regions (SARs)

The two SARs are Hong Kong and Macau, beside Guangdong Province. Both regions have a high degree of autonomy and were granted their own legal systems under the 'one country, two systems' policy. Macau ceased to be a Portuguese colony and was returned to China in November 1999. Although Portuguese is still one of its official languages it is not a compulsory school subject and it is not widely spoken. There are many fine Portuguese buildings in Macau and, along with the casinos, they are the major landmarks of the city. See the next section of the book for more information on Hong Kong.

Population

Although China is slightly smaller than Canada, its population is 40 times greater and has reached over 1.3 billion. The population density is on average 135 people per sq km. However, the population is not evenly spread and is higher in the south and east. For example, the population density in Beijing is nearly 900 people per sq km, and that of Shanghai is around 2,750 people per sq km. It is believed that the centre of Shanghai has 34,000 people per sq km. As a whole, 44% of the population is urban and 56% rural. According to the statistical estimates for 2007, the natural growth rate is about 0.6% and the birth and death rates are 1.35% and 0.7% respectively. Life expectancy is, on average, 75 for women and 71 for men.

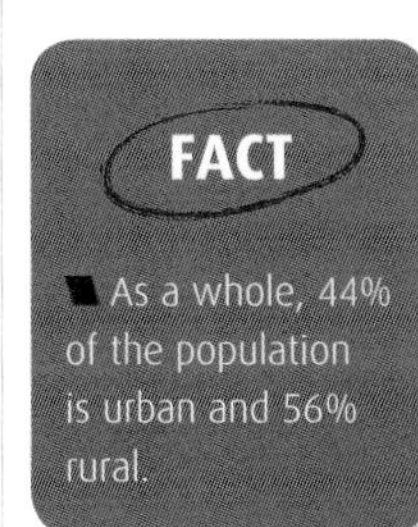

In the 1970s, the population was increasing so fast that in 1979, the government introduced the one-child policy. Ethnic minorities or couples who are both only

FACT

- As a whole, 44% of the population is urban and 56% rural.

children were allowed to have two children. The government claims that the policy was a great success and prevented at least 250 million potential births between 1980 and 2000. However, a downside has been the creation of a gender imbalance. By the end of 200, there were 51.52% males to 48.48% females. The male-female ratio has continued to rise in the last 20 years. As Chinese parents favour sons this has led to a rise in abortions of girl babies. Abortions rose from 200,000 in 1980 to 500,000 in 1987. Female infanticide was sometimes resorted to. The government has continually refined the regulations, eg allowing some in second marriages to have a second child, and likewise the parents of a handicapped child, but has said that it will stick with the basic policy in the short term.

About 70% of the population is between 15 and 64, with an increasing ratio of over 65-year-olds who currently represent 7.5% of the population. According to the world standard, in which 7% is the borderline, China is an ageing country. By the year 2050, elderly people will make up about one-fifth of the population. The ageing problem is also a result of the one-child policy.

Climate

The north and west have quite extreme weather, dominated by the dry and wet monsoon wind. The summers are hot and wet on account of the moist, warm wind from the ocean in the south. Winters are made cold and dry by the winds from the higher latitudes.

In the south and the south-east the weather is less extreme with fewer sudden seasonal changes. Summer is the season of rain and storms and temperatures can reach up to 38°C (100°F) with high humidity. Rainfall can be over 400mm in June, July and August, when typhoons are common. Spring is humid in the south, and autumn is dry. The winter is short and mild and temperatures rarely fall below 10°C in the most southerly provinces.

The north can be very cold between December and March. The temperature in Beijing drops to -10°C or less. In the far north, such as Harbin, winter can be as cold as -40°C and snow and ice are around for months at a time. Sandstorms are also a problem in winter, and summers can be very hot with temperatures as high as 40°C.

In the centre of the country, in Hubei, Hunan, Chongqing and Sichuan, it is very hot and wet from April to October, and winters are very cold and dry.

However the most extreme weather is in the north-west of China in Turpan, which is 150m below sea level, where summer temperatures have been known to rise to 47°C. In the winter temperatures fall to -20°C. The average annual rainfall is below 40mm.

In Tibet, in the south-west, the temperature can vary by 20°C from day to night. A midday temperature of 30°C can drop to - 10°C at night. Strong and cold winds commonly blow during winter but there is rarely snow. The winter lasts from November to March, and from December to February the temperature can be as low as -10°C. Rainfall is sparse and there can be less than 5mm of rain a day for six months of the year. Even in the rainy season in July and August, rainfall does not exceed 150mm.

In the winter, it can be more uncomfortable to be in the central region than in the far north of China, as no heating is permitted south of the Yangtze River, but in the north public buildings are usually heated.

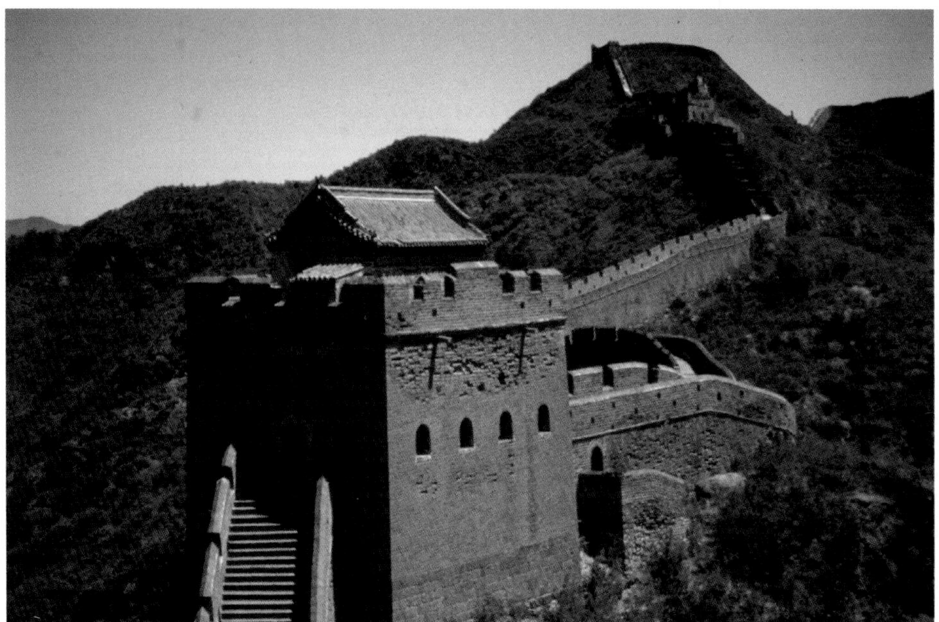

The Great Wall of China

www.travelchinaguide.com/climate provides details of temperatures and rainfall in different cities.

Pollution

This has been a big challenge for the government over the last 15 years. According to a report by the China Environmental Monitoring Center in 2003, about 40% of the seven major river valleys, including the Yangtze River, the Yellow River, the Huaihe, Haihe, Liaohe, Songhuajiang and the Pearl River have very poor water quality. The centre reported that more than one-third of the cities recorded a very poor air quality standard at level three or below. About 40% of cities including the six biggest – Beijing, Shanghai, Shenyang, Chongqing, Xian and Guangzhou – are believed to have badly polluted air. Urban areas in industrial regions such as Liaoning and Shanxi Provinces are facing even more serious air and water pollution. Air pollution in urban areas is largely due to the combustion of poor-quality coal with high sulphur content for heat and electricity generation. Inefficient use of energy, lack of emission controls and the discharge of pollutants close to ground level also further degrade the air quality. Industrial development is another major reason for water pollution in China. In October 2006 the Ministry of Land and Resources reported that agricultural land fell to 121.8 million hectares (306,800 million acres) since the start of the year.

FACT
In April 2007 the BBC reported that 10% of farmland is polluted. The BBC report described China's cities, countryside, waterways and coastlines as among the most polluted in the world.

Pollution is a threat to health and it is reported that millions die each year of respiratory disease. China has introduced a series of policies for tackling pollution. Since 1 January 2003, the Cleaner Production Promotion Law has been in effect. Since its selection for the 2008 Olympic games, reducing pollution has been one of Beijing's major development directions. The anti-pollution policies include tackling

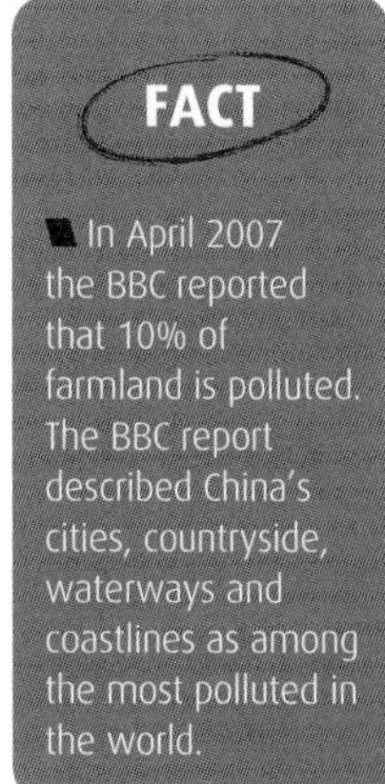

coal-smoke pollution in the city, increasing forest coverage and improving treatment of drainage water. About 20,000 municipal buses were converted to natural gas while thousands of pollution-free new buses will bring the total number of natural gas buses to 150,000 by 2008. The municipal government has also worked on the light rail system between Beijing city centre and the Olympic Park, as well as increasing the length of the subway line by four-fifths. The Chinese government remains positive about the anti-pollution projects in Beijing though a lack of obvious progress led some Olympic delegates to voice their concern for athletes' health during visits in 2007. There is a huge amount of money being spent on combating pollution in China but, as the economy continues to grow, the problem remains acute.

REGIONAL GUIDE

The aim of the following section is to introduce the varied areas of the enormous terrain of China, mentioning their general characteristics, modern and historical, in the hope that it will help you make a choice about which region appeals most to you .

Anhui

Anhui (population 64 million) is an eastern inland province, which links the economies of eastern and western China. The province straddles the basins of the

REGIONS**OF**CHINA

Beijing

Chengdu, Sichuan

Guangzhou, Guangdong

Nanjing, Jiangsu

NORTH

XINJIANG
Kashi
Kashgar
Yining
Karamay
Urumgi
Hami

TIBET
Shiquanhe
Lhasa

QINGHAI
Golmund
Xining

GANSU
Yumen
Lanzhou

NINGXIA
Yinchuan

INNER MONGOLIA
Manzhouli
Hailar
Hohhot

HEILONGJIANG
Qiqihar
Harbin

JILIN
Changchun

LIAONING
Shenyang
Dalian

BEIJING
Tainjin

HEBEI
Shijiazhuang

SHANXI
Taiyuan

SHAANXI
Xi'an
Baoji
Ankang

HENAN
Luoyang
Zhengzhou

SHANDONG
Dezhou
Jinan
Yantai
Qingdao

JIANGSU
Xuzhou
Nanjing

SHANGHAI

ANHUI
Hefei

ZHEJIANG
Hangzhou

HUBEI
Xiangfan
Yichang
Wuhan

SICHUAN
Chengdu
Panzhihua

CHONGQING
Chongqing

JIANGXI
Nanchang
Yingtan
Pingxiang

HUNAN
Changsha
Huaihua
Hengyang

FUJIAN
Fuzhou
Xiamen

GUIZHOU
Guiyang

YUNNAN
Kunming

GUANGXI
Guilin
Liuzhou
Nanning

GUANGDONG
Shaoguan
Guangzhou
Macau
Zhangjiang

HONG KONG

HAINAN
Haikou

EAST CHINA SEA

SOUTH CHINA SEA

SOVIET UNION
MONGOLIA
CHINA
INDIA
BURMA

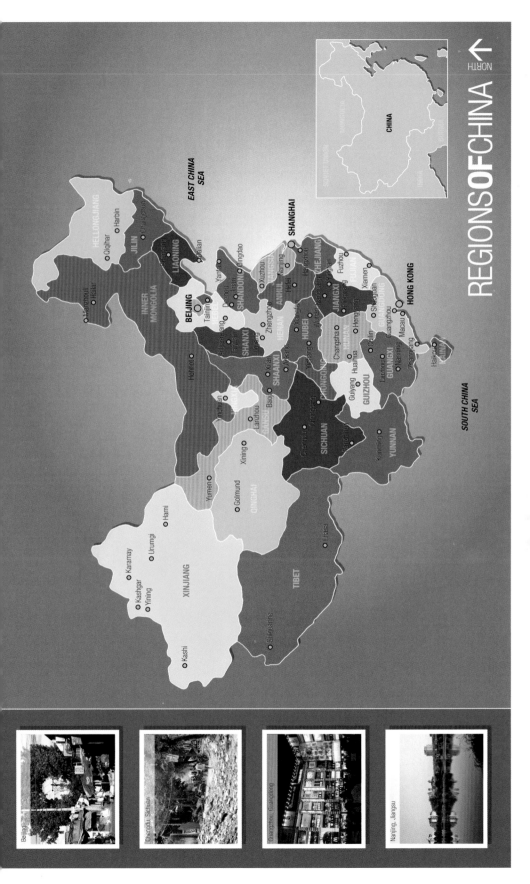

Yangtze and Huai Rivers. It was the first region of southern China to be settled by Han Chinese. The four treasures of scholarship – writing brush, ink stick, ink slab and Xuan paper – are associated with the region. The province is also famous for its dramatic mountains, which have inspired poets, mystics and painters for centuries. There are 81 universities in Anhui.

Capital city: Hefei (population nearly four million) is in the heart of the province. The city is on the Bengbu-Yuxikou railway and is joined to the Yangtze by waterway via Lake Chaohu. It is now the political, economic, and cultural centre of Anhui Province. Its industries include iron and steel, machine building, electronics, construction materials, textiles, dyes and chemicals.

Beijing

The municipality of Beijing (population approximately 15 million) is the capital city of China. It was previously known to the west as Peking. It is the second largest city, after Shanghai, and is one of four province-level municipalities. It is the country's political, educational and cultural hub. China's enormous central government is based here as well as a separate municipal government. Many of China's top universities are here, including the prestigious Tsinghua. The city has been in a constant state of reconstruction since the lead up to the 2008 Olympics, hosted by Beijing, and this has continued offer the event.

Chongqing

The municipality of Chongqing (population 31 million) is the largest and most highly populated of China's four province-level municipalities. It is a major port and is at the confluence of the Yangtze and Jialingjiang Rivers at the head of the reservoir behind the Three Gorges Dam. It is south-west China's commercial capital and a major centre of iron and steel production, motorcycle manufacturing and shipbuilding, as well as chemical and pharmaceutical production. There are 35 universities. The nearby religious cliff sculptures of Dazu and Baodingshan and the Three Gorges scenic region of the Yangtze River make Chongqing an important tourist centre.

Fujian

Fujian (population 35 million) is across the water from Taiwan and has historically been one of the provinces most open to the outside world. Recently Fujian has followed a programme of intense economic development, offering flexible measures to attract international investment and business. It is now one of China's most vibrant and prosperous provinces and home to many of China's ethnic minorities. About eight million overseas Chinese worldwide are from Fujian. There are 53 universities.

Capital city: Fuzhou (population 6.6 million) is an important commercial and manufacturing centre on the Min River. There are also many arts-related industries, including the 'three treasures of Fuzhou' (lacquer work, stone sculpting and cork cutting), famous cuisine, and Min Opera. Xiamen (formerly Amoy) is the major coastal city between Hong Kong and Shanghai. It has an international flavour and is one of China's most attractive resort cities. It is one of the four Special Economic Zones. The island of Gulangyu, a former colonial enclave, is a five-minute ferry ride from Xiamen.

Gansu

Gansu Province (population 26 million) is in the upper reaches of the Yellow River, in the middle part of the Silk Road. It is home to the largest and best-preserved site of ancient Buddhist art, the Mogao Caves near Dunhuang. It is also home to the grand Jiayuguan Pass, where the Great Wall ends in the west. The region is well known for its fruit: peach, watermelon, honeydew melon and melon seeds. It has 31 universities.

Capital city: Lanzhou (population 2.8 million) was an important strategic town on the ancient Silk Road, and is now a key link on the present Eurasia Bridge that crosses Asia and Europe. Lanzhou is the standard Yellow River crossing point. It is also a major transport terminal for the region; all trains to Xinjiang, Qinghai and Tibet pass through the city.

Guangdong

Guangdong province (population 86 million) is China's largest regional economy and a global manufacturing centre. Today Guangdong is China's wealthiest province, and contains three Special Economic Zones (Shenzhen, Shantou and Zhuhai). Rivers from all over Guangdong flow through the fertile Pearl River Delta into the South China Sea midway along the long coastline. The Pearl River Delta is one of China's most densely cultivated areas. An all-round development has taken place in finance, commerce, foreign trade, industry, and agriculture. The province has countless small and medium-sized enterprises as well as many famous large firms. It is rich in fruits, vegetables and livestock. Guangdong has 94 universities. Cantonese cuisine is famous for its delicacy and variety.

Capital city: Guangzhou (population around seven million), formerly called Canton in the west, is at the top of the river delta. Guangzhou is a famous ancient cultural city and the largest metropolis and foreign trade port in southern China. It is also an important industrial centre.

Guangxi Zhuang

Guangxi Zhuang Autonomous Region (population 45 million) is on the Beihai Gulf. It is the only western province with a coastline, and therefore has an important role in the Western Region Development Programme, as a major gateway for imports and exports. Guangxi is famed for the limestone karst landscapes in its northern reaches and its various ethnic cultures. There are 49 universities.

Capital city: Nanning (population 6.5 million) is a prosperous industrial city. It is the centre of the Zhuang culture, China's largest minority (over 15 million). The city now has an open border with neighbouring Vietnam and is a gateway to commerce with Thailand, Indonesia and Vietnam. The mild climate means that there is a year-round growing season for rice, sugar cane, and subtropical fruits such as mangos and lychees.

Guizhou

Guizhou (population over 35 million) is a beautiful mountainous province in central southern China. It has an abundance of natural resources (coal and gold are among the most important), and the highest average rainfall in China. The province therefore has significant potential, particularly for the energy sector. It is one of 12 provinces implementing the western development strategy. The province is home to more than 15 national minority peoples, and has a rich variety of cultures. Guizhou has 26 universities.

Capital city: Guiyang (population 3.22 million). The city is dominated by mist-covered hills surrounding the Wujiang Valley.

Hainan

Hainan (population 8.2 million) is a tropical island in the south of China. Hainan's warm climate, beautiful beaches and clean air, make it a popular holiday destination. It is rich in natural resources, and Hainan's inland and offshore deposits of oil and natural gas are among the highest in China. Hainan was made a Special Economic Zone in the late 1980s. National minorities make up about one million of the population. The island has 14 universities. It is China's smallest province.

Capital city: Haikou (population around 0.5 million). It is a major seaport and is the political, economic, cultural and transportation centre of the whole province. It is one of China's leading economic cities. Most tourists congregate around the coastal resort of Sanya.

Hebei

Hebei (population 68 million) surrounds the cities of Beijing and Tianjin. It has industrial and historical importance and is one of China's more developed provinces. The Great Wall cuts across Hebei's steep mountains to the north. The resort of Chengde was the largest royal summer resort of the Qing Dynasty (1644–1911) and within it, the Great Wall is among China's most visited sites. There are 87 universities.

Capital city: Shijiazhuang (population 8.6 million) is a major railway junction for northern China. The city is a centre for China's largest pharmaceutical factory and for the study of traditional Chinese medicine.

Heilongjiang

Heilongjiang (population 38 million) is China's most north-eastern province. It is separated from the Russian Federation to the north by the Amur River, and borders Inner Mongolia to the west and Jilin to the south. Petrochemicals and equipment manufacturing are its traditional industries. Gold, coal and graphite are also important minerals. The iconic DaqQing oilfield is here. The province has a great potential for windpower. Cold climate agriculture produces maize, wheat, flax and beet. Heilongjiang has China's greatest commercial production of soybeans and also the greatest number of milk-producing cows. It has 59 universities.

Capital city: Harbin (population 9.54 million). Freezing winter temperatures make it the perfect location for China's largest ice sculpture festival. Every June, it hosts a major international trade fair.

Henan

Henan (population 97.2 million) is China's most populated province. It is traditionally regarded as the historic source of Chinese civilisation and was the centre of ancient

China for at least the first half of Chinese history. Luoyang and Kaifeng were each China's capital city for many dynasties. The Buddhist Shaolin Temple, at the foot of Mount Song, and martial arts schools are in Henan. It has 82 universities.

Capital city: Zhengzhou (population 5.6 million) is a transportation hub and has abundant mineral resources, including coal and cement rock. Important industries are textile, machinery, tobacco, non-ferrous metallurgy, chemicals, building materials, food and coal. Wheat, corn, cotton and tobacco are all grown here. Mount Song lies south-west of Zhengzhou. Its beautiful rugged peaks make it one of the most famous mountains in China. Luoyang is another important city.

Hubei

Hubei (population 60.2 million) is on the middle reaches of the Yangzte River, north of Dongting Lake. Hubei has long been well developed in economic and cultural terms thanks to its central location. Hubei has both beautiful scenery and historical relics and is home to various ethnic minorities. The famed Three Gorges of the Yangzte River are here. Wudang Mountain and Jiugong Mountain are Taoist sacred places. In the east are green rice paddies, lakes, cherry blossom and, in the west, mountains with primitive forests, caves and waterfalls. Along the Yangtze River are sites of ancient battlegrounds and of Sun Yat-sen's republican revolution. There are 85 universities.

Capital city: Wuhan (population 7.81 million) is at the confluence of the Yangtze and Han Rivers. The city is made up of three towns – Wuchang, Hankou and Hanyang – which are on opposite banks of the rivers and are linked by several bridges. It is an international commercial centre of finance, industry, trade and science. With scientific, technological and educational institutions the city is also an intellectual centre. Foreign investment has brought economic growth to the area.

Hunan

Hunan (population 67 million) is in the middle reaches of the Yangtze River and south of Lake Dongting. It has long been a major centre of Chinese agriculture, growing rice, tea, and oranges. In 1982, China established its first national forest park, Zhangjaijie National Forest Park, in a particularly scenic area of north-west Hunan. Hunan's cuisine is 'chilli hot'. One well-known historic Hunanese figure is Quyuan, a third century AD official who drowned himself in the Miluo River. His death and the search for his body started the tradition of the Dragon Boat Festival. Mao Zedong was born in Shaoshan. Former Premier Zhu Rongji also comes from Hunan.

Capital city: Changsha (population nearly 1.5 million) is a famous cultural centre with many historical sites and places of interest. Changsha's urban areas are the industrial, trade and financial centres of the province. Its rural areas are famous for grain production and pig farming. Among China's 32 large cities Changsha ranks eighth in terms of economic capacity.

Inner Mongolia

Inner Mongolia, or Nei Menggu Autonomous Region, (population 23 million in an area more than 10% of China) is a Special Economic Zone. Han Chinese are the

majority ethnic group followed by the Mongols, who make up around 20% of the population. The Han Chinese arrived in waves during the 19th and 20th centuries and, for the most part, have settled along the Yellow River as well as in central and eastern Inner Mongolia. The pastoral economy of the Mongols was collectivised during the Maoist years, so they no longer live as nomads. Main sources of livelihood are agriculture and stockbreeding (Sanhe horses and oxen and fine-wool sheep) but also forestry, coal mining and steel industries. Apart from wheat, oats, millet, sorghum, maize, potato and rice, a wide range of cash crops are grown, including soybeans, linseed, rapeseed, castor-oil plants and sugar-beets. The Greater Hinggan range has one-sixth of the country's total timber reserves. There are abundant natural resources, especially mineral resources and its reserves of rare earth and natural alkali rank first in China.

Capital city: Hohhot (population over 0.75 million) has an ethnically mixed population. Mongolian folk songs and wrestling are popular forms of entertainment, seen at their best during the Naddam Fair. Hohhot is the political, cultural and industrial centre of the region. Manufacture of wool and leather products, metal, building materials, engineering and chemical industries all play an important role.

Jiangsu

Jiangsu (population over 74 million) has over 1,000km of coastline along the Yellow Sea and covers the lower reaches of the Yangtze River; it is called 'the land of fish and rice'. It is one of China's largest regional economies and is famous for its shoal exploitation and grain crops in the north. In the sout h, many cities are well known for machinery, electronics, chemicals, automobiles, textiles and tourism. Two great waterways flow through the province: the Yangtze River from west to east and the Beijing-Hangzhou Grand Canal from north to south. It has 112 universities.

Capital city: Nanjing (population 5.2 million) is on the south bank of the Yangtze River. It is a historical political centre, the capital of early southern regimes and was the southern capital during the Ming dynasty. It was also the seat of the nationalist government in the 20th century. Today Nanjing houses manufacturing and production facilities for some of the world's leading multinational corporations. The picturesque cities of Wuxi and Suzhou, famous for their gardens and canals, are also in Jiangsu.

Jiangxi

Jiangxi (population 43 million) is an inland province on the Yangtze River and is known as the 'cradle of the revolution'. The Communist party began its famous

'Long March' from here. Poyang Lake, in the north, is China's largest freshwater lake and also the largest winter habitat for white cranes. It is one of China's richest agricultural areas. The Grand Canal, built by the Tang dynasty (618–907), put it on the main trade route between northern and southern China. Jiangxi is an important source of tungsten and there are both light and heavy industries here. The province has 66 universities.

Capital city: Nanchang (population 1.38 million) is on the Ganjiang River. For centuries, it was a storage and distribution centre for high-quality porcelain from nearby Jingdezhen. Jingdezhen remains a national centre for porcelain.

Jilin

Jilin (population 27 million) borders North Korea. It is rich in natural resources, particularly Chinese herbal medicines. The economy is mainly derived from its forest industry.

Some of China's best ski resorts are here and the province is home to a major Ice Lantern Festival in winter. There are 42 universities.

Capital city: Changchun (population 2.78 million) started about 200 years ago as a small trading town. Pu Yi, the last Qing emperor, lived in Changchun in an Imperial Palace between 1931 and 1945. It has many large and important enterprises, including the First Automotive Work and Changchun Bus Works.

Liaoning

Liaoning (population 42 million) in the north-east is China's closest gateway to the Korean Peninsula. Proximity to the sea has long given it commercial as well as strategic advantages. Liaoning was one of the first of China's provinces to industrialise. In recent years it has become a popular destination for Chinese tourists, largely thanks to the resort city of Dalian. It has 71 universities.

Capital city: After 1644 Shenyang (population 4.9 million) became the secondary capital of the Manchu dynasty for 350 years. It is also called Mukden in the north-eastern dialect of Manchu. Today the rich deposits of coal, iron ore and non-ferrous ore throughout Liaoning Province make Shenyang one of China's major industrial centres. Dalian is one of China's most important ports.

Ningxia

Ningxia Hui Autonomous Region (population 5.8 million) is in a remote area of central China. Stock raising and agriculture are the main economic activities. Home to the Muslim Hui people; Ningxia has a rich cultural heritage. The northern section, through which the Yellow River flows, is top-quality agricultural land. Wheat, sorghum, rice, beans, fruit and vegetables are cultivated. Wools, furs, hides, and rugs are exported, and there is some coal mining. Desert lakes yield salt and soda. The chief cities – Yinquan, Wuzhong, and Shicui shan – are all on the Yellow River. Other towns on the camel caravan routes are still important avenues of trade. There are 13 universities.

Capital city: Yinchuan City (population 413,000) is also called 'Phoenix City' and is famous as a cultural centre beyond the Great Wall. The products of the Ningxia plain are shipped from here. Textiles, chemicals, rubber and machinery are manufactured in the vicinity. Marco Polo is thought to have visited Yinchuan in the 13th century.

Qinghai

Qinghai (population 5.4 million) has the source of the Yellow River at its centre, while the Yangtze and Lankang Rivers have their sources in the south. There are 44 national minorities in Qinghai accounting for 44% of the province's total population. Qinghai Lake is the largest inland salt lake in China. The province is one of the five largest pasturelands which horses, yaks, and sheep graze on. In recent years, the Qinghai Tourism Administration has opened some routes, including the Southern Silk Road from Xining to Dunhuang, and the Ancient Road from Xining to the Yushu Tibet Autonomous Prefecture. It has 11 universities.

Capital city: Xining (population one million) is an important stop along the Qinghai-Tibet railway line, and a good stopping place for travellers to Tibet. Xining was once an important station on the Silk Road and has some interesting historic sites.

Shaanxi

Shaanxi (population 37 million) is one of China's oldest inhabited areas. The fertile strip of land along the Wei River, a tributary of the Yellow River, was where Chinese civilisation developed. The capital of 13 dynasties was in this province for over more than a millennium. The region has plentiful natural resources especially oil and coal. There are 62 universities.

Capital city: Xian, formerly Chang'An, (population six million) is home to cultural and historical treasures, the most famous being the terracotta warriors guarding the Ch'in emperor's tomb. As the city is the most important in north-west China, there are a lot of shopping outlets, big shopping centres, department stores and supermarkets for locals and tourists alike in and around Xian.

Shandong

Shandong (population 91 million) extends from the lower reaches of the Yellow River to the sea, forming the Shandong Peninsula. Confucius was born here and annual festivals are held in his hometown of Qufu to mark his birth. During the 2008 Beijing Olympics, the coastal city of Qingdao hosted water sports events and building and investment is high in the run-up to this global event.

Shandong is a key producer of grain, cotton and oil crops and is also well known for its tobacco, fruit, peanuts, silks, meat, and marine products. Its major mineral deposits include coal, petroleum, iron, aluminium and gold. The coastal area is abundant in salt, though fishing stocks have depleted in recent years due to the overexploitation. Shandong's many industries include oil extraction (the second largest source of crude oil in China is the Shengli Oilfield in northern Shandong), processing, machinery, electric power, chemicals, foodstuffs, textile, arts and crafts, and papermaking. As well as important rail transport links, Shandong has a dense highway network. It has 97 universities.

Capital city: Jinan (population four million) is an important educational centre. The seaside resort Qingdao – formerly a colonial outport for the Japanese and Germans – is home to the eponymous Tsingtao beer and the now-global Haier brand of white and electrical goods. It is the province's leading industrial centre and with a huge container port, is well linked to outside cities, especially in Korea. Zibo is an important coal-mining centre and also produces porcelain and glassworks.

Shanghai

Shanghai municipality (population 18.7 million), once a small fishing village is now China's biggest industrial centre, an important seaport, and mainland China's undisputed commercial and financial centre. Shanghai is the most cosmopolitan city in the country and was once known as the 'Paris of the east'. China's first stock exchange was re-opened here in 1990. Shanghai's Grand Hyatt is the highest hotel in the world.

Shanxi

Shanxi (population 33 million) was one of the earliest centres of Chinese civilisation and has numerous temples, cave-temples and monasteries. For centuries Shanxi was a centre of trade and banking and was famous for its merchants. The province is one of China's traditional industrial centres, accounting for two thirds of China's coal reserves. It has 56 universities.

Capital city: Taiyuan (population 2.2 million) is mostly on the eastern bank of the Fen River and is an industrial city.

Sichuan

Sichuan (population 87million) is on the upper reaches of the Yangtze River. With its rich natural resources, it has the strongest economy in western China and the most established industrial sector in the region. It is famously home to the giant panda (the Giant Panda Research Base is in Chengdu), has five world heritage sites, and is known for its spicy cuisine. It is also former CCP leader Deng Xiaoping's home province. Sichuan has 68 universities.

Capital city: Chengdu (population 11 million) was one of China's first centres of printing and it is here that the first paper money was printed in the fifth century. Chengdu is the main inland access city for Tibet.

Tibet

Tibet (population 2.7 million) is one of five autonomous regions in China. The country has long fascinated foreigners and its inaccessibility has added to the mystery. It contains most of the Himalayan mountain range, and with an average elevation of 4,900m (16,000ft), it is often called the 'roof of the world'. China recently opened a new railway, linking Tibet's capital Lhasa with the neighbouring province of Qinghai. The line climbs 5,072m (16,640ft) above sea level, making it the highest railway (in terms of elevation) in the world. Its final 710-mile section cost $3 billion and took four years to construct. There are four universities in Tibet. Tibet has a harsh natural environment but beautiful scenery including empty plains and high snowy mountains.

China's rule over Tibet is disputed by many exiled Tibetans, who see the increasing Han Chinese presence in Tibet as a threat to the Tibetan culture and way of life. Periodic uprisings and protests occur in Tibet, including in 2008, seeking more independence and self-governance.

Potala Palace, Tibet

Capital city: Lhasa (population 373,000) has long been the cultural and religious centre of Tibet. The grand Potala Palace, former winter residence of the Dalai Lama, dominates the city and is a symbol of the unified supreme authority of politics and religion. It attracts thousands of tourists a day.

Xinjiang

Xinjiang (population 19.3 million) is one of five autonomous regions. It is China's largest province making up more than a sixth of the country's territory and a quarter of its external borders. Minority groups form 60% of its population, with the Uighurs, Muslims of Turkish origin, making up 47%. The region produces grain, cotton, sugar beet and livestock; it has a relatively well-developed industrial structure. It has two major deserts: the Taklamakan and the Gobi, which are separated by the Tian Shan mountain range. There are 28 universities in Xinjiang.

Capital city: Urumqi (population one million) is the world's most landlocked city, being farther from the sea than any other major city on earth.

Yunnan

Yunnan (population 44 million) is one of China's most culturally varied provinces with more national minority peoples than any other part of China. It has a diverse topography – alpine mountain ranges to tropical rainforests – and has the greatest number of plant species in China. Its main industries are tobacco, biology and mining. There are 43 universities. Yunnan has more poverty-stricken areas than anywhere else, though projects are being put in place to alleviate this situation.

Capital city: Kunming (population 3.74 million) is on the edge of Lake Dianchi. The extraordinary Stone Forest is accessible from here.

Zhejiang

Zhejiang (population 47.2 million) produces the renowned Longjing tea, and is the second largest silk producer in China. It was in Zhejiang that the internationally prized grey-green celadon ware was manufactured. There were two famous kilns in Zhejiang as long ago as the 11th and 12th centuries. There are 67 universities in the province.

Capital city: Hangzhou (population 6.4 million) was once capital of the southern Song dynasty. It is one of China seven ancient capitals and is still one of the country's most attractive cities. The Lingyin Temple, one of Buddhism's 10 most famous ancient temples, is in the city.

OVERVIEW**OF**HONG KONG

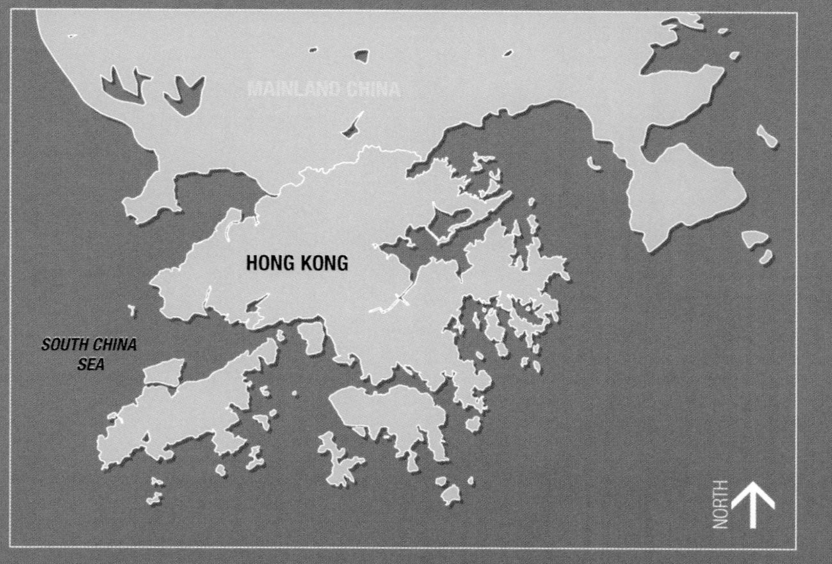
MAINLAND CHINA
HONG KONG
SOUTH CHINA SEA
NORTH

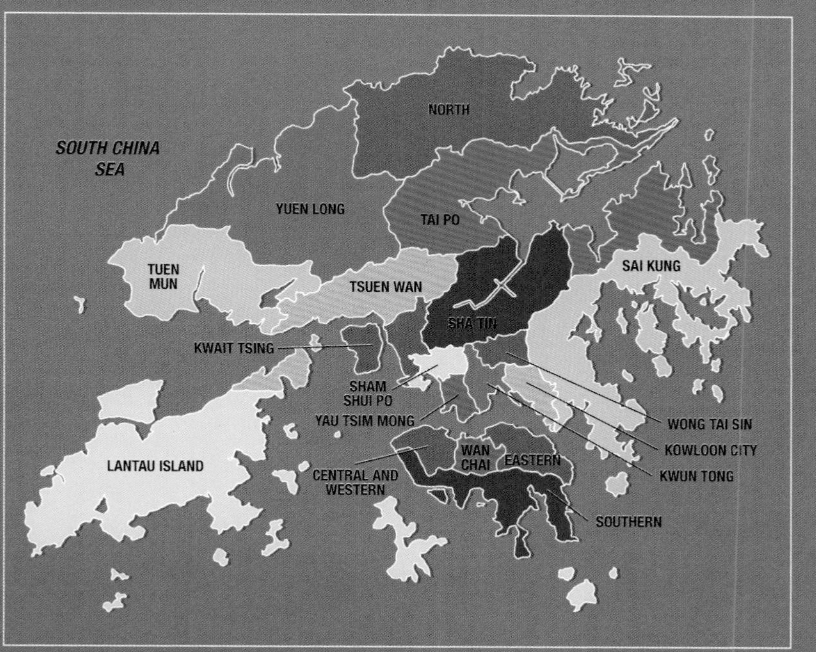
SOUTH CHINA SEA
NORTH
YUEN LONG
TAI PO
TUEN MUN
TSUEN WAN
SHA TIN
SAI KUNG
KWAIT TSING
SHAM SHUI PO
YAU TSIM MONG
WONG TAI SIN
KOWLOON CITY
KWUN TONG
LANTAU ISLAND
CENTRAL AND WESTERN
WAN CHAI
EASTERN
SOUTHERN

存德大押

Why Live & Work in Hong Kong?

ABOUT HONG KONG

It is not surprising that Hong Kong is popular amongst foreigners for travelling, working, or even settling down, as it is a vibrant commercial and cultural centre. Breathtaking modern architecture, the Big Buddha on Lantau Island, the mesmerising city lights by the harbour at night, the permanent buzz of activity, and an almost unlimited choice of food and fashion are all very impressive to foreigners. The excellent infrastructure makes it easy to travel around the city, and access to mainland China is good. Since English is one of the official languages (the others are Cantonese and Mandarin Chinese), it is easy to get by, and travel around the city is cheap. Many locals have been taught English at school and are generally friendly and helpful. People are accustomed to the mix of cultures and nationalities; racial discrimination is rare and is almost never directed against westerners.

There is excellent healthcare in Hong Kong, and apart from an increasingly polluted atmosphere, the standard of general cleanliness is high. There is a range of hospitals – some government, some private, some subvented by charities. There are many international schools in Hong Kong that are of a good standard. It is difficult for foreign children to get a place in a local Cantonese-speaking school, but it has been done.

There is a lively cultural scene and a very popular annual arts festival, which takes place at around Chinese New Year for a month. All the general release films are shown in Hong Kong's many cinemas, as well as some 'art' films. Throughout the year there are concerts of Chinese and western music performed by the local orchestras and performers as well as visiting overseas orchestras. There are also dramatic performances in various venues. The theatres are technically state-of-the-art.

Eating out – even for breakfast – is very much part of the culture. There are restaurants of just about every level of expense and sophistication where you can get the cuisine from almost every region of China. In the business districts it is sometimes hard to get a table at lunchtime, although the same restaurants will be much quieter in the evening. There is also a great variety of other restaurants: French, Russian, Italian, Middle Eastern, Japanese, Korean, Mexican, Thai, Indonesian, Indian, Spanish, sandwich bars, fast food (the busiest McDonalds in the world is in Hong Kong) and of course the ubiquitous Irish pub.

Hong Kong is a very social place with people getting together in bars, restaurants and in each other's homes. Try Lan Kwai Fong in Central (the central business district of Hong Kong) on a Friday night, and Staunton Street in Soho for its open-fronted restaurants and cosmopolitan atmosphere.

PROS AND CONS OF LIVING IN HONG KONG

Some of the things that attract foreigners to live and work in Hong Kong are that the tax rate is low, the infrastructure is very modern and you can get anything you need in the shops. The simple tax regime is also very attractive. There is no sales tax and many industries import cheap raw materials from China, which helps them to maintain their competitiveness.

Hong Kong has a very different culture to the west, and yet westerners can get more or less anything familiar, even if it costs more than at home. For a large part of the year the weather is fairly hot and it is possible to wear light clothes and go swimming. Hong Kong is a very cosmopolitan city, even though it is predominantly Chinese.

Pros:

- Very low tax rates
- Good infrastructure
- Warm weather
- Cosmopolitan culture
- No significant racial tension
- Reasonable living costs
- Very low crime rate
- English is one of the official languages
- Easy access to mainland China
- High standard of living

Cons:

- No government pension
- Expensive housing
- Overcrowding
- Air-pollution
- Far away from the USA and Europe
- Long working hours

Despite over a century of privileges for westerners, there seems to be no racial tension nowadays. Indeed some westerners observe that since 1997 taxi drivers and other folk who work in shops are friendlier to expats than they were before. It is as though now that westerners are no longer the 'colonial masters' they can be made welcome as foreigners and shown the kind of courtesy normally extended to visitors.

Hong Kong is also a good base from which to explore the region. There are flights to China, of course, and all major Asian cities. Thus, China (also accessible by bus, train or ferry), Taiwan, Thailand, Indonesia, Japan, and other countries of the region can easily be visited. There are often cheap package deals advertised. You can get the visa required for China in a matter of a few days (see visa information).

All the major general release films are shown in Hong Kong, and there are occasional concerts with performances by local musicians and international artists. In spite of, or maybe because of, the very crowded nature of many areas the crime rate is quite low. There are nearly always people about. You will find that

local people have quite a fear of crime and of being robbed or mugged but this is not born out by the incidence of crime. Violent crime is particularly low. However, given that there isn't the same level of censorship in Hong Kong as there is on the mainland, both Chinese and English-language media reports crimes in all their gory detail and the stories are on everyone's lips, especially if westerners are involved.

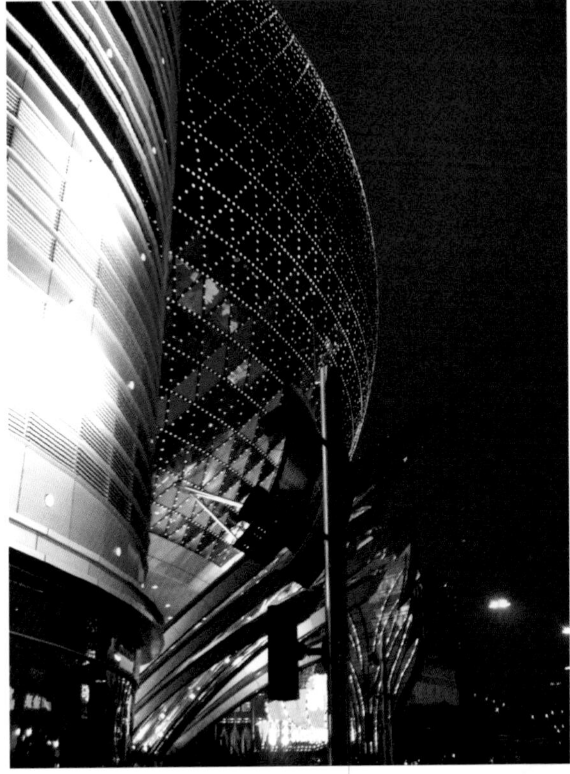

One of the official languages is English so it is possible for westerners and other foreigners to get by without Chinese. Some of the old-style colonialists never learnt any Cantonese at all (or ate any Chinese food) even if they lived here for over 20 years. In the days when there were Chinese live-in domestic helpers (amahs), it was not uncommon for the European children in their care to learn the language. Although it is possible to get by without, if you don't speak any Cantonese you'll inevitably miss a lot of the local culture.

Apart from the cost of accommodation and private medical care, living costs are fairly reasonable. This includes the cost of food, transport and clothing. The standard of living for most foreigners is high. International firms pay high salaries, often with perks attached. A foreigner working for an international company on 'expat terms' will also be provided with accommodation or accommodation allowance, sometimes with education allowances for children and with passages home every year or so.

Most of the foreigners in Hong Kong are of working age: it is not a popular place for foreigners to retire as there is no government pension, only occupational ones. There are, however, some foreigners that stay after retirement, who have invested in property in their working life, or who are married to a local spouse.

Since the city is already very overcrowded and land is at a premium, buying or renting a house or flat independently can be very expensive. Apart from this major consideration, living costs in Hong Kong are not high when compared to the USA and the UK.

The weather is never too cold in Hong Kong – almost never below 10°C – but it can be unpleasantly hot and humid in the summer, when it also rains a good deal. However, almost all restaurants, shopping centres, shops, cinemas and even public transport are air-conditioned.

Poor air quality might be a problem to foreigners. Due to the large number of vehicles in the city, and the presence of Chinese factories across the northern border with Hong Kong, the problem of air pollution is serious. What was once often a clear blue sky is now mostly a foggy pall. Even the once-stunning views from the mountains of the New Territories are now shrouded in murk. It may take some time to get used to it and if you end up staying, be warned that some long-term visitors develop mild respiratory problems.

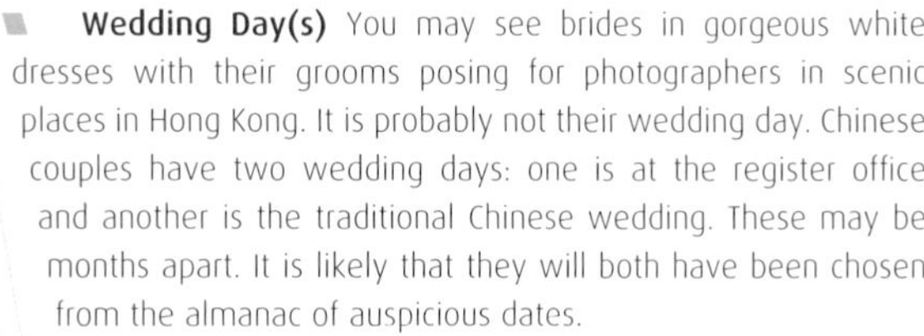

The strong work ethic of the local labour force ensures that the economy is robust, but it could be difficult for foreigners to cope with. It is common to work for over 10 hours a day, and working overtime is so common that in some cases you do not even get paid for it.

- **Wedding Day(s)** You may see brides in gorgeous white dresses with their grooms posing for photographers in scenic places in Hong Kong. It is probably not their wedding day. Chinese couples have two wedding days: one is at the register office and another is the traditional Chinese wedding. These may be months apart. It is likely that they will both have been chosen from the almanac of auspicious dates.

PERSONAL CASE HISTORIES

Jennifer Atkinson – solicitor

How did you come to be living and working in Hong Kong?

I spent a year working in Hong Kong. I was seconded to the Hong Kong office of the firm I worked for at the time, Clifford Chance (solicitors), for my final six months of training, but I arranged to stay for a further few months in order to gain more experience and an extra qualification.

What was your first impression of Hong Kong?

I first visited Hong Kong in February. My first impressions are very memorable: Kai Tak was the only airport in Hong Kong at the time and of course the weather in February was rather miserable – damp and grey with low cloud. As I looked down out of the plane window I was really depressed! Everything looked so dirty and grey. I thought, 'What have I just flown half the way round the world for if it's as horrible as this?'

The friend I was visiting was lucky enough to be staying in the Mandarin Oriental at the time and he sent a hotel car to collect me from the airport. It was a Rolls Royce Silver Shadow! So I had a journey in this car from Kai Tak to the Mandarin with such mixed feelings: the city looked so dirty and miserable and wet, but the car was so luxurious and it was such a treat to be driven around by someone else.

What was your visa status? Was it difficult to get such a visa?

I have a British passport, so this was not a problem for me. I got a year's entitlement to remain with my British passport.

What sort of place did you live in? Was it easy to find accommodation?

I lived in a flat with another trainee solicitor, which was rented on our behalf by Clifford Chance, so I don't know what the rental amount was. The firm had rented this flat for a number of years, along with several others in the same block. It was a two-bed apartment in Happy Valley and it was small but comfortable.

What was the social life like? Was it easy to make a new group of local friends?

For us trainee solicitors, the social life revolved around the office and among the trainee solicitors from other firms. I tended to socialise with the other trainee solicitors from my firm who had come out from London at the same time as me, and also with the young local solicitors from Clifford Chance. To this extent, there was a ready-made social group.

I suppose it was a typical expat social scene: we would go out for the evening once or twice a week to Lan Kwai Fong or Wanchai, and one or two weekends per month we would be invited to go out on the firm's junk. We would occasionally go to the cinema at Pacific Place. We would also spend some time entertaining clients of the firm by going for evenings out to restaurants or on the junk.

While this sounds as if I lived quite an expat lifestyle, I spent the majority of my free time alone, exploring the city and the countryside, and on most weekends spent some time walking, alone, in the New Territories, which is fantastic hiking country.

What do you like best about Hong Kong?

I love Hong Kong for its delicately balanced mix of east and west. It is the ideal place for a first-time visitor to Asia from Britain, as, while on the one hand it is a Chinese city, on the other, there is enough English spoken and written there to be able to lead the sort of life you would recognise at home. Also, I like the fact that it is so easy to get out of the city and into the countryside, such as the New Territories. This is a lot more difficult in London, for example. Also, Hong Kong is well placed for getting to other Asian destinations for the weekend or for a holiday – I went to China, Vietnam, Macau and the Philippines during my year in Hong Kong.

What do you like least about Hong Kong?

I suppose there are two things I dislike about Hong Kong. One is the rather limited cultural life. The number of exhibitions or concerts to go to is very small compared to life in London, and because they are less frequent, the tickets sell out very quickly.

The other aspect I dislike is that most of the expats have a very blasé attitude to the place. In a lot of cases, these people only go to the office and the nightclub and do very little else. This must give a very bad and shallow impression, and one that I don't want to associate myself with. In fact, the opposite was true of my local friends in Hong Kong: they were very bright, very interesting people. I expect that both these sets of people are exactly the ones you would expect to come into contact with most frequently as an English professional working in Hong Kong.

What advice would you have for anyone thinking of coming to live and work in Hong Kong?

First, I'd say pay a lot of attention to where you live. If you want the standard expat package, stay in the Midlevels, but I particularly enjoyed living away from that scene where the majority of your neighbours are not expats.

Secondly, don't worry about not being able to get things you rely on at home and having to bring a lot of things with you. I don't think there was anything I could not get in Hong Kong that I needed – either in terms of clothing and footwear, or in terms of food.

Finally, learn a little bit of Cantonese: at the very least learn how to say your address (so you can get home in a taxi from anywhere) and the numbers from zero to nine (so you can understand the prices of things and so you can phone directory enquiries which at the last count only had one English-speaking line and many more Cantonese-speaking lines).

Mark Adams – university lecturer

How did you come to be living and working in Hong Kong?

I found myself 'addicted' to Hong Kong after my first visit in the early 1960s. It has seemed like my adopted home although I never lived continuously here until I arrived in 1991. But I had managed to spend a year here on some 'academic mission' in just about every decade over that time and felt a need to experience the historic changeover first hand. I met Joyce [my wife] here while I was on a sabbatical year and came to know the people at the philosophy department quite well. So when I was offered a job, I was excited to accept it.

What was your first impression of Hong Kong?

It was about as totally 'other' as an impression could be. I arrived here almost directly from my life on the insanely, remote and sparsely populated desert north-slope plateaus of the High Uintah Mountains in eastern Utah. Our nearest neighbours were about three miles away and I would usually visit my neighbour 'friend' on horseback. I arrived in Hong Kong the day before a visit from some royalty (I think it was Princess Margaret) and the streets were crammed. I remember thinking as I struggled with the crowds on Nathan Road that I was seeing in this hour more people than I had seen in my entire life up to this point.

What is your visa status? Was it difficult to get such a visa?

I haven't had too much trouble with visa status except for the time spent in immigration. All of my earlier visits were on full-time visas and I was on an employment visa until I got permanent residence.

What sort of place do you live in? Was it easy to find accommodation?

I am still in university accommodation and I pay about HK$8,700 (£562/$1,118) per month in rent. There was a regular Hong Kong University (HKU) 'bidding' process for the available flats in operation when I arrived and it was relatively straightforward to get assigned a place. Since then, the system has become much less transparent and we have had trouble moving to more suitable places.

What is the social life like? Was it easy to make a new group of local friends?

The university does have a kind of built in community. We have made friends primarily through work and our child's various school situations and friends.

What do you like best about Hong Kong?

It's hard to say a single thing – it certainly is the package: Chinese people and culture, food, social life, language, energy and excitement, modernity, efficiency, rate of change, street life and colour, weather, beauty of the setting (harbour and peaks in a tropical forest), international character and 'sense' of the rest of the world.

What do you like least about Hong Kong?

Bureaucracy, air pollution, crowding, uncertain commitment to democratic/freedom principles.

What advice would you have for anyone thinking of coming to live and work in Hong Kong?

Do it! Be patient. Everyone who comes from the west gets exhausted by Hong Kong after about six months then again at around two years. Then it grows on you and it's hard to leave – probably the next most common decision to depart comes after about seven years. Almost everyone who stays over two years is sorry to leave and dreams of schemes to return.

Michiel Gen – exchange student

How did you come to be living in Hong Kong?

I came to study, an exchange programme at HKU.

What was your first impression of Hong Kong?

Very impressive skyline, bustling cosmopolitan atmosphere, the most efficient and affordable public transport system I have ever seen. Very fast pace of living.

What was your visa status? Was it difficult to get such a visa?

Student visa. It wasn't difficult to obtain one, as HKU took care of the entire procedure.

What sort of place did you live in? Was it easy to find accommodation?

Student hall. I can't remember the exact rent (HK$1,000–HK$1,200 per month) but it was quite cheap compared to private accommodation. I believe it was heavily subsidised by the university. The size of the accommodation left something to be desired according to European standards. Single room size was about 2m by 4m. It was easy to get this accommodation – the university arranged everything.

What was the social life like? Was it easy to make a new group of local friends?

My social life was very active. There was a sizeable contingent of expats and other exchange students with whom it was easy to make contact. Making friends with Chinese students proved a little more difficult as they seemed rather shy and reluctant to speak English (with the exception of the authors of this book!). I decided to choose the more difficult (yet rewarding) path by focusing on meeting local people and spending less time with westerners. After all one of the reasons why I chose to go to Hong Kong was to learn about other cultures. I made a number of Chinese friends with whom I'm still in regular contact.

What do you like best about Hong Kong?

The food. Enormous variety of, naturally Cantonese cuisine but also other Chinese, Japanese, other Asian and western styles. The local varieties being more affordable than others.

What do you like least about Hong Kong?

The climate in summer (too hot and humid). Dress accordingly!

What advice would you have for anyone thinking of coming to live and work in Hong Kong?

Make some local friend.s, learn some Cantonese, learn to eat with chopsticks, allow people a way out of discussions and debates which allows them to save face an important concept in China.

PHILIPS
SAMSUNG
NEC
ONWARD
762P.
GOLDEN STAR

Before You Go

VISAS, WORK PERMITS AND CITIZENSHIP

Due to overcrowding, Hong Kong has never been very keen to attract permanent immigrants. In fact, the government has been busy preventing illegal immigrants from entering Hong Kong, especially during the 1980s and the early 1990s. There were mass influxes of illegal immigrants from mainland China in the early 1960s and 1970s and they were allowed to stay in Hong Kong and became legal residents, but since October 1980 the government has prohibited illegal immigrants from the mainland from remaining in the city. However, a great number of illegal immigrants continue to take the risk and enter Hong Kong to take up employment. The government has spent many years fighting illegal employment and introduced several laws in the 1990s to prohibit employers from hiring illegal immigrants. Apart from those from the mainland, there were also a great number of Vietnamese refugees seeking shelter in the 1970s, 1980s and 1990s. Many of them came to Hong Kong to seek the help of the authorities to settle in third countries. Around 140,000 Vietnamese were settled overseas with the help of the Hong Kong government between 1975 and 2000. However, it has been getting more and more difficult to convince other countries to accept the refugees permanently, and many of those who came in the 1990s did not really qualify as refugees in the first place. The number of Vietnamese arrivals did not decrease until the Hong Kong government abolished the 'Port of First Asylum' policy in 1998.

It is not easy to obtain long-term residence in Hong Kong. Some professionals are allowed in to work and thus stay while they are working in Hong Kong. Alternatively, you could be a dependent of a permanent resident or of a professional who is allowed to work in Hong Kong. If you have enough financial assets you can also consider the Capital Investment Entrant Scheme.

Foreigners are always able to enter Hong Kong for short-term visits. Tourism has been an important industry for the city since the early 1980s and attracted more than 25 million visitors in 2006. The government has granted visa-free visits to nationals of about 170 countries and territories to make it easy to travel to Hong Kong. Most of the foreigners are permitted a visa-free period from seven days to three months. British nationals can stay without a visa for six months.

Following the hand-over from British rule to Chinese rule in 1997, the Hong Kong and mainland governments have been working on simplifying the immigration procedures between the two. Visiting quotas for Chinese citizens have been removed to make travelling to Hong Kong easier, particularly for residents of Guangdong and Shanghai. The government has been looking for more professionals from mainland China and launched the Admission Scheme for Mainland Talents and Professionals in July 2003. In October the same year, the government launched another scheme to attract capital investors. Even though the scheme is not limited to Chinese citizens, it is believed that most potential applicants will be from mainland China.

Visas

Visit, transit or business visit

Many foreigners enjoy a visa-free period, for travel to Hong Kong and as long as you hold a valid passport during your stay, you can buy a flight ticket and visit Hong Kong at anytime. Americans, Australians and most Europeans can stay in Hong Kong without a visa for up to 90 days while British citizens enjoy a longer visa-free stay for up to 180 days. Visitors are not allowed to engage in any employment or become a student at a school, university or other educational institute during their stay.

'Business visit' refers to a visit related to business but does not entail employment. Staff of multi-national corporations and joint-venture companies going to Hong Kong for orientation, product update or an exchange programme can apply for a business visit visa instead of a training or employment visa.

An onward ticket with a clear destination is required for application for a transit visa. However, no onward ticket is required if the destination of the onward trip is mainland China or Macau.

Required documents:

- ID936 form with parts A, B, C and D completed
- A photocopy of your travel document, the page with personal particulars, date of issue and expiry date
- Evidence of employment (if any) and financial standing
- Copy of identity card for the reference/sponsor (if any), or copy of the Business Registration Certificate of the company if it is a business visit

Employment for professionals or entry for investment purpose

An application for an imported worker or domestic helper is not covered in this section. Please see *Employment as a domestic helper* later in this chapter.

Applicants for an employment or investment visa are supposed to possess a special skill or knowledge or have experience of value to Hong Kong that is not readily available locally. The applicant is supposed to be in a position to make a substantial contribution to the local economy. Before issuing a visa, the Immigration Department considers whether the applicant is suitably qualified with the relevant experience for the job, whether the terms and conditions of employment are comparable to those in the local market, and whether the job can be filled locally.

These entry arrangements do not apply to nationals from Afghanistan, Albania, Bulgaria, Cambodia, Cuba, Laos, Mongolia, Democratic People's Republic of Korea,

Romania and Vietnam. Chinese nationals holding PRC passports can apply only if the applicant has been residing overseas for at least one year immediately before submission of the application.

Required documents for employment:

- ID936 form with parts A, B, E, F and G completed
- Photocopies of travel document, the page with personal particulars, date of issue and expiry date
- Proof of academic qualifications and experience relevant to the post
- A copy of the service contract or letter of appointment with details of the post, salaries and benefits and employment period

Required documents for investment:

- Documents listed under *Supporting documents for Employment* (complete part J instead of part G in the ID936 form)
- Business registration certificate
- Business registration particulars
- Partnership agreement
- Certificate of Incorporation
- Memorandum and Articles of Association
- Returns on directors
- Allotment of all shares
- Returns on shareholders
- Office purchase/tenancy agreement and the size
- Current staff list
- Company profile
- Proof of business activities/transactions
- Import and export customs declaration
- Current financial standing and source of finance of both the company and the applicant
- Trading profit and loss account
- Trial balance sheet up to last month and projected turnover in the coming year
- A full CV/résumé of applicant
- A full job description of the post that the applicant will take up
- Provision of housing for the applicant and the remuneration/honorarium the applicant will receive
- Actual monetary investment of the applicant in the company
- A detailed business plan

Capital Investment Entrant Scheme

- Terms relating to the Capital Investment Entrant Scheme.
- **Approval-in-Principle** A preliminary and provisional grant of approval in writing given by the director to the applicant to enter and/or remain in Hong Kong pursuant to the scheme.
- **Director** Director of the Immigration Department.

- **Entrant** An individual who has been granted formal approval by the director.
- **Formal Approval** A confirmed grant of approval in writing given by the director to the Applicant to enter and/or remain in Hong Kong pursuant to the scheme.
- **Market Value** The best price obtainable for the exchange of assets or property between a willing buyer and a willing seller in a transaction.
- **Net Assets/Net Equity** The two terms are interchangeable, meaning any asset, property or equity after deducting the amount of lien and encumbrance secured on or attached to it.
- **Premissible Investment Assets** Real estate and specified financial assets, including equities, debt securities, certificates of deposits, subordinated debt, Eligible Collective Investment Scheme.
- **Date of Completion** The date of payment on completion, or the last instalment if payment is made by more than one instalment.

FACT
Since 2003 foreigners have been permitted to enter and stay in Hong Kong as a Capital Investment Entrant.

Since 2003 foreigners have been permitted to enter and stay in Hong Kong as a Capital Investment Entrant. 'Investments' here only refer to investments in real estate or specified financial assets (equities, debt securities, certificates of deposits, subordinated debt, Eligible Collective Investment Scheme); other forms of investments do not count under this scheme. In addition, the entrants of the scheme are not allowed to engage in running any business.

To be a Capital Investment Entrant, you must be 18 or above, and have net assets or net equity with a market value of not less than HK$6.5 million (£400,000/$800,000) throughout the two years before you lodge an application. Moreover, you should have started investing within the six months before submission of your application, or will invest within six months after the granting of approval-in-principle. A three-month stay as a visitor will be granted after obtaining the approval-in-principle, and it can be extended for another three months if evidence of active progress in investment is shown. When the entrant has provided proof that the requisite level of investment has been made, a formal approval will be granted and he or she can stay for two years. A further extension of two years will be granted if the entrant can demonstrate further evidence for the continuation of investments. Further extensions, in units of two years, will be granted on the same principle. After the entrant has stayed in Hong Kong continually for seven years, he or she can become a permanent resident.

Entrants are allowed to bring their spouse and children under the age of 18 with them to Hong Kong, as long as they are capable of supporting their dependents without relying on any return from the permissible investment assets, from employment in or carried out in Hong Kong, or from any public assistance. Dependents of entrants are prohibited from taking up employment until they become permanent residents but children are allowed to study in local schools.

Entrants are not required to top-up the value of investments even if the market value of the assets falls below HK$6.5 million. However, even if the market value of the investments rises above HK$6.5 million, the entrants are not allowed to withdraw or remove any appreciation from the investment assets without sacrificing the right to stay under the scheme.

As well as the application form ID967, you should provide any document, for example transaction records, related to your investment to the Immigration

Department when you apply to be an entrant. Moreover, you also need to keep the records of your investment and provide written materials to the director for assessing your eligibility and entitlement under the scheme. The Immigration Department usually takes four to six weeks to process an application.

Employment as an imported worker

The Supplementary Labour Scheme (SLS) allows employers to import workers from outside Hong Kong if the employer experiences genuine difficulties in filling the vacancies locally. Workers imported under the SLS are restricted to those at the technician, craftsman, supervisor and experienced operative levels. SLS does not apply to some categories of jobs for which the supply in the local market is plentiful. For further details of the excluded categories, please visit the Immigration Department website (www.immd.gov.hk). Employers have to apply directly to the labour department for approval-in-principle before they make the visa arrangements for their imported workers. The visa application has to be made within three months after the approval-in-principle is obtained.

Required documents:

- ID936 form with parts A, B, E, F, H and I completed
- Photocopies of travel document, the page with personal particulars, date of issue and expiry date
- A set of standard employment contracts signed between the applicant and employer
- Academic qualifications and experience relevant to the post
- Proof showing the applicant is physically fit for the job.

Employment as domestic helper

Domestic helpers in Hong Kong are mainly from the Philippines, Thailand, or Indonesia. The employer has to provide a document stating the salary offered when applying for a visa for a domestic helper, as the Hong Kong government has set a minimum wage to protect them. The applicant should have more than two years' working experience as a domestic helper and must be physically fit for the job. The employer has to be financially capable of providing accommodation and guaranteeing the applicant's maintenance and repatriation upon the termination of the contract.

Required documents:

- ID936 form with parts A, B, E and F completed
- Photocopies of travel document, the page with personal particulars, date of issue and expiry date
- Standard employment contracts signed by both employer and applicant
- A testimonial of previous working experience
- Proof showing the applicant is physically fit for the job.

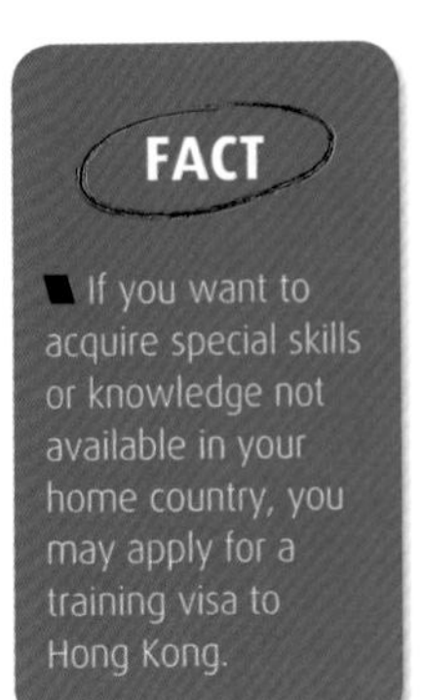
FACT
If you want to acquire special skills or knowledge not available in your home country, you may apply for a training visa to Hong Kong.

Training

If you want to acquire special skills or knowledge not available in your home country, you may apply for a training visa to Hong Kong. A visa for entering Hong Kong for the purpose of training is usually limited to a period of 12 months. The applicant should receive training at their chosen company's premises until the end of the agreed period and the trainee will return to his/her home country after that. It will be easier to get the visa if there is a contract between the sponsor and the trainee, and if the sponsor is a well-known company.

Entry arrangements do not apply to nationals from Afghanistan, Albania, Bulgaria, Cambodia, Cuba, Laos, Mongolia, Democratic People's Republic of Korea, Romania, Vietnam, and mainland China.

Required documents:

As for an Employment visa. p.255

Education

There are over 1,500 foreign students (not including those from mainland China and dependants of other visa holders) coming to study in Hong Kong every year. You must apply for a student visa before coming to Hong Kong unless you are a Chinese resident of the mainland or Taiwan. Except for tertiary education, foreign students can only be admitted to private schools but not public or suppported schools. Children going to pursue primary education in Hong Kong must be between the ages of six and 11. Applicants who are below the age of 20 can be admitted to secondary schools in Hong Kong. The applicant must hold a letter of acceptance from the school before applying for the student visa. Moreover, the applicant has to name a local sponsor who agrees to support and provide accommodation for the student.

Required documents:

- ID936 form with parts A, B and E completed
- Photocopies of travel document, the page with personal particulars, date of issue and expiry date
- A letter of acceptance from the school
- A letter of consent from one of the applicant's parents, if the applicant is under the age of 18
- A copy of the sponsor's Hong Kong identity card and/or travel document
- Evidence of the sponsor's financial standing
- An undertaking that the sponsor is prepared to act as the guardian in Hong Kong and that the applicant will be staying with him, or evidence that a place has been provided in a recognised boarding school.

Working Holiday Scheme

At the moment, this scheme only accepts applications from Australian and New Zealand citizens and there is a quota of 200 for each country every year. The aim of the scheme is to facilitate cultural and educational exchange between Hong Kong and the participating countries. The applicant must be aged between 18 and 30 and the main intention must be to have a holiday, not to work. Applicants have to show that they are financially capable of supporting themselves during their stay in Hong Kong and have a return ticket for the end of the stay. Successful applicants are allowed to stay for a period of not more than 12 months. They may take up short-term employment but they are not allowed to work for the same employer for more than three months. They are allowed to enrol in study or training course(s) of not more than three months (New Zealand citizens can only enrol in one course while there is no limit for Australian citizens). A person can only apply for the scheme once and an extension of stay will not normally be considered. It usually takes two weeks to process the application.

Required documents:

- Completed application form ID940
- A photocopy of travel document, the page with personal particulars, date of issue and expiry date
- Financial proof of a sufficient amount for maintenance during the stay in Hong Kong, eg bank statement, saving accounts passbooks, etc
- A photocopy of your return ticket or financial proof of having an amount equivalent to the return airfare
- A cashier order/bank draft for payment of the visa fee (which will be returned to the applicant if the application is unsuccessful)

Residence as a dependent

Dependents can be the spouse, unmarried children (aged below 18) and parents (60 or above) of a Hong Kong resident (the sponsor). Widows and widowers can apply as dependents to join their relatives in Hong Kong when they reach the age of 60. The applicant has to show a satisfactory relationship with the sponsor. The sponsor must have the right of abode in Hong Kong and be able to support the dependent at a reasonable living standard, and provide him/her with suitable accommodation in Hong Kong. Successful visa applicants of employment as Capital Investment Entrants, professionals entitled to work in Hong Kong, and visa holders for entry for investment, training, study as a full-time undergraduate and postgraduate can also bring their spouses and unmarried dependent children under the age of 18 (but not parents) to Hong Kong. The dependents are not permitted to take up employment during their stay in Hong Kong. Imported workers, domestic helpers and successfully applicants for the Working Holiday Scheme are not allowed to bring in their dependants.

FACT
Dependents can be the spouse, unmarried children (aged below 18) and parents (60 or above) of a Hong Kong resident (the sponsor).

Required documents:

- ID936 form with parts A, B and I completed
- Photocopies of travel document, the page with personal particulars, date of issue and expiry date
- A copy of sponsor's Hong Kong identity card
- Evidence of the sponsor's financial standing
- Evidence of the applicant's relationship with the applicant
- Evidence of sponsor's accommodation

Application methods

For visa applications for employment, investment (Capital Investment Entrant Scheme is not included), education, visit, training and residence, you have to fill-in the relevant parts of application form ID936 with a photograph affixed to it. The size of the photograph must not be larger than 55mm x 45mm and not smaller than 50mm x 40mm. The photograph must be taken full face and without a hat, against a plain background of mid-range colours (white, pink or light blue are the most common). Supporting documents should be presented along with the application. It usually takes four to six weeks to process an entry visa. See supporting documents under each visa section.

Where to send your application:

- Applications for transit or a visit should be sent to: Hong Kong Immigration Department, Visitors Section, 6/F, Immigration Tower, 7 Gloucester Road, Wan Chai, Hong Kong.
- For application of Capital Investment Entrant Scheme, send your application to: Other Visas and Permits Section, Immigration Department, 7/F, Immigration Tower, 7 Gloucester Road, Wan Chai, Hong Kong.
- Any other applications should be sent to: Hong Kong Immigration Department, Receipt and Dispatch Unit, 2/F, Immigration Tower, 7 Gloucester Road, Wan Chai, Hong Kong.
- Applicants can also hand in the application form in person to the nearest Chinese diplomatic and consular missions in their place of residence.

i A visa application form can be downloaded from the Immigration Department's website: *www.immd.gov.hk.*

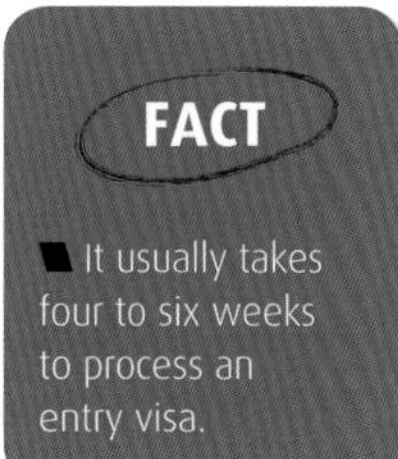

Fees for visas

Type of visa	US$	GBP£
Ordinary visa	$160	£80
Transit visa	$84	£42
Working Holiday Scheme	$160	£80
Capital Investment Entrant Scheme	$160	£80
Change of conditions of stay/extension of limit of stay	$160	£80
Declaration of nationality change	$145	£73
Naturalisation as a Chinese national	$3,140	£1,570

Hong Kong citizenship

Unlike Canada and Australia, there is no points system for migrating to Hong Kong. To become a Hong Kong citizen, you have to enter Hong Kong with valid travel documents, and have to reside in Hong Kong for a continuous period of seven years. You will need to apply for the Hong Kong Identity Card and make a declaration adopting Hong Kong as your permanent place of residence. After becoming a permanent resident, you are entitled to vote and receive social security. You can also apply for a HKSAR passport while keeping your original foreign passport. Contact the Immigration Department (www.immd.gov.hk) for further enquiries on Hong Kong citizenship.

THE LANGUAGES

English and Cantonese are the official languages in Hong Kong, and Cantonese is spoken by more than 90% of the population. Apart from English-speaking foreigners there is also a small proportion of people from India and the Middle East who speak their own languages too. The thousands of Filipino women working in Hong Kong as domestic helpers speak Tagalog and other dialects. You will find them chatting and singing on Sundays in Statue Square in Central.

The written Chinese language was standardised over 2,000 years ago. However, in 1956 the written characters were simplified in mainland China. The result is that Chinese people in Hong Kong and Taiwan still use the traditional, more complicated characters. Most Hong Kong people can manage to recognise simplified characters, but for foreigners it might be a challenge to manage both.

Government documents and official signs are bilingual. Restaurants usually have an English menu and products in shops usually have English descriptions as well as the Chinese ones.

Mandarin *v.* Cantonese

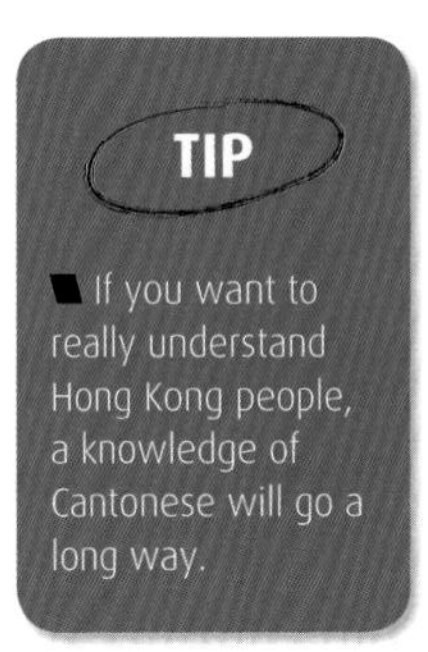
TIP
If you want to really understand Hong Kong people, a knowledge of Cantonese will go a long way.

Even though the official spoken language in the People's Republic of China is Mandarin, people in Hong Kong speak Cantonese, as do most people in Guangdong Province. Since Hong Kong was a British colony before 1997, neither the government nor the public placed much emphasis on Mandarin. Hong Kong started to take the Mandarin language more seriously when the economy of mainland China opened to the west in 1984. It was not easy for a foreign merchant to trade with mainland companies at that time and hence Hong Kong acted as a middleman to facilitate the trading. It became very useful to be able to speak Mandarin. In addition, many factories moved from Hong Kong to mainland China after the 1980s in order to minimise production costs and people started to realise the importance of learning Mandarin. This was especially so after the handover in 1997, and after the economic downturn in 1998. Mainland China is a very big market and it has been easier to do business with the motherland since the handover. Many companies started to expand their business to the mainland and it is necessary to send staff to the offices on the mainland to monitor the business and facilitate trade with local companies. In the economic downturn, looking for jobs in mainland China became an alternative to looking in Hong Kong. Hence, suddenly, learning Mandarin has become as important as acquiring IT proficiency. Moreover, the Hong Kong government states that being 'biliterate (Chinese and English) and trilingual (Cantonese, Mandarin and English)' is one of the main directions for education. Mandarin is clearly here to stay.

That said, you will find that many Hong Kong people learn and use Mandarin more or less out of necessity, and Cantonese still dominates daily usage. It is uncommon for two Cantonese speakers to converse in Mandarin. In Hong Kong, many young Chinese people even prefer to speak English if they cannot communicate in Cantonese. Government officials make their speeches to the public in Cantonese; news reports are in Cantonese; local movies, TV series and songs are mainly in Cantonese. The language also reflects the culture of Hong Kong, and

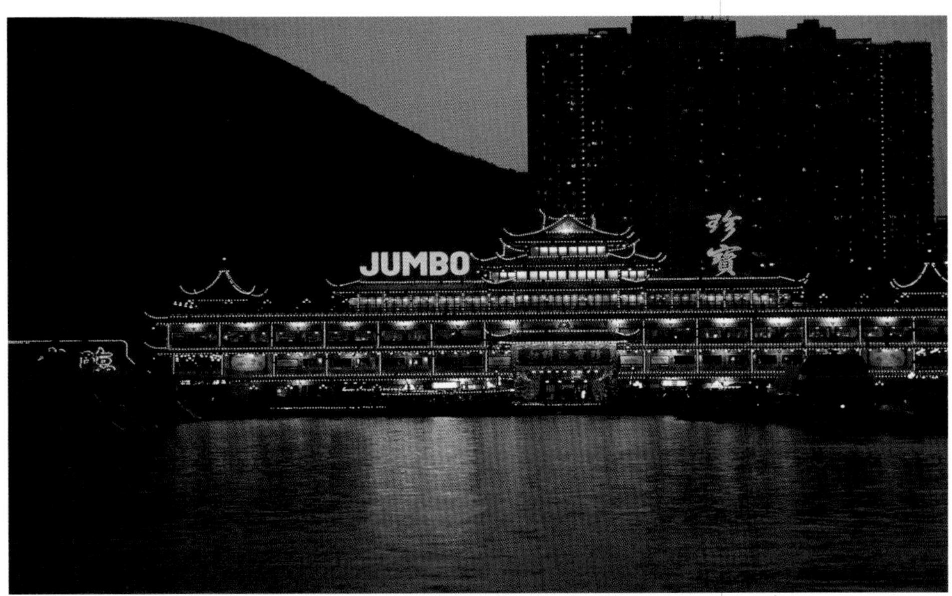

you may not be able to find an equivalent word in Mandarin for a Cantonese term or expression. If you want to really understand Hong Kong people, a knowledge of Cantonese will go a long way.

BANKING

Banking in Hong Kong is efficient and reliable. There are a lot of different services to suit all customers. Banks, in general, open Monday to Friday, 9am–5pm, and 9am–1pm on Saturday. Most of the banks are particularly busy during lunchtime and on Saturday mornings. Try to avoid going to the banks at these times or you will need to queue for up to 30 minutes. Many banks provide online banking services and basic transactions can be done online. There is no debit card in Hong Kong but EPS, a similar system, is widely accepted in shops. Credit cards are another normal payment method and it is easy to get a credit card in Hong Kong. Cheques are normal when doing business or handling fees, but companies prefer to have salaries paid directly to the employees' accounts. ATM machines are everywhere and some banks are linked. No extra fee is needed if you use the ATM machines of linked banks to withdraw money.

How to open a bank account?

Hong Kong has over 130 different banks. You can choose from American banks to Chinese banks, or from British banks to Indian banks. However, around five to eight banks have a significant domination in the market. Many companies prefer employees to have an account with a specific bank into which they can pay salaries. Opening an account in a main bank may therefore save a lot of trouble. Moreover, these banks usually have a lot of branches in most districts. See below for a list of the main banks.

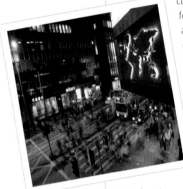

Many banks require a minimum opening balance of HK$100–HK$200 (£6–£13/$12–$25). It is best to check up with the bank for the required documents for opening an account. You will probably need a passport or other identification, and maybe a document, like the electricity bill, to confirm your mailing address. The banks usually suggest other services when you open an account, like a credit card, internet banking, phone banking or cheque account. You can apply for those according to your need. Internet banking, phone banking and a chequebook are all free of charge. Many banks waive the annual fee for credit cards to attract customers. You may also try to get your bank to waive the annual fee for your credit card if you use it frequently. Do it before the next annual fee is due. Many banks require customers to maintain a certain average monthly balance, maybe $3,000–$5,000. You will be charged an additional fee of around $20–$50 per month if your average monthly balance is below the required one. Overdrafts apply to some types of account. However, an additional fee may be required and the interest rate is usually quite high.

It is possible, and maybe better, to open an account in your own country before you go to Hong Kong. Many banks have branches in Hong Kong and are able to arrange an account in advance. Check with your home bank, so that you can have your account in Hong Kong ready before you arrive.

Main banks

Bank of China Ltd, Hong Kong: 2826 6888; www.bochk.com
The Bank of East Asia Ltd: 2842 3200; www.hkbea.com
Citibank, NA: 2868 8888; www.citibank.com.hk
Hang Seng Bank Ltd: 2198 1111; www.hangseng.com
The Hongkong and Shanghai Banking Corporation Ltd: 2822 1111; www.hsbc.com.hk
Standard Chartered Bank: 2820 3333; www.standardchartered.com.hk

Other banks

American Express Bank Ltd: 2844 0688; www.americanexpress.com/hk
Australia & New Zealand Banking Group Ltd: 2843 7111; www.anz.com
Barclays Bank Plc: 2903 2000; www.barclays.com

International money transfers

Transferring money to and from Hong Kong can be done in two ways, either by going to the bank or through electronic banking. A flat rate is required for both methods regardless of how much is to be transferred. Transferring money electronically is usually faster and cheaper, and may be done within one or two days. A bank draft takes around five days.

Currency

The dollar (HK$) is the monetary unit in Hong Kong, which is made up of 100 cents. Prices are generally presented with two decimal places, eg HK$2.50 represents two dollars and 50 cents. The smallest coin value is 10 cents. Others are HK$10, HK$5, HK$2, HK$1, 50 cents and 20 cents. There are six different value notes: HK$1,000, HK$500, HK$100, HK$50, HK$20 and HK$10.

FACT
The Hong Kong dollar is linked to the US dollar and currently has a standard exchange rate with it of US$1=HK$7.8 HK$1=US$0.128.

GETTING THERE

The cost of flying to Hong Kong varies from low season to peak season. Flying from London to Hong Kong takes 12–13 hours and costs as much as £400/$800 for a one-way ticket in high season. From the USA, airline Cathay Pacific flies non-stop to Hong Kong from both east and west coasts. The cost of flying from the east coast of America is around £500/$1,000 in high season and £400/$800 in low season. Flights fly towards the east and it takes around 16 hours to fly from New York to Hong Kong. It is quicker to fly from the west coast, which takes 14–15 hours, since flights go westwards instead. The prices for tickets in high season

and low season for flying from the west coast are around £450/$900 and £350/$700 return respectively.

The peak season runs from mid-June to September (and also over Christmas). You will get the cheapest tickets in October, November and March. In general, the earlier you book, the cheaper the fare. Indirect flights stopping in Singapore or Taiwan are usually cheaper. There are some online search engines specifically for air tickets and they usually provide better offers than booking directly from airlines.

Getting to the city centre from Hong Kong International Airport is easy. You can take buses or the Airport Express (operated by MTR, Hong Kong's underground railway) for just HK$100 (£6/$12). You can also take a taxi which will cost more – about HK$300 to Central from the airport.

- **Octopus Cards** It is a good idea to buy yourself an Octopus card when you arrive at the airport at the customer service desk. This is an electronic stored value card that you can use for nearly all public transport and for small purchases in convenience stores. It is an immensely convenient way to pay for travel as you simply swipe it across the meter, which automatically deducts the correct amount. It does away with the business of fumbling for change. There are even wristwatches with the Octopus card incorporated in it. It was introduced in the autumn of 1997 and there are currently 14 million in circulation. When you leave you can return it and reclaim your HK$50 (£3.20/$6.40) deposit and any unused stored money.

Airline websites

Air Canada: www.aircanada.ca
Air France: www.airfrance.com
Air New Zealand: www.airnz.com.au
American Airlines: www.aa.com
Australia Airlines: www.australianairlines.com.au

British Airways: www.britishairways.com
Cathay Pacific Airway: www.cathaypacific.com
China Airlines: www.china-airlines.com
Delta Airlines: www.delta.com
Emirates Airlines: www.emirates.com
EVA Air: www.evaair.com
Finnair: www.finnair.com
Oasis Hong Kong: www.oasishongkong.com
Singapore Airlines: www.singaporeair.com

Other useful websites

www.cheapflights.co.uk
www.expedia.co.uk
www.priceline.com
www.onlinetravel.com
www.statravel.com
www.traveljungle.co.uk
www.travelsupermarket.com

Useful resources

The Association of British Travel Agents (ABTA): 020 7637 2444; corporate@abta.co.uk; www.abta.com
American Society of Travel Agents (ASTA): 703 739 2782; askasta@astahq.com; www.astanet.com
Hong Kong Tourism Board: *(Hong Kong)* 2807 6543; info@www.hktb.com; *(London)* 020 7533 7100; lonwwo@hktb.com; *(New York)* 212 421 3382; nycwwo@hktb.com; *(Toronto)* 416 366 2389; yyzwwo@hktb.com; www.discoverhongkong.com
Registrar of Travel Agents, Hong Kong: 3151 7945; targr@edlb.gov.hk
STA Travel: *(Hong Kong)* 2736 1618; www.statravel.com.hk; *(UK)* 0870 1 600 599; www.statravel.co.uk; *(USA)* 800 781 4040; www.statravel.com
The Travel Industry Council of Hong Kong (TIC): (+852) 2807 1199; www.tichk.org

PLANNING AN INTERNATIONAL MOVE

Even though it is probably cheaper to buy new furniture and electrical appliances for your new home in Hong Kong, you may want to bring your beloved sofa or antiques with you. If you are moving from the UK, The British Association of Removers can provide a list of removers according to your current location. There are many removers in different parts of the USA and other countries as well. The cost depends greatly on the distance travelled and the weight/bulk of your possessions. Many companies also provide services for shipping vehicles.

Removal and relocation companies

Allied International: *(USA)* 800 323 1909; *(UK)* 020 8219 8000; *(Australia)* 3 9797 1600; *(Vancouver)* 800 795 2920; *(Toronto)* 866 267 9106; *www.alliedtoallied.com*
Allied Van Lines, Inc, USA: 800 323 1909; insurance@alliedintl.com; www.alliedvan.com
The British Association of Removers: 020 8861 3331; www.removers.org.uk
Excess Baggage PLC, UK: 020 8324 2000; sales@excess-baggage.com; www.excess-baggage.com
Sterling Corporate Relocation, UK: 020 8841 7000; mail@sterlingrelocation.com; www.sterlingrelocation.com
Sterling Corporate Relocation, Paris: 1 49 39 47 00; relocation@sterling-intl.fr; www.sterlingrelocation.com

Customs

Only a few commodities like liquor, tobacco, hydrocarbon oil and methyl alcohol are taxed when imported into Hong Kong. Bringing your household and personal belongings to Hong Kong is duty free as long as you can show the Customs and Excise Department that they are for personal use and not for trade. It is advisable to have a doctor's letter if you are on prescription drugs.

Importing a car

There is no customs tax for imported vehicles from other countries, whether they are for sale or personal use. However, it is generally not permitted to import left-hand-drive vehicles to Hong Kong as the road system is designed for right-hand-drive vehicles. If there is some reason why you have to import your left-hand-drive vehicle, you can apply for an Import Licence from the Left-Hand-Drive Vehicles or the Outboard Engine Licence Office. Right-hand-drive vehicles are not subjected to any licence when imported in to Hong Kong. You need to make a declaration within 14 days of importation, and are also required to submit an Import Return (CED336) and a Declaration on Particulars of Motor Vehicles Imported for Personal Use (CED336A) to the Customs and Excise Department within 30 days of the importation of a right-hand-drive vehicle. Forms can be obtained from the Custom and Excise Department (Motor Vehicles Valuation Group/Office of Dutiable Commodities Administration), Transport Department and Home Affairs Department.

Because of the potential congestion in such a built up area, running a car in Hong Kong is very expensive and is discouraged. Even though there is no customs tax for importing your vehicle, you are required to pay the First Registration Tax, which applies to all motor vehicles for use in Hong Kong, and also to pay a registration fee. You need to pay vehicle licence fee and levy for Traffic Accident Victim Assistance for licensing your vehicle as well. First Registration Tax is calculated according to the published retail price. For private cars, 35% will be the tax on the first HK$150,000 (£12,000/$19,000) of the published retail price, then 65% for the next HK$150,000, 85% on an additional HK$200,000 and 100% on the remaining taxable value. The First Registration Tax is a once-only charge. If the price of the vehicle is expressed in foreign currency, the foreign currency exchange rate will be taken on the date of importation of the vehicle.

- **What your car says about you** High status cars are popular in Hong Kong as part of the ethos of conspicuous consumption. The only people who drive old bangers can be regarded as dodgy types. A European university lecturer who used to ride a motorbike from Kowloon to his place of work in the New Territories was regarded by his Chinese colleagues as quite eccentric.

- Because of the potential congestion in such a built up area, running a car in Hong Kong is very expensive and is discouraged.

Useful resources

Left Hand Drive Vehicles/Outboard Engine Licence Office: 2723 3196; www.info.gov.hk/customs
Motor Vehicles Valuation Group: 2231 4391; www.info.gov.hk/customs
Office of Dutiable Commodities Administration: 2852 3049; www.info.gov.hk/customs
Transport Department: 2804 2600; www.info.gov.hk/td

Pets

You have to apply for a special permit to bring your pets to Hong Kong. Your pets should be given certain vaccinations, like Infectious Canine Hepatitis and Canine Parvovirus for dogs and Feline Panleucopaenia (Infectious Enteritis) and Feline Respiratory Disease Complex (Cat Flu) for cats.

You have to submit an application form to the Agriculture, Fisheries and Conservation Department, plus a permit fee of approximately HK$500 (£32.30/$64.25) for the first animal and around $100 for every additional one. Overseas applicants should submit the fee with a bank draft in Hong Kong currency payable to 'The Government of the Hong Kong Special Administration Region'. It takes about five working days to process the permit and it will be mailed to your home.

- Apply to: the *Agriculture, Fisheries and Conservation Department*, (+852) 2708 8885; www.afcd.gov.hk

Setting Up Home

CHOOSING WHERE TO LIVE

Hong Kong people spend a rather large proportion of their salary on mortgage repayments or rent. According to government statistics, the median mortgage payment and loan repayment to income ratio is 28% while median rent to income ratio is 14%. About half the population own their own houses or apartments.

Hong Kong is an extremely crowded area with a population of around 6.8 million living in an area less than 1,105 sq km, which is about two-thirds the size of London. What makes the overcrowding worse is its uneven distribution. The population density in Kowloon, for instance, is a staggering 43,200 people per sq km. With this kind of density, tower blocks seem to be the only answer. Residential buildings are usually about 30-storeys tall, or higher. All, of course, have elevators. People tend to prefer the higher floors (you're less likely to be burgled), so the higher the flat, the more expensive it is. The major determinant of the price or the rent, however, is location. More scenic districts like Mid-Levels and Discovery Bay are very expensive. Apartments in Causeway Bay and Central are also quite expensive as they are close to the business centres. You will find cheaper apartments in the New Territories and the outlying islands although they are still far from cheap by any standards. Many local people choose to live in public rental apartments, which are managed by the government to provide cheap accommodation for low-income households.

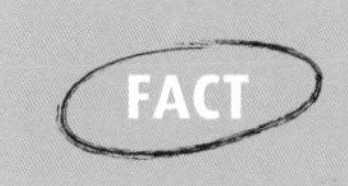

- About 50% of the people actually own the property they live in.

If you want to buy or rent an apartment, it is probably easier to do so through real estate agents, especially if you are not familiar with the local legal procedures. All the real estate agents are licensed and you can ask to see their licence before engaging them as your representative.

Types of properties

Hong Kong people are not a mobile group like Americans and Europeans. They usually spend a very long time in the same place and hence buying an apartment or a house and living there for over 30 years is very common. Apartments in Hong Kong are typically small. It is common to find a family of four or five living in a small apartment of around 300–500 sq ft (28–46 sq m). They usually have a living room, one or two bedrooms, a kitchen and a bathroom. Some bigger and more luxurious houses may have three bedrooms, with one of them en suite, but it is not common among middle or low-income groups. It is considered a real luxury for people to have a house with a garden. If you are really rich, you can look for a proper house in Mid-Levels, Stanley, Sai Kung or Tai Po. They do exist, though they usually come at an incredibly high price. The price for a flat of 3,000 sq ft (280 sq m) is around HK$28 million (£1.8 million/$3.6 million), which is around HK$9,500 per sq ft (£660/$1,200 per sq ft).

Electrical appliances like refrigerators, air-conditioners, washing machines, televisions and microwave ovens are a basic necessity for any household. Computer and broadband network connections are the norm for most households as well.

Although the transport system is good, many people still prefer to have a car. The population to car ratio is 15:1, which is on average one car for every five families.

FACT

- Although the transport system is good, many people still prefer to have a car. The population to car ratio is 15:1, which is on average one car for every five families.

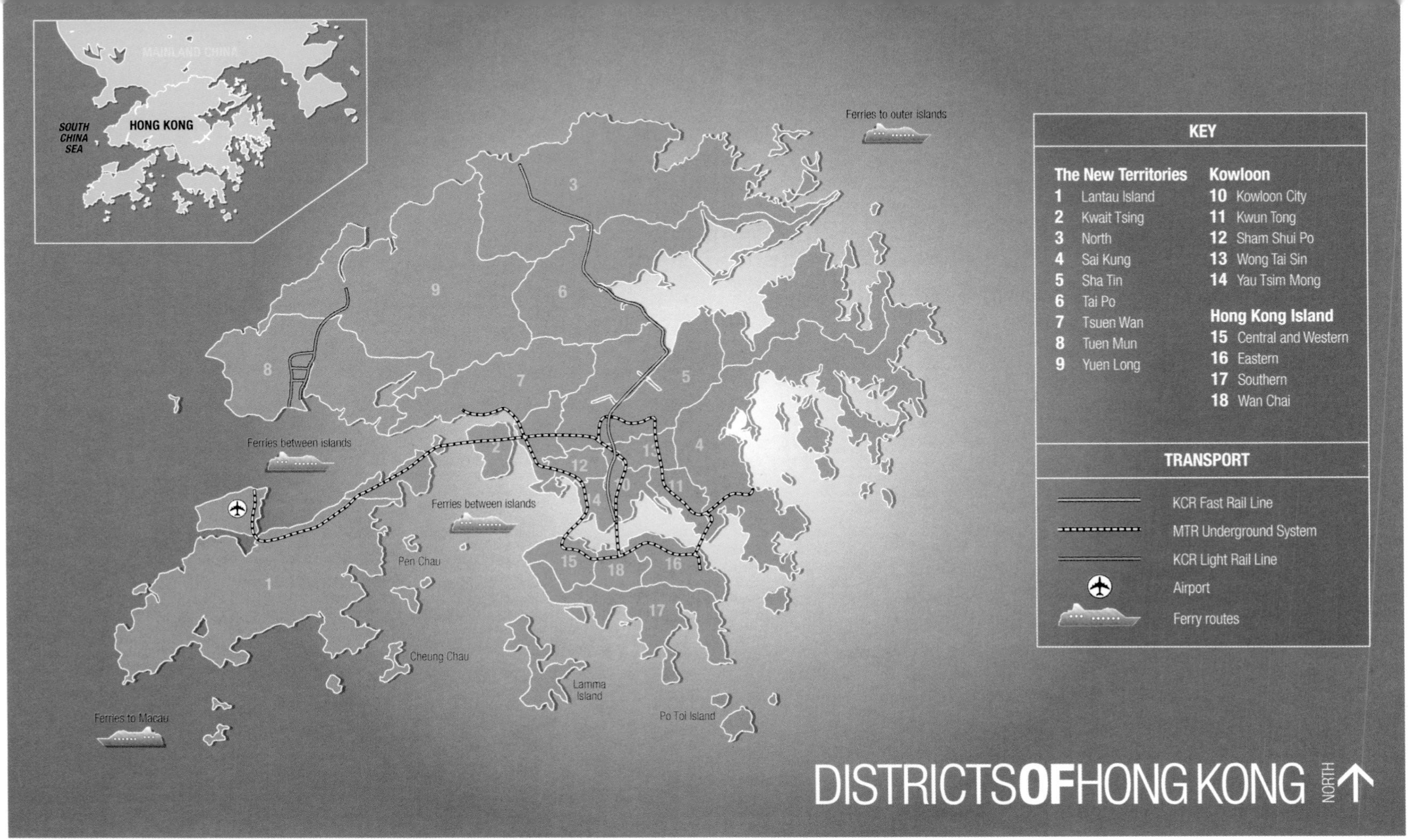

DISTRICTS OF HONG KONG
NORTH
KEY
The New Territories
1 Lantau Island
2 Kwait Tsing
3 North
4 Sai Kung
5 Sha Tin
6 Tai Po
7 Tsuen Wan
8 Tuen Mun
9 Yuen Long
Kowloon
10 Kowloon City
11 Kwun Tong
12 Sham Shui Po
13 Wong Tai Sin
14 Yau Tsim Mong
Hong Kong Island
15 Central and Western
16 Eastern
17 Southern
18 Wan Chai
TRANSPORT
KCR Fast Rail Line
MTR Underground System
KCR Light Rail Line
Airport
Ferry routes
MAINLAND CHINA
HONG KONG
SOUTH CHINA SEA
Ferries to outer islands
Ferries between islands
Ferries between islands
Ferries to Macau
Pen Chau
Cheung Chau
Lamma Island
Po Toi Island

NEIGHBOURHOODS OF HONG KONG

Hong Kong officially takes the title Special Administrative Region (SAR), but few could argue that this is a country in miniature. Broadly speaking, the SAR comprises several mountainous islands and a chunk of 'mainland' peninsula. The peninsula itself is divided into northerly and southerly sections. There's Kowloon – the original British concession – at the southern tip, and the New Territories, an expansive area of mountains and small towns that leads up towards the mainland border.

> If you want the standard expat package, stay in the Midlevels, but I particularly enjoyed living away from that scene where the majority of your neighbours are not expats.
> **Jennifer Atkinson**

With its stunning skyline, Hong Kong Island is the high-rise-studded symbol of Asian affluence. The island may represent just a fraction of the territory's overall bulk, but most of the money and power are packed into its limited confines. The urban strip that runs along the northern fringe is one of the most densely populated areas in China. In contrast, the Outlying Islands and New Territories offer rugged wilderness and breathing space away from the urban milieu. Excellent English-language signs make navigation easy, wherever you are, and the bus, train, metro and ferry routes stretch to all corners.

Hong Kong is technically divided into three major regions: Hong Kong Island, Kowloon, and the New Territories and Outlying Islands. These are subdivided into 18 administrative districts, each with its own local council. Hong Kong Island has four districts, Kowloon five and the New Territories nine. However, such is the density in certain pockets that several districts could easily be divided again. Central and Sheung Wan, for example, are both side by side within the Central and Western District but have very different characters.

Despite talk of Hong Kong being the ultimate east *vs.* west melting pot, the SAR retains an overwhelmingly Chinese flavour and expatriates generally cluster together in certain zones. Thanks to its proximity with the international business districts in Central, the Mid-Levels remains most popular with westerners, particularly those on executive salaries. The fashionable dining scene in nearby Soho is largely a product of moneyed residents being close at hand.

As ever in urban China, proximity to one's work must be a consideration. Commuting in the Hong Kong rush hour is slightly more bearable than it is on the mainland, mainly due to the fact people are less likely to push and queue jump. However, the sheer number of people always makes it a squeeze. What you will get for your monthly rental varies greatly, so it is equally important to look at which areas are within your budget.

Hong Kong property prices have been sky-high since the 1980s. Though there was a slump in the late 1990s and the early part of the 20th century, the market has made something of a comeback in recent years. Like Shanghai, given the extraordinary cost of buying a flat, it's still possible to find apartments that are relatively inexpensive to rent. Don't expect too much room though.

All prices below are per month, and based (approximately) on a two-bedroom (80–120 sq m) property in a relatively new apartment complex. The price range will reflect several factors, including the exact size of the apartment, its age and general condition, views, location relative to metro stops and whether it comes with furniture and other amenities. In Hong Kong, a 100 sq m apartment would be considered very large, hence the high prices quoted. Most singles and couples (and even familes with children) will live in smaller (and therefore cheaper) apartments than those quoted below. The price comparisons shown relate to Hong Kong only – in relation to the mainland they would nearly all be in the top price tier.

> Currency conversion: HK$10,000 = £646/$1,285

Central

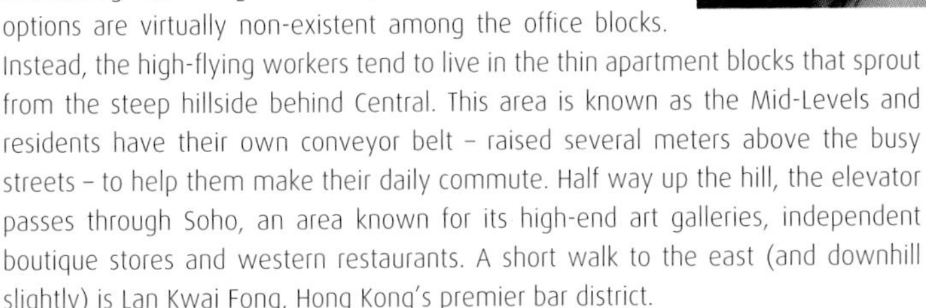

Central represents Hong Kong's land of luxury. It's a shopper's paradise, with hundreds of famous fashion names loitering behind polished glass façades, as well as corporate HQ to hundreds of international companies. Many have taken up home in the shimmering skyscrapers that populate the sea-level part of Central. The 88-floor Two IFC (International Finance Centre) building is the jewel in the crown, though office space abounds everywhere. The attractive Legislative Council Building, a relic of the colonial era and still the fully functioning seat of government, is also here. Residential options are virtually non-existent among the office blocks. Instead, the high-flying workers tend to live in the thin apartment blocks that sprout from the steep hillside behind Central. This area is known as the Mid-Levels and residents have their own conveyor belt – raised several meters above the busy streets – to help them make their daily commute. Half way up the hill, the elevator passes through Soho, an area known for its high-end art galleries, independent boutique stores and western restaurants. A short walk to the east (and downhill slightly) is Lan Kwai Fong, Hong Kong's premier bar district.

Best for: Businessmen, arty types, partygoers
Less good for: Families, anyone without expat salary packages
Price factor: HK$30,000–HK$55,000

Sheung Wan

Sheung Wan, or the Western District, lies just to the west of Central. It's paired with Central in the same administrative district, but the two neighbourhoods couldn't be more different. Sheung Wan is one of Hong Kong's most traditional areas where the shops sell herbal medicine and dried preservatives by the sack load. The fragrant backstreets of Sheung Wan offer up traditional markets and delightful colonial buildings, which rub shoulders with Hong Kong's modern, glitzy constructions. The Western Market is a good example. Built in 1906, this distinctive Edwardian building fell into disuse before being declared an historical monument in 1990 and restored. Next to it is the Sheung Wan Fong piazza surrounded by traditional shopping streets. Residential options are limited and apartments are still expensive and on the small side. Even so, prices are slightly cheaper here than in the Mid-Levels. Hong Kong University (HKU) has its campus in Sheung Wan.

Best for: Traditionalists, workers in Central
Less good for: Families
Price factor: HK$25,000–HK$45,000

Wanchai

Wanchai, the area immediately east of Central, was once famed as Hong Kong Island's den of depravity (particularly during the Vietnam War era). Plenty of escort bars remain but the overall mood is now fairly salubrious. It's possible to take a ferry directly to or from Tsim Sha Tsui in Kowloon, making it useful for transport. The boat docks beside the Sydney Opera House-styled Hong Kong Convention and Exhibition Centre, the venue for some major shows. As in Central, an elevated pedestrian walkway guides passengers from the waterfront into the urban jungle. All the land north of Hennessy Road in Wanchai has been reclaimed from Victoria Harbour. Apartments are in good supply here but, as ever in this part of Hong Kong Island, space is tight.

Best for: Partying
Less good for: Families
Price factor: HK$25,000–HK$45,000

Causeway Bay

A few kilometers east of Wanchai is Causeway Bay, a melting pot of consumerism. The imposing Times Square building is a veritable skyscraper of a shopping mall while nearby are Jardine's Bazaar and Jardine's Crescent which contain a warren of shop-cum-cubicles that sell cheap clothes. For its energy alone, Causeway Bay is one of Hong Kong's most vibrant and exciting neighbourhoods. Nearby is the wonderfully claustrophobic Happy Valley Racecourse. Evening horseracing meetings are held here most Wednesdays between September and June. Central Library, located on the northern fringes of Victoria Park, has one of the best English-language collections in Asia. There's also free internet and stunning views across Victoria Harbour.

Best for: Shoppers, bookish types, gamblers
Less good for: Families
Price factor: HK$25,000–HK$50,000

The Peak

Hong Kong's take on Beverley Hills, the Peak area is where celebrities and tycoons ensconce themselves in homes that cost silly money. Mount Austin Road is the thread which binds it all together and leads to the peak's 552m summit from where there are breathtaking views down to the harbour and across to Kowloon. The peak is connected with Central by the Peak Tram, a creaking funicular railway that dates to 1888 and hauls (mainly) tourists up and down the steep hillside. The uppermost station links directly into the Peak Tower which has a viewing platform as well as tourist attractions, like Madame Tussaud's and Ripley's Believe It Or Not Odditorium. Just across Peak Road is the Peak Galleria, home to several expensive restaurants and shops. Anyone who wants to stay up here overnight (or longer) should make sure their bank balance looks healthy first.

Best for: Tycoons, space, views
Less good for: Traditional atmosphere
Price factor: HK$30,000–HK$60,000

Stanley

The historic village of Stanley lies across the mountains, close to Hong Kong Island's most southerly point. This is one of the few areas populated prior to British rule and is now best known for its busy market. There is a pleasant beach close by and some great walking trails in the hills behind town. The area throngs with tourists by day, but this is – at heart – a seaside village and there's much to recommend it if you want something a little more laidback than can be found in the north. There are good bus links with Central but consider buying your own car if you are serious about settling here.

Best for: Families, walks
Less good for: Singles, access to central areas
Price factor: HK$25,000–HK$45,000

Aberdeen

Another of Hong Kong Island's famous seaside towns, Aberdeen has unique character due to the number of seafaring vessels that can be found bobbing in the harbour. This was once home to a legion of 'boat people' who lived on floating sampans and junks. Most have now moved ashore, though boats remain for fishing and tourism. Ocean Park, one of Asia's best marine parks, is located nearby.

Best for: Families
Less good for: Singles
Price factor: HK$25,000–HK$40,000

Repulse Bay

Repulse Bay, to the south side of Hong Kong Island, is a sandy strand is popular for sunbathing and swimming. The hills behind the bay are strewn with luxury apartment blocks. Like Victoria Peak, this area is an enclave for the rich. 'Luxe-Hong Kong' is still well within reach, but great sea views offer a feeling of tranquility. These are best enjoyed from a private room. In the public areas, things can get very hectic, especially on weekends when thousands of day-trippers descend. The Repulse Bay Hotel, a replica of a once-famous colonial resort hotel, houses some fine restaurants, including The Verandah.

Best for: Beach lovers
Less good for: Peace and quiet, shoppers
Price factor: HK$35,000–HK$45,000

Tsim Sha Tsui to Yau Ma Tei

With its historic buildings and modern museums, Tsim Sha Tsui (on Kowloon's southern tip) is arguably Hong Kong's most cultured locale. Moving north, top-end hotels and plush shops begin to rub shoulders with hideous apartment blocks, like the infamous Chungking Mansions. Street hawkers ply their trade here in huge numbers, offering tailor-made suits, 'Rolex' watches and digital cameras – all of which are in bountiful supply. Nathan Road is the main vein that connects the several districts of this area. The street has been virtually sealed from the elements due to the number of overhanging hoardings. Temple Street Market, close to the Jordan MTR station, is Hong Kong's most famous night market. The quality of accommodation in this area will vary greatly. New apartments are very expensive, but cheaper digs in older blocks can sometimes be found.

Best for: Arty types, foodies
Less good for: Congestion, hawkers
Price factor: HK$ 30,000–HK$50,000

Mongkok

Mongkok is one of the most crowded and lively districts in Kowloon. It's historically a working-class neighbourhood and gone is the slick sophistication of Hong Kong Island or Tsim Sha Tsui. What emerges is a riot of commercialism set against a backdrop of crumbling tenement blocks and crackly neon signs. Mongkok retains an authenticity that is perhaps lacking in other areas of Hong Kong; small shops and stalls abound. Mongkok has benefited from efforts at urban regeneration and there's a certain youthful 'hip-ness' in parts, evident in the likes of Langham Place – a 15-storey mall that houses lots of indie brands. However, much of the accommodation here is in old buildings and facilities may not be as slick as elsewhere. Prices, on the other hand, might be that bit cheaper.

Best for: Traditional atmosphere, transport
Less good for: Congestion
Price factor: HK$25,000–HK$40,000

Sai Kung

A small town located at the beginnings of the beautiful Sai Kung Peninsula in the east of the New Territories, Sai Kung has a strong seaside flavour. There's an independent community feel in its markets, noodle shops, restaurants and bars and, for those who do not crave the thrills and excitement of Kowloon and Hong Kong Island, there would be scant reason to leave. Which is perhaps a good thing given the relative paucity of public transport. On Sundays thousands of Hong Kong's Filipino residents flock to Sai Kung to worship at the nearby Catholic church. There are a handful of Hong Kong's more spectacular golf clubs lurking close by. Much of the Sai Kung peninsula has been declared a country park making Sai Kung arguably the best spot in Hong Kong to enjoy the pleasures of the countryside without having to forego all of the perks of urban life.

Best for: Families, the great outdoors
Less good for: Transport
Price factor: HK$15,000–HK$30,000

Sha Tin

Sha Tin was formerly a sleepy market town but now looks more like some kind of futuristic hive of skyscraping apartment blocks and vista-gobbling housing projects. It is home to Shatin Centre Street and the impressive New Town Plaza shopping centre. As a new town, it lacks the glamour and history of the more built-up areas in the south but, thanks for the KCR railway that runs through town, it's fairly easy to reach both Kowloon and the mainland border. However, the town is far

enough away from both to make the trip irritating if it is a daily commute. There are numerous cultural, recreational and sporting facilities close at hand: swimming pools, recreation centers, athletics grounds and football pitches among them. Sha Tin is also home to Hong Kong's biggest horse racing venue.

Best for: Families
Less good for: Foodies, culture
Price factor: HK$20,000–HK$35,000

Cheung Chau

Loitering off the south-east coast of Lantau, the tiny island of Cheung Chau has some of Hong Kong's cheapest accommodation. In its busy harbour, promenade restaurants and low-rise buildings, Cheung Chau has a laid-back atmosphere that feels a world away from Hong Kong Island, which can be seen across the sea on a clear day. The harbour front comes alive in the evenings when the long row of restaurants move business outdoors and set up beside the water. The seafood here is some of the best in Hong Kong, while the alleys behind Praya Street are the complete epitome of Hong Kong's oft-cited 'traditional way of life'. The island is also a car-free zone, making it a great spot to clear the lungs, especially around the beautiful coastal pathways.

Best for: Families, beaches, price
Less good for: Ease of access
Price factor: HK$10,000–HK$30,000

RENTING A PROPERTY

It is more usual for a foreigner to rent an apartment or house, rather than buying one immediately, when he or she first arrives. Moreover, it is usually cheaper, if you do not plan to stay for a long period, or if you are not yet sure of what you want. You can find both furnished and unfurnished flats in Hong Kong. It is easiest to look for a flat or house through real estate agents. Many real estate agents put the details of vacant flats or houses on their websites so you can have a look before contacting the agents. Some owners prefer to put an advertisement in newspapers instead, but it is not very common these days. You may find some on-street advertisements as well, which is more common around rural villages in the New Territories or some older districts. Be careful when dealing with these owners, particularly if you are looking for a flat in older Kowloon districts like Yau Ma Tei and Shum Shui Po. There have been complaints that some advertisements were merely posted to lure people to a place where they can easily be robbed. Universities usually have a notice board for leasing and it would be easier to check up there, instead of with real estate agents, if you are looking for a room or a flat to share. Some of them may be offered to students only, but you can always ask.

Renting costs

Like many other cities, rental costs are mainly determined by the location and size of the apartment or house. In general, renting an apartment in Hong Kong Island is more expensive than most parts of Kowloon and the New Territories. An apartment in Causeway Bay or Wanchai, at the heart of Hong Kong Island, costs around HK$8,000 (£500/$1,000) for an apartment of 500 sq ft (47 sq m). Expect to pay a minimum of HK$10,000 a month for an apartment of 800 sq ft (75 sq m) in these busy areas.

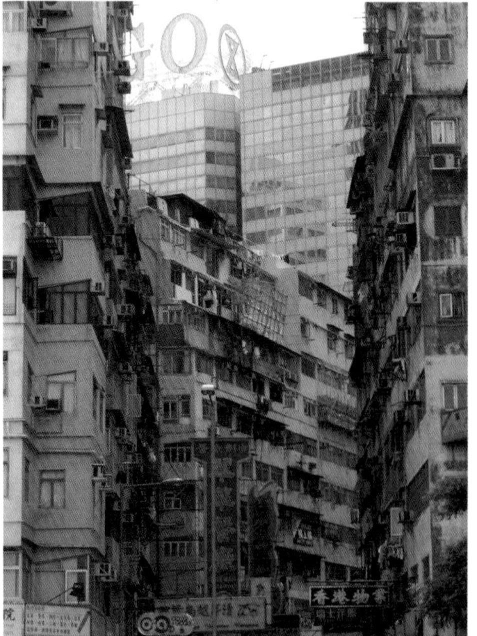

West Hong Kong Island is a good option if you prefer to live on Hong Kong Island. For apartments of about the same size, the monthly rent is HK$2,000–HK$3,000 cheaper if you are living in Sheung Wan or Kennedy Town instead of Causeway Bay. There is also some cheaper housing in the New Territories and the outlying islands. It is possible to rent a house of 700 sq ft for HK$3,000–HK$4,000 in rural villages, like those in Yuen Long, Tai Po or Sheung Shui. However, you must pay extra attention to checking the facilities before signing the tenancy agreement, as these houses are usually very old. You will find quiet houses facing the sea in Sai Kung, but prices vary a lot depending on the location, size and distance from the beaches, etc. If you are looking for deluxe apartments or houses, the Peak and the surrounding region will be your focus. Alternatively, Discovery Bay, located in Lantau Island and 30 minutes by ferry from Central, has been getting more and more popular amongst the high-income group.

Tenants usually have to pay a maintenance fee for buildings with security guards at the lobby. The fee varies from hundreds to thousands of Hong Kong dollars, depending on how expensive the basic rent is.

Property and rental prices in Hong Kong fluctuate a good deal so the above figures should be taken as a rough guide only.

Tenancy agreements

It is important to read the tenancy agreement carefully before signing, as the law in Hong Kong tends to favour the landlord rather than the tenant, which may sound a bit unusual. The landlord usually takes a deposit of a month's rent in advance on top of the first month's rental payment. The landlord will hold the deposit until you move out. Bills are usually not included. It would be wise to make sure to what extent you are responsible for damaged furniture during your rental period and make it a written statement on the tenancy agreement. The tenancy agreement may not state the exact rental period but it is important to discuss this with the landlord. You should make sure that the period of notification required in case either side wants to end the tenancy is written in the tenancy agreement. You will probably have to inform the landlord at least a month before you are moving out but it all depends on the agreement between you and the landlord. The landlord should inform you if there is an increase in rent at least a month in advance before the end of the tenancy agreement or the commencing date of the new rent. If a tenant fails to pay the rent within 15 days after the rent is due, the landlord can apply to the court for an order for eviction of the tenants.

Real Estate Agents

Centanet: info@centaline.com.hk; www.centanet.com
Century 21 Hong Kong Ltd: 2869 7221; www.century21-hk.com
Evergreen Management Co Ltd: www.homehksar.com. Specialises in housing in Mid-Levels and the Peak.
Hutchison Whampoa Properties Ltd: 2128 7500; www.hwpg.com
Karlson Property Consultants Ltd: 2342 2261; www.karlson.com.hk
Sun Hung Kai Properties Ltd: 2827 8111; shkp@shkp.com; www.shkp.com.hk

BUYING A PROPERTY

The government provides loans for households to purchase property. There are different policies to help middle and low-income households to purchase their own property. For people living in public housing, the Hong Kong government has launched the Tenants Purchase Scheme, which was designed to help public housing residents to buy the rented apartments. Under a current scheme the tenants of public residential complexes can buy the flats they are currently occupying at very affordable prices.

It is quite common to buy an apartment before the construction is finished. The builders advertise when there are going to be new residential avenues and set out dates for purchasing. You can see long queues outside the building sites on the

dates for selling. For details please see *Buying property under construction* later in this chapter.

How to find a property

The most convenient way to find a property is through real estate agents. You can either visit or call them or visit their websites for enquiries. There are also advertisements in newspapers and magazines, with dates for registration, when there are new residential sites for sale. See above for a list of major agents.

Mortgages

In Hong Kong, banks are the main providers of mortgage services. In general, a buyer can borrow around 70% of the value of the apartment from banks and some provide mortgages of up to 90%. There are several types of mortgage provided by the banks including Floating Rate Mortgages, Fixed Adjustable Rate Mortgages and Mortgage Insurance Programmes. Fixed Adjustable Rate Mortgages are mortgages originating in a fixed gross mortgage rate, which is fixed for the first year or for up to three years. After the end of the fixed term, the borrowers can choose to continue another fixed term under the gross mortgage rate at that time, or change to Floating Rate Mortgage, where the mortgage rate can be adjusted from time to time according to the market rate.

The Mortgage Insurance Programme was launched in 1999, with the Hong Kong Mortgage Corporation Ltd (a government authority established in 1997) providing the mortgage insurance. Under this programme the banks can provide the borrowers with a mortgage of up to 90%. However, the Mortgage Insurance

Programme only applies to borrowers who buy properties as owner-occupiers but not as investments. Some of the buyers will choose to have a second mortgage, which in general provides a further 15%–20% loan on the value of the property, if the first mortgage is 70% or less of the property value.

The interest rate and repayment period are the two major factors to consider when choosing a mortgage provider. Banks provide different types of mortgages to fit the needs of borrowers and the repayment period can be up to 30 years long. In general, the more you can borrow, the higher the interest rate. You should bear in mind that there is usually a minimum repayment period, and extra costs may be incurred if you repay the entire mortgage before the minimum repayment period expires. Some builders have agreements with specific banks to provide mortgages to buyers at a better rate, but it may not necessarily be the best deal available. It is better to go through the different mortgage plans of different banks before choosing the one that suits your needs. There is a list of mortgage providers in the Hong Kong Mortgage Corporation Ltd website and you can also visit the banks' websites.

Hong Kong Mortgage Corporation Ltd: www.hkmc.com.hk. With information of different kinds of mortgages and a list of mortgage providers.

Buying a property under construction

Buying a property before it is completed is quite common in Hong Kong. It is called buying *lou fa* (house flowers), presumably analogous to buying flowers and waiting for them to blossom later on. When a new, residential building under construction is up for sale, interested buyers have to register with the builder and present a cheque for 5% of the average selling price of the apartments in the building. The builder will then arrange a date for the registered buyers to select their desired apartments. The buyers have to sign a temporary contract with the builder after they have selected the apartments. The cheque they have handed in earlier will be used as part of the deposit for the apartments they buy. If the buyers fail to find a desired apartment or they are absent on the date for selecting an apartment, the cheque they have handed in during registration will be returned to them. Otherwise, the buyers will have to sign a standard contract with the builder within three days. In general, the builder will cancel the temporary contract if the buyers do not sign the standard contract within three days and the cheques in this case will not be refunded. The contract is drawn up by a lawyer for the builder and is approved by the Land Department, which should clearly state the selling price, date for the apartment to be finished, payment method, compensation if the apartment is not finished on time, etc. The contract will then be sent to the buyers' lawyers before the buyers sign it. The apartments are technically owned by the builders until the construction is finished and is approved by the government. The builder has to notify the buyers to take possession of their apartments within a month and the buyers, in general, have to complete all the transaction procedures 14 days after the builder sends the letters.

Buying a completed property

The procedures for buying a completed property are simpler than buying a property under construction – at least you do not need to register and sign a temporary contract with the builder. However, most new apartments are sold while they are still under construction and hence most completed properties you can find are not new but are pre-owned. Most owners sell their properties through real estate agents, which means the buyers and the owners do not usually negotiate directly over the selling price. It is important to check with the real estate agents to see if the furniture, electrical appliances, etc are included in the selling price. Take a careful look at the property before signing the contract, since, as elsewhere, both the seller and agents will tend to show you only the best aspects of the property.

Checking a property

No one wants to find that they have bought an apartment with cracks in the walls or a bathtub that leaks. It is very important to check everything in your new home carefully. Check the sink and bathtub to see if the draining system is working properly. Is there any gap between the door and doorframe? Do the keys fit the doors well? Are the electrical appliances supplied working properly and are they exactly the make that the builder or the owner promised to offer (some builders supply electrical appliances as an offer to buyers)? Mark down the readings of

electricity and water used during your tests, to see if the meters are working. If there is anything wrong with the property, you should ask the builder or the owner to fix the problems as soon as possible.

Property in wills

If someone dies without a will, under the current Intestates' Estates Ordinance in Hong Kong, his or her movable personal property goes to the spouse and the residuary estate (other than movable personal properties) is divided into two halves: one goes to the spouse, and the other half goes to the children. If he or she does not have any children, the second half of the residuary estate goes to the parents, or to the siblings if the parents have already died. For the deceased who has no spouse but children, the residuary estate will be held in statutory trusts for the children. If the deceased is still single when he or she dies, the residuary estate goes in sequence to parents, siblings, grandparents and then uncles and aunts, until one of the groups claim the residuary estate.

SERVICES AND UTILITIES

Utility companies provide good services even though there is not much competition. Electricity and gas bills come every two months while telephone bills and water bills come every three months and four months respectively. You can pay most of the bills through PPS (a 24-hour bill payment service that allows you to settle over 150 bills by a tone phone) or the internet at anytime. Funds will be automatically transferred from your bank account to the receiver's account upon your transaction. Some banks also provide bill payment services through the electronic banking system.

PPS: Customer Services Department; 2311 9876; hotline@eps.com.hk; www.ppshk.com

Electricity

The electricity supply in Hong Kong is 220 volts (50 Hz) and is provided by two companies: The Hong Kong Electric Company Ltd (HEC) and CLP Power Hong Kong Ltd (CLP Power). Electricity in Hong Kong Island and Lamma Island is provided by the HEC while CLP Power is responsible for providing electricity to Kowloon, the New Territories and other outlying islands. The charges of the two companies are not the same and HEC is slightly more expensive than CLP Power. The electricity companies take a meter reading from households every month and there is a minimum charge even when no electricity is consumed in that period. In general, electricity charges are higher in the summer if you use air-conditioning (which nearly everybody does). Electrical appliances with flat three-pin plugs are common and recommended. Nowadays two-pin plugs are considered unsafe and shops in Hong Kong are prohibited from selling them. Round-pin sockets are not very common and you may need to use an adaptor. Electrical appliances are relatively cheap when compared to Europe or North America, due to the low taxation and easily available

Asian products. You might want to buy new electrical appliances instead of bringing them all the way from home.

Electricity providers

CLP Power Hong Kong Ltd: 2678 8111; clp-info@clp.com.hk; www.clpgroup.com
The Hongkong Electric Company Ltd (HEC): 2887 3411; mail@hec.com.hk; www.hec.com.hk/hec

Gas

There are two types of gas supply in Hong Kong: Liquefied Petroleum Gas (LPG) and Towngas. Gas is the main fuel for cooking and can also be used on other appliances such as water heaters and dishwashers. Most households use a piped-in system but a very small number of households are still using bottled gas. Gas bills are sent to piped-in gas users every two months.

Gas suppliers

Shell Hong Kong Ltd: 2435 8388; www.shellgas.com.hk
Towngas: 2880 6988; www.hkcg.

Water

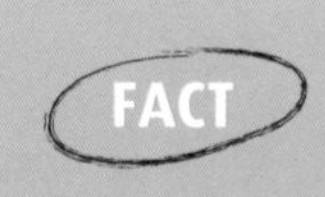

Local numbers consist of eight digits and there is no area code within Hong Kong. Making a local call with a fixed line is free of charge.

The water supply in Hong Kong is provided by the Water Supplies Department. Since Hong Kong has such a large population, there is not enough water in the reservoirs for all households. The government has to import water from Dongjiang in Guangdong Province. The water has undergone a series of treatments – a small amount of chlorine is added to it – before being supplied to households. Many people buy bottled water even though there is no problem with drinking tap water in Hong Kong. Flushing water is seawater and is provided free of charge, unless you specifically request drinking water for flushing. Meters for all households are installed in a certain area of each building and a water bill is sent to households every four months.

For enquiries about water supply, call Water Supplies Department hotline on 2824 5000 or visit the website www.info.gov.hk/wsd

Telephones

Home telephones are cheap in Hong Kong. There is no per-minute charge for making local calls but there is a basic monthly fee of about HK$100 (£6/$12). Local numbers consist of eight digits and there is no area code within Hong Kong. Making a local call with a fixed line is free of charge. Hong Kong Telephone Company Ltd was the only provider for home telephone services before July 1995, but the government has opened the telecom market to other companies and there are now nine companies licensed to provide a home telephone service.

For details of the current telephone service providers, visit the Telecommunications Authority's website: *www.ofta.gov.hk*

The installation fee for a new line is around HK$400–HK$500 and you can add another line for an additional HK$400. It is possible to take the old telephone number with you when you move to a new flat in Hong Kong, for a charge of HK$300. Call waiting, call forwarding, conference calling, voice mail services, etc are available with an additional charge of around HK$15–HK$20 for each service. The telephone companies quite often give promotional offers to customers, especially to new ones, but be careful. The company may ask you to pay a lump sum at the beginning for future reductions of the telephone fee. Take a careful look at the later bills to check if the amount you need to pay is the same as the sales mentioned. There are, disappointingly, many complaints about 'miscalculations' of fees, especially for sales plans that spread across a number of months. Call the customer service centres if you have any enquiry about the bills.

■ Local numbers consist of eight digits and there is no area code within Hong Kong. Making a local call with a fixed line is free of charge.

Telephone companies

CM Ltd: 2209 1709; www.chinaone.com.hk
Eastar Technology Ltd: 2908 8086; www.etns.net
HKC Network Ltd: 2890 7866
Hong Kong Broadband Network: 128 100; hmtelsupport@hkbn.net; www.ctinets.com
Hutchison Global Communications Ltd: 2128 2828; suggestion@hgc.com.hk; www.hgc.com.hk
New World Telecommunications Ltd: 2138 2138; www.newworldtel.com
PCCW: 2888 2888; general@pccw.com; www.cwhkt.com
TraxComm Ltd: 2993 8333
Wharf T&T Ltd: 2112 1121; cc@wharftt.com; www.wharfnewtt.com

International calls

Making international calls from Hong Kong is the same as from other countries: country code + area code (omit the zero of the area code) + the number. Cantonese, English, Mandarin and Japanese instructions are available when making international calls using public telephones. Local telephone companies provide a home international calls service as well. These companies are keenly competitive and therefore they always provide promotional calling rates to attract customers. However, these promotion schemes are usually under constraints. Most of them provide low rates only during non-business hours, on Sundays and on public holidays. Prices for calls made during business hours can be multiples of those in non-business hours.

You can either use the long-distance telephone service from telephone companies, or use a pre-paid long-distance phone card for making international calls at home. However, these cards have no standard call rates and the rates vary widely, and the expiry date might be another problem. The cards usually expire in three to six months. Check the call rates and expiry date carefully before buying. Purchasing from big telephone companies will usually be safer. The access numbers of these cards are usually free to call and instruction in English is available.

Pay phones

Pay phones are common and apart from the telephone boxes in the street, pay phones can also be found in convenience stores, KCR and MTR stations. HK$1, HK$2, HK$5 and HK$10 coins are accepted in most telephones but be aware that some of the telephones only accept phone cards or credit cards. Phone cards are available in stored values of HK$50, HK$100 and HK$200 and can be found in telephone company retail shops and convenience stores.

If a public telephone cannot be found nearby but you need to make a local call, there are usually telephones in Chinese restaurants (places for having dim-sum and Chinese tea). Although these telephones are supposed to be used by customers only, no one really checks or minds.

The emergency number in Hong Kong is 999

Television

As in China, there is no TV licence requirement in Hong Kong. For more on the television channels available in Hong Kong, go to the *Media and Communications* section in Daily Life.

Useful Telephone Numbers

Public and company phone number enquiry: 1083
Taxi stations: (Hong Kong Island/Kowloon) 2760 0455; (New Territories) 2457 2266; (Lantau Island) 2984 1328.
URBTIX (for reserving cultural programmes tickets): 2926 1133; www.lcsd.gov.hk/CE/Entertainment/Ticket
Weather forecast: 187 8066/2926 1133

 MOVING IN

Furniture

If you plan to import various items of furniture, see Planning an international move in *Before you go*. It is often cheaper and easier to fit out your new home when you are in Hong Kong.

Insurance

Many people prefer to have a home insurance plan to reduce the loss in case of accidents such as fire. Both insurance companies and banks provide different kinds of home insurance policies. Some cover a single event like fire protection, and there is also a combined one that covers different kinds of losses like burglary, fire, damage to home decoration and even medical expenses for domestic helpers.

Useful Resouces

American International Assurance Co Ltd: 2232 8888; www.aia.com.hk
The Bank of East Asia Ltd: 2842 3200; www.hkbea.com
Hang Seng Bank Ltd: 2198 1111; www.hangseng.com
Blue Cross (Asia-Pacific) Insurance Ltd: 2163 1000; www.bluecross.com.hk
The Hongkong and Shanghai Banking Corporation Ltd: 2822 1111; www.hsbc.com.hk
ING General Insurance International: 2850 3030; www.ing.com.hk/gi
Prudential Assurance Co Ltd: The Cityplaza Taikoo Shing, Shau Kei Wan. Standard Chartered Bank: 2820 3333; www.standardchartered.com.hk

Help in the home

There is a huge pool of foreign domestic workers (mostly from the Philippines, Thailand, or Indonesia), so it is not difficult to get help in the home. Their contracts and minimum salary are strictly controlled by the Labour Department to prevent exploitation.

For visa regulations, please see page 254.

美東豆肽片
修補・美肌・免疫
活性植物小蛋白
比燕窩更易吸收
AOBO
3102 3631
CAFE
2890 6799
易找換店FOREIGNEXCHANGE
¥ € $ £
£ € $
廣滙通訊
MULTI-LINK

Daily Life

CULTURE SHOCK

> I remember thinking as I struggled with the crowds on Nathan Road that I was seeing in this hour more people than I had seen in my entire life up to this point.
> **Mark Adams**

When you arrive in Hong Kong you may be hit by the heat and humidity, the crowds, the fog of pollution – an atmosphere that is very different from the one you have come from. All this can be exciting but also disorienting. If you have arrived from a very different time zone you will also have the effects of jet lag to contend with.

However, some expats say that when they first go to work in an office in Hong Kong everything seems reassuringly similar and the locals they come across seem very westernised. It is only after about six months that they realise that the traditional culture is in fact very different.

Hong Kong has some of the most densely populated urban areas in the world, and yet the population is on the whole very orderly and tolerant. Even in the densest areas, on a Sunday or public holiday in the shopping districts, the crowd has a peaceful and completely unthreatening feel to it. Nevertheless you should make sure that your valuables are not easy to pickpocket.

Hong Kong people are non-confrontational, but also do not particularly like engaging with strangers. This even extends to people not holding a door open for the person behind them after having gone through it, and not waiting for people to come out of a lift before entering it. It is almost as if strangers are invisible. There is still something of a 'me first' attitude that may be left over from the refugee days.

FOOD AND DRINK

Hong Kong people like to eat out in restaurants (hence the enormous number in Hong Kong), and like to buy fresh food in the 'wet' markets for home cooking.

People say that the food in Hong Kong is a genuine comfort when you are missing home. You can find cuisines from most parts of the world: Italian, French, Spanish, American, Japanese, Korean, Indian, Thai, Malay, Singaporean, Brazilian, Middle Eastern or Greek, etc. As for Chinese food, you can easily find over 10 different styles in Hong Kong. Hong Kong people like to eat out in restaurants (hence the enormous number in Hong Kong), and like to buy fresh food in the 'wet' markets for home cooking. You will never find it difficult to find a restaurant for your favourite food. Rather, it is often hard to choose from the varied choices. Seafood is a particular highlight. For some of the best, and cheapest, seafood in Hong Kong, head to one of the outlying islands, in particular Cheung Chau where outdoor eateries line the harbour.

Street and fast food

Fast food is very common in Hong Kong too. Apart from McDonald's, KFC or Burger King, you can try the local fast-food restaurants (not those that serve dim-sum, but small restaurants serving quick meals, called *cha-chaan-tang*) or Chinese noodle shops, which both serve cheap and good food.

Foreigners may also find *dai-pai-dong* interesting. These are on-street restaurants that place tables and chairs in the open areas in front of their kitchens, and are usually located inside public residential estates. There are some good ones in Shatin, Fo Tan and Yau Ma Tei. Table manners are not of much concern in these places, but the dishes are usually cheap and very tasty. The potential problem is that there may not be an English menu for foreigners. The waiters or waitresses are usually middle-aged locals who don't speak English. Therefore, it would be good to learn the names of the dishes you want to try from your local friends, or ask them to go with you – it is well worth it even if you have to pay the bill.

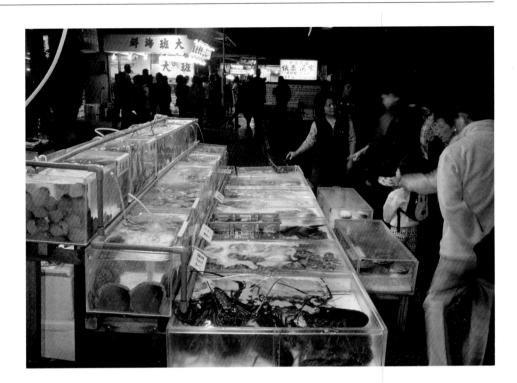

For real local specialties, there are tons of street snacks like fish balls (which do not really taste like fish, *yu-daan*), fake shark fin soup (made with soya beans, cooked with meat and other ingredients like the real shark fin soup, *woon-chai-chi*), rice rolls (*cheung-fan*), etc. These are all very tasty! There are many small food stalls selling these snacks in Mongkok, Causeway Bay and Wan Chai. They are often very cheap but food cleanliness is sometimes a concern.

For some of the best, and cheapest, seafood in Hong Kong, head to one of the outlying islands, in particular Cheung Chau where outdoor eateries line the harbour.

Bars, pubs and clubs

Bars and pubs are common in Kowloon and Hong Kong Island, particularly in Central (Lan Kwai Fong), Wanchai (Jaffe Road) and Tsim Sha Tsui. You may find some small pubs in the New Territories but they are rare. Pubs usually open from 4pm or 5pm until very late, maybe 3am in the morning. Alcohol is only sold to over 18s. You will find that drinks, for instance beer, served at bars and pubs are much more expensive than in supermarkets and convenience stores – sometimes tenfold or more. You can drink outside on the streets as long as you do not disturb others.

You will probably be taken aback at where you end up if you ask a taxi driver to take you to a nightclub. 'Nightclub' in Hong Kong is often used to refer to a hostess bar or a similar expensive place where you can find prostitutes. Hong Kong people call the western version of nightclubs 'discos'. There are many discos in the pub area in Wanchai and are also in Tsim Sha Shui and Mongkok.

Coffee shops are popular with those who want to sit comfortably and chat, which can be a bit difficult given the crowdedness of the city. Apart from big coffee shop chains like Pacific Coffee and Starbucks, there are also some small but pleasant coffee shops in Hankow Road, Tsim Sha Tsui.

SHOPPING

Many tourists like visiting Hong Kong because they find it a shopper's paradise. Shops usually open from 11am to 9pm or 10pm, seven days a week. There are lots of shopping centres in different parts of Hong Kong and you can find almost all you need. For designer clothing, go to Park Lane in Tsim Sha Tsui. You can still get tailor-made suits in some tailor shops, even though most people prefer cheaper ready-made ones, or designer labels. Kwun Ki is the largest clothing store with branches in different districts. If you are looking for some cheap and cool clothing, visit Fa Yuen Street in Mongkok or Granville Road in Tsim Sha Tsui or the Wanchai end of Queen's Road East. You will be amazed by the prices of the clothes. Do not expect the quality to be good (although you may be pleasantly surprised) but there is certainly a lot of choice. However, shoe sizes for women tend to stop at 38 (UK5/US7.5) and it is difficult to find shoes at size 40, (UK6.5/US5) or above.

Electrical appliances are, in general, cheaper than in the USA and Europe. It is better to go to the big electrical chain stores like Fortress or Broadway if you are not familiar with the small shops, even if the price is usually more attractive there. Be careful when buying electrical appliances in tourist areas like Tsim Sha Tsui zand Causeway Bay as the price is usually marked up for tourists.

You can probably get furniture at reasonable prices in Hong Kong. Ikea provides a great selection but small furniture shops sometimes stock the same kinds of items at a lower price.

> I don't think there was anything I could not get in Hong Kong that I needed – either in terms of clothing and footwear, or in terms of food.
> **Jennifer Atkinson**

Local specialities

- There is a street full of shops selling goldfish near Fa Yuen Street.
- You can find lots of sports shops in Sai Yee Street, just next to Fa Yuen Street.
- The Jade Market is in Yau Ma Tei, behind the Kowloon Central Post Office. You can get good deals for jade, if you know how to recognise the best quality.
- In Sheung Wan in Hong Kong Island, there are many shops selling dried seafoods, which are great for cooking or as presents for the Chinese New Year. Since the competition is keen, the quality is in general very good although the price may not be significantly lower than elsewhere.
- Gold and jewellery is a must-buy for visitors from mainland China. The gold sold in Hong Kong is under strict supervision, and the guaranteed quality attracts many tourists from mainland China. Moreover, the jewellery designs are also more fashionable and there is more choice.

Useful resources

Visit the shops' websites for branches information.

Broadway: Shop 714, Times Square, Causeway Bay; 2506 1330; www.ibroadway.com.hk

Fortress: 1st Floor, Cavendish Centre, 23 Yip Hing Street, Wong Chuk Hang, Hong Kong; 2555 5788; fortress@asw.com.hk; www.fortress.com.hk

Ikea: 3125 0888; www.ikea.com.hk

Kwun Ki: 1, Yee Wo Street, Causeway Bay, Hong Kong; 2576 2505; customer hotline (for enquiry on addresses and telephone numbers of other branches): (852) 2793 1393

Books and bookshops

The prices of books in Hong Kong greatly depend on where they are published. Books from China and Taiwan are usually cheap but are mainly in Chinese. In general, English books are more expensive. A medium-length (around 200–300 pages) English novel costs around HK$80–HK$160 (£5–£10/$10–$20). Dymock's Book Sellers, Swindon Book Co, Bookazine and Page One are the major bookshops selling English books. You are more likely to find academic and literary works in the university bookshops. Even if they do not have the book you are looking for, they can order it for you although there may be a surcharge for those who are not university staff or students.

There is a huge book fair in Hong Kong every year in late July to early August, which is held in the Hong Kong Convention and Exhibition Centre in Wanchai. The entry fee is around $20 and books are usually at a discount. Avoid visiting on the first day or the weekends if you do not want to queue for hours before you can get into the exhibition halls.

Bookstores

Contact the individual companies for branch details.

Academic & Professional Book Center: Shop 623, Grand Century Place (Mongkok Railway Station), Mongkok, Kowloon, Hong Kong; 2398 3044

Bookazine: Shop 309-313A, Prince's Building, Central, Hong Kong; 2522 1785; shonee@feml.com.hk; www.bookazine.com.hk

City University Bookshop: Level 4, Academic Block, City University of Hong Kong, Tat Chee Ave., Kowloon Tong, Kowloon, Hong Kong; 2777 0122; apcityu@netvigator.com

Dymocks Booksellers: Shop 115-116, Prince's Building, 10 Chater Road, Central, Hong Kong; 2826 9248; erictfho@dymockspb.com.hk; www.dymocks.com

Page One: Basement 1, Times Square, 1 Matheson Street, Causeway Bay, Hong Kong; 2506 0383

Swindon Book Company: 310 and 328 Ocean Centre, Harbour City, Tsim Sha Tsui, Kowloon, Hong Kong; 2730 0183; www.swindonbooks.com

MEDIA AND COMMUNICATIONS

Newspapers

There are over 10 local newspapers in Hong Kong and three of them are in English. *The Standard* and *Asian Times* are focused primarily on business news. The *South China Morning Post* is the pick of the bunch and covers all the usual sections, it also has good features of topical and regional interest. Many of its wider-interest features are bought in from the London press. Some international newspapers may be found in shops in Central, Admiralty and Tsim Sha Tsui but they are not common on newspaper stands.

The Hong Kong government website (*www.news.gov.hk/en*), reports some of the top stories in English every day, and may be an alternative way to get local news.

Main newspapers

Asia Times: 2585 7119; editor@atimes.com; www.atimes.com
South China Morning Post: 2565 2222; www.scmp.com
The Standard: 2798 2798; www.thestandard.com.hk

Magazines

As with newspapers, there are not many locally published English magazines but a wide range of international magazines is available. *HK Magazine* and *bc magazine* are published locally. The former is a lifestyle publication for affluent urban professionals, and the latter is an entertainment guide including information about gigs, cinema, eating out and sports. International magazines like *Time* (which has an Asian edition), *Newsweek, Asiaweek* and *The Economist* are popular among locals. Women's magazines including *Marie Claire, Cosmopolitan* and *Elle* are very successful as well. Many different kinds of magazines such as *PC World, Arts of Asia, Rider Magazine* and *The Voice*, etc are also available. In general, there are more English magazines in big bookstores, such as Page One, than in the newspaper stands or convenience stores.

Television

Television is everywhere and provides cheap entertainment as there is no TV licence fee. There are four main channels broadcast by two companies: Television Broadcasts Ltd (TVB) and Asia Television Ltd (ATV). All four channels are free of charge but there are advertisements between and during programmes (sometimes every 10-15 minutes). Of the four channels, Pearl and ATV World are broadcast in English. Popular current British and American TV series are broadcast in peak hours. Programmes about current affairs and documentaries are also very popular.

Hong Kong Cable Television Ltd (Cable TV) is the largest pay-TV company. There are more than 32 channels including BBC, CNN, National Geographic Channel and Discovery Channel. Programmes run 24 hours a day and are very varied. Channels for movies, music, sports, news, children and travel can all be found on Cable TV. The monthly fee for Cable TV depends on how many channels are subscribed to. For further details, visit the website *www.wharfcable.com*.

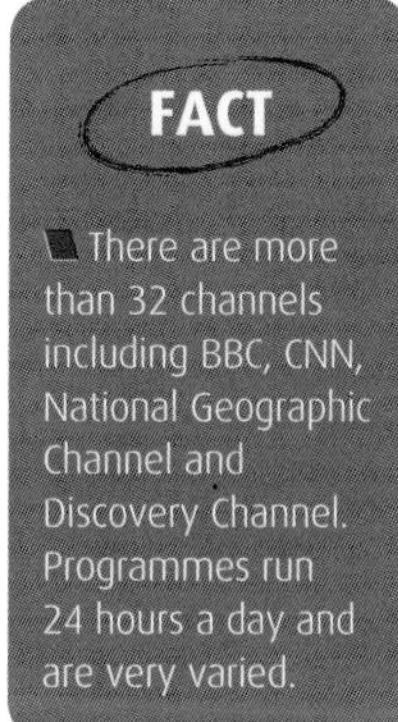
FACT
There are more than 32 channels including BBC, CNN, National Geographic Channel and Discovery Channel. Programmes run 24 hours a day and are very varied.

 TV programme schedules can be found in daily newspapers or on the company websites. For TVB, it is *www.tvb.com*; and for ATV *www.hkatv.com*.

Radio

There are four radio stations in Hong Kong offering around 10–15 channels. However, most of them are broadcast in Cantonese. There are only three radio channels that are broadcast in English, which include RTHK (Radio Television Hong Kong) Radio 3 (AM 567/AM 1584/FM 106.8/FM 97.9), Radio 4 (FM 97.6–98.9), and Metro Broadcast Metro Plus (AM 1044). RTHK Radio 3 provides a greater variety of information than the other two channels. The programmes cover news, current affairs, music, entertainment, etc. RTHK Radio 4 is mainly a music channel and programmes are bilingually broadcast. The presenter explains the text in Cantonese after presenting it in English. You can tune in to all kinds of music: western classical music, contemporary music, Chinese music, jazz and more any time of the day. Metro Plus is like RTHK Radio 4 in that music is the main focus. However, Metro Plus is aimed at people from other Asian countries. There are programmes broadcast in Mandarin, Filipino, Indonesian and Indian languages every week.

POST

The Hong Kong postal service is cheap and efficient. It usually takes one working day to deliver local letters and four to seven days to deliver letters to the UK and the USA.

Post offices open 9:30am–5pm, Monday to Friday, and 9:30am–1pm on Saturday. If you need the postal service on a Saturday afternoon or on Sunday, the Central Post Office in Central is in service until 6pm on Saturdays and 9am–2pm on Sundays.

Parcels usually take seven to 10 days to reach the UK and the USA by air, and around 45 days by surface mail. The cost for sending parcels to Hawaii is lower than sending to other US states and the size limit for sending parcels to the USA (including Puerto Rico) is different from sending parcels to other countries.

Mail is usually delivered once a day from Monday to Saturday. Stamps can be purchased at convenience stores as well as post offices, and the prices are the same. Mailboxes are green and can be found in main streets and most residential complexes. Mailboxes can also be found inside train stations and MTR stations, but remember the mailboxes inside MTR stations are behind the station gates.

> Information about postal costs and size/weight limits are available at The Hong Kong Post website www.hongkongpost.com.

SpeedPost is an alternative to other express delivery companies like UPS and FedEx. It promises overnight delivery to 92 destinations. There is also an express service for local post.

Post offices also have PayThruPost service, which accepts payments for more than 20 government bills, including tax bills, electricity bills, home telephone (and some mobile phone) bills, gas bills, etc. Payment by cash, cheque, cashier order or EPS are all accepted. For further details of the PayThruPost service, call the Hong Kong Post enquiry hotline on 2921 2222.

HEALTH

Hospitals

All Hong Kong public hospitals are managed by The Hospital Authority (HA). The Accident and Emergency (A&E) service was free before April 2003, but many people chose to use the A&E service even in non-emergency cases and so the demand was overwhelming. Now, patients are charged for this service.

Stamp collectors

There are many limited edition stamps issued for festivals or special events in Hong Kong every year. There are long queues outside post offices when a new stamp is issued. The Hong Kong Post provides ordering services for stamp collectors every year. Credit card is the only accepted payment method for this service and the minimum ordering amount is HK$50 (£3.23/$6.42). The deadline for ordering next year's stamps is usually around September. Delivery of new stamps is provided at a cost of around HK$10 per delivery, or you can collect your stamps at a designated post office.

- A regularly updated list of all hospital charges can be found at the HA website www.ha.org.hk or telephone 2882 4866

There are four levels of emergency in the A&E unit. A wait of two or three hours for people who are classified as third or fourth emergency levels is usual. The HA introduced the A&E service charge of HK$100 (£6/$12), aiming to reduce the pressure on A&E. Recipients of Comprehensive Social Security Assistance (CSSA) will be exempt from payment of their medical expenses for public healthcare services. Non-CSSA recipients who cannot afford medical fees can apply for a fee waiver from the Medical Social Workers of public hospitals and clinics.

The charges are less for local residents with a Hong Kong Identity Card. If you do not have a Hong Kong Identity Card, the charges will be much higher, and highest of all in private hospitals.

The demand for public health services is huge. Prepare to wait for at least two months for a non-urgent operation. Private hospitals are an alternative but the charges may be much higher. Consulting private clinics costs around HK$150–HK$250 per attendance and dental services are from HK$150–HK$1,500 depending on what treatments you need.

- **Emergencies** The emergency number in Hong Kong is 999. The operator will direct the line to the relevant departments. An ambulance will generally arrive within 10 minutes. Many buildings have a direct connection with fire stations; if the fire alarm rings, the fire station will send firemen to the building even if no one calls 999.

- The emergency number in Hong Kong is 999.

Health insurance

Even though the charges in Hong Kong hospitals are low if you are a local resident, many people prefer to have personal health insurance. Usually, people buy health insurance through insurance agents, although some companies have health and dental benefit packages for their employees. Big insurance companies like AIA, Blue Cross and AXA are reliable and offer more varied insurance plans.

Traditional medicine

Traditional Chinese medicine is officially recognised in Hong Kong and it is now part of the medical student's curriculum at the Chinese University and the University of Hong Kong. There are also acupuncturists who can help with all kinds of complaints. The best way to find a good practitioner is to ask your Chinese colleagues and acquaintances.

Useful resources

American International Assurance Co Ltd: 2232 8888; www.aia.com.hk
AXA Asia Pacific Holdings Ltd: 2519 1111; www.axa-chinaregion.com
Blue Cross (Asia-Pacific) Insurance Ltd: 2163 1000; www.bluecross.com.hk
Eagle Star Life Assurance Co Ltd: 2967 8393; www.eaglestar.com.hk/eng
ING General Insurance International: 2850 3030; www.ing.com.hk/gi
New York Life Insurance Worldwide Ltd: 2881 0688; www.newyorklife.com.hk
Prudential Assurance Co Ltd: 2977 3888; www.prudential.com.hk
Royal & Sun Alliance Insurance Ltd: 2968 3000; www.royalsunalliance.com.hk

EDUCATION

Hong Kong's education system is very similar to that of the UK. The Hong Kong government provides nine years of free education, from Primary One to Secondary Three (ages six to 15), for all Hong Kong children. The academic year starts on 1 September and ends in mid-July for both primary and secondary schools. Primary and secondary school students have 90 days of holiday a year, including the summer holiday.

The education system

Pre-primary education

Although it is not compulsory in Hong Kong, most children (over 90%) attend childcare centres, nurseries or kindergartens. Childcare centres and nurseries are for children from infancy to six and are under the supervision of the Social Welfare Department. The minimum age for entering kindergarten is three years old and all kindergartens are under the supervision of the Education and Manpower Bureau. Every kindergarten, childcare centre or nursery has to get a licence before it provides an education service. Syllabus and school fees are set by the organisations themselves. Fees can vary from hundreds of dollars to around HK$5,000 (£20–£300/$40–$600) a month. Parents can apply for subsidies from the Social Welfare Department and the Education and Manpower Bureau for their children's school fees.

Opening hours for childcare centres and kindergartens can be very different. Both half-day and full-day schools exist. Some stay open until 6pm for working parents.

There are usually fixed timetables in kindergartens and childcare centres. Basic knowledge like the weather, shapes, colours, etc will be taught in pre-school education. Children are encouraged to learn social skills through games, singing and physical exercises. Parents have become more concerned about the development of creativity and thinking skills in recent years, and schools are putting more focus on these aspects as well. Reading and writing of simple words may start as early as the age of four or five.

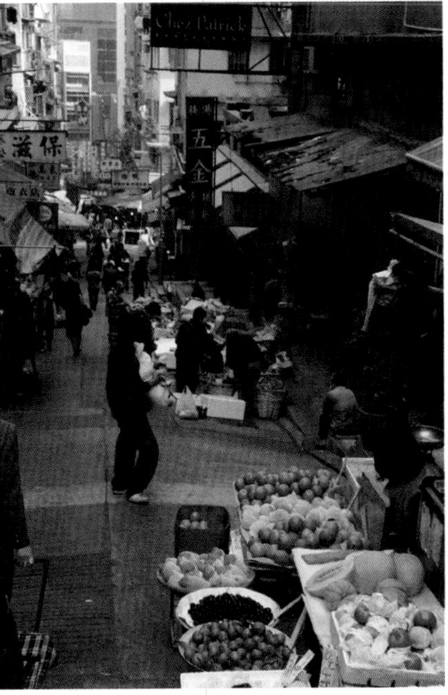

Primary schools

Primary education is compulsory for all children. There is a strict minimum age limit for Primary One admission. The child has to be at least five years and eight months old to enter primary school. Most primary schools require students to wear a school uniform; primary education is more standardised compared to pre-primary education. Children have to acquire language, mathematics, general knowledge and simple science skills during their six years of primary school education. English is a compulsory subject and students in most schools take Chinese as well. Some schools provide other languages such as French or Japanese as a second language for non-Chinese students. Subjects like art, music, physical education and civil education are also included in the timetable. Extra-curricular activities are provided as supplementary subjects for children to develop different skills as well as to enjoy themselves.

Most of the schools in Hong Kong are funded by the government. There are no school fees for government-run and government-subsidised schools and their syllabus is set under the supervision of the government.

Children studying in Direct Subsidy Scheme (DSS) schools and private schools have to pay school fees even if they are within the age range for free education provided by the Hong Kong government. DSS schools are non-profit-making and also under the monitoring of the government but they have more freedom when designing their own syllabus and usually they have better school facilities, like computers and swimming pools. Less than 10% of the primary schools are operated by private organisations and they are not under the supervision of the government. School fees are more expensive in private schools, and may amount to several thousand a month.

When choosing a primary school, you may want to pay attention to whether the school has any link to a particular secondary school. If a primary school and a secondary school are linked, students can usually get a place at that secondary school more easily. Many parents plan very carefully when choosing a primary school, as they want their children to enter the desired linked secondary school, which they believe may provide a better learning environment and better facilities.

Secondary education

The first three years, usually called junior levels, of the secondary school education is, like primary school education, compulsory and free of charge. Most students prefer

English in school

Both primary and secondary schools in Hong Kong are separated into EMI (English as the medium of instruction) and non-EMI. Foreign children may find it very difficult if all subjects except English are taught in Chinese. Around two-fifths of secondary schools but less than one-fifth of primary schools are EMI. However, secondary schools are allowed to choose the language of instruction starting from Secondary Four. Therefore, the number of schools using English as medium of instruction in senior levels may exceed two-fifths of the total number of secondary schools.

to continue their studies after Secondary Three. Compulsory subjects include: two languages, mathematics, elementary sciences, history, geography and public affairs. Art, music, physical education, computer studies, home economics and design and technology are also common subjects. Students choose their streams of studies starting from Secondary Four (the start of senior level). They are mainly divided into two streams – arts and sciences. Arts students usually take humanities and social science subjects like economics, literature and geography; while science students study advanced levels of mathematics, physics, chemistry, biology, computer studies, etc. English and general mathematics are required in both streams. Art and music are voluntary subjects starting from senior level, which means most students are not examined on these subjects. Secondary Five students are required to sit for a public examination, the Hong Kong Certificate Examination of Education (HKCEE), to see if they are eligible for further studies.

The HKCEE is similar to GCSEs in the UK or SATs in the USA. Students take six to 10 subjects in their examination and the best six will be taken as reference for assessment. The passing grade is E and a student should pass all exams if he or she wants to pursue further studies. However, the requirements are usually higher (like two Cs and four Ds) due to limited places for Secondary Six. Secondary Six and Seven are taken as the preparation for tertiary education but not all Secondary Seven students are able to get a place in universities. They will have to sit another examination, the Hong Kong Advanced Level Examination (HKALE) to fight for a place.

Starting from Secondary Four, students need to pay school fees. It is usually several hundred dollars a month for government-funded schools. As in primary schools, most of the secondary schools require students to wear school uniform.

International schools

International schools are more popular with foreign residents. There are not many EMI primary schools and many local schools only provide Chinese as the second language, which is very difficult for a foreign child to learn. Besides, many of these students are used to western education where more focus is put on personal

Homework and examinations

Many people complain that Hong Kong students are under too much pressure. Apart from public examinations like HKCEE and HKALE, students have to sit internal school examinations every term. Some schools even have additional mid-term tests. There are usually two to three terms in each academic year, which means some schools have up to six examinations a year, plus quizzes and dictations.

Homework is given every day and there may be as many as five to eight pieces of homework a day. Many children find it difficult to adapt to the Hong Kong education system if they are from western countries. International schools, however, have a lighter workload compared to local schools and may be more suitable for foreign children.

development, creativity and thinking skills. Pupils at international schools in Hong Kong are mainly taught by native English speakers and the class size is usually smaller. The schools have good facilities and learning environments but the school fees are higher than local schools. The English Schools Foundation, which runs well-regarded primary and secondary schools, is less expensive than other private schools as they receive some government funding.

Below are contact details for the main interational schools in Hong Kong:

American International School: 125 Waterloo Road, Kowloon Tong, Kowloon, Hong Kong; 2336-3812; aisadmin@ais.edu.hk; www.ais.edu.hk

Christian Alliance, PC Lau Memorial, International School: 2 Fu Ning Street, Kowloon City, Hong Kong; 2713 3733; info@cais.edu.hk; www.cais.edu.hk

Concordia International School: 68 Begonia Road, Yau Yat Chuen, Kowloon, Hong Kong; 2397 6576; adm@cihs.edu.hk; www.cihs.edu.hk

ESF schools: www.esf.edu.hk

Hong Kong International School: 23 South Bay Close, Repulse Bay, Hong Kong; 2812 5000; admiss@hkis.edu.hk; www.hkis.edu.hk

Hong Lok Yuen International School: 20th Street, Hong Lok Yuen, Tai Po, New Territories, Hong Kong; 2658 6935; info@hlyis.edu.hk; www.hlyis.edu.hk

German Swiss International School: 11 Guildford Road, The Peak, Hong Kong; 2849 6216; gsis@gsis.edu.hk; www.gsis.edu.hk

Kellett School: 2 Wah Lok Path; Wah Fu, Pokfulam; Hong Kong; 2551 8234; kellett@kellettschool.com; kellettmain.kellettschool.com

Singapore International School: 23 Nam Long Shan Road, Aberdeen, Hong Kong; 2872 0266; secretary@singapore.edu.hk; www.singapore.edu.hk

Yew Chung Education Foundation (Primary and Secondary Section): 10 Somerset Road, Kowloon Tong, Kowloon, Hong Kong; 2338 7106; inquiry@ycef.com; www.ycef.com

Vocational training

Some students choose to attend vocational training institutes after Secondary Five, especially if they do not do very well in the HKCEE. The aim of the courses provided by the vocational institutes is to help students to develop a technical skill for a future career. Students need to attend pre-employment and also in-service education and training. The Hong Kong Institute of Vocational Education (IVE), the Vocational Training Council (VTC), the School of Business and Information Systems (SBI) and its training and development centres are the recognised institutes providing vocational training at the moment.

Higher education

Universities

There are eight universities providing around 65,000 (both full-time and part-time) places for students each year. In general, the universities expect the students to complete their degree in three years, except for some longer courses like medicine and dentistry. Apart from their specialised subject (their 'major'), students are required to take classes of different disciplines as well. An academic year is usually divided into two semesters, September to Christmas/January, and February to June. Students take examinations after each semester.

For local residents fees are around HK$42,000 (£2,700/$5,400) a year. Students can apply for a government grant and loan for paying the fee if the family income is low. Fees for foreign students are HK$70,000 per year (2006–2007 prices).

Hong Kong Institute of Education (HKIEd)

This is an institute recognised by the government for providing education and training for those who plan to be primary or secondary teachers. Students take two major subjects in preparation for teaching. One can either apply to the institute after Secondary Five with HKCEE results that meet the entry requirements, or apply after passing HKALE. Those who enter the institute after Secondary Five will take three years to finish the certificate, and it takes only two years for those who attended HKALE. HKIEd also provides a part-time certificate course for current teachers. The institute was approved by the government to offer a degree course, Bachelor in Education for primary and secondary education a few years ago.

Hong Kong Academy for Performing Arts

This is the only tertiary institution in Hong Kong solely for the provision of professional education, training and research facilities for the performing arts, theatre technical arts, and film and television. The academy provides both diploma and degree courses in dance, drama, music, technical arts, traditional theatre together with film and television for students. The academy organises performances by their students, which are open to the public and are part of their training.

Useful higher education resources

The Chinese University of Hong Kong: 2609 7000; www.cuhk.edu.hk
City University of Hong Kong: 2788 7654; www.cityu.edu.hk
Hong Kong Baptist University: 3411 7400; www.hkbu.edu.hk
The Hong Kong Polytechnic University: 2766 5111; www.polyu.edu.hk
Hong Kong University of Science and Technology: 2358 8888; www.ust.hk
Lingnan University: 2616 8888; www.ln.edu.hk
Open University of Hong Kong: 2711 2100; www.ouhk.edu.hk

The University of Hong Kong: 2859 2111; www.hku.hk
The Hong Kong Academy for Performing Arts: 2584 8500; PR@hkapa.edu; www.hkapa.edu
Hong Kong Institute of Education: 2948 8888; www.ied.edu.hk
Vocational Training Council: 2836 1000; vtcmailbox@vtc.edu.hk; www.vtc.edu.hk

WOMEN'S ISSUES

In spite of centuries of imposed inferiority, Chinese women are now holding their own. There are many in high places in business and government and the academic world. The age-old preference of sons over daughters seems to have more or less receded. Undoubtedly the professional success of many Chinese women, who are also married and mothers, is due to the easy availability of live-in domestic help and care for the children. Among non-professionals, it tends to be the grandmothers who are roped in as child-minders and who are often paid to do it.

Western women are taken seriously as professionals and generally treated with respect, though not usually with door-opening courtesy. Unlike in Mediterranean or Middle Eastern countries, a western woman will not generally find herself being looked up and down. In general Hong Kong is a safe place for women (and children), though there are occasional reports of muggings and harassment. Best to ask around until you yourself get the feel of what is safe and acceptable.

SOCIAL SECURITY

Even though the tax rate in Hong Kong is low, social security and benefits are good. Unlike Canada or the USA, Hong Kong does not require citizens to pay additional tax for social security and benefits.

Comprehensive Social Security Assistance (CSSA)

This scheme is intended to help low-income individuals or families to live up to a prescribed level to meet their basic needs. Applicants must be Hong Kong residents and have resided in Hong Kong for at least a year before applying. The Social Welfare Department will assess the capital assets of the individual or family and then decide if the applicant is eligible. There is an additional requirement for adults aged 15–59 in normal health. They should be working or actively looking for a paid job if they apply for CSSA. The standard rate for a family with physically healthy parents and two children is about HK$5,000–HK6,000 (£320–£385/$640–$770) a month. The family can apply for additional grants for rent allowance, water and electrical charges allowances and school fee grants. The assistance is a bit more for those aged over 60, disabled, single parents and those medically certified as in ill health.

Social Security Allowance (SSA) Scheme

This scheme is for people aged 65 or above who have lived in Hong Kong continuously for five years or more after they turned 60. Elderly people who are under the capital asset limit will receive a monthly allowance of HK$625–HK$705. For those who have a disability, the allowance will be between HK$1,120 and HK$2,240.

Criminal and Law Enforcement Injuries Compensation Scheme (CLEICS)

If an innocent person is injured or has died as a result of a crime of violence, or by a law enforcement officer using a weapon in the execution of his duty, he or she can apply for CLEICS. This scheme is not limited to Hong Kong citizens. Victims who are able to show they were legally permitted to stay in Hong Kong at the time of the incident, and have to receive treatment for at least three days can apply for it. It is non-means-tested financial assistance. In the case of death, the compensation will be given to the dependents of the victim.

Traffic Accident Victims Assistance Scheme (TAVAS)

This is another financial assistance not solely for Hong Kong citizens. Victims of road accidents, even if they caused the accident, can apply for it. As with CLEICS, applicants must show they were legally permitted to stay in Hong Kong when the accident happened, and received treatment for at least three days after the accident. Financial assistance will be provided to dependents of the victims in case of death.

Emergency Relief (ER)

In the event of natural and other disasters, the Social and Welfare Department will provide material aid including hot meals, blankets and other essential relief articles. There is also financial assistance called the Emergency Relief Fund (ERF), providing cash assistance for persons in need of urgent relief as a result of natural or other disasters.

The Social Welfare Department also provides supporting services to single parents, new immigrants, disabled, elderly and young people, and general community service to the public. For further details of these services, visit the Social Welfare Department website at www.info.gov.hk/swd.

CRIME

The crime rate in Hong Kong is extremely low. While violent crime is rare, foreigners should still exercise their common sense concerning pickpocketing. Take care of your personal belongings, particularly when you are in a crowded area or public areas like bars and restaurants and the airport. Criminals may sometimes work in a group, so that one of them attracts your attention while the other makes off with your belongings.

Complaints concerning deception during retail or other commercial transactions are not unusual as well. Some shops do not show the prices for the products in the display window and then demand a price according to the perceived wealth of the customers. It is not a crime if you and the shop agree on a deal, even if you later found out that you paid a much higher price than the locals. It is only a crime if the shops give you wrong information on what you pay, the model number, the functions of the products and so on. Shops like these are more concentrated in tourist areas like Tsim Sha Tsui and Causeway Bay. You are advised to visit several shops before buying something and it is safer to buy electrical products in big stores like Fortress and Broadway.

There are around 35,000 policemen in Hong Kong, around one per 200 Hong Kong citizens. They wear a dark blue uniform and are armed. It is not difficult to find a police officer on the street and they are generally very helpful. You can ask them for directions if you lose your way. You are required to carry your Hong Kong Identity Card with you if you have one, or your passport if you are just visiting. The emergency telephone number is 999.

- There are around 35,000 policemen in Hong Kong, around one per 200 Hong Kong citizens. They wear a dark blue uniform and are armed.

CARS AND MOTORING

The number of vehicles in Hong Kong is just as astonishing as the population. There are over 440,000 vehicles on the roads every day. This does not include public transportation like buses and taxis. It is estimated that, by 2011, the number of vehicles in Hong Kong will be around one million! Although the number of vehicles has not yet reached this number, congestion is already a serious problem.

> During rush hours, it can easily take you an hour to complete what should be a 15-minute ride.

Hong Kong is currently running a Driving-Offence Point System. Points will be incurred when a driver commits driving offences, like speeding or jumping traffic lights. If 13 points or more are incurred within two years, disqualification from holding a driving licence applies. The first disqualification lasts for three months and six months for subsequent convictions.

The Hong Kong driving system is the same as the British and people drive on the left. Traffic light runs turn from red to red-and-amber, and then to green; and green to amber and then red. Unlike the UK or other European countries, you are not supposed to put your vehicle in motion when the red-and-amber is on, even where there is no pedestrian crossing the road, and right-hand/left-hand turns on a red light are not allowed.

Road signs in Hong Kong are in English and Chinese and are usually up above the road, while the speed limit is posted on the side of the road.

- **Motorcycles** Motorcyclists in the first year of obtaining their licence are required by law to undergo a 12-month probation period. They have to put 'P' plates at the front and rear of their motorcycles. They are not allowed to carry passengers on the back, exceed the speed of 70kmph and cannot drive on the offside lane of expressways when there are three or more lanes. A full driving licence will be granted after a year to those whose performance is satisfactory.

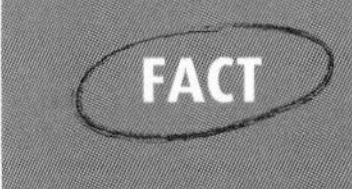

- Road signs in Hong Kong are in English and Chinese and are usually up above the road, while the speed limit is posted on the side of the road.

Driving licences

People holding an international driving licence issued outside Hong Kong are allowed to drive in Hong Kong for 12 months starting from the date of arrival. The Transport Department grants a temporary driving licence to people from some areas. If you hold a driving licence issued by your country, you should check up with the Transport Department within three months of your arrival. You cannot apply for the temporary driving licence more than three months after your arrival. In that case, you have to apply for a full Hong Kong driving licence instead which lasts for 10 years up to the age of 70 (after which time you need a doctor's certificate, as in the UK) and is very expensive. Contact the Transport Department website www.td.gov.hk for online applications.

Driving regulations

Hong Kong's road system is basically a copy of that of the British, since Hong Kong was a British colony when the road system was built. People coming from the UK should not have much difficulty driving in Hong Kong, but people from America and other European countries will need some adjustment, the most important of which is probably to learn to drive on the left side. Drivers and passengers are required to wear seat belts while the vehicle is in motion. Using hand-held mobile phones when the vehicle is in motion is an offence and will attract a penalty of up to HK$2,000 (£129/$257). The speed limits on expressways and highways are usually 80kmph–100kmph and 50kmph–70kmph in the city area. The lane on the far right-hand side is the fast lane, which is prohibited for lorries. Police have speed cameras to catch speeding drivers, who risk incurring penalty points and a fine.

Drink-driving

Drink-driving is strictly prohibited and is a criminal offence in Hong Kong. Ten demerit-offensive points will be incurred for the first conviction. The driver may be disqualified from driving for a period of time. The maximum penalty for drink-driving is a heavy fine plus up to three years imprisonment. The police can stop a driver for a breath test if the driver is suspected to be drink-driving or has committed a traffic offence. A breath test is also given to drivers who are involved in traffic accidents. Further alcohol tests on blood and urine may be necessary. Failure to do the tests without reasonable excuse will incur penalties. The alcohol limit is 50mg per 100ml of blood. This limit is lower than that of the UK and the USA (80mg of alcohol per 100ml of blood). You will probably reach the limit after a glass of wine or one pint of beer.

Parking

Parking is often a difficult problem in Hong Kong. There are limited parking areas along the roads in the city area. Parking meters only accept parking cards, which you can buy from convenience stores. The maximum period for parking on a meter is two hours for each payment. Car parks do not necessarily have any space at busy times. Vehicles parking in any prohibited area may be towed away and the owner may have to pay a fine.

Breakdowns and accidents

There are emergency telephones on every expressway, highway and inside the tunnels for drivers whose vehicles have broken down. Calling for help from a mobile phone may be a safer and quicker way. If your vehicle breaks down on the expressway or highway, try to move it to the side of the road and put the hazard lights on. If it is not possible to move your vehicle, leave the hazard lights on and get out of your vehicle to a safe place to wait for help. It is a good idea to carry the numbers of companies for vehicle repair services, so that you can call them to tow your vehicle away for repair directly.

When there is a traffic accident, the car owners can settle the loss among themselves if no one is injured in the accident and the private property damage is minor. Car owners have a right to make a report to the police within 72 hours. In any case, you must call the police if someone gets hurt, or if the accident involves more than two vehicles, government properties or a government vehicle.

For information on importing your car, see page 268.

Useful breakdown contacts

AA Towing Services Company: 2382 4444
Auto Power Towing Company Ltd: 2668 2999
Compass Auto Club: 2234 5999
Shun Chong Towing Service Ltd: 2338 0982; www.yp.com.hk/shunchong
Universal Towing Service Company Ltd: 2519 8731; www.yp.com.hk/universaltowing

Car registration

All vehicles must register with the Hong Kong Licensing Office of the Transport Department. You are required to pay First Registration Tax and a registration fee for your vehicle, and to pay a vehicle licence fee and levy for the Traffic Accident Victim Assistance Fund. First Registration Tax is a once-only charge but it can add up to nearly half of the value of your car. You should note that registration of a left-hand drive vehicle will normally not be accepted.

For further details about driving licences and vehicle licences, visit the Transport Department website *www.info.gov.hk/td*

Useful contacts

Driving-Offence Points: 2804 2594
Driving Test: 2804 2583
Licensing Information (24-Hour Interactive Voice Hotline): 2804 2600
Police force hotline: 2527 7177
Transport Department Headquarters: 2804 2600

OTHER TRANSPORT

Even though Hong Kong is smaller in size than other big cities like New York or London, its transportation is up to international standards and its quality is even better than many other international cities. According to the results of Skytrax Research in London, global air travellers picked Hong Kong International Airport (HKIA) as the world's best airport for five consecutive years (2001–2005), but in 2006 it came second to Singapore's Changi Airport. HKIA was also named Cargo Airport of the Year, 2003, by the trade publication *Air Cargo News*. The rail system is well developed and has a good connection to mainland China. Buses are frequent and cover almost all areas of Hong Kong.

Plane

Flights to mainland China are mainly operated by Chinese airlines, which include Air China and China Southern Airlines. Dragon Air is the only Hong Kong-based airline that runs domestic flights to mainland China. Recently, more people have been flying to mainland China from Shenzhen's airport instead of Hong Kong International Airport as this usually saves around HK$1,000–HK$3,000. To cover this demand, there are lots of bus and ferry services direct from Hong Kong to Shenzhen's Bao'an Airport. There are also some special offers from travel agents, especially in low season.

Octopus cards

Hong Kong introduced a stored value card, Octopus, in 1997, akin to London's Oyster cards. Octopus can be used on most city transport, except red minibuses, the Peak Trams and taxis. Initial stored value Octopus of HK$100 (£6/$12) is available for adults, HK$50 for students and HK$20 for the over 60 and children under 12, in addition to a deposit of HK$50 when a new card is purchased. Octopus can be recharged when the stored value is used up. The maximum stored value is HK$1,000 while a minimum stored value is HK$50. There are machines for recharging the Octopus in all KCR and MTR stations, and it can also be done in some convenience stores (7-Eleven and Circle K). The deposit will be refunded when you return the Octopus card to the company. There is also a personalised Octopus, which stores personal data inside the card and can be recharged directly from a bank account when the stored value is used up. Octopus can be purchased from KCR and MTR stations.

Useful resources

China Travel Net Hong Kong Ltd: Room A, 2/F, Tak Bo Building, 62–74 Sai Yee Street, Mongkok, Hong Kong; 2789 5401; enquiry@chinatravel1.com; www.chinatravel1.com

Dragon Air Ticketing Office: Room 4609–4611, 46/F, COSCO Tower, 183 Queen's Road Central, Hong Kong; 2868 6777; www.dragonair.com

Energy Tours: Room 309–331, 3/F, Bank Centre, 636 Nathan Road, Mongkok, Kowloon; 2782 0380

Hong Tai Travel: 5/F, United Centre, Admiralty MTR Station; 2108 8888; www.hongthai.com

Kwun Kin Tours: Room 407–411, Block B, Hunghom Commercial Centre, 37 Ma Tau Wai Road, Hunghom; 2362 2022; custom@kwankin.com.hk

Wing On Travel: Room 1707, 17/F, Lane Crawford House, 70 Queen's Road Central, Central; 2189 7689; www.wingontravel.com

Train

There are two railway companies in Hong Kong, The Kowloon-Canton Railway Corporation (KCR) and the Mass Transit Railway (MTR).

KCR

KCR currently operates four domestic rail services, the East Rail, the West Rail, the Ma On Shan line and the Light Rail.

The East Rail is a main link for the New Territories and Kowloon. There are 13 stations along the railway, beginning at Tsim Sha Tsui East, a new station linked to Tsim Sha Tsui itself by a long subway, and ending at the border at Lo Wu. An East Rail train consists of 12 compartments and can accommodate over 2,000 passengers. A single trip costs from HK$3.5 to HK$33 for an adult. East Rail also operates intercity passenger services to Guangzhou on its own train, and provides access for other intercity trains running to and from Guangzhou, Shanghai and Beijing. The Beijing-Kowloon Through Train and the Shanghai-Kowloon Through Train operate on alternate days with a total journey time of about 26 and 23 hours respectively. Tickets are HK$500–HK$1,200, depending on which class you are travelling. The Guangzhou-Kowloon line is much cheaper. Tickets are HK$130–HK$230.

The West Rail, which began operating in December 2003, runs from Nam Cheong in Kowloon toward the western extremity of the New Territiories at Tuen Mun.

The Ma On Shan railway branches off from the East Rail after the Tai Wai station and runs along the northern coast of part of the Sai Kung Peninsula in the east of the New Territories.

The Light Rail, provides passenger services for the fast-developing North West New Territories (Yuen Long and Tuen Mun). There are 57 stops in total. The Light Rail is not unlike some European underground railways. A Light Rail train can accommodate around 200 passengers. The fare depends on the number of zones covered (HK$4–HK$6).

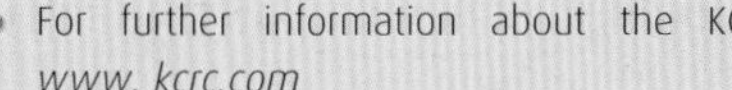

For further information about the KCR, visit the company website *www. kcrc.com*

MTR

The MTR route covers most parts of Hong Kong Island, Kowloon and southern New Territories. Each train consists of eight compartments and has a capacity of 2,500 passengers. The fare is HK$4–HK$13. Rates are likely to be in the higher bands if your journey crosses Victoria Harbour from Kowloon to Hong Kong Island. The MTR company also operates the Airport Express running between Hong Kong International Airport and Central. It also provides in-town check-in services to many major airlines up to 100 minutes before the flight takes off. Passengers of some airlines can even check in and get the boarding pass one day prior to departure. It only takes 23 minutes to get to the airport by MTR from Central. However, it is much more expensive than taking the airport buses. It costs HK$100 from Central to the airport by MTR, but it costs around HK$30 or less if you take the bus.

TIP

The East Rail of KCR and MTR are connected at Kowloon Tong Station.

For further information about MTR services, visit the MTR customer website *www.mtr.com.hk*

Bus

Apart from trains, the bus is also a popular and easy way to get around the city. Double-decker buses are very common in Hong Kong due to the high population density. Almost all buses in Hong Kong are air-conditioned. Hong Kong is very mountainous, so many tunnels have been built to connect different parts of Hong Kong. In general, buses passing through tunnels, which carry charges, are more expensive. There are three bus companies in Hong Kong. All three companies provide a point-to-point bus route enquiry online. If you type in where you want to board the bus and your destination, the point-to-point enquiry service can provide you with the bus details such as bus numbers, duration of the trip, where the bus stops are and the price, etc.

Long Win Bus Co Ltd, a wholly owned subsidiary company of Kowloon Motor Bus Group (see the KMB website), and Citybus operate bus routes to and from the airport.

Bus companies

The Kowloon Motor Bus Company Ltd (KMB): 2745 4466 (enquiry hotline); www.kmb.com.hk

First Bus: 2136 8888; www.nwfb.com.hk

Citybus Ltd: 2873 0818 (enquiry hotline); www.citybus.com.hk

Tram

If you are not in a hurry, and for a relaxed and old-world feel, take a tram. Trams are the cheapest transportation in Hong Kong with a flat fare of HK$2 for adults and

■ Trams are the cheapest transportation in Hong Kong with a flat fare of HK$2 for adults and HK$1 for children under 12 and senior citizens aged 65 or above.

Minibus

Minibuses are small buses that can accommodate 16 passengers. Destinations are written in Chinese and English on the front panel of the bus. There are two types of minibus in Hong Kong: 'red minibuses' and 'green minibuses'. Green minibuses are green and beige in colour. They have fixed routes but can stop anywhere that it is permitted to stop. You usually pay, either by Octopus or coins, when you get on the minibus. The drivers will not take your money directly as they are hired by the minibus companies and have a monthly salary. Red minibuses are red and beige in colour. They have fixed routes but the drivers may change the routes slightly according to the traffic situation. There are no fixed stops and a passenger can get off anywhere along the route, except in restricted areas marked by double yellow lines along the road. Passengers pay the driver directly when they get off. Octopus is not accepted at the moment. Unlike the green minibuses, many red minibuses run after midnight. The fares of red minibuses vary sometimes, especially on festivals or after midnight or at peak times. In contrast to most double-decker drivers, drivers of minibuses are sometimes unable to speak much English.

HK$1 for children under 12 and senior citizens aged 65 or above. They have been operating on Hong Kong Island since 1904. Hongkong Tramways Ltd operates six overlapping routes on 13km of double track along the northern shore of Hong Kong Island between Kennedy Town and Shau Kei Wan, and about 3km of single track around Happy Valley.

Another Hong Kong tramway is the Peak Tram, operated by Peak Tramways Company Ltd since 1888. The 1.4km line runs between Central and the Peak. A single trip for adults costs HK$22. A return trip is HK$33.

Taxi

Taxis are numerous and can be hailed anywhere that it is permitted to stop. Red taxis serve Hong Kong Island and Kowloon; green ones, the New Territories; and blue taxis, Lantau Island. The fare is shown on the meter. Additional charges apply to cross-harbour tunnels, Lion Rock Tunnel, Junk Bay Tunnel and Aberdeen Tunnel, and there is a HK$5 charge for each piece of luggage. Drivers normally accept Hong Kong dollars only though this may be changing now that the Chinese yuan has overtaken the dollar in value.

Ferry

The Star Ferry, which has connected Hong Kong Island and Kowloon since 1898, runs regularly between 6.30am and 11.30pm. It is one of the cheapest and most scenic ferry rides in the world, and takes approximately eight minutes.

It is a wonderfully relaxing journey as you cross one of the busiest harbours in the world.

First Ferry operates services to the outlying islands including Cheung Chau and Lantau Island from a new pier, directly in front of the landmark 88-storey IFC2 tower. Hong Kong & Kowloon Ferry Ltd also provides regular services between Lamma and Hong Kong Island. First Ferry operates ferries between Hong Kong and Macau; however, there are only a limited number of ferries every day. TurboJET provides more frequent ferries to Macau as well as providing connections to Shenzhen and Guangzhou.

Ferry companies

The Star Ferry Company Ltd: 2367 7065; sf@starferry.com.hk; www.starferry. com.hk

Hong Kong & Kowloon Ferry Ltd: 2815 6063; www.hkkf.com.hk

First Ferry: Central Pier No6; 2131 8181; www.nwff.com.hk

TurboJET: 2859 3333 (enquiry hotline); www.turbojet.com.hk

TAX

Hong Kong has a very low tax rate when compared to most countries, and the items that are taxed are limited. This is very attractive for people moving to Hong Kong. The tax rates for locals and foreigners are the same.

Income tax

Full-time employees of a company in Hong Kong, whether a local company or a foreign owned one, have to pay full tax. The amount paid depends on annual income and deductions. Annual income includes: salaries; commission; allowances; tips; salary tax paid by employer; value of a place of residence provided by the employer; share option gains; awards and gratuities; and payments received from retirement schemes. The annual income is counted from 1 April of the previous year to 31 March of the current year.

There are several deductions that can be claimed before tax. These deductions include allowances, concessionary deductions and outgoings and expenses. Approved charitable donations, mandatory contributions (pension contributions) or occupational retirement schemes, home loan interest and elderly residential care expenses can be claimed as concessionary deductions. However, voluntary mandatory contributions are not counted in concessionary deductions. For some employees, like insurance representatives, certain types of expenses are necessary in the production of the assessable income. It is possible for them to claim a deduction if they can prove their expenses are wholly, exclusively and necessarily for the employment. If buying a uniform and joining a professional body is a pre-requisite for the employment, deduction can also be claimed. Self-education and depreciation allowances on plant and machinery, related to producing an income, are also counted as outgoings and expenses.

Tax Allowances	
Year of assessment 2006/2007	**HK$**
Basic allowance	100,000
Married person's allowance	200,000
Child allowance (for each of the first nine children)	40,000
Dependent brother/sister allowance (for each qualified brother/sister)	30,000
Dependent parent/grandparent allowance (for each qualified parent)	30,000
Additional dependent parent allowance (for each qualified parent)	30,000
Single parent allowance	100,000
Disabled dependant allowance (for each qualified dependant)	60,000

The biggest deduction from annual income is allowances and everyone can claim the types and amount of allowances as shown in the below table. Tax rates are in a graduated system. The higher the net income (annual income minus the deductions), the more tax you pay.

Every taxpayer is responsible for filling in their tax form and returning it on time. Failure to do so without good reason will be subject to a penalty. One can also use the Tele Tax, provided by the Inland Revenue Department, to file the return. Tax will not be deducted from your salary directly, but can be paid by telephone, internet, bank ATM machines, by post or in person.

Other taxes

Property tax

This tax applies to owners of land or buildings in Hong Kong. Payments received by the owners, which include rent, payment for the right of use of premises under licence, lump sum premiums, service charges and management fees paid to the owner. Property Tax will be imposed on this net assessable value after deducting expenditures. The rate for the tax in 2006/2007 will be 16%.

Year of assessment 2006/2007	
Net chargeable income (HK$)	**Rate**
On the first HK$30,000	2%
On the next HK$30,000	7%
On the next HK$30,000	13%
Remainder	19%

Profit tax

Persons or corporations carrying on a trade, profession or business that derives profit from Hong Kong have to pay profit tax. It is not limited to local or international corporations. The key point is if the profit is derived from Hong Kong. Profit tax for corporation businesses and incorporated businesses are 17.5% and 16% respectively.

Stamp duty

Stamp duty is imposed on certain types of documents, which are mainly a conveyance on sale, agreement for sale of residential property, lease of immovable property, and transfer of Hong Kong stock.

Business registration

Everyone carrying on a business must register the business. 'Business' means any form of trade, commerce, craftsmanship, profession, calling or other activity carried out for the purpose of gain. Clubs and organisations providing social and recreational activities for members, have to apply for business registration no matter whether the aim is to make a profit or not.

Hotel accommodation tax

In Hong Kong, 3% of all accommodation charges is for hotel accommodation tax. It is usually included in the listed prices.

Betting duty

This is charged on horse racing, lotteries and football betting at rates of 12%–50%. The bookmaker, not the individual gambler, is liable for tax on earnings.

Estate duty

Estate duty is chargeable when someone dies. Everything the deceased owned is taken into account, the share property jointly owned by the deceased and others, and property that the deceased gave away anytime during the three years before death.

For more information about taxes in Hong Kong, visit this website *www.info.gov.hk/ird*

Working in Hong Kong

FINDING A JOB

A guide to the market

The unemployment rate before 1998 was very low, below 3% of the population. However, it has been rising since 1998, and reached a peak of 8.7% in July 2003, after the outbreak of SARS (Severe Acute Respiratory Syndrome); the highest recorded rate in Hong Kong's history. Airlines, restaurants, hotels and retail shops were hit badly and many of them closed down. The average monthly salary of all industries in June 2003 (up to supervisory levels) dropped by HK$400 (£26/$52) to HK$600.

Hong Kong experienced an economic downturn after September 11 (2001) and the government decided to cut the salaries of civil servants in April 2002 and announced a suspension of employment for the public sector. This means some retired or resigned positions were not replaced. The government also chose not to recruit new executive officers or administrative officers, which was customary every year before 2002. Many companies have cut overtime payments and reduced salaries; they also now prefer contract or part-time employment, which is more flexible and entails fewer fringe benefits. Middle-aged workers and teenagers with low qualifications find it particularly difficult to get a job as more competitive candidates are willing to lower their expected salary and take up less professional jobs. From about 2005 salaries were no longer being cut, but nor were they increasing. The unemployment rate in 2007 was 5%–6%.

The import/export trade is recovering well and tourism, finance and banking are now major areas of development in Hong Kong.

Skills and qualifications

In general, Hong Kong employers expect to see proof of your professional qualifications. Degrees and certificates issued by US and British universities are usually recognised in Hong Kong. For professions like law, medicine, teaching, etc, you may have to pass the relevant exams or their equivalents and register with the authorities before you can carry out your work. Details for each profession will be discussed later in this chapter.

Since tertiary education has become increasingly common, employers are quite keen to look for university degree holders to fill basic job positions (in some cases including personal secretaries/clerks). Even if you are being interviewed for a position that does not require a university degree, the employer is usually happier to see some certificates or evidence of training related to the job.

Although most industries take formal qualifications seriously, there are some exceptions. Experience and other hands-on skills are more important in some jobs like journalism, hairdressing, insurance and art.

Computer skills are welcomed, if not necessary, in almost all industries. It is impossible to find a clerical job these days without good computer skills. Most shops use computers for record keeping and shop assistants are thus often required to operate computers.

Good language skills are useful for work in Hong Kong as well. Fluent English and Mandarin are particularly important in business-related jobs.

Salary guide

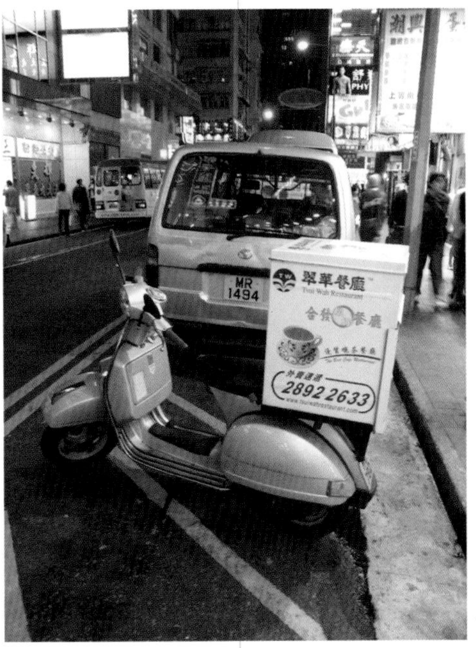

The biggest advantage of working in Hong Kong is the low tax rate, which means the amount you earn is almost equal to what you take home. However, there is no legally stipulated minimum level of salary for local employees in Hong Kong, except for imported domestic helpers. Therefore, the salary discrepancy is generally wide. Moreover, salaries in Hong Kong have been stagnating since around 2004. A general clerk in the government earns over HK$10,000 (£639/$1,277) per month, while the same position in a small company can receive as little as HK$6,000 per month. The salary of a primary school teacher (HK$17,100 per month) is higher than that of an administrative supervisor of a company (HK$16,500 per month).

In general, people working in finance companies, banks, education, and computer-related business earn higher salaries than in other fields. Civil servants also enjoy high salaries and extremely good job security. The average monthly salary of all industries (excluding managerial and professional positions) is HK$10,600. The figure looks quite impressive, especially given the low taxation rate. However, many lower-level positions like cleaning workers earn HK$5,000 or less, even though they work for 10 hours or more a day.

Salaries are usually paid at the end of each calendar month. Employers, in general, prefer to pay by direct debit through banks than by cheque. Pension contributions are automatically deducted from the salary, but income tax is not.

Job search resources

Many newspapers have a job section on a particular day of the week. The *South China Morning Post (SCMP)* has a classified section every Wednesday and Saturday, as well as an online version at www.classifiedpost.com. *Ming Pao* is a Chinese newspaper, but half of the job advertisements are in English. There is a section on Tuesdays and Thursdays especially for teaching jobs. Specialist publications like *Career Times* and *Recruit* are also available. They are free and are available in all underground (MTR) stations. *Recruit* is issued twice a week, on Tuesdays and Fridays, and you can find the *Career Times* every Wednesday and Saturday. Both publications have online versions (www.recruit.com.hk and www.careertimes.com.hk). Try *The Guardian* and *The Economist* if you plan to look for a job before coming to Hong Kong.

Crimson Publishing has a series of publications about working abroad, including tips on looking for jobs and directories for companies in different sectors. *Summer Jobs Worldwide* (2007) and *Work Your Way Around the World* (Susan Griffith, 2007) provide information for short-term employment. If you are interested in working as a volunteer, take a look at *The International Directory of Voluntary Work* (Guy Hobbs, Vacation Work 2006). For Crimson Publising's full list of titles, visit www.crimsonpublishing.co.uk.

Employment agencies

There are many employment agencies in the USA and the UK, which look for overseas employment for their clients. You have to join and pay a membership fee for posting your CV/résumé on an agency's website. The agency will contact the employers you are interested in for you. If you are already in Hong Kong, there are also local employment agencies to help you with job hunting.

Useful resources

Beyond Recruitment: www.staffservice.com/eng
Expats Direct Ltd, UK: Stockton Business Centre, 70 Brunswick Street, Stockton on Tees, TS18 1DW; 01642 730822; info@expatsdirect.com; www.expatsdirect.com
Gemini Personnel Ltd: 15/F Silver Fortune Plaza, 1 Wellington Street, Central, Hong Kong; 2525 7283; www.gemini.com.hk
Inter Career Net, New York: 420 Lexington Avenue, Graybar Building Suite 1750, New York, NY 10170; 800 859 8535; admin@rici.com; www.intercareer.com
VIP International, UK: VIP House, 17 Charing Cross Road, London, WC2H 0QW; 020 7930 0541; vip@vipinternational.co.uk; www.vipinternational

Recruitment websites

Ambition: www.ambition.biz. Provides details of jobs in finance, accounting and marketing.
Best Job Hong Kong: www.bestjobshk.com
Career Times: www.careertimes.com.hk
Civil Service Bureau: www.csb.gov.hk. Provides details about government vacancies.
Classified Post: www.classifiedpost.com.hk
Hong Kong Jobs: www.hkjobs.com
Interactive Employment Service of the Labour Department: www.jobs.gov.hk
JobsDB: www.jobsdb.com
Jobs Financial: www.jobsfinancial.com
JobOK: www.jobok.com
Recruit Online: www.recruit.com.hk

Employment regulations

Non-residents require a work permit in order to work in Hong Kong. You should present your work permit to immigration when you arrive. For imported workers and domestic helpers, the employers are responsible for getting the work permit before their employees arrive. Visitors are not allowed to take up any employment during their stay in Hong Kong. Dependents of residents, or those of professionals approved to stay in Hong Kong, cannot take up employment unless they become permanent residents themselves. If you have a Working Holiday Visa, you can work in Hong Kong but you must not work with the same employer for more than three months during your stay. For further details about work regulations, see *Visas, work permits and citizenship* in Before you go.

Recruitment procedures

Letters of application

An employer may not explicitly state that they require a letter of application in the job advertisement, but it is usually better to send one. You should briefly explain your interest in the position and why you are a suitable candidate. Your letter should be in a fairly formal tone and should highlight relevant achievements in past jobs. Common sense applies. You need to be clear and polite, but not be excessively modest.

CV/Résumé

A CV/resumé is the summary of what you have done, usually in a table or as a list of points. It should provide the details for the employers to decide if you are the candidate the company is looking for. It is important to make it easy to read as the Hong Kong labour force is big and employers typically receive many applications. You should make the headings prominent and readable at a glance. Use action words, and focus on relevant experience rather than putting everything in.

Education and work experience should be in chronological order (or its reverse). Avoid leaving unexplained periods of unemployment as they may lead to undesirable assumptions. You should also include details of referees in your résumé (names, addresses, contact numbers and email addresses).

These days it is usually not necessary to include a photograph. Similarly you do not need to mention your expected salary unless you are explicitly required to.

Interview

Normally, employers in Hong Kong invite you for interviews only if they think you are reasonably suitable. The employer will want to know more about you than

The Hong Kong Convention and Exhibition Centre

can be shown on the application letter and résumé, and also to meet you face to face. You should be familiar with your résumé and should do some research on the organisation and the whole field of its operation. Being familiar with current issues related to the business will also be to your advantage. Think about some possible questions that may come up in the interview and practise the answers. You should think of one or two sensible questions to ask them to show your interest in the company – intelligent questions will leave a good impression. If you are not familiar with the location, check it on the map to see how to get there and how long it takes. Punctuality is clearly very important and the traffic in Hong Kong can be tricky. Many employers will ask the opinions of the receptionist after interviews, so you should be polite and pleasant to them also. Employers in general prefer candidates who are positive and confident, who dress smartly and are pleasant.

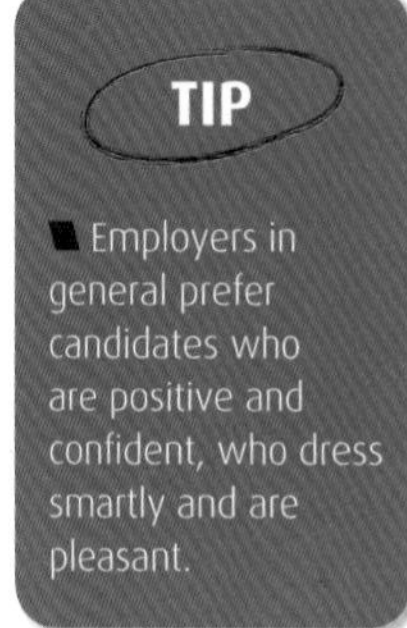
TIP
Employers in general prefer candidates who are positive and confident, who dress smartly and are pleasant.

Companies usually do not pay for travel costs if you are applying for a job overseas. Depending on the post you are applying for, you may ask for a phone interview or a net meeting instead if you are applying from abroad.

Some common interview questions

- Tell me something about yourself.
- Why do you want to come to Hong Kong?
- What are your expectations for this job?
- In what way have you added value to your organisation in your current or past positions?
- What makes you want to change your job?
- What do you think are the most important qualities for this job? Do you posses these qualities? Can you give me some examples?
- Do you have any questions? (Try not to say 'no'!)

ASPECTS OF EMPLOYMENT

Employment contracts

An employment contract is an agreement made between employer and employee and it can be in the form of a written statement or an oral agreement. An employment contract is not required by law but it is recommended, as it protects both employee and employer. An employment contract should include information about wages, working hours, allowances, overtime rates, holidays, sick leave, sick leave allowances and the period of employment. It should also include the length of notice required to terminate the contract and compensation for failure to give such notice. The employer should give a copy of the written contract to the employee for reference. Even in the case of an oral agreement, employers have to provide employees with such information in writing if they are requested to do so.

All employees, whether they are working full-time or part-time, are covered by the Employment Ordinance. They are entitled to basic protection including statutory holidays, wage protection and protection against anti-union discrimination. Employees who are employed under a continuous contract are further entitled to benefits such as rest days, paid annual leave, sickness allowance, severance payment and long service payments. Employers cannot modify the contents of the employment contract without the consent of the employees. Employers should also provide employees with a copy of the written amendments of the contract after obtaining the consent of employees.

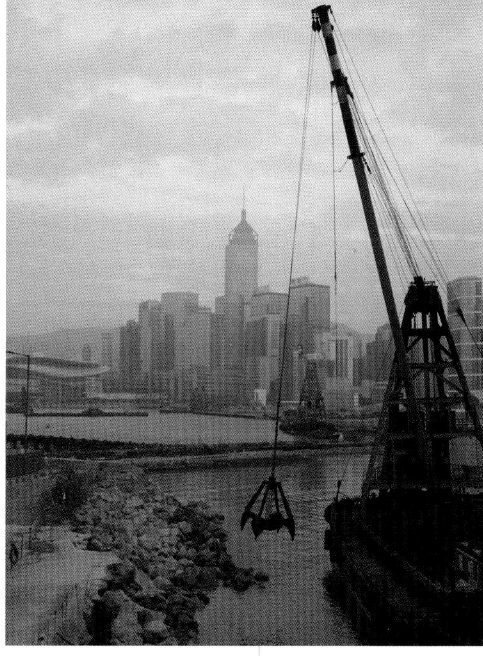

Working practices

It is important not to over-generalise about work practices in all industries but many of them share some common features. Hong Kong people are reputedly quick. They walk very quickly, eat quickly and are expected to work quickly as well. Many employers expect employees to finish their work before going home, even when it goes beyond normal working hours. Do not be surprised if a friend in Hong Kong tells you that he or she works in the office until 10pm everyday, as it regularly happens. Being punctual is a general requirement in all disciplines. Some companies require employees to sign in formally every morning. This practice was very common in manufacturing industries in the 1980s and some companies still use this system to check employees' punctuality. You are supposed to phone the company with an acceptable reason if you expect to be late by over 30 minutes.

If you need to take sick leave, you should call the company in the morning, and you should provide a medical certificate the next day when you are back at work. It is not usual for Hong Kong companies to have regular coffee breaks in the morning, where people gather together socially and chat. However, many companies do have a short tea break at around 3pm and it is common to order food and drinks to be delivered to the offices. More and more offices are smoke-free these days and it is thought to be inconsiderate to smoke in the office, even if it is not explicitly stated that the office is smoke-free.

Usually, a month's notice should be given before resignation. It may take longer, for example three months, if you are in a higher position, but this all depends on the employment contract. It is common to use first names amongst colleagues, but address your clients and bosses by their last names, especially the first time you meet them. Some companies allow employees to dress in casual wear on Fridays but this is by no means universal.

Working hours and overtime

In many companies, official working hours are generally from 9am to 5pm or 6pm, around eight to nine hours with an hour lunch break. However, you should be warned that many employers expect employees to work overtime if work has not been finished during working hours.

TIP
Some companies allow employees to dress in casual wear on Fridays but this is by no means universal.

Benefits

Hong Kong companies are not very generous when offering fringe benefits for employees, unless you work for the government. The legal requirements concerning these are not particularly strong either. Some bigger companies may have deals with insurance companies, banks or shops to provide discounts for employees. Discounted medical or dental care packages are becoming more common, and extra paid holidays are also a common benefit. Cash rewards exist but they are usually under certain specific conditions. Some employers provide an extra month's salary to employees at the end of the year, normally during the month prior to the Chinese New Year. There are also bonus schemes in some companies that reward employees according to their performance at the end of the year. Childcare services or childcare allowances are not common in Hong Kong. It is not usual for a company to provide a car for employees unless they work in a very high position in a large company. Travel expenses for business trips are usually covered by companies and employees are usually allowed to use the flyer mileages on private trips.

Some industries require employees, like nurses and security guards, to work shifts and each shift is between eight and 12 hours. Due to the economic downturn in the last few years, many companies have cut overtime payments substantially in order to reduce running costs, so employees in many cases receive no overtime payment despite working after normal working hours. Even so, not many employees refuse to work overtime as the unemployment rate has been increasing for three consecutive years; it was over 8% after the SARS outbreak in spring 2003, four times that in 1997.

Holidays

Under the Employment Ordinance, every employee is granted 12 statutory days holiday every year (see the chart below for details). Employees under continuous contract are also entitled to one rest day in every period of seven days. If a statutory holiday falls on an employee's rest day, the employer should give a rest day on the day following the statutory holiday. It is illegal for the employer to fail to grant rest days to employees or compel employees to work on those days. Failure to grant rest days for employees will incur a substantial fine. All that said, the government is now moving to create a five-day working week culture in Hong Kong, scaling back the hours worked by civil servants. Even though private business has not been compelled to follow suit, a five-day working week is now more and more common.

An employee is also entitled to annual leave with pay, if he or she is employed under a continuous contract of 12 months. The number of days leave is dependent on the number of years of service. There should be at least seven days of leave for the first two years of service and the number increases by one day per extra year of service in the company, until it reaches the maximum of 14 days. Some companies may offer more annual leave to employees but this is not very common. If an employer requires an employee to work on a statutory holiday or annual leave period with the consent of the employee, the employee should get holiday pay or annual leave pay, which is equal to the average daily wage. However, without the employees' consent employers are prohibited to make any form of payment in place of granting employees holidays.

The 12 statutory holidays

- New Year (1 January)
- Lunar New Year's Day (falls in mid-January to mid-February)
- The second day of Lunar New Year (falls in mid-January to mid-February)
- The third day of Lunar New Year (falls in mid-January to mid-February)
- Ching Ming Festival (5 April)
- Labour Day (1 May)
- Tuen Ng Festival (June)
- Hong Kong Special Administrative Region Establishment Day (1 July)
- The day following Chinese Mid-Autumn Festival (September/October)
- National Day (1 October)
- Chung Yeung Festival (October)
- Chinese Winter Solstice Festival (22 December) or Christmas Day (25 December) (at the option of the employer)

Popular vacation times for Hong Kong residents are the weeks of Christmas and Easter, as well as the Chinese New Year, when many establishments close for the entire week. Chinese New Year is by far the most important holiday and you are likely to find almost everything closed.

Popular vacation times for Hong Kong residents are the weeks of Christmas and Easter, as well as the Chinese New Year, when many establishments close for the entire week. Chinese New Year is by far the most important holiday and you are likely to find almost everything closed.

Sick pay

Employees under continuous contracts are also entitled to paid sick leave and sickness allowance. Employees are granted two paid sickness days each month in their first 12 months of employment. The number of paid sickness days will then increase to four each month. Paid sickness days can be accumulated up to 120 days maximum. You will be paid at the normal rate for taking sick leave so long as you have not used up your paid sickness days. Employers in general do not deduct from

the salary of employees if they take one or two days more than the accumulated paid sickness days they have.

Sickness allowance is equal to four-fifths of the normal wages and is granted to employees who take sick leave for four or more consecutive days. An employee is able to claim the sickness allowance if he or she can provide a certificate issued by a registered medical practitioner or a registered dentist, and the maximum paid leave for sickness is 36 days. Employers can request an investigation if the amount of sick leave taken is more than 36 days, even if certificates are provided.

For information on maternity leave, see *Women in work* later in this chapter.

Trade unions

There are around 660 trade unions in Hong Kong and every trade union has to register with the Registry of Trade Unions.

Trade unions in Hong Kong are not as powerful as they are in western countries, as Hong Kong trade unions have no right to organise collective bargaining. Employers, in general, refuse to recognise trade unions and there have been cases where staff have been laid off after trade disputes, which is very likely to be related to their roles in the trade unions. Unfortunately, even though employees should be protected from anti-union discrimination under the Employment Ordinance, it can sometimes be tricky to prove that the staff were laid off due to their roles in the unions. Moreover, the ordinance only ensures that a worker has the right to sue the employer for compensation but does not entitle him or her to reinstatement if he

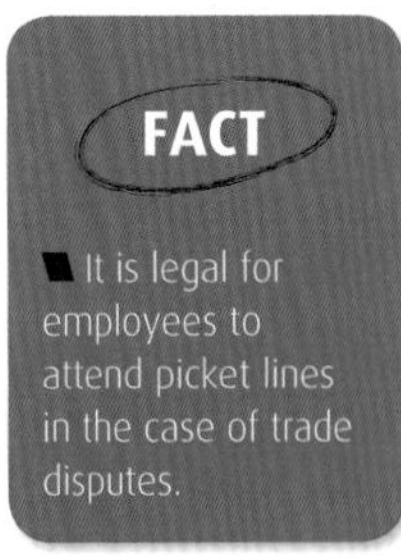

FACT

- It is legal for employees to attend picket lines in the case of trade disputes.

or she is dismissed for strike action. It is, however, illegal for employers to prohibit employees from joining trade unions and taking part in union activities outside working hours. It is legal for employees to attend picket lines in the case of trade disputes.

Even though trade unions today are not as powerful as they were, many employees still join unions to enjoy the benefits provided by them and taking part in activities held by trade unions provides a chance to make new friends.

WORKING CULTURE AND BUSINESS ETIQUETTE

Office culture

A typical Chinese office in Hong Kong will strike a westerner as amazingly crowded and ingenious in terms of how many desks and chairs can be fitted in to a relatively small space. As a rule, the 'rank and file', so to speak, will work in an open-plan setting, while the superiors and supervisors will have tiny offices symbolically separated from the main area. Everyone will have a computer and a phone on their desk and there will be piles of paper on every available surface. Somewhere in all this there will be the means for making tea, coffee, a distilled water container and possibly a microwave oven.

The atmosphere will likely be cheerful and businesslike among workmates, and deferential to the supervisor who will most probably be addressed by a title rather than by name. In crowded Hong Kong, an office may be spread over several floors, sometimes with another company in between. The toilet will be shared and will be in a common area outside the office and accessed by a key.

More upmarket companies will have bigger offices, usually also open-plan. The décor will probably be more sophisticated and modern and the floors carpeted. The bosses will have bigger and more luxurious offices. If the office is on an upper floor in a high-rise building the bosses' office is likely to have stunning views over Hong Kong.

The office may well be arranged according to the principles of feng shui. This means that a practitioner may have been consulted and advice given on the arrangement of desks, so that there should be no sharp edges or inauspicious sights to be seen out of the windows. The current writer knows one boss' office where the window was completely blocked out and filled with bookshelves so that the sharp angle of the building opposite did not have harmful influences.

Typically, Hong Kong people work long hours, often longer than the standard 42 hours per week. No one who is serious about their work leaves on the dot.

Typically, Hong Kong people work long hours, often longer than the standard 42 hours per week. No one who is serious about their work leaves on the dot.

Business culture

Doing business in Hong Kong is, on the whole, more straightforward than in China because of the lengthy British influence. Most businessmen will speak reasonably good English and if they don't they will have access to someone who does and who can interpret for them. Nevertheless, when doing business in Hong Kong it is very

important to understand protocol, etiquette and acceptable ways of behaving. Hong Kong, although superficially westernised, is at heart a very different culture, and what is acceptable back home may shock or offend in Hong Kong. If you want to do business successfully it is important to tread carefully. On the whole what is acceptable or not acceptable is more rigidly circumscribed than it is in the UK or USA.

Business etiquette

Both English and Chinese should be used for business documents. A company logo printed on your business card will impress your Hong Kong associates. Give your business card to everyone who gives you theirs. If you don't you might as well tell them you're not interested in doing business with them – that's what they will assume. Give and receive with both hands, look at the one you have been given with interest before you put it on the table or in your wallet.

If you have to give bad news to a Hong Kong associate, you should do it in private so that no one else can hear. It is very important to be tactful and in control at all times and never cause yourself or your associates to 'lose face'. Making a comment that suggests ignorance on your associate's part could mean that a deal is off. This is also true if you swear or lose your temper in a meeting. Your tone should always be neutral and pleasant and your words carefully chosen. Never boast, raise your voice or pile on the pressure.

Business meetings

Make appointments well in advance and make sure that you are on time. This is essential as lateness suggests lack of respect. If you should happen to be late it is not good enough just to make a rather casual apology. Even if you were late through no fault of your own (the taxi got lost, the bus broke down, an accident blocked the road etc) you need to apologise again and again so that your associate does not lose face. If your Hong Kong associate is late for the meeting, take care not to show any annoyance or irritation if you want to be regarded as a reasonable person.

At many business meetings you will be served a cup of Chinese tea, often in a ceramic mug with a lid. Drink it whether you like it or not but always wait for the host to start drinking his or hers first; it is considered rude not to be appreciative and accept it.

TIP

- Never ever show temper, irritation, annoyance, let alone anger when you are with Chinese people, either friends or business associates. It is regarded as embarrassing for others. In Chinese culture people who cannot control their own emotions in public are not well thought of.

Businesswear

For formal business occasions business suits in dark colours are appropriate for both men and women. Bright colours with busy patterns, such as on a tie, are generally frowned upon as inappropriate and frivolous. Women should wear modest but smart dress. Professional Chinese women tend not to wear plunging necklines and tight-fitting clothing. Do not wear blue or white at social functions as these are traditional mourning colors.

Name cards

In Hong Kong everyone has a name card with their name in Chinese on one side and English on the other. You should also get one made if the company you work for does not automatically do this for you. These will be exchanged within minutes of meeting someone new in either a social or a business setting. You need to present it and receive it with both hands. Both hands are also used when giving and receiving a present.

Get used to the kind of language that is used in business meetings and learn to understand what certain expressions really mean. The word 'no' is rarely used, for instance. Be aware that 'maybe' or 'we'll see what happens' are more likely to mean a negative outcome. The word 'yes' can be used for 'we need time to think about it' or even 'I understand what you're saying'.

Never ever show temper, irritation, annoyance, let alone anger when you are with Chinese people, either friends or business associates. It is regarded as embarrassing for others. In Chinese culture people who cannot control their own emotions in public are not well thought of.

Casual conversation before a business meeting has started is acceptable but avoid any personal topics such as asking about the associate's spouse and children, financial status or what he/she is doing at the weekend. These types of questions are viewed as far too intimate.

Before the meeting, make sure that you understand how to use your associates' names. In Chinese usage, the family name comes first. Therefore, you should address an individual by his title, or 'Mr' and the first name you see on the name card. A woman does not usually take her husband's family name so avoid using 'Mrs' and her husband's family name. Use titles such as 'Professor' or 'Dr' if this is appropriate. Make sure your pronunciation is exact. Practise this before the meeting.

TIP

- When you are in someone else's house don't go overboard praising anything in the home such as a picture, or vase etc. If you overdo it you may have the embarrassment of finding yourself being presented with it.

Hospitality

Giving gifts is appropriate during business transactions or in social settings, but the custom is to give and receive. If you have been given a gift you will be thought of as lacking in manners if you do not give one in return. Whether giving or receiving a gift, you need to do it with both hands rather than one. It is not done to open a gift in front of others (it looks greedy), especially in front of the presenter. Thank the person for the gift instead, then put it on one side and open it later. Many westerners are very disconcerted when the gift they have given is politely accepted and thanks given but then apparently ignored.

Age is a major consideration in relations with people in Hong Kong. At a dinner or meeting always greet people by starting with the oldest person present and work your way down to the youngest. The older you are the more respect you are shown. Passing over an older associate to converse with someone younger is very bad manners, unless you have already acknowledged the senior person beforehand.

If a banquet is given in your honour then it is an obligation that later you invite your hosts to a banquet. Even if this has not happened to you, giving a banquet is still a very good gift to give an associate or business partner.

If you are invited to someone's home for a meal you should take a present, but take care. Sweets and chocolates, or a basket of fruit make for excellent gifts, as does an item of handmade craft. Avoid anything personal such as perfume. As the Chinese word for clock sounds like the word for death it is obviously not a good idea to give one. Blankets represent a loss of future prosperity. Green hats, unwrapped gifts and gifts with blue wrapping paper are also inappropriate for various cultural reasons. If you are around at Chinese New Year it is the custom to give gifts of cash to children of friends and associates and persons whose services you use. The present should be given only in a red envelope, which you can get in any shop selling stationery (but make sure it has the characters for the traditional New Year greeting – *Gong Hei Fat Choi* – rather than, say, a wedding sentiment), and the money should be bills and amounts in even numbers. You can get crisp new banknotes at a special counter in banks.

When you are in someone else's house don't go overboard praising anything in the home such as a picture, or vase etc. If you overdo it you may have the embarrassment of finding yourself being presented with it.

Given the likelihood of your having dinner with local business associates, it is a good idea to learn to use chopsticks before you go to Hong Kong (if you don't already know how to). It is a common practice to belch after a meal and is considered a compliment to the cook, so don't be surprised! You can do it too to show your appreciation of the food you have eaten. Leave a bit of food on the plate to give the impression that you have had plenty to eat. Good food and plenty of it is very important to Chinese.

Business correspondence

When writing business letters in Hong Kong, always err on the side of formality – likewise with emails. Re-read what you have written to make sure that you have made your points clearly and without ambiguity. Remember that the person you are writing to has different cultural expectations and also that, usually, English is not his or her first language. Sometimes it might be a good idea to get your letter translated into Chinese, although at the same time you don't want to suggest that the recipient's English is in any way deficient. It is a fine balance.

WOMEN IN WORK

The balance between men and women in work has changed a great deal in the last two decades. Women did work in the 1960s and 1970s but they were expected to be full-time mothers once they had children. Moreover, girls in many families did not have the opportunity for education, which made it difficult for them to look for a job. More girls received education only after the government introduced the nine years of free education for all children up to the age of 15 in 1978. Since then, more women have been provided with an increasing number of job opportunities.

About half of the female population in Hong Kong now works, and accounts for 44% of the total labour force. Women nowadays are very competitive and are doing better than men in many aspects of work. Opportunities provided to men and women have been made more and more equal. Many jobs are open to both sexes now: the fire service is a recent example, and more women take up other 'traditional men's jobs', like becoming helicopter pilots and joining the police force.

The government has been working hard to eliminate gender discrimination. The Sex Discrimination Ordinance was set up in 1995 in order to protect women from being deprived of the same rights as men. Job advertisements are not allowed to set gender as a requirement for a post. If anyone, man or woman, is treated unfairly due to his or her gender, the Sex Discrimination Ordinance applies.

Another ordinance, the Equal Opportunities Commission, was set up in 1996 to expand this protection to other groups that were treated unfairly in the past. This new law aims to eliminate discrimination for disability, age or the status of the family. The Convention on the Elimination of All Forms of Discrimination Against Women (CEDAW) was established in the same year and women have been provided with stronger protection under these two new laws ever since. Before the introduction of the laws, it was not difficult to find cases where older women or women with children were less favoured by employers, even though this might be difficult to prove. The situation has now improved as employers are, in general, more concerned about the problem, and women are more willing to speak out with the support of the legal system.

After the establishment of the Women's Commission in 2001, women's concerns have been taken into account when the government formulates policies. The Commission was established to promote the well being and interests of women, and to arouse community concern over perceptions about what women should or should not do.

Sexual harassment does exist in the workplace. Most of the cases of sexual harassment in Hong Kong are related to unwanted touching, sexual jokes about gender and remarks about the body or features relating to gender. There are also complaints about receiving unwanted letters, phone calls or photos (through emails) of a sexual nature, and of unwanted kissing – but complaints of pressure for sexual activity are rare. Unfortunately, although both the Sexual Discrimination Ordinance and Equal Opportunities Commission protect women from being sexually harassed, not many women report their unpleasant experiences. About half of all women ignore harassment and only 40% of them show the harasser how much they object. Only a small percentage report the matter to employers or take legal action.

Maternity leave

Every female employee under a continuous contract is entitled to maternity leave. Maternity leave is a continuous period of 10 weeks and the employee can choose to start her leave two to four weeks before the expected date of confinement. If confinement occurs later than the expected date, the employee will enjoy further leave. She can have another four weeks' leave (as maximum) on grounds of illness or disability due to pregnancy or confinement. Employees who work with companies for 40 continuous weeks or more before commencement of maternity leave are entitled to maternity leave pay of 10 weeks. The amount is equal to four-fifths of the normal wages, if proper notice and medical proof are provided to the employer after pregnancy is confirmed.

Absence for medical examination in relation to pregnancy, post medical treatment or miscarriage should be counted as sick leave with sick leave allowance equal to four-fifths of normal wages. The Employment Ordinance protects employees from being laid off because of their pregnancy; it is an offence for an employer to dismiss an employee for her pregnancy and will incur a hefty fine. The law also requires an employer to remove heavy, hazardous or harmful work, eg working in a slippery environment or requiring the pregnant employee to lift heavy objects, if she is working in such situations during pregnancy.

TEMPORARY WORK

Activity leader/organiser

Community centres or other organisations have many activities like camping, indoor camping (a stay in a recreational centre with accommodation facilities) and workshops every year, especially during the summer vacation. Activity organisers and leaders are recruited for preparing and running the activities. These kinds of employment are usually project-based and employees are paid after the end of the activity. Keep an eye on the notice boards of city halls and community centres if you are interested in being an activity organiser or leader. This is also a good way to meet young people. Advertisements for programmes held during summer vacations are usually placed around May. You will need to check whether you need a work permit for one of these jobs.

Nanny/housework helper

Nannies are not in great demand in Hong Kong as many middle-class or wealthy people can afford to hire a live-in domestic helper, usually from south-east Asia, to look after the children as well as doing the housework. Moreover, most childcare centres and kindergartens open for quite long hours for the convenience of working parents. However, some families prefer a part-time nanny instead of a live-in domestic helper, especially during an economic downturn. Some parents require nannies to help their children with homework and revision as well. If English is your native language, you can capitalise on this, as most middle-class parents are quite keen to develop their children's language skills.

Part-time housework helpers have become popular with working couples or individuals in the last few years. They usually work a few hours a day, three to five days a week, tidy up the employer's house and do some housework, including laundry and cleaning. Some employers require their helpers to cook dinner as well. In this case, wages are higher and the cost of buying raw materials can be claimed. The wages for a housework helper are around HK$70 (£4.50/$9) per hour. Be warned however that it is illegal to employ a part-time helper who is not a Hong Kong resident.

Seasonal employment

If you have a work permit, there are more part-time jobs available before and during festivals like Christmas, Chinese New Year and Valentine's Day. Department stores and shops are busier before these festivals, and extra staff are required for cashier work or for wrapping presents. Restaurants and bars usually need more staff as well, since many of them extend their opening hours during festivals. The wages are usually not high, but there are plenty of job opportunities. You need to check with the Immigration Department whether you are eligible for work.

Try the following department stores:

Citistore: City Landmark II, TWTL 301, Tsuen Wan, NT, Hong Kong; 2413 8686; www.hld.com/english/associate/citistore (visit the website for information on other branches)

Jusco, AEON Stores (HK) Co Ltd: 3/F, Stanhope House, 738 King's Road, Quarry Bay, Hong Kong; recruitment@jusco.com.hk; www.jusco.com.hk (visit the website for other branches information)

Lane Crawford: Pacific Place, 88 Queensway, Admiralty, Hong Kong; 2118 3668; www.lanecrawford.com (visit the website for information on other branches)

Mitsukoshi Hong Kong: Hennessy Centre, 500 Hennessy Road; Causeway Bay, Hong Kong; 2576 5222; www.mitsukoshi.com.hk

Seiyu (Shatin) Co Ltd: New Town Plaza Phase III, 2–8 Shatin Centre Street, Shatin, New Territories, Hong Kong; 2694 1111; cs@seiyu.com.hk; www.seiyu.com.hk

Sincere Co Ltd: 173 Des Voeux Road Central, Sheung Wan, Hong Kong; 2544 2688; mktg@sincere.com.hk; www.sincere.com.hk (visit the website for information on other branches)

Sogo Hong Kong Co Ltd: 555 Hennessy Road, Causeway Bay, Hong Kong; 2833 8338; www.sogo.com.hk

Wing On Centre: 211 Des Voeux Road Central, Sheung Wan, Hong Kong; 2852 1888; www.wingonet.com (visit the website for information on other branches)

Yueh Wa Store: 301–309 Nathan Road, Kowloon, Hong Kong; 2384 0084; www.yuehwa.com (visit the website for information on other branches)

Sales

In general, shop assistants change their jobs frequently and shop owners are always looking for new employees to fill positions. Therefore, it is not difficult to get a temporary job as a shop assistant, if you do not mind the low wage, and you are eligible to apply for work.

On-street promotion counters are a common promotion method in Hong Kong, particularly for telecommunications and banks. Short-term promoters are employed to set up counters in different districts to persuade people to use particular credit cards or join the internet services of a telecommunication company. Some staff are paid hourly while some are paid a premium salary plus commission.

Teaching English or foreign languages

Even though students have English lessons at schools, many parents still prefer to have a private native English teacher for their children. In order to make learning

English more interesting, some schools (mainly private schools) employ foreigners to carry out activities conducted in English, so the students can learn English is a non-classroom situation.

There are many foreign-language centres in Hong Kong and it is not too difficult to find a job as a foreign language teacher. However, private language teachers (except for English) are not in great demand. French, German, Spanish, Italian and Japanese are the next most popular languages in Hong Kong.

If you are looking for students to teach, you can place an advertisement on the notice boards in universities and also in supermarkets, which is free of charge.

Voluntary work

It is very easy to be a volunteer in Hong Kong, unless special qualifications and skills are required. There are many charitable organisations that provide a wide variety of services. Many organisations like HOPE Worldwide and The Community Chest are very concerned about problems in China, and they organise on-site services in some poor regions in China as well as raising funds in Hong Kong. If you are interested in helping poor people in China, these programmes would probably be what you are looking for. Travel expenses, lodging and meal costs are normally covered by the organisations. Apart from joining the programmes organised by charitable organisations, you can also approach a location where you want to work directly. Small organisations such as orphanages, centres for the elderly and mental disability centres usually welcome volunteers to organise activities for their members or just to make regular visits.

Useful resources

The Community Chest of Hong Kong: 2599 6111; chest@commchest.org; www.commchest.org
Friends of the Earth: 2528 5588; www.foe.org.hk
Green Power: 2314 2662; info@greenpower.org.hk; www.greenpower.org.hk
HOPE Worldwide Hong Kong: 2588 1291; enquiry@hopeww.org.hk; hk.hopeworld wide.org
Medecins Sans Frontieres: 2338 8277; office@msf.org.hk; www.msf.org.hk
Oxfam: 2520 2525; info@oxfam.org.hk; www.oxfam.org.hk
Rotary International: 2576 8882; ric@rotary3450.org; www.rotary3450.org
WWF Hong Kong: 2526 1011; wwf@wwf.org.hk; www.wwf.org.hk

PERMANENT WORK

Civil servants

A civil servant is eligible for a great number of allowances and benefits, in addition to a high salary. Therefore, more than half of university graduates sit the civil service selection examination every year. Even when Hong Kong was in economic recession after 1998 no civil servant was laid off, even though there were massive lay-offs in many industries. However, it is now getting more difficult to get a government job as, in order to cut costs, the government is reducing the number of new recruits. Moreover, the government is encouraging early retirement and resignation by paying compensation to employees who retire early.

FACT
Hong Kong people call their jobs a 'rice bowl' and a job as a civil servant is called 'the iron bowl' because the job security is so good.

Finance and banking

Finance and banking are among the industries with the best prospects in Hong Kong. Hong Kong is one of the most important financial centres in the world and it was second in the world's per capita holding of foreign currency in 2006. There are more than 180 different banks in Hong Kong and the banking business has expanded the scope of its services in recent years. Electronic banking is one of the main developments. More and more bank services can be used through the internet, and the banks are putting more effort into making electronic banking safe and quick. The industry requires all sorts of professionals from different areas to ensure that business runs smoothly, which means you may be able to join the industry if you are an expert in accounting, marketing, risk management, advertising or information technology.

Information technology

Many students in Hong Kong choose to study computer science or information science at university because of the career prospects. The general public is positive about the development of information technology and the industry showed that it is doing well even under the economic downturn of the last few years. More and more services are being computerised every day, and the Hong Kong Identity Card is just one example. Due to the phenomenal growth rate of mainland China, there are also many opportunities for Hong Kong IT professionals to provide their services there or even develop their careers in the mainland.

Law

The legal system in Hong Kong is similar to that of the UK. To practise law in Hong Kong you have to be registered with the Law Society of Hong Kong. Foreign lawyers, who offer their services to the public as a practitioner of foreign law other than solicitors or barristers, are prohibited from practising Hong Kong law. They are also prohibited from joining a partnership with, or being employed by, Hong Kong solicitors. Foreign lawyers can be employed as foreign legal consultants by a Hong Kong solicitor. An overseas lawyer, who is entitled to practise law in an overseas jurisdiction, may be able to be admitted as a solicitor in Hong Kong. Both foreign and overseas lawyers have to register with The Law Society of Hong Kong before practising or working. For more information about the requirements for being a lawyer in Hong Kong and the registration procedures, visit The Law Society of Hong Kong's website.

The Law Society of Hong Kong: 2846 0500; sg@hklawsoc.org.hk; www.hklawsoc.org.hk. Check this website to see if you are eligible to be a solicitor in Hong Kong.

Medicine

Doctors working in public hospitals are very well paid, but they usually work very long hours. Some work for 18 hours in one shift and also have to be on call at night for patients who need urgent treatment. Private doctors, in general, earn a higher income than hospital doctors, and their working hours are also more flexible. A doctor with qualifications from another country has to register with the Registrar of Medical Practitioners, and may be asked to pass some tests before he or she can be a recognised doctor in Hong Kong. For further details about being a doctor in Hong Kong, refer to the Medical Registration Ordinance (*www.mchk.org.hk/ch161*).

There are two kinds of nurse in Hong Kong: Registered Nurse (RN) and Enrolled Nurse (EN). Nurses are also paid well in Hong Kong. Someone from overseas who is interested in being a nurse in Hong Kong must hold a relevant qualification and must register with the Nursing Council of Hong Kong.

If you are interested in working in Hong Kong hospitals, as a doctor or nurse, the Hospital Authority (*www.ha.org.hk*) will provide you with more details.

Useful resources

The Medical Council of Hong Kong: 2873 5131; mc-dc@dh.gov.hk; www.hkam.org.hk
Hospital Authority: 2882 4866; www.ha.org.hk
Nursing Council of Hong Kong: 2314 6900; info@nurse.org.hk; www.nurse.org.hk

Teaching

The salary starting point is for a teacher in Hong Kong is comparatively high. This is not determined according to the supply and demand of the job market, which means the salary in teaching is more stable than many other industries. Therefore, being a teacher is particularly attractive during an economic downturn. Long vacations are another positive factor.

The government has proposed many policies designed to improve the quality of primary and secondary education in the last decade. It is more difficult to be a teacher nowadays than in the 1980s or the early 1990s. If you were a university graduate in the 1980s, it was not difficult to find a teaching job. However, now you have to either have a recognised degree/diploma in education or a certificate in education in addition to a first degree (if your first degree is not in education) to qualify as a primary or secondary school teacher. Moreover, you have to pass the Language Proficiency Requirement for Teachers if you plan to teach English or Mandarin.

The government introduced the mother tongue (Chinese) as the medium of instruction in 1997. The Native-speaking English Teacher (NET) Scheme was introduced at the same time, as the government wants to keep up the students' standard of English after switching to Chinese as the medium of instruction. One NET is provided to each primary or secondary school with 40 classes or fewer (two NETs for a school with more than 40 classes) to teach English as well as helping the English panel develop an English curriculum. The NETs are also expected to bring more variety to English teaching in schools. Visit the Education and Manpower Bureau (www.emb.gov.hk) for details of duty, qualifications required and application method to be a NET.

The salary of a university lecturer in Hong Kong is one of the highest in the world. The starting salary for a lecturer is over HK$40,000 (£2,500/$5,000) per month and the universities generally provide a strong fringe benefit package, usually including housing allowances, and medical care.

INDUSTRY OVERVIEW

Finance and banking

There are more than 180 banks in Hong Kong and the number of branches is over 1,500. Hong Kong is the third largest international banking centre in Asia in terms of the volume of external transactions. It also has the second highest per capita holding of foreign currency in the world. The Hong Kong stock market plays an important role in the world as well. The stock markets in New York, London and Hong Kong open continuously one after another, making a full day's schedule. Hong Kong is the ninth largest stock market and also the seventh largest exchange market in the world.

Apart from ordinary banking services, banks also provide insurance, loans and investment services to customers. Some of the banks in Hong Kong have branches or have arrangements with banks in other countries, to provide overseas banking services at reasonable charges. The banking sector alone provides around 80,000 jobs in Hong Kong.

FACT

More than 10% of the GDP of Hong Kong comes from finance and insurance.

Import/export

Hong Kong's main trading partners are mainland China, the USA, Japan and the UK. Clothing and accessories from Hong Kong are famous for their quality and low prices.

Dozens of mao figures - a popular tourist purchase

Apart from clothing and accessories, electrical machinery, apparatus and appliances, and electrical parts are also major export items. The main import items are raw materials and semi-manufactured goods, which are mostly bought from mainland China.

Many industries experienced a seriously hard time during the outbreak of SARS. However, the amount of import/export trade during the same period did not drop – in fact it even increased. This helped Hong Kong's economy to recover quickly. Hong Kong and mainland China signed the Closer Economic Partnership Arrangement (CEPA) in late June 2003. CEPA grants Hong Kong products duty-free access to the mainland and additional market access for Hong Kong companies in the mainland. It is believed that the CEPA will further boost the import/export trading between Hong Kong and mainland China. In 2005 trade was up 9.6% from the previous year.

Teaching

Since the handover to mainland China in 1997, the government has been working hard to produce students that are 'biliteral (English and Chinese) and trilingual (English, Cantonese and Mandarin)'. Apart from encouraging primary and secondary schools to include Mandarin as one of the subjects, most of the secondary schools were asked to use Chinese as the medium of instruction (using Chinese books and lessons conducted in Cantonese) in junior levels. Nevertheless, school principals can decide to use English or Chinese, or both, to teach senior students. You may find at senior levels some topics of a subject are taught in English and some in Chinese. Many principals, teachers, students and parents found it difficult to adjust to the new system, as the change has been too fast. Students in particular found it difficult to switch between the languages for instruction.

Getting a teaching job is more difficult now. From September 2004, all teachers are required to be degree holders and have a certificate in education. Moreover, graduates who want to teach English or Mandarin have to pass the language proficiency requirement before teaching in primary and secondary schools. The government encourages schools to teach the Chinese language in Mandarin and it is believed that it will become a compulsory policy in a few years' time.

A substantial number of students have moved from mainland China in the last few years, and more schools have changed to a whole-day from a half-day schedule. Since then, the demand for teachers in general increased but the distribution of students is uneven throughout different districts. The number of students in particular districts, like Shatin and Taipo, went down in the last few years and many of the teachers in these districts were laid off due to the reduction in the number of classes.

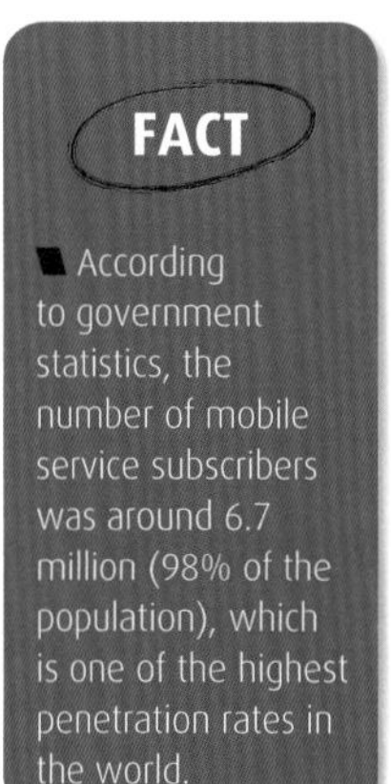

Telecommunications

Hong Kong is the second largest telecommunications market in Asia; however, telecom companies in Hong Kong face keen competition and the telephone markets are quite saturated. According to government statistics, the number of mobile service subscribers was around 6.7 million (98% of the population), which is one of the highest penetration rates in the world. International Direct Dialing (IDD) services and residential fixed line telephones also face severe competition. According to the same government statistics, the telephone density was 56 lines per 100 people, which was the highest amongst Asian countries. The telecom companies compete to attract customers from other companies by lowering their rates and improving the quality of services. More staff are employed then to do strategic planning, promotion and systems maintenance and upgrades.

More than half of all households have access to the internet at home, with broadband gaining an increasing presence. Internet service providers are actively seeking potential customers through setting up promotion counters in different districts and sending staff to households for promotion.

Tourism

Tourism is very important to the Hong Kong economy and is one of the main focuses for development in the next 10 years. There was a continuous increase in the number of visitors before the outbreak of SARS in March 2003, which was a hung blow to tourism and tourism-related businesses, for example, airlines and retail. However, the city is recovering at a faster rate than many expected. The number of visitors recorded in the first three months of 2006 was 6.2 million, up 13.8% from 2005 and, in the first few months of 2007, numbers were up by another 5.3%.

The government has recently completed a number of major projects for developing tourist attractions and facilities. Foremost among them is Hong Kong Disneyland which opened in 2005. Since then, the 5.7km-long Ngong Ping Skyrail has become the longest cable car ride in the world, running from Tung Chung to the Big Buddha over Lantau Island's mountainous terrain. The Hong Kong Wetland Park in the New Territories and the Tsim Sha Tsui Promenade are also big draws.

According to statistics, about a half of the visitors to Hong Kong in the first few months of 2007 were from mainland China. It is believed that there will be more mainland visitors to Hong Kong in the coming few years as residents of Guangdong can apply to visit Hong Kong as individual visitors without going through agencies.

There was no specific qualification required to be a tourist guide in the past, but all tourist guides must now go through training and only those who complete the training and pass the examination will be qualified to work as guides.

DIRECTORY OF MAJOR EMPLOYERS

Accounting

Deloitte Touche Tohmatsu: 2852 1600; www.deloitte.com
Ernst & Young: 2846 9888; www.ey.com
KPMG: 2522 6022; www.kpmg.com.hk
PricewaterhouseCoopers: 2289 8888; www.pwchk.com

Engineering

Far East Engineering Services Ltd: 2898 7331; www.fareast.com.hk
Gammon Skanska Ltd: 2516 8823; hongkong@gammonskanska.com; www.gammonskanska.com/hk

Jardine Engineering House: 2807 1717; jec@jec.com; www.jec.com
Maunsell Group: 2605 6262; Tony.Shum@maunsell.com.hk; www.maunsell. com.hk
Ove ARUP: 2528 3031; andrew.chan@arup.com; www.arup.com.hk
Shui On Construction and Materials Ltd : 2398 4888; corpcomm@shuion.com.hk; www.shuion.com

Food and beverages

Café de Coral Holdings Ltd: Foo Tan, Sha Tin; 2693 6218
Double Rainbow: 2506 4278; www.yp.com.hk/doublerainbow
Double Star Café: 2628 3126
Hard Rock Café: 2375 1323
Maxim's: 2101 1333; pr@maxims.com.hk; www.maxims.com.hk
McDonald's Restaurants Ltd: 2880 7300; www.mcdonalds.com.hk
Pacific Coffee: 2536 4860; www.pacificcoffee.com
Pokka Corp Ltd: 2367 4101
Swire Coca-Cola Ltd: 2636 7888; www.swirepacific.com
Tsingtao Beverage Co Ltd: 2850 6882
Vitasoy International Holdings Ltd: 2466 0333; www.vitasoy.com.hk

Hotels

The Excelsior Hong Kong: 2894 8888; info-exhkg@mohg.com; www.mandarinoriental.com
Grand Hyatt Hong Kong: 2588 1234; info@grandhyatt.com.hk; hongkong.grand.hyatt.com
Holiday Inn Hong Kong, Golden Mile: 2369 3111; reserv@goldenmile.com; goldenmile-hk.holiday-inn.com
Hyatt Regency Hong Kong: 2311 1234; general.hkgrh@hyattintl.com; hongkong.regency.hyatt.com
Island Shangri-La Hotel Hong Kong: 2877 3838; isl@shangri-la.com; www.shangri-la.com
Kowloon Shangri-La Hotel Hong Kong: 2721 2111; ksl@shangri-la.com; www.shangri-la.com
Mandarin Oriental Hong Kong: 2522 0111; mohkg-reservations@mohg.com; www.mandarinoriental.com
The Marco Polo Hongkong Hotel: 2113 0088; hongkong@marcopolohotels.com; www.marcopolohotels.com
The Peninsula Hong Kong: 2920 2888; pen@peninsula.com; www.peninsula.com

Insurance

American International Assurance Co (Bermuda) Ltd: 2232 8888; www.aia.com.hk
AXA Asia Pacific Holdings Ltd: 2519 1111; www.axa-chinaregion.com
Blue Cross (Asia-Pacific) Insurance Ltd: 2163 1000; www.bluecross.com.hk
Eagle Star Life Assurance Co Ltd: 2967 8393; www.eaglestar.com.hk/eng
ING General Insurance International: 2850 3030; www.ing.com.hk/gi
New York Life Insurance Worldwide Ltd: 2881 0688; www.newyorklife.com.hk
Prudential Assurance Co Ltd: 2977 3888; www.prudential.com.hk
Royal & Sun Alliance Insurance Ltd: 2968 3000; www.royalsunalliance.com.hk

Law

Baker & Mckenzie: 2846 1888; hklaw@bakernet.com; www.bakernet.com
Deacons: 2825 9211; hongkong@deaconslaw.com; www.deaconslaw.com
Freshfields Bruckhaus Deringer: 2846 3400; perry.noble@freshfields.com; www.freshfields.com
Herbert Smith: 2845 6639; contact.asia@herbertsmith.com; www.herbertsmith.com
Jones Stokee and Master: 2843 2211; jsm@jsm.com.hk; www.jsm-law.com
Linklaters: 2842 4888; nrees@linklaters.com; www.linklaters.com
Lovells: 2219 0888; may.law@lovells.com; www.lovells.com
Simmons and Simmons: 2868 1131; tracey.lees@simmons-simmons.com; www.simmons-simmons.com
Richards Butler: 2810 8008; law@richardsbutler.com.hk; www.richardsbutler.com

Nurseries and kindergartens

Deborah English Kindergarten: 3403 4393; www.deborah-intl.com
Deborah International Play School: 2994 8998; www.deborah-intl.com
Highgate House School: 2849 6336; info@highgatehouse.edu.hk; www.highgatehouse.edu.hk
Olympic International Pre-School: 2338 8175
Po Leung Kuk Tam Au Yeung Siu Fong Memorial Kindergarten: 2311 3871; plktaysfk@hknet.com; www.kids-club.net/edu/taysfmkg
Rosaryhill Kindergarten: 2835 5122; rhs@rhs.edu.hk; www.rhs.edu.hk
Small World Christian Kindergarten: 2525 0922; smallworld@swck.edu.hk; www.swck.edu.hk
Sun Island: info@sunisland.com.hk; www.sunisland.com.hk
The Woodland Group of Pre-School: 2559 4855; enquiry@woodlandschools.com; www.woodlandschools.com.hk
Victoria (South Horizons) International Nursery: 2884 3781
York English Kindergarten: 2338 2544

Teaching

American International School: 2336 3812; aisadmin@ais.edu.hk;www.ais.edu.hk
Christian Alliance: *PC Lau Memorial, International School*: 2713 3733; info.cais.edu.hk; www.cais.edu.hk
Concordia International School: 2397 6576; adm@cihs.edu.hk; www.cihs.edu.hk
English Schools Foundation: www.esf.edu.hk
Hong Kong International School: 2812 5000; admiss@hkis.edu.hk; www.hkis.edu.hk
Hong Lok Yuen International School: 2658 6935; info@hlyis.edu.hk; www.hlyis.edu.hk
German Swiss International School: 2849 6216; gsis@gsis.edu.hk; www.gsis.edu.hk
Kellett School: 2551 8234; kellett@kellettschool.com; www.kellettschool.com
Singapore International School: 2872 0266; secretary@singapore.edu.hk; www.singapore.edu.hk
Yew Chung Education Foundation (primary and secondary section): 2338 7106; inquiry@ycef.com; www.ycef.com

Telecommunications
City Telecom: Champion Bldg, Sheung Wan; 2854 1268
Ericsson Ltd: 2590 2388; www.ericsson.com.hk
Nokia Ltd: 2597 0100; careline.hk@nokia.com; www.nokia.com.hk
Orange: 9753 5458; feedback@orangehk.com; www.orangehk.com
Sunday: 2113 8118; www.sunday.com

STARTING A BUSINESS

Why Hong Kong is a good place to start a business

Hong Kong has been a popular city to set up a business for the last three decades. Many international companies choose Hong Kong as a base in order to develop their business in Asia. Hong Kong is one of the most important economic centres in the world and is also a gateway to the fast-growing mainland Chinese market. It is also the world's freest economy.

The infrastructure and taxation systems are also very attractive. The tax system in Hong Kong is simple and the corporate tax rate is only 17%, which compares very favourably with other economies such as Japan, South Korea, Singapore and mainland China. In Hong Kong there is no withholding tax on dividends or interest, nor is there capital gains tax or sales tax.

There are more than 180 banks in Hong Kong. Many of them are internationally renowned and provide worldwide finance services. Also, thanks to the nine-year mandatory free education system and the eight local universities in the region, the workforce in Hong Kong is generally well educated.

How to start a business in Hong Kong

Preparation from scratch

There are a number of factors to consider when you plan to start a business. Obviously, you have to decide what kind of business you want to set up and which is the appropriate form of business ownership. A considerable amount of research has to be done before making a decision. In doing so, you could consult the statistics produced by the government, universities and trade associations. If necessary, you could even consult a market research company. If you are short on budget, there are some government loan schemes that you might be able to apply for. On the other hand, if you decide to borrow money from banks, you should get information from different banks and choose the one that suits you best.

The Hong Kong Trade Development Council has a special unit for Small and Medium Enterprises (SMEs). There is a free advisory service, which you can book via the council's website: www.tid.gov.hk

The Trade and Industry Department also has a lot of information about setting up a business in Hong Kong, including information for funding schemes and business licences.

Useful resources

Census and Statistics Department: www.info.gov.hk/censtatd
Hong Kong Trade Development Council: 2584 4333; hktdc@tdc.org.hk; www.tdctrade.com/sme
Small and Medium Enterprises (SME) Service Station: 1830 668; www.tid.gov.hk

Market research companies

DN Acorn Ltd: 2881 5250; hongkong@acornasia.com; www.acornasia.com
Fusion Consulting: 2107 4299; www.fusionc.com
Strategic Focus: 2832 7861; davidhui@strategicfocus.com.hk; www.strategicfocus.net
Synovate-Asia Pacific Hong Kong: 2881 5388; hongkong@synovate.com; www.synovate.com

Accountants

A limited company must appoint an accountant for auditing. Even though sole proprietorships and partnerships are not required to hire an accountant, it may still be beneficial to do so, especially if you are inexperienced in running a business. Apart from doing the auditing, a good accountant can also provide useful advice on how best to manage your money. Some experienced accountants may even help their clients to analyse their business plans and help to reduce the risks. There are a great number of accountants in Hong Kong and their charges vary significantly. Look them up in the Yellow Pages to find one which fits your budget.

Useful resources

Deloitte Touche Tohmatsu: 2852 1600; www.deloitte.com
Ernst & Young: 2846 9888; www.ey.com
KPMG: 2522 6022; www.kpmg.com.hk
PricewaterhouseCoopers: 2289 8888; www.pwchk.com
Yellow Page Online: www.yp.com.hk

Choosing a location for your business

A good location brings you more business. Unlike starting a business in a big country, weather and geographical factors are not as important when you are selecting a location for your business in Hong Kong. The major factors to consider are your budget, the size and type of office, shop or factory you need, who your targeted customers are and where they are likely to be.

Central, Admiralty, Wanchai and Causeway Bay are particularly popular for setting up an office. International trading, banking and finance providers are active in these areas and you can find the offices of many local and international companies there. However, rents in these areas are, very high. If you are looking for a cheaper office, there is more choice in towns in the New Territories like Shatin and Tsuen Wan, or to the east of Hong Kong Island like Chai Wan.

If you are trying to sell goods to young customers or tourists, you may want to consider setting up in Tsim Sha

Tsui, Causeway Bay or Mongkok. Factories can only be set up in certain areas such as Tai Po, Yuen Long, Tseung Kwan O, Tsuen Wan, Cheung Sha Wan and Kwun Tong.

Raising finance

Apart from personal savings, banks are the main funding providers for starting a business. However, if you have never run a business before, or do not have a track record of assets and cash flow to use as reference, it is not easy to obtain the funding. Obviously, you have to convince the banks that your business will be profitable and you will be able to pay back the loan. You will normally be required to prepare a business plan, in which you should outline the business you want to start, along with the details of the market research you have done, and your views and aspirations about the future of the business. You also have to include a detailed financial budget, in which you have to list the start up costs, daily running cost, salaries, cash flow schedules, expected income, etc.

If you have contacted the suppliers and obtained a quote for the goods, it will be a good idea to include it in the plan. In general, the more details you can provide, the more likely the banks are going to be convinced. You should also include CV/résumés for yourself and other active members in the business. Your experience and skills are assessed by the bank when considering an application for a business loan. A business plan should be for five years or more, especially if you are applying for a long-term loan. You should be positive when you present the business plan but not unrealistic. Show the bank you understand both your strengths and weaknesses.

Even if you have enough money to start the business yourself, some of the short-term financial schemes provided by banks may help you to maintain a better cash flow. It is good to get as much information about the different kinds of funding you can obtain from the banks even though you may not need it in the end. More information provides you with more flexibility and it is better to be prepared to face financial problems before they occur.

Investment incentives

More than 98% of the business establishments in Hong Kong are small and medium enterprises (SMEs), which means they have fewer than 100 employees. Although each of them hires only a small number of people, together the jobs they provide create 60% of private business sector employment. For this reason, the government has some special funding schemes for SMEs.

Regularly updated information on SME investment incentives can be found at www.smefund.tid.gov.hk

SME Loan Guarantee Scheme (SGS)

There are three types of loans available:

- **Business Installation and Equipment Loans** This loan could be used for acquiring installations and equipment needed in business operations. The maximum guarantee limit is HK$2 million (£130,000/$260,000), or 50% of the loan approved by the participating lending institute concerned, whichever is less. The maximum guarantee period is five years.
- **Guarantee for Associated Working Capital Loans** This loan could be used to meet additional operational expenses arising from, or in relation to, the business installations and equipment acquired, or to be acquired under the SGS. If the applicant has applied for Business Installation and Equipment Loans from a participating lending institute, the Associated Working Capital Loan must be provided by the same institute. The maximum amount of the loan is 50% of the Guarantee for Business Installations and Equipment Loan, or 50% of the Associated Working Capital Loan approved by the participating lending institute, depending on which is less. The maximum guarantee period is two years.
- **Guarantee for Accounts Receivable Loans** These should only be used for meeting the working capital needs arising from provision of credit terms to the customers. An applicant is granted a guarantee of HK$1 million or 50% of the approved loan as maximum, whichever is less. As with the *Guarantee for Associated Working Capital Loans*, the guarantee period is up to two years.

SME Export Marketing Fund (EMF)

This is set up to help SMEs expand their businesses through active participation in export promotion activities. SMEs can apply for grants to participate in overseas trade fairs or exhibitions and study missions. This also applies to local trade fairs or exhibitions that are export-oriented. However, the promotion activities must be organised by experienced and reputable export promotion organisations or companies, which are directly relevant to the applicants' business. There is no limit to the number of applications for a single applicant but the total amount granted is limited to HK$80,000.

SME Training Fund (STF)

STF aims to provide grants to encourage SMEs to provide relevant training to their employers and employees. It also aims to assist the SMEs to enhance their human resources and hence improve their capabilities and competitiveness. There are two categories: one for employers' training and one for employees' training. The maximum cumulative amount of grant for an SME to support employers' training is HK$10,000 and HK$20,000 for employees. The amount of grant for each successful application will be 70% of the training expenses directly incurred or the balance of the accumulative grant for respective categories, whichever is lower. The training must be given by professional training organisations.

SME Development Fund (SDF)

SDF aims to provide support to projects carried out by non-profit-distributing organisations operating as support organisations, trade and industrial organisations, professional bodies or research institutes to enhance the competitiveness of the SMEs in Hong Kong. The total amount of funding for an approved project is up to HK$2 million, or 90% of the total project expenditure as a maximum, whichever is lower. The fund can be spent on manpower, equipment and other direct costs for carrying out the project. In general, the project should be completed in two years even though longer support may be considered if the applicant is able to show that the project cannot be carried on due to a lack of financial support after the cessation of SDF.

In order to apply for SGS, EMF and STF, your company must be registered in Hong Kong and the number of persons employed (including individual proprietors, partners, shareholders actively engaged in the work of the business and employees who get paid), has to be fewer than 50 for non-manufacturing business and 100 for manufacturing business. To apply for SDF, your organisation must be non-profit-distributing (which means profits are not distributed to its directors, shareholders, employees or any person). It can be operating as a support organisation, professional body or research institute. For further details of the above funding schemes and their application methods, visit The Trade and Industry Department website: www.smefund.tid.gov.hk.

Business registration

Every business or branch of business in Hong Kong must be registered with the Business Registration Office of the Inland Revenue Department. This must be done within one month of the commencement of the business. You will get a Business Registration Certificate after that, which must be displayed in a prominent place in the place where the business is carried out.

The Business Registration Certificate is renewable every year. The Business Licence Information Service (www.licence.tid.gov.hk), run by the government, is very useful for checking the required licenses, permits, certificates and approvals related to particular businesses.

Useful resources

Business Licence Information Service: 2398 5133; enq@licence.tid.gcn.gov.hk; www.licence.tid.gov.hk
Business Registration Office: 2594 3146; www.info.gov.hk/ird

Company registration

Not all companies have to be registered with the Companies Registry, which keeps a record of company names and details. Only limited companies are required to be registered. Other business structures, such as partnerships, can also register their company names if they want. The name of a new company must not be the same as any name registered on the Registrar's Index. You are required to provide the Memorandum and Articles of Association of your company; a statutory declaration of compliance; a proforma stating your company's name, the presenter's name, contact telephone number, fax number and address; and the prescribed fee for the registration. You can also deregister your company or change the company name. Contact the Companies Registry for more details.

 *Companies Registry*: 2234 9933; www.info.gov.hk/cr

Trademark registration

Even though a trademark registration is not legally required, it is strongly recommended if there is a chance that the pirate industry may take advantage of your business. A new design of certain goods, for instance, can be registered. However, the trademark registration does not apply to computer programmes, protected layout designs (topographies), and designs for articles of a literary or artistic character.

 For more details about trademark registration, contact the Intellectual Property Department (2803 5860; enquiry@ipd.gov.hk; www.info.gov.hk/ipd).

Business structures in Hong Kong

Sole proprietorship

If you are going to start a small business and you are the only director of the company, sole proprietorship is an easy way to begin. The legal procedure for setting up a sole proprietorship is far easier than setting up a limited company. All you need to do is look for an office and get the business registered.

Sole proprietorship is conducted by one person and this person is also the beneficiary of all profits produced by the business. The profit tax rate for sole proprietorship is 15.5%, which is lower than that for limited companies. Sole proprietorships are not required to prepare audited accounts but are required to keep sufficient records for at least seven years. The biggest disadvantage of sole proprietorship is its unlimited liability. The owner is not legally separated from the company and thus the owner is personally responsible for all the losses of the company. Sole proprietors may also find it difficult to raise capital, as banks are very wary of providing loans to sole proprietors.

Partnership

Partnerships are similar to sole proprietorships in many ways, but there have to be at least two owners (maximum 20). Partnerships are also easy to set up. The partners have to come up with an agreement on how to run the business, and state clearly the duties and rights of each partner. It is easier to raise funds from banks for starting a partnership compared to starting a sole proprietorship business. As with sole proprietorship, owners of a partnership business have unlimited personal liability and each partner is fully liable for any business debt, even if the debt is incurred by just one of the partners. Therefore, it is very important to find trustworthy partners.

Profits are shared among the partners according to the agreement made and the profit tax rate of partnerships is the same as for sole proprietorships at 15.5%.

Limited company

There are two types of limited company in Hong Kong: private limited companies and public limited companies. More than 99% of the investors set up business by forming a private limited company. A private limited company has a maximum of 50 shareholders and the right to transfer shares is restricted. There are 50 or more shareholders in a public limited company and there is no restriction on share transfers. Under certain conditions, public limited companies can also invite the public to subscribe to the shares.

A limited company is legally separated from the owner(s) and thus the owners are not personally responsible for the debts of the company. Limited companies are comparatively easy to obtain funds for since there can be such a large number of shareholders. Morever banks are more willing to issue loans to these companies.

However, limited companies, both private and public, are subject to a slightly higher profit tax rate of 17.5%. Limited companies are also more complicated to set up. A limited company needs to register the company name, prepare the Memorandum and Articles of Association, prepare and execute a Declaration of Compliance after the Memorandum and Articles of Association has been printed and signed, prepare the company stamp, statutory books, etc. A limited company is also required to submit annual audited accounts and hence it has to appoint auditors. The information of public limited companies (but not private limited companies) will be filed with the Companies Registry and is available for public scrutiny. They are also required to keep minutes of meetings for inspection if necessary.

It is not easy to close down a limited company, which can only be closed down by liquidation. A company has to appoint a liquidator to evaluate the assets of the company and then distribute payments to creditors and shareholders. It often requires a solicitor and an accountancy firm to handle the process, which can be very costly.

Franchising

Franchising may be a good choice for your first business venture as the franchisors provide a great deal of support to the franchisees. The failure rate of franchising is low when compared to other forms of business. Even though you are not familiar with running a business, an experienced franchisor is able to help as the framework is already set up and market research has been done. Moreover, a franchisor is usually well known to the public and holds a certain market share. A franchisor usually takes care of all the promotions and advertisements, which saves money and time. Franchisors usually have fixed procedures for running a business and require the franchisees to follow the management style. Having specific steps to follow can be extremely valuable if you are not experienced in running a business. On the other hand, there will be much less flexibility and your profit will have to be shared with the franchisor. In Hong Kong, franchising is particularly common in fast-food businesses and convenience stores. Some well-known franchising businesses in Hong Kong are McDonald's, 7-Eleven and OK (convenience stores).

Useful resources

Hong Kong Trade Development Council: 2584 4333; hktdc@tdc.org.hk; www.tdctrade.com/sme

Small and Medium Enterprises (SME) Service Station: 1830 668; www.tid. gov.hk

Import/export

There is no customs tariff in Hong Kong and only a few items, such as tobacco, liquor, methyl alcohol and hydrocarbon oil, are subjected to excise duties. Import and export licences are not common and they are required only to fulfill obligations under international agreements or requirements for importing countries. However, if you import or export prohibited goods, you must, of course, obtain licences in advance. The Trade and Industry Department will provide you with more details on prohibited goods and the procedures for applying for the appropriate licences. Import and export declarations are required within 14 days from the import or export of all goods. If you plan to run a textile and clothing business, bear in mind that there is a quota for exporting to certain countries.

Trade and Industry Department: 2392 2922; enquiry@tid.gov.hk; www.tid.gov.hk

Ideas for a new business

Although things are slowly changing, Hong Kong people in general perceive western goods as stylish and of high quality. Apart from a few electronic gadgets, many people prefer to buy western-made goods if they can afford to. You will probably have to capitalise on this perceived image of western products to compete with the much lower prices of goods imported from Asia.

Hong Kong people also like new ideas. They are eager to try new and interesting things. For instance, *Tamagotchi*, a Japanese portable digital toy for keeping virtual pets, was extraordinarily popular amongst all ages back in the 1990s. However, a craze also often dies pretty quickly. If you are the owner of a business, especially a trendy one, it is important to keep bringing out new alternatives for your customers.

Fashion and clothing

Clothing is one of the things for which people's perception really makes a difference. Mainland Chinese brands used to be unheard of in Hong Kong but changes are afoot as China's fashion industry grows. Many local companies still basically sell mainland products with a Hong Kong label attached to them. Expensive as they are, western designer labels, on the other hand, are extremely popular among young people.

Import/export

Hong Kong has a world reputation for being the gateway to the fast-growing, ever-expanding, billion-people market of mainland China. Although China has now opened its market and joined the World Trade Organisation, a lot of import/export business is still done through Hong Kong, where finance, banking and legal services are excellent. In June 2003, a new Mainland and Hong Kong Closer Economic Partnership Arrangement (CEPA) was signed, which means trading between Hong Kong and mainland China is even more barrier-free.

Bars/restaurants

Hong Kong people love dining out. Although you may find Asian food tasty and often (but not always) cheap, there are plenty of middle-class young locals or tourists who fancy sampling western cuisines. In fact, Hong Kong people are so spoilt and obsessed with the variety of food offered by the city that you can see people paying literally 10 times the price for a meal, 'just for a change'. There are lots of opportunities for classy restaurants serving authentic western cuisines.

Similarly for bars and pubs, while beer in supermarkets can be as cheap as a tenth of the price of a pint on tap, going out is associated with a certain image of being hip and posh. However selecting a good location is very important, as Hong Kong people do not drink as frequently nor as much as westerners. When they do, they often hang out around Wanchai, Central or Tsim Sha Tsui, where you will also find the tourists.

> **FACT**
>
> Under the Equal Opportunity Ordinance, it is illegal to reject a job application due to age, sex, disability or the family role of a candidate. Be careful when placing job advertisements, as the information contained in your ad must not suggest discrimination.

Guided tours

Interestingly, Hong Kong people rarely travel solo. They prefer to join guided tour packages and have everything taken care of for them, including having someone to show them around in groups. This is especially true for older people, who have the money to spend but not the language ability to get by easily in a foreign country. Just as you might find their city fascinating, they might be equally impressed with your country too.

RUNNING A BUSINESS

Employing staff

Due to the government's policy of non-intervention, there is no minimum wage in Hong Kong and an employer can negotiate the salary with an individual employee. Salaries are usually paid once a month through direct deposit to the employees' bank account. Employees, such as construction workers, may be paid weekly or even daily if the number of working days is variable.

Under the Equal Opportunity Ordinance, it is illegal to reject a job application due to age, sex, disability or the family role of a candidate. Be careful when placing job advertisements, as the information contained in your ad must not suggest discrimination.

Employees' right to join unions is protected by law. An employer is not allowed to force an employee to join or withdraw from a union, nor can an employer prohibit an employee from joining the activities organised by trade unions outside office hours.

Even though employment training is not compulsory, many companies provide it to help their staff to adapt to the new working environment and help them to develop the skills required for the job. In addition, many people view employment training as a kind of employment benefit and take it into consideration when looking for a job.

See earlier in this chapter for further details concerning employing staff.

Pensions

The establishment of a pension scheme in Hong Kong is very recent. The Mandatory Provident Fund (MPF) scheme, a compulsory pension scheme, came into full operation on 1 December 2000. With the exception of civil servants, judicial officials, and teachers in subsidised or grant schools, statutory pensions or provident funds schemes were not available to the general public before the MPF. Only very few companies had provident funds schemes as a benefit for employees before MPF.

FACT
The minimum age for work in Hong Kong is 15.

Employees and self-employed people have to join the MPF if they are aged between 18 and 65, and are employed for 60 days or more with the same employer. Both the employee and employer have to make a contribution of 5% of the employee's salary. Failing to contribute the minimum 5% is illegal.

Additional voluntary contributions are accepted. Under the current system, an employee whose monthly income is HK$5,000 (£320/$640) or below is exempt from MPF and the mandatory contributions are capped at 5% of relevant income, for which there is a ceiling of HK$20,000. This means the maximum monthly contribution (each) for employer and employed is HK$1,000. The same principle applies to self-employed people as well. These figures are subject to change and it is better to check for updated information with the MPF Schemes Authority (MPFA), the authority set up by the government for regulating, supervising and monitoring the operation of the MPF system. MPF funds are managed by trustees and all trustees must register with the MPFA.

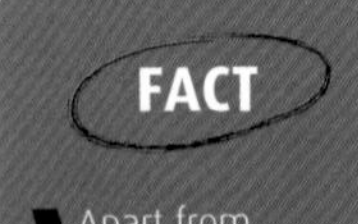

■ Apart from the basic salary, employers have to contribute at least 5% of the salaries of the employees to a pension scheme.

An employee is allowed to transfer the accrued benefits to another scheme when taking up new employment in a different company. The benefits derived from MPF cannot be accessed before the retirement age of 65, or early retirement at 60 or above. You can access the benefits before 65 if there is a particular reason, like death or permanent departure from Hong Kong.

Employees can claim a tax deduction under salaries tax for the mandatory contributions made to the MPF scheme. The maximum deductible amount for each year of assessment is HK$1,200.

 *Check the MPF's website for the most updated information:* www.mpfahk.org

Taxation

The simple taxation system is one of the great advantages of running a business in Hong Kong. Compared to other countries, the tax rates in Hong Kong are very low and there are only a few taxes that have to be paid when running a business. All persons, corporations, partnerships and trustees who carry out trade or business in Hong Kong are subject to profits tax. Even if you are running a company whose head office is overseas, you are still liable for profits tax if your company's income is earned in Hong Kong. You are required to make a profits tax return every year, usually in April. The tax rates for residents and non-residents are the same. It is 17.5% for a limited and 15.5% for an unlimited businesses. There is no special tax or licence required unless you are importing or exporting certain specified goods.

Employers are also responsible for providing an annual return of remuneration for employees (for filling in their personal tax returns) within one month from the date of issue, which is normally in April each year. In addition they are required to notify the commissioner of the Inland Revenue Department in writing within three months of a new employee starting work, and one month prior to an employee leaving. When an employee is going to leave Hong Kong for over a month and not for business purposes, the employer has to report to the Inland Revenue Department at least one month before the departure of the employee. Moreover, the employer should temporarily withhold the payment of salary and other remuneration to the employee until the Inland Revenue Department issues a 'letter of release'.

There is a more detailed illustration of the taxation system of Hong Kong in the *Tax* section of Daily Life.

Time Off

PUBLIC HOLIDAYS

New Year	*1 January*
Ching Ming Festival	*5 April*
Good Friday	*date varies*
The day after Good Friday	*date varies*
Easter Monday	*date varies*
Labour Day	*1 May*
Hong Kong Special Administrative	
Region Establishment Day	*1 July*
National Day	*1 October*
Christmas Day	*25 December*
Boxing Day	*26 December*

There are some other public holidays which are based on the Chinese lunar calendar and therefore do not have a simple fixed date in the western calendar.

- Chinese New Year, late January/February. Holiday starts from the day before the New Year to the third day of the New Year.
- The Buddha's Birthday, May
- Tuen Ng Festival, May/June
- The day following Mid-Autumn Festival, September/October
- Chung Yueng Festival, around October

SOCIALISING

Hong Kong is a very social place, and most foreigners find it friendly and easygoing. People are generally willing to help and are well disposed towards foreigners. Though it is not very common for Hong Kong people to start a conversation with a stranger at the bus stop or on a train, if you take the initiative, they will usually keep up a conversation with you if there is no language barrier.

> My social life was very active. There was a sizable contingent of expats and other exchange students with whom it was easy to make contact. Making friends with Chinese students proved a little more difficult as they seemed rather shy and reluctant to speak English. I decided to choose the more difficult (yet rewarding) path by focusing on meeting local people and spending less time with westerners. After all one of the reasons why I chose to go to Hong Kong was to learn about other cultures. I made a number of Chinese friends with whom I'm still in regular contact.
>
> **Michiel Gen**

East meets west

Even though Hong Kong is a cultural mix of east and west, the oriental tradition has a bigger influence. In a casual meeting or at a party, people usually introduce themselves by their first names and expect to be called by that name. Most people have English names and it is fine to call them by that name, if that is how they have introduced themselves. However, if you meet someone in business and trade at more formal meetings, like an interview, people usually introduce themselves by their surname and their position. It is better to call them Mr or Ms and their last name, unless they ask to be called by their first names. In universities, students usually call their teachers 'professor' even if they know each other well.

Handshaking is common in all situations when you first meet someone. Both men and women shake hands. Hugs and pecks on the cheek are not very common among locals, especially with older people. Young people accept it as a way of showing friendliness to foreigners but they do not do it much with local friends.

Social and recreational clubs have long waiting lists – although you may work for a company that has a corporate membership. If that is the case it is worthwhile going along and taking part in some of the events. There will be plenty of local Chinese members as well as other expats.

FACT

- Shaking hands is the usual greeting. Kissing and hugging is not usual in public, even between family members.

Manners and customs

It is not usual for Hong Kong people to drink wine at meals although it is getting more and more widespread among middle-class businessmen. More traditional Chinese women tend not to drink wine or any alcohol. In any event, chocolates or a box of desserts make a better present than wine. Traditionally, a Chinese meal consists of a number of dishes served more or less simultaneously that are shared by everyone. It is also normal to have soup both before and after dinner.

Chopsticks are the usual eating utensils and it is well worth learning how to use them if you don't already know. Traditionally, Chinese people would not expect to share the bill if you are invited for dinner in a restaurant. You may consider a reciprocal dinner invitation if you would like to thank your hosts.

You are more likely to be invited to a restaurant than to a meal at home by Chinese colleagues and acquaintances. The home is a private family space and it is a sign of real friendship to be invited to it. It is also the case that most ordinary homes in Hong Kong are extremely small.

You may well, however, be invited to a wedding banquet in a Chinese restaurant. These are usually grand affairs with many round tables, each of which seat 12 people. The tables are arranged in a strict hierarchy with the bride and groom and their close family in the centre of the banqueting hall. The meal will be made up of many courses served by a waiter one after the other. The traditional gift brought to the banquet by the guests consists of money, preferably new bank notes, in a special red envelope, on which are printed the Chinese characters for 'double happiness'. The amount of the gift should be at least the equivalent of what it has cost them to feed you.

Making friends

The work place or university (if you are a student) is a good place to start making friends. You may find that some of the locals are a bit shy in the beginning but that is probably part of the culture. Most of them are, however, very friendly to westerners. Bars and pubs are good places to make friends, although Hong Kong people in general do not drink as much as people do in the west. You may want to stay away from Central, and hang out in Kowloon and Wan Chai if you want to meet the locals in bars and pubs.

Even though many adults in Hong Kong are too busy to take much physical exercise, many of them enjoy watching sports, particularly football and basketball. It can be a good topic to start a conversation with new acquaintances. There are many sports centres, mainly operated by the government, that provide training courses for different sports at low fees, which is a good chance to make friends as well as to learn a new sport. If you are not a big fan of sports, city halls and other cultural

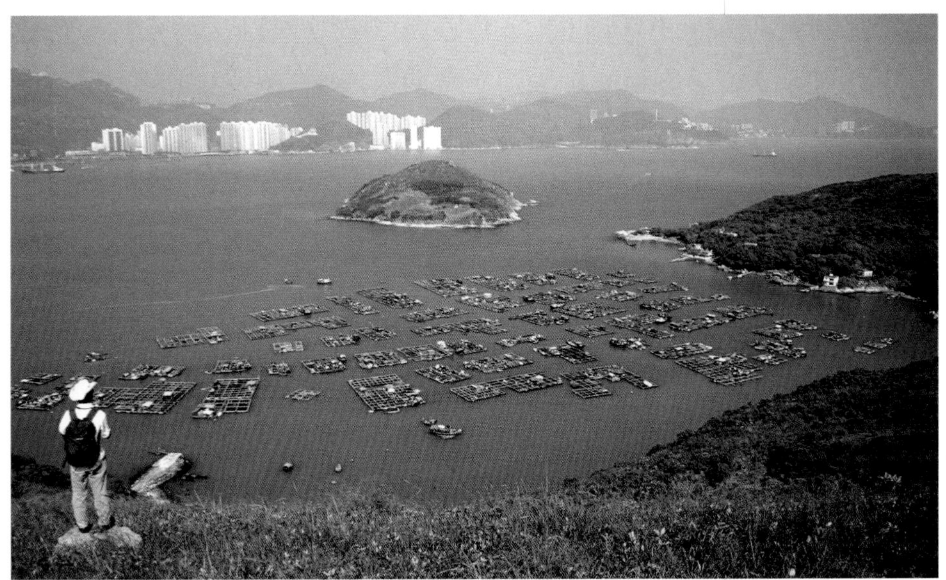

organisations also organise regular cultural activities or courses at low prices for the public. If you are interested in cultural activities, the Hong Kong Fringe is also a good place to hang out and meet a mix of locals and expats.

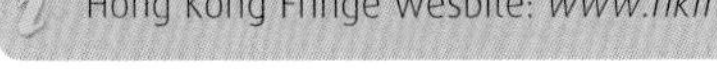

Hong Kong Fringe wesbite: *www.hkfringe.com.hk*

Relationships

There are plenty of partnerships, short-term and long-term, involving a local Chinese person and a westerner. More of them involve a western male and Chinese female, perhaps partly because there are more young single foreign males in Hong Kong than females. A book has been written about mixed marriages by Dan Waters called *One Couple, Two Cultures* (MCCM Creations, 2005). Waters is in his 80s and has been married for at least 50 years to his Chinese wife. Be prepared for different cultural assumptions that may not surface at first.

ENTERTAINMENT AND CULTURE

Cinema

Movies are a popular entertainment in Hong Kong. You can see Chinese films from mainland China as well as many from the sizeable homegrown film industry, once one of the largest in the world and still a force to be reckoned with. European, Japanese and Korean movies are as popular as the latest Hollywood offerings.

Movies usually have English and Chinese subtitles and you can book the tickets online or by telephone. You can buy tickets three days in advance, or sometimes seven days for very popular movies. If you prefer to stay away from the mainstream movies, try Cine-Art House and Broadway Cinematheque, both of which show many non-Hollywood and non-local movies.

There are many shops selling DVDs of variable quality, but usually fairly inexpensively.

Useful addresses

Broadway Cinematheque: Phase 2, Properous Garden, No 3, Public Square's Street, Yau Ma Tei, Kowloon, Hong Kong; 2388 3188

Broadway cinemas: www.cinema.com.hk

Cine-Art House: 30 Harbour Road, Wanchai, Hong Kong; 2827 4778

Cityline: www.cityline.com.hk (for booking tickets online)

Hong Kong Film: www.hkfilms.com (for addresses and telephone numbers of all cinemas in Hong Kong)

UA cinemas: www.uacinemas.com.hk

Art and museums

Hong Kong has some of the best museums in China. There are many interesting exhibitions about the history and development of Hong Kong. Hong Kong Museum of History is an interesting place with models and photos of old Hong Kong as well as Chinese traditions. You will find collections of arts, culture and traditions in the Hong Kong Heritage Museum. Otherwise, the biggest collection of Chinese painting and western painting is in the Museum of Art, spectacularly located at the tip of Tsim Sha Tsui facing the skyline of Central. It is very possible to spend two to three hours there.

The Hong Kong Space Museum is definitely worth a visit. Like the Museum of Art, it is located at the tip of Tsim Sha Tsui and has one of the largest planetariums in the world. 'Sky shows' are held in the IMAX theatre and are great for the kids.

A recent splendid addition to Hong Kong's museums is the Hong Kong Maritime Museum, which opened in 2005. It contains exhibitions about Hong Kong's importance as a sea-faring centre and port. It is currently housed in Stanley in the Murray Building. The Murray Building is a 19th-century building, once government offices, which was taken stone-by-stone from Central and reassembled at its present site.

> The number of exhibitions or concerts to go to is very small compared to life in London, and because they are less frequent, the tickets sell out very quickly.
>
> **Jennifer Atkinson**

In addition to the afore-mentioned museums, there are also the Hong Kong Museum of Coastal Defence, Hong Kong Science Museum, Art Museum of the Chinese University of Hong Kong, University Museum and Art Gallery (the University of Hong Kong), Police Museum, The Hong Kong Racing Museum and Tai Po Kau Interactive Nature Centre.

There are many cultural centres or city halls with different performances every night. Some internationally famous productions or dance groups have performances, like *The Phantom of the Opera* and *Chicago*. Another recent addition to the Hong Kong Island skyline is the distinctive Sydney Opera House-styled Hong Kong Convention and Exhibition Centre, which has staged major cultural performances.

The Fringe Club in Central is a good place to check out if you are keen on the arts, especially those that are a bit alternative.

Museums

Art Museum The Chinese University of Hong Kong: Shatin, NT Hong Kong; 2609 7416; www.cuhk.edu.hk/ics/amm

Hong Kong Convention and Exhibition Centre: 2 Harbour Road, Wanchai; 2582 0200; www.hkac.org.hk

Hong Kong Heritage Museum: 1 Man Lam Road, Sha Tin, Hong Kong; 2180 8188; www.heritagemuseum.gov.hk

Hong Kong Maritime Museum: Murray Building, Stanley; 2813 2322; www.hkmaritimemuseum.org

Hong Kong Museum of Art: 10 Salisbury Road, Tsim Sha Tsui, Kowloon, Hong Kong; 2721 0116; enquiries@lcsd.gov.hk; www.lcsd.gov.hk/CE/Museum/Arts

Hong Kong Museum of Coastal Defence: 175 Tung Hei Road, Shau Kei Wan, Hong Kong; 2569 1500; hkmcd@lcsd.gov.hk; http://hk.coastaldefence.museum

Hong Kong Museum of History: 100 Chatham Road South, Tsim Sha Tsui, Kowloon, Hong Kong (next to the Hong Kong Science Museum); 2724 9042; hkmh@lcsd.gov.hk; www.lcsd.gov.hk/CE/Museum/History

Hong Kong Police Museum: 27 Coombe Road, The Peak, Hong Kong; 2849 7019; www.info.gov.hk/police

The Hong Kong Racing Museum: 2F, Happy Valley Stand, Happy Valley, Hong Kong; 2966 8065; museum@hkjc.org.hk; www.hongkongjockeyclub.com

Hong Kong Science Museum: 2 Science Museum Road, Tsimshatsui East, Kowloon, Hong Kong, 2732 3232; www.lcsd.gov.hk/CE/Museum/Science

Hong Kong Space Museum: 10 Salisbury Road, Tsim Sha Tsui, Kowloon, Hong Kong; 2721 0226; www.lcsd.gov.hk/CE/Museum/Space

University Museum and Art Gallery: The University of Hong Kong, 94 Bonham Road, Pokfulam, Hong Kong; 2241 5500; www.hku.hk/hkumag

About Hong Kong

THE PEOPLE

Family tradition

Hong Kong Chinese people in the family will call each other by their family position such as 'older brother', 'third sister-in-law' etc. The old lady who claimed that she couldn't remember the name of her husband, who had died after three years of marriage, had probably never used his name.

Traditionally, as with other Chinese groups, most Hong Kong young people remain living with their families until they marry. Once they are working they are likely to contribute a substantial proportion of their earnings to the household.

For the last two or three generations marriage has been a matter of personal choice. The average age at marriage is currently 30 for males and 27 for females. The fertility rate is the lowest in the world with 0.9 babies per woman. This is a far cry from the previous generation as most of these women will themselves be likely to have several brothers and sisters.

Sometimes a married couple will continue to live in the flat of the parents of one of the partners – traditionally the husband's but not always nowadays. They will move out when they have saved enough to buy or rent a flat of their own. Later the old couple or widowed father or mother may go to live with the younger generation. These days the most common household unit is the nuclear family. The second most common, though a long way behind, is the single person unit and most of these people will be over 40.

Wherever they live, Hong Kong people will be likely to get together often for family meals, for the grandparents to help substantially with the care of the grandchildren and for brothers and sisters to be in frequent contact.

Trends in society

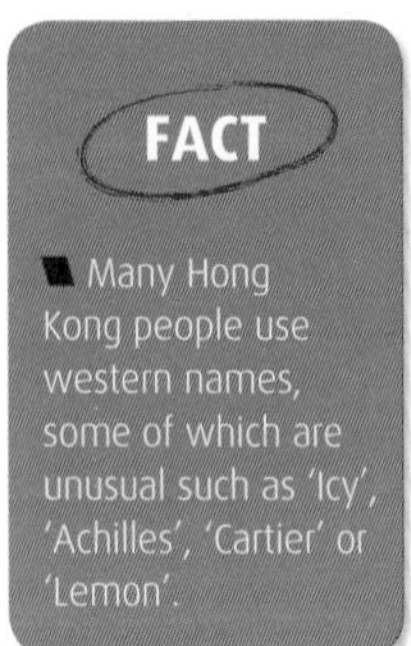

FACT
Many Hong Kong people use western names, some of which are unusual such as 'Icy', 'Achilles', 'Cartier' or 'Lemon'.

Until a few years ago 100% of Chinese people had black hair. Nowadays young people bleach their hair red, blonde and all the colours in between. You see very few grey heads in Hong Kong because the elderly touch it up all the time, both men and women, which seems odd in a culture which is supposed to revere old age. Foreign children with blonde hair find it disconcerting that local people touch their hair. It is thought that as the hair is golden it could bring luck and money to those who touch it.

Generally speaking, Hong Kong people work hard and efficiently, are always busy and are supremely interested in money. It has been deplored that employees show little loyalty to the company they work for and will readily move jobs for a relatively small salary increase.

A casual glance can tell that most people are middle class or aspiring to be middle class. They are 'clean and neat', as one foreign visitor put it, and well dressed, often fashionably so.

HISTORY OF HONG KONG

Human activity on Hong Kong Island dates back to around 3000BC. The discovery of a brick tomb in Lei Cheng Uk suggests that people from the mainland came and settled in Hong Kong in the Han Dynasty (206BC–AD220). It is clear that a significant number of people migrated from mainland China to Hong Kong in the Song Dynasty (960AD–1279AD), as coins, fishing and farming utensils that are characteristic of that period have been found.

Trade between China and the west began in the 16th century. Even though the Portuguese were the first to reach China, it was the British who dominated foreign trade in the southern region of Guangzhou.

Many of the British trade companies developed very rapidly and the British East India Company, the biggest company trading with southern regions at that time, started to sell opium in Guangzhou to further increase its profits in the beginning of the 19th century. The opium business was very successful (in monetary terms) and the result was that the health of Chinese people in Guangzhou was severely damaged. Another issue for the Chinese was that opium was often paid for in silver, which meant that a lot of silver was leaving China. Although the Chinese government had banned the drug trade in 1799 this had little effect as it was still easily imported from the south. The ban was not successful as demand for the drug was huge and smuggling was rife. The British continued to enjoy huge profits from the sale of opium until the government official Lin Zexu was appointed by the emperor to stop the trade in Guangzhou in 1839. Lin and his troops used force to compel the foreign factories to surrender the stocks of opium, and in one historic scene he burned all the collected opium in front of the public to show the determination of the emperor to ban the opium trade. The British were not impressed, and this led to the First Opium War (1839–1842), which resulted in a century-long colonial period for Hong Kong.

Hong Kong Island was occupied by the British in January 1841 while China was in a very unfavourable position in the war. After negotiations between the British captain and the governor of Guangdong Province, Hong Kong was awarded to the British under the Convention of Chuen Pi. Hong Kong was officially ceded to the British in 1842 after the two governments signed the Treaty of Nanjing, and it then became a colony.

After the First Opium War, a series of conflicts between China and the British followed. The British were backed by the French, the Russians and the Americans. A combined force of the British and the French invaded China, sparking the Second Opium War (1856–1860), which culminated in them storming the Forbidden City in Beijing. They forced the emperor to agree to the Convention of Beijing, which ceded the Kowloon Peninsula and nearby Stonecutters Island to the British. The British were concerned that Hong Kong could not be defended unless the surrounding area was also under its control, and so asked for a lease of the New Territories for a period of 99 years in 1898.

Despite its turbulent and dishonourable colonial beginnings, Hong Kong developed rapidly in industry and commerce. One exceptional period was during

the Japanese occupation in the Second World War, which lasted for three years and eight months (1941–1945) and was a time of inflation and disruption to the economy. There was also a serious labour movement in 1967 (during the Cultural Revolution in China), in which a great number of militant workers went on strike for fair treatment, but this turned into more of a riot than a prolonged protest.

Apart from these events, Hong Kong has largely been a peaceful place. It developed as a warehouse and distribution centre for trade between the British and southern China in the 19th and 20th centuries. Industrialisation initially involved the production of cotton textiles, but gradually diversified to include woollen goods and, in the late 1960s, man-made fibres and complete garments. Hong Kong has become a major exporter of high technology goods and since the late 1980s, Hong Kong has been transformed into one of the world's leading economies.

In December 1984, the People's Republic of China (PRC) and the British government signed the Sino-British Joint Declaration, in which the British government agreed to hand over the entire colony when the lease on the New Territories ended in 1997. The first wave of emigration then took place, even though the PRC agreed that Hong Kong would be allowed to retain its pre-1997 social, economic and legal systems for at least 50 years after 1997. There was a second and larger wave of emigration after the suppression of the Tiananmen Square protest on 4 June 1989, which affected many Hong Kong people deeply. The emigrants consisted mostly of middle-class people, and their destinations were western countries like Canada,

Australia, or the UK. However, many of them returned to Hong Kong after some years once they had fulfilled overseas residence requirements.

Hong Kong is now a Special Administrative Region of China. One thing that makes Hong Kong significantly different from other Chinese provinces or cities is that it has its own independent judiciary system. Since Hong Kong was returned to China, the city is running in a 'One Country, Two Systems' mode, which means it runs according its own Basic Law, which was set out by the Sino-British government and the Central People's Government in 1990, before the return of Hong Kong.

The British colonial period ended on 1 July 1997 and Hong Kong was handed over to the PRC. Tung Chee-hua was the first chief executive of the Hong Kong Special Administrative Region government. Even though it is part of the PRC, the Basic Law is thought of as Hong Kong's 'mini constitution'.

GEOGRAPHICAL INFORMATION

Hong Kong is situated in the south-eastern tip of mainland China, facing the South China Sea. It is a very condensed city with an area of only 1,105 sq km, which makes it about the same size as the City of Los Angeles, two-thirds the size of London and half that of Milan.

Regional divisions

Hong Kong is divided into three regions: Hong Kong Island, Kowloon and the New Territories and outlying islands.

Hong Kong Island is the main financial district of the city and is also the earliest developed area in Hong Kong. Many banks and companies are located in Central, Wanchai and Causeway Bay. There are many shopping centres and restaurants, and it is usually where the tourists first set foot. Hong Kong Island is separated from the New Territories and Kowloon, although, a good transport system links the areas very efficiently.

Kowloon lies to the south of the New Territories and consists of the smallest area (46.9 sq km) of the three regions, but with the highest population density. The crowded district of Mongkok is popular with teenagers as there are a lot of trendy shops and a great number of people go to Wong Tai Sin temple complex to make a wish and to make offerings at Chinese New Year.

The New Territories and outlying islands occupy around 80% of the area of Hong Kong (around 970 sq km). The New Territories are situated in the middle-to-northern part of Hong Kong, and consist of many new towns and some old villages. The main connections between mainland China and Hong Kong, Lo Wu and Lok Ma Chau are located in the New Territories. The largest outlying island, by a considerable margin, is Lantau, followed by Lamma and Cheung Chau. Lantau lies to the south-west of the New Territories (and is connected by the mighty Tsing Ma Bridge). Cheung Chau and Lamma are to the west of Hong Kong Island. Hong Kong International Airport is located on Lantau Island.

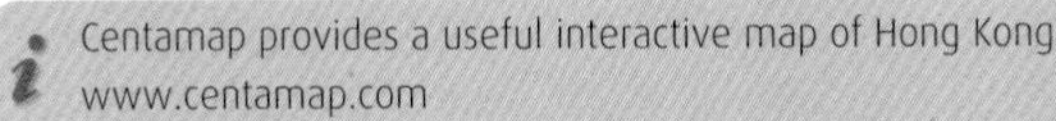

Centamap provides a useful interactive map of Hong Kong:
www.centamap.com

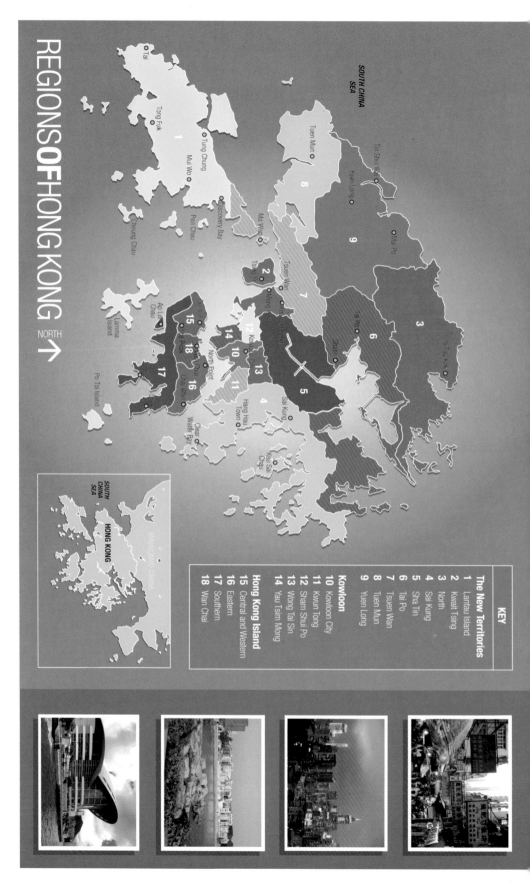

REGIONS**OF**HONG KONG

KEY

The New Territories
1 Lantau Island
2 Kwait Tsing
3 North
4 Sai Kung
5 Sha Tin
6 Tai Po
7 Tsuen Wan
8 Tuen Mun
9 Yuen Long

Kowloon
10 Kowloon City
11 Kwun Tong
12 Sham Shui Po
13 Wong Tai Sin
14 Yau Tsim Mong

Hong Kong Island
15 Central and Western
16 Eastern
17 Southern
18 Wan Chai

Population

According to government statistics of 2006, there are 6.9 million people living in Hong Kong with an average population density of 6,430 per sq km. The population density can be up to 43,220 per sq km in Kowloon.

The population growth rate is quite stable at around 1% per year. The female population comprises around 52%. The bulk of the population (72%) is aged between 15 and 64; those under 15 make up 16% and the elderly (aged 65 or above) make up about 12% of the population. The elderly population is likely to increase and the younger population to decrease in the next 20–30 years. The median age is 38 and is likely to increase to 49 in this period. Hong Kong has experienced a continuous decline in mortality during the last two decades, with a corresponding increase in expectation of life. Over the last 20 years, the life expectancy for males has increased from 72 to 78, and for females, from 78 to 84 years.

Approximately 90% of the population are Cantonese, originating from Guangdong Province, and around 2% is Filipino. The rest mainly come from other Asian countries (Thailand and Indonesia) while westerners are a minority in Hong Kong, accounting for around only 1% of the total population. It is only in recent years that residents being born actually are in Hong Kong, unlike their immigrant parents or grandparents.

Climate

Hong Kong is quite hot in summer and the temperature can be above 30°C in July and August. However, air conditioning is ubiquitous (and is even claimed by some to be too cold) so it will not be too uncomfortable unless you stay outdoors most of the time. Winter falls between December and February with an average temperature of 13°C–15°C. You may experience a few colder days during the winter but the

temperature rarely falls below 10°C. Temperatures range from 15°C–25°C in other months throughout the year. Since Hong Kong is a peninsula, the humidity is quite high, and averages 70%. Summer is the rainy season, which starts in June or July. Summer is also the typhoon season when the weather can be very unsettled.

Since Hong Kong lies just south of the Tropic of Cancer, sunrise and sunset times do not vary by more than a couple of hours throughout the year, and hence there is no daylight-saving season in Hong Kong.

Air pollution in Hong Kong is quite serious due to the large number of vehicles and the emission from factories over the border with China. Many foreigners take a long time to get used to the poor air quality. Air pollution is particularly serious in Causeway Bay, Wanchai, Mongkok, Sham Shui Po and the factory areas. The Environment Protection Department takes the Air Pollution Index everyday and you can find the index in weather forecasts and also newspapers. It is advisable not to go to crowded areas, for example Causeway Bay and Mongkok, if the Air Pollution Index is over 100, which means the quality of air is very poor.

Since Hong Kong lies just south of the Tropic of Cancer, sunrise and sunset times do not vary by more than about a couple of hours throughout the year, and hence there is no daylight-saving season in Hong Kong.

POLITICS AND ECOMONY

Politics

The government of the Hong Kong Special Administrative Region (HKSAR) is headed by the chief executive, who is elected by a broadly representative Election Committee appointed by the Central People's Government. The chief executive has to lead the government, decide on government policies, issue executive orders, etc. Under the chief executive are the Executive Council and Legislative Council. The Executive Council assists the chief executive in policy making, while the Legislative Council is mainly responsible for enacting laws, examining and approving budgets, taxation and public expenditure, and monitoring the work of the government. The chief executive, the Executive Council and the Legislative Council work very closely with each other. The chief executive is expected to consult the Executive Council before making important policy decisions, introducing bills to the Legislative Council, making subordinate legislation or dissolving the Legislative Council. The Executive Council also advises on principal legislation before it is introduced into the Legislative Council and has the power to make subsidiary legislation under a number of ordinances passed by the Legislative Council. However, the expenditure of public funds for policies decided by the Executive Council has to be approved by the Legislative Council. The Legislative Council is also given the power to impeach the chief executive.

Executive Council (Exco)

This comprises 14 principal officials, including the chief secretary of administration, secretary for justice, financial secretary and 11 secretaries from different departments, appointed under the Accountability System. There are another five non-officials in the Exco as well. All the members of the Exco have to be Chinese citizens who are permanent residents of HKSAR with no right of abode in any foreign country. The Exco usually meets once a week to discuss important policy decisions.

Legislative Council (Legco)

This has 60 members: 24 from geographical constituencies through direct elections, 30 from functional constituencies and six members through an Election Committee comprising of 800 elected representatives of the community. Apart from enacting laws, examining budgets, approving taxation and public expenditure, (as mentioned above), the Legco is also responsible for receiving and debating the policy address of the chief executive, raising questions on the work of the government, debating issues concerning public interests, receiving and handling complaints from Hong Kong residents and endorsing the appointment and removal of the judges of the Court of Final Appeal and the chief judge of the High Court. The Legco meets every Wednesday afternoon – while in session – in the Chamber of the Legislative Council to conduct its business. The chief executive attends a special council meeting to brief Legco members on policy issues and to answer questions from members. All Legco meetings are open to the public.

The history of political parties in Hong Kong is very short, as political parties were illegal before 1990. There were no direct elections for Legco before 1990. Members were either appointed by the governor or selected by functional constituencies at that time.

Political parties in Hong Kong are mainly divided into either pro-democracy or pro-China (mainland) groups. Hong Kong Democratic Party (DP) is the most popular political party in Hong Kong. It is a pro-democracy party and has the greatest number of members in the Legco. The DP has made strong criticisms of the HKSAR

government and is not popular with the PRC government. Some of the DP members have been branded as 'subversive' and are not welcome to visit mainland China. The Frontier, established in 1996, is another pro-democracy party and has been getting more popular in Hong Kong. Its major principle is that Hong Kong people should have the right to elect their own government, which is not the case at present. Other pro-democracy parties include the Association for Democracy and People's Livelihood and the Citizens Party. The basic principle of all the pro-democracy parties is to have the direct election of chief executive and members for Exco and Legco. They are all fighting for 'a high degree of autonomy' and 'Hong Kong people ruling Hong Kong', which they believe are implied by the notion of 'One Country, Two Systems'.

The Democratic Alliance for the Betterment of Hong Kong (DAB), formed in 1992, is the leading pro-China group in Hong Kong. It explicitly opposes the direction of the pro-democracy parties. In one dramatic case, for example, after the pro-democracy parties announced that a demonstration against a government proposal would start in Victoria Park, the DAB decided to have a party in exactly the same place to celebrate the Special Administrative Region Establishment Day. Other pro-China parties include the New Century Forum, the Hong Kong Progressive Alliance and the Liberty Party. Some people take the Liberty Party and the Hong Kong Progressive Alliance as pro-business rather than pro-China parties as their common and main principle is to ensure 'stability and prosperity', but this also implies avoidance of

upsetting the main Chinese government as Hong Kong does a lot of business with mainland China. That is why they are also usually classified as pro-China.

Below are the websites of the main political parties in Hong Kong:

Association for Democracy and People's Livelihood: www.adpl.org.hk

Citizen Party: www.citizensparty.org

Democratic Alliance for Betterment of Hong Kong (DAB): www.dab.org.hk

The Democratic Party (DP): www.dphk.org

The Frontier: www.frontier.org.hk

The Hong Kong Progressive Alliance: www.hkpa.org.hk

Liberty Party: www.liberal.org.hk

Economy

During the 1940s, before the communists took control of China in 1949 and ended the civil war, many wealthy and skilled people went to Hong Kong to avoid becoming victims of the war. Since then, Hong Kong has been getting more and more economically important and it is now one of the world's major financial centres. Since 2000, Canada's Fraser Institute has named Hong Kong as the world's most open economy. The Heritage Foundation also gave the same honour to Hong Kong. In 2001, Hong Kong was the world's second highest per capita holder of foreign currency. The GDP expanded by 7.5% in 2005, by 6.9% in 2006 and was around $188.8 billion in 2006. There has been steady growth, even after the global downturn and the events of September 11 in 2001.

In the 1950s, Hong Kong developed into a manufacturing centre with new immigrants from China bringing skills, capital and labour to the city. At that time, Hong Kong was focused on heavy manufacturing, such as shipbuilding. Plastics, textiles and toys replaced heavy manufacturing in the 1960s. Many of these goods were exported to other countries, as they were of high quality and low price. The textile industry was still important in the 1970s but there were also some new industries such as electronics, clocks and watches. Since the 1980s Hong Kong has been changing to a tertiary industry society. Tourism, banking and cargo services have been major contributors to the economy. One of the reasons for Hong Kong changing from a manufacturing society to a commercial centre was the high cost of land and labour for manufacturing. Many of the factory owners chose to move their premises to mainland China to reduce costs.

The 1990s was a golden time for Hong Kong. It was prosperous with a low unemployment rate (around 2% on average in the early 1990s) and there was a great deal of investment from foreign countries, establishing Hong Kong as an important bridge between mainland China and the west. Since then, import/export businesses have grown rapidly. Hong Kong and three other regions in Asia (Singapore, South Korea and Taiwan) were named the 'four little dragons' in the early 1990s as they grew rapidly economically and became more and more important globally.

Not long after its return to China, Hong Kong experienced an economic downturn, as did many other countries at that time. The real estate market and the stock market collapsed and many property owners experienced financial difficulties for some years to come. The unemployment rate in 1998 doubled from that of 1997, from 2.2% to 4.7%. The economy recovered a little in 2000 and 2001 but it then slowed again after September 11. Since the Hong Kong currency is tied to the US currency at a fixed rate, the US economy has a big impact on the financial markets in Hong Kong.

The unemployment rate has been rising since then and it reached its highest after the outbreak of the fatal, flu-like infectious disease, SARS (Severe Acute Respiratory Syndrome), in mid-March 2003. Unemployment increased to a record breaking 8.7% in July 2003; the disease killed 300 people, hit the economy badly and many small companies closed down. The catering, retail trade and airline companies suffered the most, since tourists avoided Hong Kong during the outbreak. The number of tourists dropped by over 50%. Even local people avoided visiting restaurants and other crowded public areas like cinemas and boutiques. Fortunately, since then Hong Kong has recovered faster than expected. The unemployment rate dropped to 5.6% in 2006, and visitor arrivals were 6.6 million in the first quarter of 2007. There was a 5.2% growth in retail sales volume in June 2006.

The government is upbeat about the future of the economy. The Closer Economic Partnership Arrangement (CEPA) between China and Hong Kong was concluded in late June 2003, which grants Hong Kong products duty-free access to the mainland and additional market access for Hong Kong companies to the mainland. CEPA is believed to be beneficial both to the mainland and to Hong Kong. The Capital Investment Entrant Scheme, launched on 27 October 2003, is attracting investment from other countries to Hong Kong. In addition, the low tax rate and government policy of non-interference are still very attractive to foreign companies for investment and trade. The government allows market forces to set wages and prices, and does not restrict foreign capital or investment. It does not impose export performance or local content requirements, and allows free repatriation of profits. Hong Kong is a duty-free port, with very few barriers to trade in goods and services. Moreover, merchandise exports have been growing solidly, even during the outbreak of SARS, which has helped Hong Kong recover from the outbreak. At the moment, mainland China, the USA, the EU and Japan are the major export markets for Hong Kong.

- At the moment, mainland China, the USA, the EU and Japan are the major export markets for Hong Kong.

Financial services, logistics, tourism and producer services have been contributing significantly to the Hong Kong economy and and are to be reinforced and further strengthened in the future. The government aims to elevate Hong Kong from its traditional intermediary role, to become an active major hub connecting China and international markets. Strengthening its ties with the Pearl River Delta will be essential for the Hong Kong economy as well.

Some accolades ascribed to Hong Kong's economy in the past few years:

- World's freest economy
- World's second highest per capita holder of foreign currency
- The second largest source of outward foreign direct investment (FDI) in Asia and 10th in the world
- World's fifth largest holder of foreign exchange reserves
- The 10th largest exporter of commercial services in the world

- The 10th largest trading economy in the world
- World's busiest container port
- World's busiest airport for international cargoes
- The largest venture capital centre in Asia
- The second largest stock market in Asia (after Japan) and the ninth largest in the world
- The third largest foreign exchange market in Asia and seventh in the world

RELIGION

There is no official religion in Hong Kong, but all major religions are represented and all are tolerated. There are official public holidays to celebrate events in the calendar of Christianity and Buddhism. Many Hong Kong people would claim to have no religious beliefs and yet are adherents of many of the practices of what is known as Chinese popular religion, which includes ancestor worship, worship of many minor deities such as the Kitchen God, and also follow Chinese New Year traditions. There is no given Chinese religious text and the line between religion and superstition is a fine one. There is also an overlap between the trappings associated with various religions. For instance a bride will wear a white western-style dress associated with a Christian wedding for part of the ceremony and then change into the traditional Chinese red embroidered gown for later.

The world's largest statue of Buddha is in Hong Kong on Lantau Island. It is 34m high and made of bronze. It is part of the Po Lin Monastery complex, which is always thronging with worshippers and tourists.

There are hundreds of Chinese temples in Hong Kong, many Christian churches including one Anglican and one Catholic cathedral, a synagogue, a Sikh temple, a Hindu temple and four mosques.

Itokin
伊都锦

SILK

KTV

Appendices

USEFUL BOOKS AND FILMS

Fernandez, JA and Shengjun L, *China CEO: A Case Study Guide for Business Leaders in China* (Wiley: 2007)
Gifford, R, *China Road: a Journey into the Future of a Rising Power* (Random House: *2007)*
Griffith, S, *Teaching English Abroad* (Crimson Publishing: London 2008)
Harper, D et al, *Lonely Planet China (*Lonely Planet Publications: Australia 2007)
Hunter, A and Sexton, J, *Contemporary China* (Palgrave Macmillan: New York 1999)
Lam, MN and Graham, JL, *China Now: Doing Business in the World's Most Dynamic Market (*McGraw-Hill: 2006)
Williamson, A, *The Chinese Business Puzzle* (howtobooks: UK 2003)
Insider's Guide to Beijing. Immersion Guides published annually and available in Foreign Language Bookstores in Beijing. Something similar about Shanghai is due to be launched there at the Expat Fair in September 2007.
Paul Merton in China (BBC DVD of the 2007 TV series)

OFFICIAL REPORTS AND GOVERNMENT INFORMATION

China Benefits and Employment Terms (Watson Wyatt Worldwide: Hong Kong 2001)
*China Statistical Yearbook 2003: compiled by China National Bureau Statistics of China (*China Statistics Press: Beijing 2003) Latest edition 2006
China Watch 2004: Annual Country Forecast (Orbis Publications, LLC: Washington DC 2003)
Hong Kong Yearbook (Hong Kong SAR: published annually)
Macau Statistical Yearbook 2002 (Macau SAR: Macau 2002)
Macau's Advantages (Macau Policy Research Institute: Macau 2002)
Reaching for a Renaissance (*The Economist:* 31 March 2007)

CONVERSIONS

Weights and Measures: Metric Conversion

Conversion Chart										
LENGTH (NB 100 cm to 1m, 10 mm to 1 cm)										
cm	1	2	3	5	10	20	25	50	75	100
inches	0.4	0.8	1.2	2	4	8	10	20	30	39
DISTANCE										
mile	1	5	10	20	30	40	50	75	100	150
km	1.6	8	16	32	48	64	80	120	161	241
km	1	5	10	20	30	40	50	100	150	200
mile	0.6	3.1	6.2	12	19	25	31	62	93	124
SPEED										
kmph	10	20	30	40	50	60	70	80	90	100
mph	6	12	19	25	31	37	44	50	56	62
TEMPERATURE										
centigrade (°C)			10	20	30					
farenheit (°F)			50	68	86					

Time

Mainland China

Even though China is such a huge country and geographically covers several time zones, time is nationwide and is based on Beijing time. It is eight hours ahead of Greenwich Mean Time (GMT), and is the same in Hong Kong and Macau. China used to have daylight saving time, but this was abolished in 1992. Xinjiang, in the far west, sometimes operates an informal local time, two hours behind Beijing time.

Hong Kong

Hong Kong is eight hours ahead of Greenwich Mean Time and seven hours ahead during British Summer Time.

Photo Credit List

2	Delivery rickshaw in Shanghai	Courtesy of Philip Ideson	pideson@aol.com
4	Chinese cuisine	Courtesy of Lidia Camacho	http://www.flickr.com/sublime
5	City lights – the Huangpu District	Courtesy of Staffan Holgersson	http://www.flickr/com/photos/staffh/
6	Ming Pearl Tower, Shanghai	Courtesy of John	http://www.flickr.com/photos/meckleychina/
7	Shangri La	Courtesy of Robert Law	robert_law42@hotmail.com
8	Starbucks in Shanghai	Courtesy of Philip Ideson	pideson@aol.com
9	Delivery rickshaw in Shanghai	Courtesy of Philip Ideson	pideson@aol.com
26	Zhabei District	Courtesy of Montrasio Inmternational Ltd	www.montrasio-international.com
27	Chinese newspapers	Courtesy of Lidia Camacho	http://www.flickr.com/sublime
30	General merchandise market, Beijing	Courtesy of Alex Yang	www.shopping-in-beijing.com
31	Loaded	Courtesy of John Meckley	http://www.flickr.com/photos/meckleychina/
33	Pedal rickshaw	Courtesy of W Fung, The Society of Anglo Chinese Understanding, www.sacu.org	
37	'Chinglish' sign	Courtesy of Sarah Riddle	
37	Old and new mingle on the streets	Courtesy of Sarah Riddle	
38	Chinese currency	Courtesy of Steven L. Mullen	slmullen@gmail.com
43	Trendy hairdressers	Courtesy of Sarah Riddle	
46	City lights – the Huangpu District	Courtesy of Staffan Holgersson	http://www.flickr/com/photos/staffh/
49	Real estate window	Courtesy of Andrea Boudville	
49	An older district in China	Courtesy of Beth law	
52	Century Park Shanghai	Courtesy of Benjamin Noggle	http:\\www.BenjaminNoggle.com
53	View over traditional roofline	Courtesy of Beth Law	
53	The Pudong District	Courtesy of Philip Ideson	pideson@aol.com
54	Hongkou District	Courtesy of John Meckley	http://www.flickr.com/photos/meckleychina/
55	Jing'an District and Temple	Courtesy of Lillis Taylor	www.liltayinchina.com
55	French Concession District	Courtesy of Terence Chua	terence.ym.chua@gmail.com
56	Zhongshan Park	Courtesy of Shun-che (Mark) Chang	kramchang@gmail.com
56	Street scene	Courtesy of Beth Law	bethlaw@hotmail.co.uk
58	City lights – the Huangpu District	Courtesy of Staffan Holgersson	http://www.flickr/com/photos/staffh/
59	Lujiazui	Courtesy of HKMPUA	http://www.flickr.com/photos/hleung/
60	near M50, Shanghai	Courtesy of John Meckley	http://www.flickr.com/photos/meckleychina
61	Older apartment blocks	Courtesy of Robert Law	robert_law42@hotmail.com
62	Pending development	Courtesy of Beth Law	bethlaw@hotmail.co.uk
65	Modern apartment block	Courtesy of Pierston Hawkins	
69	Typical kitchen in Chinese flat	Courtesy of Sarah Riddle	
70	Shanghai telephone box	Courtesy of Dauchi Fukagawa	www.flickr.com/photos/fukagawa
73	Wanchai	Courtesy of Luica Mak	wwww.tcn.co.uk/mak
76	City junction	Coursesy of Helen Li	
78	City junction	Courtesy of Helen Li	
79	Banned Activities	Courtesy of Beth Law	bethlaw@hotmail.co.uk
81	Dong Fu supermarket	Courtesy of Sarah Riddle	
81	Market stalls	Courtesy of Beth Law	bethlaw@hotmail.co.uk
	Pedestrian Hall, Guangzhou	Courtesy of John Meckley	http://www.flickr.com/photos/meckleychina/
83	Yak milk for sale in Western China	Courtesy of Sarah Riddle	
83	Food shop	Courtesy of Beth Law	bethlaw@hotmail.co.uk
84	Pedestrian mall, Guangzhou	Courtesy of John Meckley	http://www.flickr.com/photos/meckleychina
88	Fresh ingredients	Courtesy of Pierston Hawkins	
104	Police Officer	Courtesy of Harald Groven	
106	City junction	Courtesy of Helen Li	
108	Traffic Warden Chengdu	Courtesy of Benjamin Cole	www.flickr.com/photos/skyshanghai/
109	Xujiahui gridlock	Courtesy of John Meckley	http://www.flickr.com/photos/meckleychina/
112	Shanghai Transregion Maglav Train	Courtesy of John Meckley	http://www.flickr.com/photos/meckleychina/
113	The N525, Shanghai to Nanzhou	Courtesy of John Meckley	http://www.flickr.com/photos/meckleychina/
114	Metro Entrance in Shanghai	Courtesy of Philip Ideson	pideson@aol.com
119	Parked bikes	Courtesy of Beth Law	bethlaw@hotmail.co.uk
124	Fisherman with bird	Courtesy of W Fung, The Society of Anglo Chinese Understanding, www.sacu.org	
125	Hair salon	Courtesy of W Fung, The Society of Anglo Chinese Understanding, www.sacu.org	
127	A work meeting	Courtesy of Sarah Riddle	
128	Grain market	Courtesy of W Fung, The Society of Anglo Chinese Understanding, www.sacu.org	
129	Yak Bar	Courtesy of W Fung, The Society of Anglo Chinese Understanding, www.sacu.org	
132	Agricultural equipment is not always up-to-date	Courtesy of Pierston Hawkins	
133	Workers at a row of plaster shops in south-west China	Courtesy of Perston Hawkins	
140	Boazi making at a local restaurant	Courtesy of Sarah Riddle	
143	Officials attend the breaking ground on an important construction site Courtesy of Sarah Riddle		
145	A work presentation	Courtesy of Sarah Riddle	
147	An outdoor work presentation	Courtesy of Sarah Riddle	
158	Teaching English	Courtesy of Sarah Riddle	
165	Power lines	Courtesy of Beth Law	bethlaw@hotmail.co.uk
166	Peasant farmer threshing rice	Courtesy of W Fung, The Society of Anglo Chinese Understanding, www.sacu.org	
167	Construction	Courtesy of Nick Kozak, www.nickkozak.com	

191	Preparing for compulsory work aerobics Courtesy of Sarah Riddle		
198	Exercise machines are found in parks	Courtesy of Pierston Hawkins	
200	Pinned up newspaper	Courtesy of W Fung, The Society of Anglo Chinese Understanding, www.sacu.org	
201	Sound of Music Poster	Courtesy of W Fung, The Society of Anglo Chinese Understanding, www.sacu.org	
202	Promenading on the Bund	Courtesy of W Fung, The Society of Anglo Chinese Understanding, www.sacu.org	
203	Exercise machines are found in parks	Courtesy of Pierston Hawkins	
204	Terracotta army	Courtesy of W Fung, The Society of Anglo Chinese Understanding, www.sacu.org	
206	Great Wall of China	Courtesy of W Fung, The Society of Anglo Chinese Understanding	www.sacu.org
207	Great Wall of China	Courtesy of W Fung, The Society of Anglo Chinese Understanding, www.sacu.org	
209	Fruit stand in Beijing	Courtesy of Alex Yang	www.shopping-in-beijing.com
214	Backyard	Courtesy of Robert Law	robert_law42@hotmail.com
215	Village scene	Courtesy of Beth Law	bethlaw@hotmail.co.uk
219	In the shade	Courtesy of Robert Law	robert_law42@hotmail.com
220	Lake	Courtesy of Robert Law	robert_law42@hotmail.com
221	Nanjing	Courtesy of Lidia Camacho	http://www.flickr.com/sublime
224	Rock formation	Courtesy of W Fung, The Society of Anglo Chinese Understanding, www.sacu.org	
230	Street scene, Shanghai	Courtesy of Beth Law	bethlaw@hotmail.co.uk
233	Jokhang temple, Lhasa, Tibet	Courtesy of Pierston Hawkins	
234	Potala palce, Lhasa, Tibet	Courtesy of Pierston Hawkins	
241	A Symphony of Lights	Courtesy of Hong Kong Tourism Board	
242	Local snack	Courtesy of Hong Kong Tourism Board	
244	Street scene	Courtesy of Pierston Hawkins	
250	Star ferry – Courtesy of Hong Kong Tourism Board		
253	Star Ferry	Courtesy of Hong Kong Tourism Board	
252	Shopping street in Sheung Wan	Courtesy of Graham Northfield	grahamnorthfield@hotmail.com
261	Floating restaurant at Aberdeen Harbour	Courtesy of Hong Kong Tourism Board	
262	Hong Kong at night	Courtesy of Pierston Hawkins	
263	The Noonday Gun in Causeway Bay	Courtesy of Graham Northfield	grahamnorthfield@hotmail.com
265	Tsing Ma Bridge from the airport to HK Island	Courtesy of Hong Kong Tourist Board	
268	Aberdeen Harbour	Courtesy of James Lin	http://jameslin.name/
273	Central Hong Kong	Courtesy of Shinya Ichinohe (Shinyai)	www.flickr.com/shinyai/
275	Causeway Bay	Courtesy of Andrew Buckingham	http://www.flickr.com/photos/abuckingham
276	The Peak	Courtesy of Didier Lahely	http://anteneo.vox.com
277	Repulse Bay Apartments	Courtesy of Bebiano da Silva	
278	Mongkok	Courtesy of Richard Yuan of Chicago, USA yuan 2003@ gmail.com	
279	Cheung Chai	Courtesy of Carrie Chow	http://wwwflickr.com/photos/carriechow/
282	Stanley	Courtesy of Janet Brown	
284	Apartment block in Shui Fai Ta	Courtesy of Graham Northfield	grahamnorthfield@hotmail.com
289	Sai King Pier	Courtesy of Edwin Lee	edwin_lee@vodafone.ie
	Central Hong Kong	Courtesy of www.bluehongkong.net	www.bluehongkong.net
290	Hong Kong telephone box	Courtesy of Tim Wang	jiazi@msn.com
292	Causeway Bay	Courtesy of Andrew Buckingham	http://www.flickr.com/photos/abuckingham
295	Fresh seafood	Courtesy of Hong Kong Tourism Board	
296	Choosing your dinner at the Rainbow Restaurant	Courtesy of Graham Northfield	grahamnorthfield@hotmail.com
297	Marks & Spencer	Courtesy of Graham Northfield	grahamnorthfield@hotmail.com
298	Shopping at night	Courtesy of Hong Kong Tourism Board	
300	HK Post Box	Courtesy of Toby Oxborrow	www.oxborrow.net
313	HMTR train platform	Courtesy of Hong Kong Tourism Board	
315	A modern junk	Courtesy of Graham Northfield	grahamnorthfield@hotmail.com
316	Trams in Central Hong Kong	Courtesy of www.bluehongkong.net	
317	Star Ferry	Courtesy of Hong Kong Tourism Board	
323	Delivery motorbike	Courtesy of Pierston Hawkins	
325	Hong Kong Convention and Exhibition Centre	Courtesy of Hong Kong Tourism Board	
329	Incense shop in central Hong Kong	Courtesy of Pierston Hawkins	
330	Power plant on Lamma Island	Courtesy of Pierston Hawkins	
332	Fishing boats in Lamma Harbour	Courtesy of Pierston Hawkins	
341	Hong Kong is a shopping mecca	Courtesy of Pierston Hawkins	
343	Beach strollers in front of power plant	Courtesy of Pierston Hawkins	
347	Busy shopping street	Courtesy of Pierston Hawkins	
348	Busy shopping street at night	Courtesy of Pierston Hawkins	
356	Hiking on Lanna Island	Courtesy of Hong Kong Tourism Board	
361	Hiking on Lanna Island	Courtesy of Hong Kong Tourism Board	
362	Hong Kong Sevens	Courtesy of Graham Northfield	grahamnorthfield@hotmail.com
367	Big Buddha in Lantau Island	Courtesy of Graham Northfield	grahamnorthfield@hotmail.com
368	View of Central Hong Kong from the East	Courtesy of Graham Northfield	grahamnorthfield@hotmail.com
371	Hong Kong at night	Courtesy of Graham Northfield	grahamnorthfield@hotmail.com
373	Hong Kong offers natural settings	Courtesy of Pierston Hawkins	
373	Sai King Tin Hau temple	Courtesy of Hong Kong Tourism Board	
374	Temple Lantau Island	Courtesy of Graham Northfield	grahamnorthfield@hotmail.com
376	The beach at Stanley	Courtesy of Graham Northfield	grahamnorthfield@hotmail.com

INDEX

Index

Index

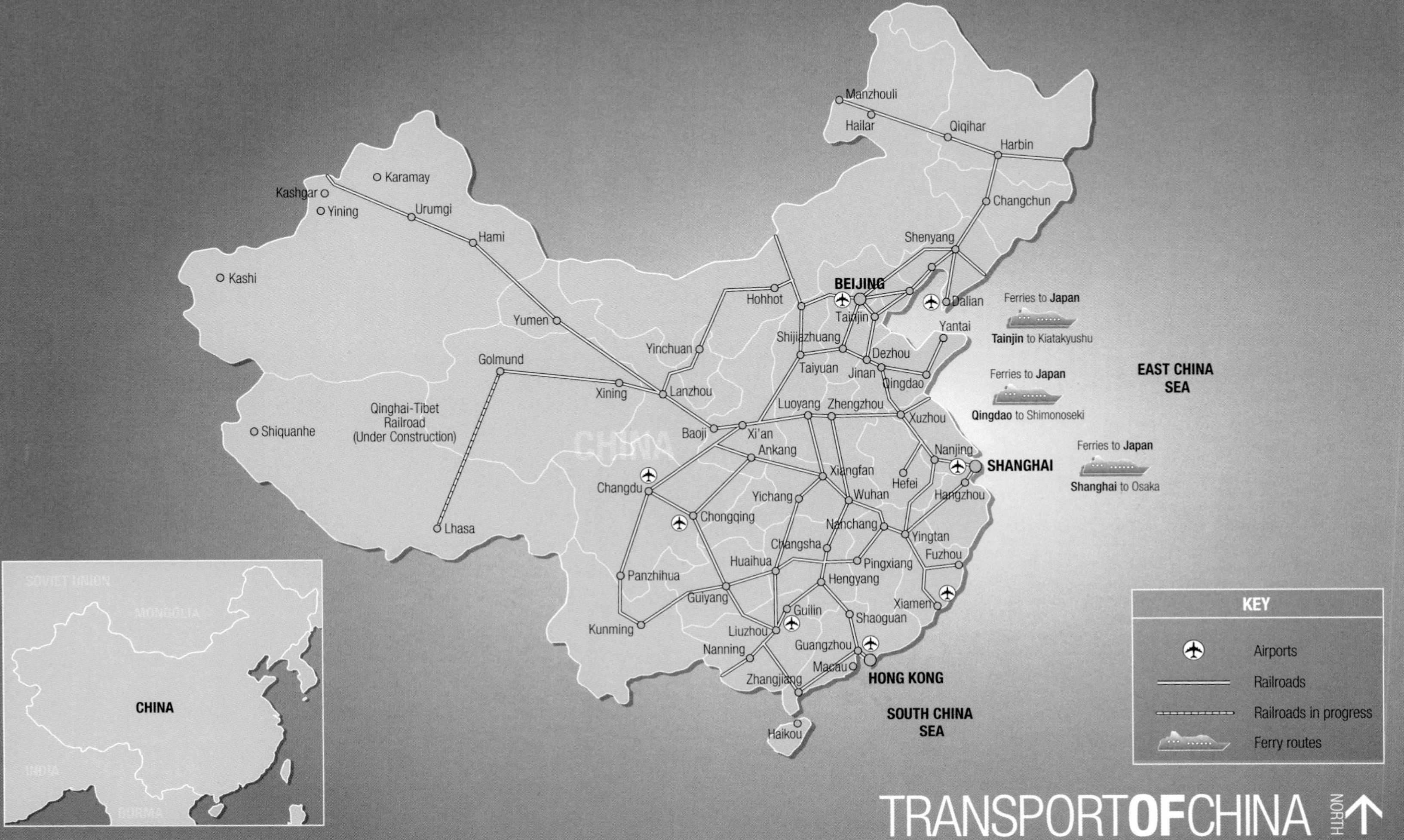
TRANSPORT OF CHINA
NORTH
KEY
Airports
Railroads
Railroads in progress
Ferry routes
Manzhouli
Hailar
Qiqihar
Harbin
Changchun
Shenyang
Karamay
Kashgar
Yining
Urumgi
Hami
Kashi
BEIJING
Dalian
Tainjin
Hohhot
Yumen
Yinchuan
Shijiazhuang
Dezhou
Yantai
Golmund
Taiyuan
Jinan
Qingdao
Xining
Lanzhou
Luoyang
Zhengzhou
Xuzhou
Shiquanhe
Qinghai-Tibet
Railroad
(Under Construction)
Baoji
Xi'an
Ankang
Nanjing
SHANGHAI
CHINA
Xiangfan
Hefei
Changdu
Yichang
Wuhan
Hangzhou
Chongqing
Lhasa
Nanchang
Yingtan
Changsha
Fuzhou
Huaihua
Pingxiang
Panzhihua
Hengyang
Guiyang
Xiamen
Guilin
Shaoguan
Kunming
Liuzhou
Guangzhou
Nanning
Macau
HONG KONG
Zhangjiang
Haikou
SOUTH CHINA
SEA
EAST CHINA
SEA
Ferries to Japan
Tainjin to Kiatakyushu
Ferries to Japan
Qingdao to Shimonoseki
Ferries to Japan
Shanghai to Osaka
SOVIET UNION
MONGOLIA
CHINA
INDIA
BURMA

CHINA HONG KONG CITY
Ferry Service to Macau & Mainland China
HK China Ferry Terminal
HARBOUR CITY
Victoria Harbour
Ocean Centre
Harbour City Ocean Terminal
Bus Terminus
Chung Wan (Central District)
Sheungwan
Wing Lok Street
Wing Lok St
Bonham Strand E.
Pier Road
Runsey St
Hillier St
Gilman's Bazaar
Central Market
CONNAUGHT RD CENTRAL
DES VOEUX RD CENTRAL
QUEENS RD CENTRAL
Harbour View St
General Post Office
Edinburgh Pl
City Hall
CHATER RD
Statue Square
Chater Garden
MURRAY RD
Lok Ku Rd
Hollywood Rd
Sai St
Ping Shan St
Fong
Bridges St
Aberdeen Street
Gage St
Wellington St
Staunton St
Peel St
Elgin St
Castle Rd
Seymour Rd
CAINE ROAD
Old Bailey St
Queen's Theatre
On Lan
Conduit Rd
Shelley St
Mosque St
Arbuthnot St
Central Hospital
Government House
HK Zoological & Botanical Gardens
GARDEN RD
COTTON TREE DRIVE
Museum of Tea Ware
Hong Kong Park
St Joseph's Path
Kennedy Rd
Macdonnel Rd
Bowen Road
Brewin Path
Canossa Hospital
Drake St
Tamar St
Red Cross Society Hospital
HARCOURT
Harcourt Garden
Rodney St
QUEENS WAY
Justicedr
Star
N
designmaps.com
Peak

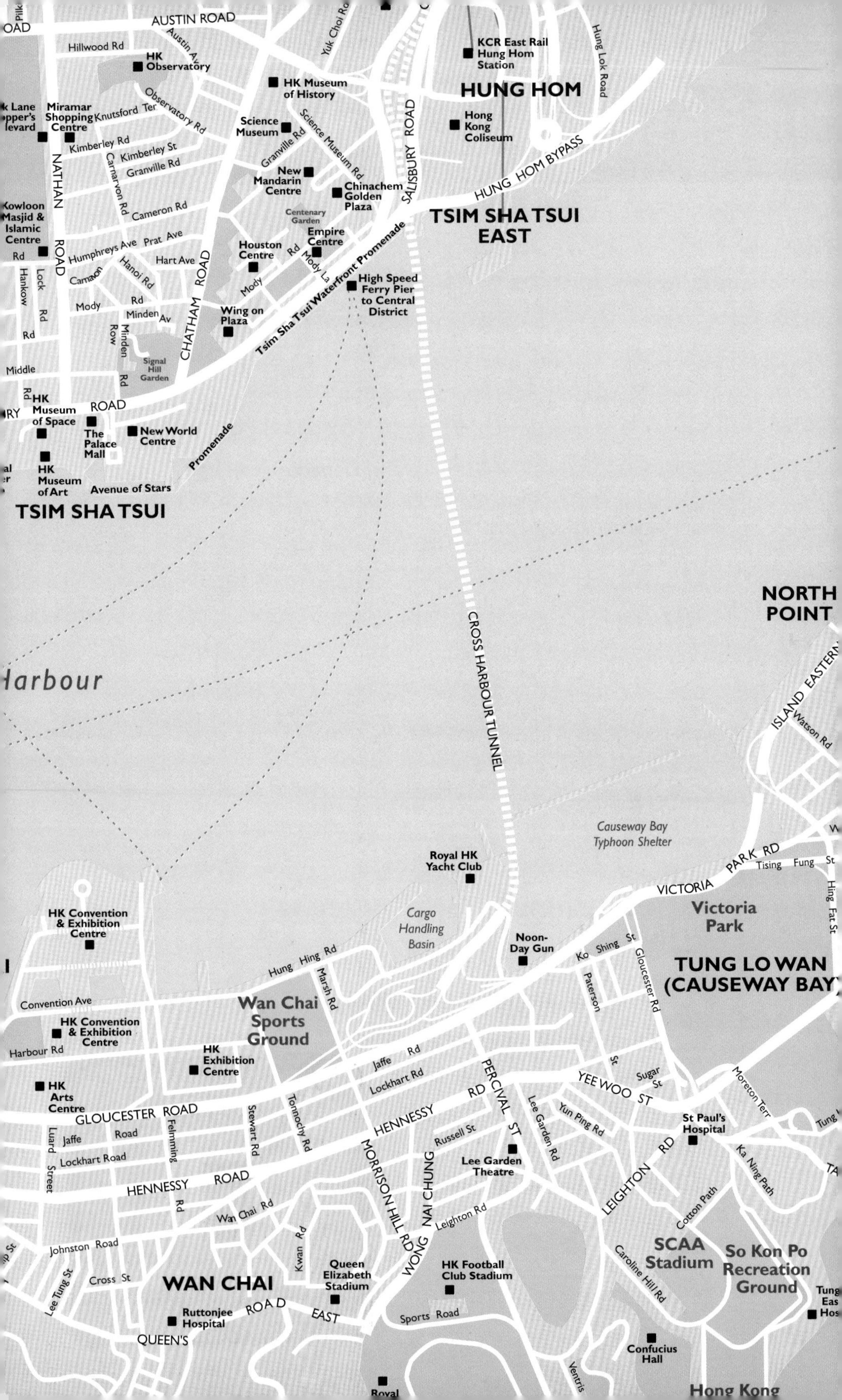
AUSTIN ROAD
Hillwood Rd
HK Observatory
Austin Av
Observatory Rd
HK Museum of History
Science Museum
Science Museum Rd
Granville Rd
New Mandarin Centre
Chinachem Golden Plaza
Centenary Garden
Empire Centre
Houston Centre
Mody La
Wing on Plaza
Miramar Shopping Centre
Knutsford Ter
Kimberley Rd
Kimberley St
Granville Rd
Carnarvon Rd
Cameron Rd
Humphreys Ave
Prat Ave
Hart Ave
Hanoi Rd
Cameron
Mody Rd
Minden Av
Minden Row
Signal Hill Garden
NATHAN ROAD
CHATHAM ROAD
Kowloon Masjid & Islamic Centre
Hankow Rd
Lock Rd
Middle Rd
HK Museum of Space
The Palace Mall
New World Centre
HK Museum of Art
Avenue of Stars
Promenade
TSIM SHA TSUI
Tsim Sha Tsui Waterfront Promenade
High Speed Ferry Pier to Central District
SALISBURY ROAD
KCR East Rail Hung Hom Station
HUNG HOM
Hung Lok Road
Hong Kong Coliseum
HUNG HOM BYPASS
TSIM SHA TSUI EAST
Yuk Choi Rd
CROSS HARBOUR TUNNEL
NORTH POINT
Harbour
ISLAND EASTERN
Watson Rd
Causeway Bay Typhoon Shelter
Royal HK Yacht Club
Cargo Handling Basin
Noon-Day Gun
VICTORIA PARK RD
Tising Fung St
Hing Fat St
Victoria Park
TUNG LO WAN (CAUSEWAY BAY)
Ko Shing St
Paterson
Gloucester Rd
HK Convention & Exhibition Centre
Hung Hing Rd
Marsh Rd
Convention Ave
Wan Chai Sports Ground
HK Convention & Exhibition Centre
Harbour Rd
HK Exhibition Centre
HK Arts Centre
Jaffe Rd
Lockhart Rd
GLOUCESTER ROAD
Jaffe Road
Lockhart Road
Luard Street
Fenwick St
Stewart Rd
Tonnochy Rd
HENNESSY RD
PERCIVAL ST
YEE WOO ST
Sugar St
Moreton Terr
Lee Garden Rd
Yun Ping Rd
St Paul's Hospital
Russell St
Lee Garden Theatre
MORRISON HILL RD
WONG NAI CHUNG
LEIGHTON RD
Ka Ning Path
Cotton Path
HENNESSY ROAD
Wan Chai Rd
Leighton Rd
Kwan Rd
Johnston Road
Cross St
Lee Tung St
WAN CHAI
Queen Elizabeth Stadium
HK Football Club Stadium
SCAA Stadium
So Kon Po Recreation Ground
Caroline Hill Rd
Ruttonjee Hospital
QUEEN'S ROAD EAST
Sports Road
Confucius Hall
Ventris
Royal
Hong Kong

Emergency services

Fire service	**119**
Police	**110**
Ambulance	**120**

Hospitals

Beijing United Family Hospital	**6433 3960**
Huadong, Shanghai	**6428 3180**
Queen Mary, Hong Kong	**2855 3838**

Phone information

Directory enquiries	**114/116**
Operator	**106**
International access code	**0086**

Travel

Beijing Airport	**6454 1100**
Shanghai Airport	**6268 3695 (Hong Qiao), 3834 4500 (Pudong)**
Hong Kong Airport	**2181 8888**

Other information

Weather report	**121**
Asia Emergency Care Assistance	**6462 9100**
Traffic Emergency	**122**
International SOS	**6590 3419**
China Women Travel Service	**6526 2244**

Embassies

Australia

Beijing	**5140 4204**
Shanghai	**5292 5500**
Hong Kong	**2585 4457**

Canada

Beijing	**6373 8007**
Shanghai	**6279 8400**
Hong Kong	**3719 4700**

India

Beijing	**6532 1908**
Shanghai	**6275 8885**
Hong Kong	**2528 4028**

New Zealand

Beijing	**6532 4317**
Shanghai	**5407 5858**
Hong Kong	**2877 4488**

United Kingdom

Beijing	**5192**
Shanghai	**6279 7650**
Hong Kong	**2901 3000**

USA

Beijing	**6532 3831**
Shanghai	**6433 6880**
Hong Kong	**2523 9011**